# The Queen's Gambit & Catalan for Black

## Lasha Janjgava

*Translated by Graham Burgess*

First published in the UK by Gambit Publications Ltd 2000

ISBN 1 901983 37 4


DISTRIBUTION:
Worldwide (except USA): Central Books Ltd, 99 Wallis Rd, London E9 5LN.
Tel +44 (0)20 8986 4854 Fax +44 (0)20 8533 5821.
E-mail: orders@Centralbooks.com
USA: BHB International, Inc., 41 Monroe Turnpike, Trumbull, CT 06611, USA.

For all other enquiries (including a full list of all Gambit Chess titles) please contact the publishers, Gambit Publications Ltd, 69 Masbro Rd, Kensington, London W14 0LS. Fax +44 (0)20 7371 1477.
E-mail Murray@gambitchess.freeserve.co.uk
Or visit the GAMBIT web site at http://www.gambitbooks.com

Edited by Graham Burgess
Typeset by Petra Nunn
Printed in Great Britain by Redwood Books, Trowbridge, Wilts.

10 9 8 7 6 5 4 3 2 1

**Gambit Publications Ltd**
*Managing Director:* GM Murray Chandler
*Chess Director:* GM John Nunn
*Editorial Director:* FM Graham Burgess
*German Editor:* WFM Petra Nunn

# Contents

# Symbols

| | |
|---|---|
| + | check |
| ++ | double check |
| # | checkmate |
| !! | brilliant move |
| ! | good move |
| !? | interesting move |
| ?! | dubious move |
| ? | bad move |
| ?? | blunder |
| +– | White is winning |
| ± | White is much better |
| ⩲ | White is slightly better |
| = | equal position |
| ∞ | unclear position |
| ∓ | Black is slightly better |
| ∓ | Black is much better |
| –+ | Black is winning |
| Ch | championship |
| Cht | team championship |
| tt | team tournament |
| Wch | world championship |
| Ech | European championship |
| Wcht | World Team Championship |
| ECC | European Clubs Cup |
| Ct | candidates event |
| IZ | interzonal event |
| Z | zonal event |
| OL | olympiad |
| jr | junior event |
| wom | women's event |
| mem | memorial event |
| rpd | rapidplay game |
| corr. | correspondence game |
| 1-0 | the game ends in a win for White |
| ½-½ | the game ends in a draw |
| 0-1 | the game ends in a win for Black |
| (n) | nth match game |
| (D) | see next diagram |

# Foreword

This book aims to provide everything the reader needs to know to play the black side of the Orthodox Queen's Gambit and the Catalan. Our starting position arises after 1 d4 d5 2 c4 e6 *(D)*.

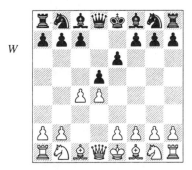

These openings have been very widely used for many years in tournaments and matches of all levels. The Orthodox Queen's Gambit has been defended by all thirteen World Champions and many other grandmasters, and underwent especially intensive testing in the matches between Kasparov and Karpov.

The first ten chapters of this book discuss the Queen's Gambit, while the final one deals with the Catalan. Throughout, the coverage is from Black's viewpoint, in as much as lines that are clearly bad for Black are not discussed in detail. However, this book does not present a narrow repertoire, with the attendant risk that one powerful novelty in a critical line could

render it worthless. After 3 ♘c3 I am recommending the 3...♗e7 move-order (meeting 4 ♘f3 with 4...♘f6), as it avoids the unpleasant form of Exchange Variation discussed in chapters 9 and 10. In the main-line position after 3 ♘c3 ♗e7 4 ♘f3 ♘f6 5 ♗g5, there are three lines offered for Black; my main recommendation is for Black to play 5...h6 and then, after 6 ♗h4 0-0 7 e3, to choose between the Lasker (7...♘e4) and Tartakower (7...b6). Both these lines are theoretically very sound, providing good prospects of full equality, with chances to play for the full point if White is imprecise or overambitious.

Given the breadth of the coverage, the book may also prove useful to players of the white pieces, though they will also need to consult other sources to build a complete repertoire.

Throughout the book I have sought to indicate which lines are most important in contemporary praxis, and to provide accurate analysis of the critical positions, and accordingly to make recommendations as to which lines the reader should adopt in his or her own games. In this task I have drawn upon not only novelties from practice, but also my own ideas and analysis, which you will find throughout these pages.

I hope that this book will prove useful not only to accomplished players, but also to a broad spectrum of chess enthusiasts.

# 1 The Alatortsev Variation

1 d4 d5 2 c4 e6 3 ♘c3 ♗e7 *(D)*

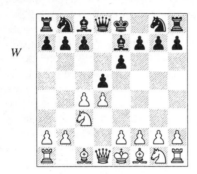

An idea of the Russian master Alatortsev. Its point is to provoke White into playing ♘f3 before developing the bishop to g5, thus rendering the Exchange Variation harmless.

**4 cxd5 exd5 5 ♗f4**

This is one of White's most aggressive systems. Black has two methods of defence:

| | |
|---|---|
| **A: 5...c6** | 6 |
| **B: 5...♘f6** | 14 |

## A)

**5...c6**

White can choose between:

| | |
|---|---|
| **A1: 6 ♕c2** | 6 |
| **A2: 6 e3** | 10 |

The former is Petrosian's move, preventing the light-squared bishop from coming to f5.

## A1)

**6 ♕c2** *(D)*

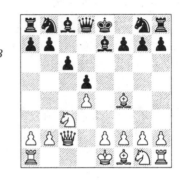

**6...♗g4**

Black tries to solve the problem of the light-squared bishop. Other continuations are also possible:

a) 6...g6 (this has a similar aim in mind):

a1) 7 0-0-0 ♘f6 8 f3 ♘a6 9 e4 ♘b4 and then:

a11) 10 ♕b3?! ♗e6 11 a3 (11 e5 ♘d7 12 a3! a5! 13 axb4 axb4 14 ♘b1 c5 ∓ Korchnoi-Spassky, Kiev Ct (6) 1968) 11...dxe4 12 d5 ♘bxd5 13 fxe4 ♕b6! ∓.

a12) 10 ♕d2 dxe4 11 ♘xe4 ♘xe4 12 fxe4 ♗e6 13 d5 cxd5 14 ♗b5+ ♗d7 15 ♗xd7+ ♕xd7 16 ♘e2 0-0! ∓ Lazarev, Shiyanovsky.

a2) 7 e4 ♗e6 8 e5 ♗f5 9 ♕d2 ♘d7 10 ♗e2 (10 ♘f3 ♘f8 11 ♗e2 h5 12 h3 ♘e6 13 ♗e3 g5 ∞) 10...h5 11 ♘f3 ♘f8 12 0-0 ♘e6 13 ♗e3 ♔f8! 14 a3 ♔g7 15 b4 ♘h6 with an equal position, Garcia Palermo-Portisch, Reggio Emilia 1984/5.

a3) 7 f3!? and now:

a31) 7...♗d6 8 ♗xd6 ♕xd6 9 0-0-0
♘e7 10 e4 ±.

a32) 7...♗e6 8 0-0-0 ♘d7 9 e4 ♘b6
10 ♔b1 ♗d6 11 ♘ge2 ♗xf4 12 ♘xf4
♘f6 13 e5 ± Mozetić-Abramović, Yugoslavia 1994.

a33) 7...♗g5!? 8 ♕d2 (8 ♗e5?! f6 9
♗g3 ♗e3!? 10 ♕d3 ♕e7 11 ♘d1 ♗h6
∞ Shirov-Magomedov, Frunze 1989; 8
♗xg5 ♕xg5 9 e4!? ±) 8...♗xf4 9 ♕xf4
♕f6 10 ♕xf6 ♘xf6 11 e4 ±.

a34) 7...♘f6 8 ♗h6 ♗f5 9 ♕d2
♘bd7 10 e3 (10 g4 ♗e6 11 ♘h3 ♗d6
12 ♗f4 ♘b6 13 ♗xd6 ♕xd6 14 ♕f4
♕e7 = Av.Bykhovsky-Geller, New
York 1990) 10...♗d6 11 ♘ge2 ♕e7 12
♘g3 0-0-0 13 ♘xf5 gxf5 14 0-0-0
♘e8 15 g3 ♕e6 16 ♗g5 f6 17 ♗h4
♘b6 18 ♕d3 ♗b4 19 ♗h3 ♘d6 20
♖he1 ♔b8 21 a3 ♗xc3 22 ♕xc3 h5 =
Petursson-Geller, Reykjavik 1990.

a4) 7 e3 ♗f5 8 ♕d2! *(D)* is also Petrosian's idea (instead of the simplifying 8 ♗d3 ♗xd3 9 ♕xd3 ♘f6 =).

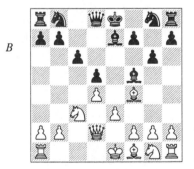

*B*

White is not troubled by the loss of
time: he has a strong position in the
centre, and hopes to exploit Black's
dark-square weaknesses on the kingside (due to the move ...g6). The g6-
pawn limits the f5-bishop and enables

White shortly to evict it from its important diagonal. Now:

a41) 8...♗d6 9 ♘ge2 ♘f6 10 f3
♗xf4 11 ♘xf4 h5 12 0-0-0 ± Rivas-
Abramović, Bor 1986.

a42) 8...♘d7 9 f3 and here:

a421) 9...g5 10 ♗g3 h5 11 e4 dxe4
(11...h4 12 ♗f2 ♗e6 13 ♗d3 ♘b6 14
♘ge2 ♘f6 {14...♕d7!?} 15 e5 ♘fd7 16
f4! ± Semkov-Geller, Plovdiv 1988)
12 fxe4 ♗g6 13 ♗d3! h4 14 ♗f2 ♘f8
15 0-0-0 ± Yakovich-Geller, Elista
1995.

a422) 9...♘b6 10 e4 ♗e6 11 e5! ±
Karpov-Kasparov, London/Leningrad
Wch (7) 1986.

a43) 8...♘f6 9 f3 and then:

a431) 9...c5 10 ♗h6 (10 ♗b5+!?
♘c6 11 dxc5 ♗xc5 12 ♘a4 ♗e7 13
♗h6 ± Petrosian-Beliavsky, Simferopol 1982) 10...cxd4 11 exd4 a6 (or
11...♘c6 12 ♗b5! ± Kasparov) 12 g4!
♗e6 13 ♘ge2 ♘c6 (13...♘bd7?! 14
♗g2 ♘b6 15 b3 ♖c8 16 0-0 ♖c6 17
h3! ± Kasparov-Short, Thessaloniki
OL 1988) 14 ♗g2 ♗f8 15 0-0 ♗xh6
16 ♕xh6 ♕b6 17 ♖ad1 0-0-0 18 ♖d2
± Kasparov.

a432) 9...0-0 and then:

a4321) 10 ♘ge2 ♘bd7 (10...♖e8
11 ♘g3 ♗e6 12 ♗e2 c5 ±) 11 g4 ♗e6
12 ♘g3 c5 13 0-0-0 (13 ♖d1?! cxd4 14
exd4 ♘e8! ∓ Howell-J.C.Diaz, Frunze
1989) 13...cxd4 14 exd4 ♘e8 15 ♔b1
♖c8 ∞.

a4322) 10 g4 ♗e6 11 ♘ge2 c5 12
h4 ♘c6 13 dxc5 ♗xc5 14 0-0-0 ♖c8
15 ♔b1 ±.

a433) 9...h5 and here:

a4331) 10 ♗d3 ♗xd3 11 ♕xd3
♘a6 (11...♘bd7 12 ♘ge2 0-0 {12...h4
13 e4 dxe4 14 fxe4 ♕a5 15 0-0 ±} 13
0-0 ♖e8 14 e4 ± Ionescu-Geller, Sochi

1986) 12 ♘ge2 ♘c7 (12...♕d7 13 0-0 ♘c7 14 ♖ab1 0-0 15 b4 ♘e6 16 ♗e5 ± Draško-Sargisian, Panormo Z 1998) 13 0-0 (13 ♗e5!? Topalov) 13...♘e6! 14 ♗e5 h4! 15 ♖ae1 0-0 16 g4! ♘d7 (16...hxg3 17 hxg3 ♘d7 18 ♔g2 ♘xe5 19 dxe5 ♔g7! {19...♕d7 20 f4 f5 21 g4! ± Topalov-Karpov, Wijk aan Zee 1998} and now 20 ♘d4 ± or 20 ♘f4 ±) 17 f4!? (17 h3 ♘xe5 18 dxe5 ♔g7 19 f4 f6 20 exf6+ ♗xf6 ∞) 17...f6! 18 ♕xg6+ ♘g7 ∞.

a4332) 10 ♘ge2 ♘bd7 11 ♘g3 ♗e6 12 ♗d3 0-0 13 0-0 ♖e8 14 ♖ae1 ± intending e4, Gulko-Anikaev, USSR 1983.

b) 6...♗d6 (D) and now:

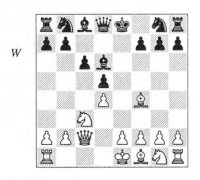

b1) 7 ♘xd5 ♗xf4 8 ♘xf4 (not 8 ♕e4+?! ♘e7 9 ♘xf4 ♕a5+ with a slight advantage for Black) 8...♕xd4 9 e3 ♕b4+ =.

b2) 7 ♗xd6 ♕xd6 8 e3 and then:

b21) 8...♘f6 9 ♗d3 ♗e6 10 ♘ge2 ♘bd7 11 0-0 0-0 12 ♖fc1 ♖fe8 13 ♖ab1 ± Beliavsky-Geller, Moscow IZ 1982.

b22) 8...♘e7 9 ♗d3 g6 10 ♘ge2 ♗f5 11 0-0 0-0 12 f3 ♗xd3 13 ♕xd3 ♘d7 14 e4 f6 15 ♖ad1 ♖ae8 16 ♖fe1 ♘b6 17 b3 ♔h8 18 ♘g3 ♘g8 19 ♘f1

♖e7 20 ♘e3 ♖fe8 = Timoshchenko-Fokin, Novosibirsk 1986.

b23) 8...♕g6 9 ♕d2 (9 ♕b3 gives White nothing due to 9...♘e7 10 ♘f3 ♘d7 11 0-0-0 ♘b6 12 h3 ♕f6 13 ♗e2 ♗e6 14 ♖hf1 ♘g6 = Knaak-Hort, Bundesliga 1994/5) 9...♘e7 (also interesting is 9...♘d7 10 f3 ♘b6 11 ♗d3 ♕h6 12 ♕f2 ♘e7 13 ♘ge2 ♘f5 14 ♘d1 0-0 15 0-0 ♗e6 16 e4 ♘e7 17 ♘g3 f5 = Kramnik-Belikov, Kuibyshev 1990) 10 ♘ge2 0-0 11 ♘g3 ♕d6 12 ♗d3 ♗e6 13 0-0 ♘d7 = Azmaiparashvili-A.Petrosian, Erevan 1989.

b3) 7 ♗g3 ♘e7 8 e3 ♗f5 9 ♕b3 (9 ♗d3 yields no advantage owing to 9...♗xd3 10 ♕xd3 0-0 11 ♘ge2 ♘a6 12 a3 ♖c8 13 b4 ♘c7 14 ♖b1 ♕d7 {14...♘e6?! 15 ♘a4 ± Granda-Lutz, Pamplona 1997/8} 15 ♗xd6 ♕xd6 16 0-0 ♖fd8!? =) and then:

b31) 9...b5?! 10 a4 b4 11 ♘ce2 0-0 12 ♖c1 a5 13 ♘f3 ♘g6 14 h4! h5 15 ♘e5 ♗xe5 16 dxe5 (16 ♗xe5? ♘xe5 17 dxe5 ♕e7 ∓ Bareev-Lputian, Lucerne Wcht 1993) 16...c5 17 ♖xc5 ♘d7 18 ♖c1 ♖c8 19 ♖xc8 ♕xc8 20 ♘d4 ♘dxe5 21 ♗e2 ±.

b32) 9...♗xg3 10 hxg3 ♕b6 and now:

b321) 11 f3 ♘a6 12 g4 ♗g6 13 ♕xb6!? (13 ♔f2 ♕xb3 = Bareev-A.Petrosian, Moscow 1989) 13...axb6 14 a3 intending ♘h3 ±.

b322) 11 ♘f3!? ♘d7 12 ♘h4 ♕xb3 13 axb3 ♗e6 14 b4 0-0 15 ♗d3 a6 16 ♘a4 h6 17 ♘c5 ♘xc5 18 bxc5 ± Gulko-Lputian, Erevan 1994.

b323) 11 ♗e2 and now:

b3231) 11...♘d7 12 g4 ♗e6 (alternatively, 12...♗g6 13 ♘h3 0-0 14 ♘f4 ±) 13 ♘h3 ♕xb3 (13...0-0-0?! 14 ♕a3! ± Bareev-Khalifman, Leningrad

1990) 14 axb3 a6 15 ♘f4 ♘g6 16 ♘xe6 fxe6 17 f4 ±.

b3232) 11...♘a6!? 12 g4 ♗g6 13 ♘f3 (13 ♗xa6 ♕xa6 14 ♘ge2 ♕b6 15 ♘f4 ♕xb3 16 axb3 a6 17 ♘xg6 ♘xg6 18 g5 0-0 19 ♘a4 ♖fe8 20 ♘c5 ♖e7 with equality, Yakovich-Burmakin, St Petersburg 1998) 13...f6 14 ♘a4 ♕xb3 15 axb3 ♘c7 16 ♘c5 b6 17 ♘a6 ♔d7 18 ♔d2 ♘e8 = Sadler-Lputian, Erevan OL 1996.

b33) 9...♘c8!? 10 ♘f3 (10 ♕xb7? ♘b6 intending ...♗c8) 10...♕b6 11 ♗e2 ♘a6 12 0-0 ♕xb3 13 axb3 ♘c7 14 b4 ♗xg3 15 hxg3 ♘d6 16 ♘d2 h5! 17 ♘b3 a6 18 f3 (18 ♘c5 ½-½ Baburin-Vaganian, Los Angeles 1997) 18...0-0-0 19 ♘c5 ♖de8 20 ♔f2 ♖e7 21 ♖fe1 ♖he8 22 ♗f1 =.

We now return to 6...♗g4 (D):

W

**7 e3**

7 f3!? seems interesting: 7...♗h5 8 0-0-0 ♘f6 9 e4 (9 e3!? ♗g6 10 ♗d3 ♘a6 11 ♗xg6 hxg6 12 g4 ∞) 9...♗g6! 10 ♗d3 0-0 11 e5 (11 ♗xb8 ♖xb8 12 e5 ♗xd3 13 ♕xd3 ♘e8 14 f4 f5 is unclear, Yrjölä-Hakulinen, Helsinki 1992) 11...♗xd3 (11...♘e8 12 ♗e3 ♘a6 13 ♗xg6 fxg6 14 f4 ♘ec7 15 h4 ∞ Shirov-Spraggett, Manila IZ 1990)

12 ♕xd3 ♘e8 13 ♗e3 ♘a6 14 f4 ♘b4! 15 ♕b1 (15 ♕e2 f5 16 ♔b1 ♕a5 17 ♘f3 ♘c7 18 ♘d2 ♕a6 = Manninen-Hakulinen, Helsinki 1992) 15...f5 16 a3 ♘a6 17 ♘f3 b5 with equality – Spraggett.

**7...♗h5 8 ♗d3**

8 ♘f3 ♘d7 9 h3 ♗g6 10 ♕d2 ♘gf6 11 ♗e2 0-0 12 0-0 ♘e4 (12...a5!? 13 ♖fc1 ♘e4 14 ♘xe4 ♗xe4 15 ♘e1! ♗b4 16 ♕d1 a4 17 ♘d3 a3! 18 b3 ♗xd3 19 ♗xd3 ± Salov-Portisch, Linares 1990) 13 ♘xe4 ♗xe4 = Salov, Ionov.

**8...♗g6 9 ♗xg6**

9 ♘ge2 ♘f6 and now:

a) 10 0-0!? 0-0 (10...♘bd7 11 ♘g3 0-0 {11...♗xd3 12 ♕xd3 0-0 13 ♘f5 ♖e8 14 ♗d6! ±} 12 ♘f5 ±) 11 ♘g3 ♘a6 12 a3 ♗xd3 13 ♕xd3 ♗d6 (or 13...♘c7 14 ♘f5 ♘e6 15 ♗g3 ±) 14 ♗xd6 ♕xd6 15 b4 ♘c7 = analysis.

b) 10 f3 ♗xd3 11 ♕xd3 0-0 12 0-0 ♘bd7 13 ♘g3 ♖e8 14 ♖ad1 ♘f8 15 ♘f5 ♘h5! = Malaniuk-Timoshchenko, Sverdlovsk 1987.

**9...hxg6 10 f3**

10 ♘f3 ♘f6 11 h3 ♘bd7 12 ♘e5 0-0 13 0-0 ♘e8 14 ♖ab1 a5 =.

**10...♗d6**

10...♘d7 11 ♘ge2 ♘b6 12 b3 (12 e4 ±) 12...♗d6 13 0-0-0 ♘e7 14 g4 (14 e4!?) 14...♕c7 (14...♘h3 15 ♗xd6 ♕xd6 16 ♘f4 ♖xf3 17 ♕e2 ±) 15 ♔b1 0-0-0 16 ♖c1 ♗xf4 17 ♘xf4 ♔b8 18 h4 ± M.Gurevich-Portisch, Wijk aan Zee 1990.

**11 ♘ge2 ♗xf4 12 ♘xf4 ♕h4+ 13 ♕f2**

13 g3 ♕xg3+ 14 hxg3 ♖xh1+ 15 ♔f2 ♖xa1 16 ♕b3! ♘d7 (16...b6 17 ♘cxd5 ±) 17 ♕xb7 ♖b8 18 ♕xc6 ♖xb2+ 19 ♘fe2 ♘gf6 ∞.

**13...♕xf2+ 14 ♔xf2 ♘f6**
The position is equal (analysis).

**A2)**
**6 e3** *(D)*

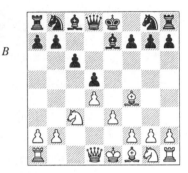

**6...♗f5**
Practice has also seen 6...♗d6, which may be OK for Black despite the loss of tempo:

a) 7 ♗xd6 ♕xd6 8 ♗d3 ♘e7 9 ♕c2 (9 ♘f3 ♘d7 10 0-0 ♘f6 11 ♕c2 0-0 12 ♖ab1 g6! = Gligorić-Portisch, Palma de Mallorca 1967) 9...♗g4 10 f3 ♗h5 11 ♘ge2 ♗g6 12 e4 dxe4 13 fxe4 ♘d7 14 0-0-0 0-0 15 g4 c5 16 h4 h5 17 e5 ♕e6 18 ♗xg6 fxg6 19 d5 ♕xe5 20 d6 ♘c6 21 ♕xg6 ♖ae8! = Lerner-Lobron, Amsterdam 1988.

b) 7 ♗g3 and then:
b1) 7...♗f5 8 ♕b3 ♗xg3 9 hxg3 ♕b6 10 ♘f3 ♘d7 (10...♘f6 11 ♘h4 ♗e6 12 ♕c2 c5 13 ♗b5+ ♘c6 14 dxc5 ♕xc5 15 ♖c1 0-0 16 ♗xc6 ♕xc6 17 0-0 ♖ac8 18 ♘f3 ± Christiansen-Ki.Georgiev, Tilburg 1994) 11 ♘h4 ♕xb3 12 axb3 ♗e6 13 b4 ♘e7 14 ♗d3 ± Knaak-Bönsch, Leipzig 1983.

b2) 7...♘e7 8 ♗d3 ♗f5 (8...♘f5!? 9 ♗xd6 ♘xd6 10 ♘ge2 ♗f5 11 ♗xf5 ♘xf5 12 ♕d3 ♘d6 13 0-0 0-0 14 f3 f5

= Seirawan-Lputian, Manila IZ 1990) 9 ♗e2 (9 ♘f3!? ♗xg3 10 hxg3 ♘d7 11 ♕c2 ♗xd3 12 ♕xd3 h6 13 0-0-0 ♕c7 14 ♔b1 0-0-0 15 ♖c1! ± Cebalo-Abramović, Yugoslavia 1985) 9...0-0 10 ♕b3 ♘c8 11 ♘f3 and then:
b221) 11...♕b6!? 12 ♗xd6 ♘xd6!? (12...♕xb3 13 axb3 ♘xd6 14 b4 ±) 13 ♕a3 ∞.
b222) 11...♕e7 12 ♘e5 ♖e8 13 0-0 f6 14 ♘d3 ♗xg3 15 hxg3 ♘d6 16 ♘f4 ♔h8 17 g4 ♗e6 18 ♕c2 ♘d7 19 ♗d3 ♗g8 20 ♖ae1 ♘f8 21 f3 ± Sakaev-Rustemov, Moscow 1998.

**7 g4**
Botvinnik's idea. The move's aim is to exploit the advanced position of the black bishop to seize space on the kingside. 7 ♕b3 ♕b6 is equal, but White has also used 7 ♘ge2:
a) 7...♘f6!? 8 ♘g3 and here:
a1) 8...♗g6 9 h4 h5 10 ♗d3 ♗xd3 11 ♕xd3 g6 12 0-0-0 ♘bd7 (12...♘a6 13 ♔b1 ♕a5 14 ♗g5 0-0-0 15 ♘f5! ♕c7 16 ♘xe7+ ♕xe7 17 e4 ± Portisch-Pietzsch, Kecskemet 1966) 13 e4 dxe4 14 ♘gxe4 0-0 15 f3 ♕a5 16 g4! ± Chekhov-Timoshchenko, USSR 1987.
a2) 8...♗e6 9 ♗d3 g6 10 0-0-0 0-0 11 h3 (11 ♘ce2?! ♖e8 12 ♖c1 ♘bd7 13 h3 ♔g7 14 f3 c5 15 b3 ♕b6 = Bronstein-Flesch, Miskolc 1963) 11...♖e8! (11...♘bd7 12 ♗h6 ♖e8 13 f4 ♗f8 14 ♗xf8 ♘xf8, Bareev-Ki.Georgiev, Pardubice 1994, 15 ♕f3! ♗c8 16 f5 g5 17 ♖ad1 ±) 12 ♗h6 ♔h8 = intending to meet 13 f4 with 13...♘g8 – Bareev.
b) 7...♘d7 *(D)* and now:
b1) 8 h3 ♗g6 (8...♘gf6 9 g4 ♗e4 10 ♖g1 ♗f3 11 ♖g3 ♗xe2 12 ♗xe2 ♗b4 13 f3 ♕e7 14 ♖g2 ♗d6 15 ♗xd6 ♕xd6, Vaiser-Timoshchenko, Frunze

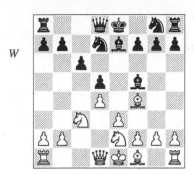

W

1987, 16 ♕d2!? 0-0-0 17 0-0-0 ±
Vaiser) 9 ♘g3 ♘f8 (9...♘gf6 10 ♗e2
a5?! 11 0-0 0-0 12 h4! h6 13 h5 ♗h7 14
f3 ± Hertneck-Sturua, Katerini 1993)
10 ♗e5 (10 h4?! ♗xh4 11 ♕b3 ♗xg3
12 ♗xg3 ♕e7 13 ♖c1 ♘e6 14 ♗h4 f6
15 ♕a4 ♕d7 16 ♗e2 ♘e7 ∓ S.Mohr-
Geller, Dortmund 1989) 10...♘e6 11
♘ge2 ♗d6 12 ♗xd6 ♕xd6 13 ♘c1
♘f6 14 ♗d3 ♗xd3 15 ♘xd3 0-0 16
0-0 ♘e4 17 ♖c1 ♘xc3 18 ♖xc3 ♖fe8
= Sadler-Lutz, Pula Echt 1997.

b2) 8 ♘g3 and then:
b21) 8...♗e6 9 ♘h5! ♗f8 (9...♔f8
10 ♗g3 ♕b6 11 ♖b1 ♗f5 12 ♗d3
♗xd3 13 ♕xd3 g6 14 ♘f4 ± Ador-
jan-Lobron, Reggio Emilia 1984/5) 10
♗g3 ♘df6 11 ♘f4 ± Portisch-Barcza,
Hungary 1978.

b22) 8...♗g6 9 ♗e2 (9 ♖c1 h5!?
10 ♗d3 h4 11 ♗xg6 hxg3 12 ♗d3
gxf2+ 13 ♔xf2 ♗g5 = Speelman-
Geller, Skara Echt 1980) and here:
b221) 9...♘f8?! 10 ♗g4 ♘f6 11
♗h3 ♘e6 12 ♗e5 ♘g5 13 ♗f5 0-0
14 h4 ± I.Sokolov-Vaganian, Tilburg
1994.

b222) 9...♕b6!? 10 ♕d2 ♘gf6
(10...h5?! 11 0-0 h4 12 ♘h1 h3 13 g4
intending f3 and ♘f2 ± I.Sokolov) 11
h4 h6 12 h5 ♗h7 13 f3 0-0 14 ♘a4

♕b4 15 ♕xb4 ♗xb4+ 16 ♔f2 ± I.Sok-
olov.

b223) 9...♘gf6 10 h4 h5 (10...h6!?
11 h5 ♗h7 12 ♗d3 ♕b6 13 ♖b1 0-0 14
♗xh7+ ♔xh7 15 ♘f5 ♖fe8 ½-½ Ador-
jan-Liang Jinrong, Shenzhen 1992) 11
♗f3 (11 ♗g5 ♗d6 12 ♖h3 ♕b6 13
♕d2 0-0 14 ♔f1 ♖fe8 15 ♔g1 ♖ac8 ∞
Portisch-Geller, Portorož IZ playoff
1973) 11...♕b6 12 ♕e2 a5 13 ♗g5
♕a6! 14 ♕xa6 ♖xa6 = Bagirov-Ler-
ner, USSR 1979.

We now return to 7 g4 *(D)*:

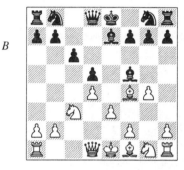

B

**7...♗e6**
The retreat to g6 gives White the
better chances: 7...♗g6 8 h4:
a) 8...♗xh4? 9 ♕b3 b6 and now 10
♖xh4! ♕xh4 11 ♘xd5 wins by force,
while 10 ♘f3 ♗e7 11 ♗xb8 (11 ♘e5!?)
11...♕xb8 12 ♘e5 ♕b7 13 ♘xc6 a6
14 ♘e5 also led to victory in Vaïsser-
Schmidt Schäffer, Munich 1992/3.
b) 8...h6 9 ♘f3 ♘d7 10 ♗d3 ♗xd3
11 ♕xd3 ♘gf6 12 ♖g1 ♕a5 13 ♘d2
♘f8 14 f3 ♘e6 15 ♗e5 ± Knaak-Rai-
čević, Athens 1992.
c) 8...h5 9 g5 ♗d6 10 ♘ge2 and
then:
c1) 10...♘e7 11 ♗xd6 ♕xd6 12
♘f4 ♘d7 (12...♗e4?! 13 ♘xe4 dxe4

14 ♕b3 ♕d7 15 ♗c4 ♘g6 16 ♘xg6 fxg6 17 ♖d1 b5 18 ♗e6 ♕d6 19 d5 +– C.Flear-A.Marić, Dubai wom OL 1986) 13 ♗e2 ♘f5 14 ♖c1 ♕b4 15 ♕d2 ± Knaak-J.C.Diaz, Hungary 1987.

c2) 10...♘a6!? 11 ♗xd6 ♕xd6 12 ♘f4 ♘c7 13 ♗e2 ♕b4!? 14 ♕d2 ♘e7 15 ♗f3 ♘e6 16 ♘ce2! ± Karpov-Portisch, Linares 1989.

**8 h4**

Botvinnik – the inventor of the plan starting with 7 g4 – considered 8 h4 most energetic, seizing even more space on the kingside. Other plans have also been tried in practice:

a) 8 ♗e5!? ♘f6 9 g5 ♘e4 10 h4 (10 ♗xg7 ♖g8 11 ♗e5 ♖xg5 ∞) 10...0-0 11 ♗d3 ♕a5 12 ♕c1 (12 ♕c2 ♘a6 13 ♕c1 ♘b4 14 ♗b1 c5 15 f3 cxd4 16 ♗xd4 ♘g3 17 ♖h2 ♘c6 18 ♔f2 ♘xd4 19 exd4 ♗d6 20 ♖g2 ♘h5 21 ♘ge2 g6 ∓ Aleksandrov-Kharitonov, Sochi 1997) 12...c5 13 f3 ♘xc3 14 ♕xc3 ∞ Kharitonov.

b) 8 ♗d3 and now:

b1) 8...♘f6 9 g5 ♘fd7 10 h4 c5 11 ♘b5 ♘a6 12 dxc5 ♘dxc5 13 ♗e2 0-0 14 ♘f3 ± K.Grigorian-Klovans, USSR 1983.

b2) 8...h5 9 gxh5 ♘f6 10 h6 g6 11 ♘ge2 ♘h5 12 ♕c2 ♘d7 13 0-0-0 ♗g5 14 ♗g3 ♕f6 15 ♔b1 ± Zheliandinov-D.Gurevich, USSR 1966.

b3) 8...♗d6 9 ♕e2 and now, rather than 9...h5?! 10 g5 ♘e7 11 ♘f3 ♗xf4 12 exf4 ♗g4 13 h3 ± Taimanov-Morović, Skopje 1970, Black should play 9...♘e7 ∞.

b4) 8...♘d7 9 h3 h5 and then:

b41) 10 gxh5 ♘df6 11 h6 (11 ♕c2 ♘xh5 12 ♗e5 ♘gf6 13 0-0-0 ♘d7 14 ♗h2 ♘b6 15 ♔b1 ♗d6 = V.Milov-Lutz, Dresden Z 1998) 11...♘xh6 12

♕c2 ♕d7 13 ♘f3 ♗f5 14 ♘e5 ♗xd3 15 ♘xd3 ♗d6 = Lputian-Geller, USSR Ch (Riga) 1985.

b42) 10 ♕f3 g5 (or 10...♕b6!? 11 0-0-0 hxg4 12 hxg4 ♖xh1 13 ♕xh1 g5 14 ♗g3 ♗xg4 15 ♖d2 and now rather than 15...♗e6?! 16 ♕h2 0-0-0 17 ♘b5! ± Miles-T.Georgadze, Porz 1981/2, Black should play 15...♘gf6 ∞) 11 ♗g3 ♘df6 12 gxh5 ♘xh5 13 ♘ge2 ♘xg3 14 ♘xg3 ♕d7 15 ♘f5 ♗f8 16 ♖g1 f6 17 0-0-0 ♘e7 ∞ Marković-Geller, Cappelle la Grande 1993.

c) 8 h3 *(D)* and now:

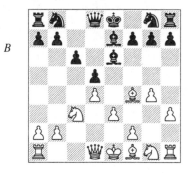

c1) 8...c5 9 dxc5 ♗xc5 10 ♗g2 ♘e7 11 ♘f3 ♘bc6 12 0-0 0-0 13 ♖c1 ♗b6 14 a3 ♘g6 15 ♗g3 ± Lputian-Magomedov, Azov 1991.

c2) 8...h5 9 gxh5 ♘d7 10 ♗e2 ♘df6 11 ♖h2! (11 ♗e5 ♗d6 12 ♖h2 ♘xh5! 13 ♗xh5 ♗xe5 14 dxe5 ♕g5 15 ♗g4 ♗xg4 16 ♖g2 ♗xd1 17 ♖xg5 ♗h5 18 ♘ge2 {18 ♖xg7? ♗g6} 18...♗xe2 19 ♔xe2 g6 is equal, Hort-Renet, France 1990) 11...♗d6 12 ♗xd6 ♕xd6 13 ♖g2 ± Korchnoi-Ivkov, USSR-Yugoslavia 1967.

c3) 8...♗d6 9 ♘ge2 ♘e7 10 ♕b3 (10 ♗xd6!? ♕xd6 11 ♘f4 ♘d7 12 ♗d3 ♖c8 13 ♕f3 0-0 14 ♕g3 with a clear advantage for White, Geller-Bradvarević, Varna 1964) 10...♗c8 11 ♗g2 ♘g6 12 ♗xd6 ♛xd6 13 h4 ♘a6 14 g5 ♘e7 15 0-0-0! (15 ♘f4?! ♘c7 16 0-0-0 ♗g4 ∞ Korchnoi-Spassky, Kiev Ct (2) 1968) 15...♘c7 (15...♗f5 16 ♘g3!) 16 e4! ±.

c4) 8...♘f6 and then:

c41) 9 ♘f3 and here:

c411) 9...h5 10 g5 ♘e4 11 ♛b3 ♛b6 12 ♛c2 ♘a6 13 a3 ♛a5 14 ♖c1 ± Geller-Pachman, Beverwijk 1965.

c412) 9...♘bd7 10 ♗d3 ♘b6 11 ♛c2 ♘c4 12 ♗xc4! (12 ♔f1 ♘d6 13 ♘d2 ♛c8 14 ♔g2 ♘d7 15 f3 ± Botvinnik-Petrosian, Moscow Wch (18) 1963) 12...dxc4 13 e4 intending ♖d1 and d5 ± – Kan.

c413) 9...0-0 10 ♛c2 c5 11 ♗g2 (11 0-0-0 ♘c6 12 dxc5 ♛a5 13 ♘d4 ♘b4 14 ♛b3 ♗xc5 15 f3 ♖ac8 16 ♔b1 ♖fe8 = Furman-Saigin, USSR 1963) 11...♘c6 12 ♖d1 ♛a5 13 0-0 with equality, Gipslis-Keller, Latvia 1962.

c42) 9 ♗d3 c5 (9...a6!? 10 ♘f3 c5 11 ♖c1 ♘c6 12 dxc5 ♗xc5 13 ♔f1 0-0 14 ♘e2 ♘e4 15 ♘e5 ♘xe5 16 ♗xe5 ♖c8 = Shaked-Portisch, Berlin 1997) 10 ♘f3 ♘c6 11 ♔f1 0-0 12 ♔g2 and here:

c421) 12...a6!?.

c422) 12...c4!? 13 ♗c2 a6 intending ...b5 ∞.

c423) 12...cxd4 13 ♘xd4 ♘xd4 (13...♗d6 14 ♗xd6 ♛xd6 15 ♘ce2 ♖fe8 16 ♖c1 ♗d7 17 ♗b1 ± Geller-Spassky, Moscow 1967) 14 exd4 ♘d7 (14...♘e4 15 ♘xe4 dxe4 16 ♗xe4 f5 17 gxf5 ♗xf5 18 ♛d3 ±) 15 ♛c2 ♘f6 16 f3 ♖c8 17 ♗e5 ♗d6 18 ♖ae1! ♗xe5 19 ♖xe5 g6 20 ♛f2 ± Botvinnik-Petrosian, Moscow Wch (4) 1963.

c424) 12...♖c8 13 ♖c1 (13 dxc5 ♗xc5 14 ♘e2 ♘e4 ∞ Bronstein-Kuijpers, Amsterdam 1968) and now Korchnoi recommends 13...a6!? = instead of 13...♖e8 14 dxc5 ♗xc5 15 ♘b5 ± Korchnoi-Karpov, Merano Wch (13) 1981.

We now return to the position after 8 h4 (D):

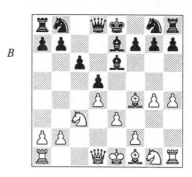

B

**8...♘d7**

Or:

a) 8...♗xh4?! 9 ♛b3 and then:

a1) 9...g5 10 ♗h2 ♛b6 (10...♗xg4? 11 ♛xb7 ♛e7 12 ♛xa8 ♛xe3+ 13 ♗e2 ♛xf2+ 14 ♔d2 +– Vaiser-Diaz, Havana 1985) 11 ♘f3 ♛xb3 12 axb3 ♗xg4 13 ♘xh4 gxh4 14 ♗xb8 ♖xb8 15 ♖xa7 ±.

a2) 9...b6 10 ♘f3 ♗e7 11 ♘e5 ♘f6 (11...g5 12 ♗g3 ♘f6 13 ♗e2 ♛c8 14 ♖c1 ♘bd7 15 ♘b5 ♘c5 16 dxc5 cxb5 17 ♛xb5+ ♔f8 18 ♘c6 ♘e4 19 ♘xe7 ♔xe7 20 ♗d6+ ♔f6 21 ♛b4 ± Yusupov-Lputian, Baden-Baden 1996) 12 g5 ♘fd7 13 g6 ♘xe5 14 ♗xe5 ♗f6! 15 ♖xh7 0-0! 16 ♗g3 fxg6 17 ♖h2 ♔f7! 18 0-0-0 ♘d7! (18...♖h8?! 19 ♖xh8 ♛xh8 20 e4! ± Gulko-Lputian, Glendale tt 1994) 19 e4 ♗e7 intending ...♘f6 ±.

b) 8...c5!? 9 dxc5 ♗xc5 10 ♘ge2
♘e7 11 ♘d4 ♘bc6 12 ♘xe6 fxe6 13
♗g2 0-0 14 0-0 ♘g6 15 ♗g5 ♗e7 ∞
Flear-Beliavsky, Szirak IZ 1987.

**9 h5 ♕b6**

Geller's idea 9...♘h6!? seems interesting: 10 ♗e2 (10 ♗h3 g5!) 10...♘b6
11 ♖c1 (11 ♘h3?! g5! 12 hxg6 hxg6
13 f3 ♗h4+! 14 ♔d2 g5 15 ♗h2 f5 ∓
Vaiser-Timoshchenko, Tashkent 1987)
and now:

a) 11...♗d6?! 12 ♘h3 ♗xf4 13
♘xf4 ♗d7 (13...♕g5?! 14 ♘xe6 fxe6
15 f4 ±) 14 ♖g1! with a slight advantage to White, Kasparov-Karpov, Moscow Wch (21) 1985.

b) 11...♘c4!? 12 b3 (12 ♗xc4 dxc4
13 ♗xh6 gxh6 ∞) 12...♘d6 ∞.

**10 ♖b1 ♘gf6 11 f3 0-0**

11...h6?! 12 ♗d3 0-0 (12...♕a5 13
♘ge2 ± Botvinnik-Spassky, Leiden
1970) 13 ♘ge2 c5 14 ♔f1 ♖ac8 (or
14...♖fe8 15 g5!) 15 g5! hxg5 16
♗xg5 ♖fe8 17 ♕e1 ± Knaak-Geller,
Moscow 1982.

**12 ♗d3 c5**

Black must try to generate counterplay in the centre.

**13 ♘ge2 ♖ac8 14 ♔f1 cxd4 15
exd4 ♘b8**

Larsen's recommendation. Worse
for Black is 15...♗d6?! 16 ♕d2 ♘e8
17 ♔g2 ♕d8 18 ♖be1 ± Beliavsky-
Geller, USSR Ch (Moscow) 1983.

**16 ♔g2 ♘c6 17 a3 ♘a5 18 g5 ♘d7**

The position is unclear.

**B)**

**5...♘f6 6 e3** *(D)*
**6...♗f5**

Another system, which has been
widely used in practice, starts with
6...0-0:

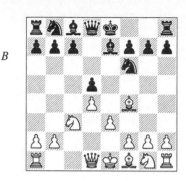

B

a) 7 ♘f3 seems interesting. 7...♗f5
and then:

a1) 8 h3 c6 (8...♘bd7!? 9 g4 ♗e4
10 g5 ♘h5 ∞) 9 g4 and here:

a11) 9...♗e4?! 10 g5! (10 ♗g2
♘bd7 11 0-0 ♗g6 12 ♘e5 ♘xe5 13
dxe5 ♘d7 ∞ Kiriakov-Korneev, Groningen 1995) 10...♘h5 11 ♗xb8! ♖xb8
12 ♘xe4 dxe4 13 ♘d2 g6 14 h4 and
White is slightly better.

a12) 9...♗g6 10 ♘e5 ♘fd7! 11
♘xg6 fxg6 (11...hxg6?! 12 ♗d3 intending ♕c2 ±) 12 ♗g2 (12 ♗d3!?)
12...♘b6 13 0-0 ♔h8 (13...g5?! 14
♗g3 ♗d6 15 ♗xd6 ♕xd6 16 e4! ±) 14
♘e2 (14 ♕d3!?; 14 ♗g3!?) 14...g5 15
♗g3 ♗d6 ∞ Karpov-Kasparov, Moscow Wch (22) 1985.

a2) 8 ♕b3!? ♘c6 and here:

a21) 9 ♕xb7 ♘b4 10 ♖c1 ♘e4 and
now:

a211) 11 ♘xe4?! dxe4 12 ♘d2 ♖b8
13 ♕xa7 ♖a8 ∓.

a212) 11 ♗e2 ♘xc3 12 bxc3 (12
♖xc3 ♘xa2 13 ♖c7 ♖b8 is equal)
12...♘xa2 13 ♖a1 ♖b8 14 ♕xc7 ♖b2
with compensation.

a213) 11 ♗xc7 ♕c8 12 ♕xc8 ♖fxc8
13 ♗a5 ♘xc3 14 ♖xc3 (14 bxc3 ♘c6)
14...♖xc3 15 bxc3 ♘xa2 16 ♗a6 ♗d8
with compensation.

a214) 11 a3 ♘xc3 12 ♖xc3 (12 axb4 ♘a2 13 ♖xc7 ♖b8! with compensation; 12 bxc3 ♘a2 13 ♖a1 ♘xc3 14 ♕xc7 {14 ♗xc7 ♕d7} 14...♕xc7 15 ♗xc7 ♖fc8 16 ♗a5 ♘b1 ∓) 12...♘a2 and then:

a2141) 13 ♖xc7 ♖b8 14 ♕xa7 (14 ♖xe7 ♖xb7 15 ♖xb7 ♕a5+ 16 ♘d2 ♖c8 ∓) 14...♖a8! (14...♖xb2? 15 ♗e2! ♗d6 16 ♗xd6 ♕xd6 17 ♘e5 ±) 15 ♕b7 ♖b8 16 ♕a6 ♖xb2 17 ♗d3 ♗b4+ ∓.

a2142) 13 ♖b3 ♖b8! 14 ♕xb8 ♕xb8 15 ♖xb8 ♖xb8 16 b4 a5 17 ♘e5 (17 b5 ♖b7; 17 ♗xc7 ♖c8 18 ♗xa5 ♖c1+ 19 ♔e2 ♖c2+ =) 17...axb4 18 ♘c6 bxa3 19 ♘xe7+ (19 ♘xb8 ♗b4+ 20 ♔d1 ♘c3+ 21 ♔c1 a2 22 ♔b2 ♗b1 intending ...♘a4+ and ...♗c3 −+) 19...♔f8 20 ♘xf5 ♖b1+ 21 ♔d2 ♖b2+ ∓ (analysis).

a22) 9 a3 ♘a5 10 ♕a2 and then:

a221) 10...c5 11 dxc5 ♗xc5 12 b4 ♗b6! 13 ♗e5! ♖c8 14 ♖d1 ♗e6 15 ♘a4! ♘c4 16 ♗xc4 ♖xc4 17 ♘xb6 axb6 18 ♕b2! ± Ruban-Makarov, USSR 1987.

a222) 10...♗e6 11 ♗e2 c5 12 ♖d1 ♘e4! (12...♘c6 13 dxc5 ♗xc5 14 0-0 ♕e7 15 ♕b1 h6, Chekhov-Timoshchenko, Frunze 1988, 16 ♕c2!? ±) 13 ♘xe4 dxe4 14 d5 ♗g4 15 ♘d2 ♗xe2 16 ♔xe2 ♕d7 with an unclear position, Timoshchenko-Kruppa, Frunze 1988.

a223) 10...c6! and here:

a2231) 11 ♘d2 c5 12 dxc5 ♗xc5 13 b4 d4 14 ♘a4 (14 ♘d1 ♘d5) 14...dxe3 15 fxe3 ♗xe3 16 ♗xe3 ♖e8 ∓.

a2232) 11 b4 ♘c4 12 ♗xc4 dxc4 13 ♕xc4 a5 14 b5 ♖c8 with compensation.

a2233) 11 ♘e5 ♘d7 12 ♘xd7 (12 b4 ♘xe5 13 ♗xe5 ♘c4 14 ♗xc4 dxc4 15 ♕xc4 a5 16 b5 ♖c8 with compensation) 12...♕xd7 13 ♗e2 ♗e6 intending ...♘c4 =.

a2234) 11 ♖c1 ♗e6!? 12 ♗d3 (12 ♘g5 ♗f5! intending ...♘h5) 12...♘h5 13 ♗g3 ♘c4 ∞.

a2235) 11 ♗e2 ♗e6!? intending to meet 12 ♘g5 with 12...♗f5 = (analysis).

a3) 8 ♘e5 c5 (8...♘bd7 9 g4 ± I.Sokolov) 9 dxc5 (9 g4 cxd4 10 exd4 ♗e6 11 ♗g2 ♘c6 12 h3 is best met by 12...♕b6! =, rather than 12...♘d7?! 13 ♘f3! ± Dokhoian-Kruppa, Sevastopol 1986) 9...♗xc5 10 ♗d3 ♗xd3 11 ♘xd3 ♗b6 12 0-0 d4 13 exd4 ♗xd4 14 ♘b5 ♘c6 15 ♖c1 a6 16 ♘xd4 ♕xd4 17 ♕b3 ♘d5 18 ♗g3 ♘a5 19 ♕c2 ♘b4 20 ♘xb4 ♕xb4 21 ♗e5 ♘c6 22 ♗c3 ♕c4 23 b3 ♕g4 24 h3 ♕g5 25 ♖cd1 ♖ad8 with an equal position, I.Sokolov-Lautier, Corrèze (4) 1992.

b) 7 ♗d3 c5 (D) and now:

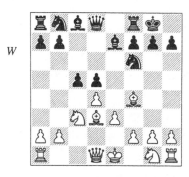

W

b1) 8 dxc5 gives White no advantage due to 8...♗xc5 9 ♘f3 ♘c6 10 0-0 d4! 11 ♘a4 ♗d6! 12 ♗xd6 ♕xd6 13 ♘xd4 ♘xd4 14 exd4 ♗g4 =.

b2) 8 ♘f3 is a popular move. 8...♘c6 9 0-0 and then:

b21) 9...cxd4 10 ♘xd4 ♗g4 (or 10...♘xd4 11 exd4 ♕b6 {11...♗g4 12 ♕b3} 12 ♖e1 ♗e6 13 ♘a4 ♕a5 14 a3 ± intending b4) 11 ♕a4 ♘xd4 (the alternative 11...♕b6 should be countered by 12 ♕b5! ±, rather than 12 ♘xc6 bxc6 13 ♗e5 ♗e6 14 ♕c2 h6 15 ♘a4 ♕b7 16 ♗d4 ♘d7 17 ♖ab1 a5! = Dokhoian-Goldin, Sevastopol 1986) 12 ♕xd4 ♕d7 13 h3 ♗e6 14 ♖fd1 ♖fc8 15 ♗e5! ± Kasparov-Tal, Skellefteå 1989.

b22) 9...♗g4 10 dxc5 ♗xc5 11 h3 ♗xf3 (11...♗h5? 12 g4! ♗g6 13 ♗xg6 hxg6 14 g5 ±) 12 ♕xf3 d4 13 ♘e4! (13 exd4?! ♘xd4 14 ♕xb7? ♘e6 −+) 13...♗e7 (13...♘xe4 14 ♗xe4 dxe3 15 ♕h5 exf2+ 16 ♔h1 f5 17 ♗xf5 g6 18 ♗xg6 hxg6 19 ♕xg6+ ♔h8 20 ♖ad1! ± G.Georgadze-Shalamberidze, Tbilisi 1987) 14 ♖ad1 and then:

b221) 14...♕b6!? 15 ♗d6!? ♘d5! (better than 15...♘xe4? 16 ♗xe7 ♖fe8 17 ♗xe4 ♖xe7 18 ♗xc6 bxc6 19 ♖xd4 or 15...♗xd6? 16 ♘xf6+ gxf6 17 ♕g4+ ♔h8 18 ♕f5) 16 ♕f5 ♗xd6 17 ♘xd6 ♘f6 18 ♘c4 ♕c7 19 e4 ± intending e5.

b222) 14...♕a5! 15 ♘g3! ± Kasparov-Karpov, London/Leningrad Wch (8) 1986.

b23) 9...c4 10 ♗c2 (10 ♗e2 ♘h5! 11 ♗e5 f6 12 ♗g3 ♘xg3 13 hxg3 ♗e6 14 ♕c2 ♖c8 15 ♖ad1 ♗b4 16 e4 ♘e7 = Kozlov-Kruppa, Frunze 1988) and then:

b231) 10...♘h5?! 11 ♗e5! f6 12 ♘g5! (12 ♗g3?! ♘xg3 13 hxg3 ♗e6 14 ♕e2 ♖e8 = Salov-Kruppa, Irkutsk 1986) 12...g6 13 ♘xh7 fxe5 14 ♘xf8 ♗xf8 15 dxe5 ♗e6 16 ♗xg6 ♘g7 17 f4 ± H.Olafsson-Einarsson, Reykjavik 1988.

b232) 10...♗g4 11 h3 ♗h5 12 g4 (12 ♗f5 ♗b4 {12...♗g6!?} 13 ♗g5 ♗xc3 14 bxc3 h6 15 ♗xf6 ♕xf6 16 g4 ♗g6 17 ♗xg6 ♕xg6 18 ♖b1 b6 19 ♘h4 ♕e6 20 ♘f5 ♘e7 = Ryskin-Pushkov, Vladivostok 1994) 12...♗g6 and here:

b2321) 13 ♗xg6 hxg6 14 ♘e5 ♗b4 15 ♘e2 (15 f3 ♖e8 16 ♕c2 ♘h7 17 ♖ad1 ♘f8 18 ♔g2 ♘e7 19 g5 ♗xc3 20 bxc3 ♘e6 = K.Nikolaidis-Mihos, Greek Cht (Poros) 1998) 15...♗d6 16 b3 cxb3 17 ♕xb3 ♖e8 18 ♘f3 ♘a5 19 ♕d3 ♘c4 20 ♖ab1 ♗xf4 21 ♘xf4 ♕d7 22 ♕b3 b6 23 ♕b5 ♕b7 = H.Olafsson-Marciano, Reykjavik 1993.

b2322) 13 ♘e5 ♗b4 14 ♗g5 ♗xc2 15 ♕xc2 ♗xc3 16 bxc3 ♖e8 17 ♘xc6 bxc6 = Vyzhmanavin-Timoshchenko, Irkutsk 1986.

b3) 8 ♘ge2 ♘c6 and then:

b31) 9 dxc5 is premature due to 9...♗xc5 10 0-0 d4!:

b311) 11 exd4 ♘xd4 12 ♘a4 (12 ♘xd4 ♕xd4 13 ♕f3 ♗g4 14 ♕g3 ♖fd8 15 ♗e2 ♗d6 16 ♗xd6 ♕xd6 17 ♕h4 ♕d7 18 h3 ½-½ Sadler-G.Georgadze, Bundesliga 1997/8) 12...♘xe2+ 13 ♗xe2 ♘d5 14 ♗g3 ♗e7 15 ♗f3 ♗e6 16 ♖e1 ♖e8 17 ♕b3 ♕a5 18 ♕xb7 ♗f6 19 ♖ad1 ♕xa4 20 ♗xd5 ½-½ Lautier-Sosonko, Lyons ECC 1991.

b312) 11 ♘a4 ♗d6 12 ♗xd6 ♕xd6 13 h3 (13 ♗b5!? ♘g4 14 ♘g3 ♖d8 15 ♗xc6 bxc6 16 ♕xd4 ♕xd4 17 exd4 ♖xd4 18 ♖fd1 ♖xd1+ 19 ♖xd1 ♗e6 20 b3 ♔f8 21 ♖d4 ♘f6 22 ♘c5 ♗d5 ±/= Lautier-Kustanovich, Tel-Aviv sim 1998) 13...♖d8 14 exd4 ♘xd4 15 ♘xd4 ♕xd4 16 ♗e2 ♗xh3 17 ♕xd4

♖xd4 18 ♘c5 ♗f5 19 ♘xb7 ♖b4 20 ♘d6 ½-½ Vaïsser-Marciano, France 1993.

b32) 9 0-0 a6 (9...♗g4 10 dxc5! ♗xc5 11 ♖c1 a6 12 ♗g5 ♗e7 13 ♗b1 ± Draško-Constantini, Montecatini Terme 1998) 10 dxc5 ♗xc5 11 ♖c1 (11 ♗g5 is unconvincing due to 11...♗e7! 12 ♗xf6 ♗xf6 13 ♘xd5 ♗xb2 =) and then:

b321) 11...♗e6 12 ♗b1 (12 ♘a4!?) 12...♗d6 13 h3 ±.

b322) 11...♗a7 12 ♗g5! h6 13 ♗h4 d4 14 exd4 ♘xd4 15 ♘e4 ±.

b323) 11...♗e7 12 ♗b1 (12 h3!? ♗e6 13 ♗c2 ♖c8 14 ♗b3 h6 15 ♗h2 ♕a5 16 ♘d4 ♖fd8 17 ♘xe6 fxe6 18 e4 ± Sadler-Gabriel, Altensteig 1992) 12...♗e6 13 ♘d4 ♖c8 14 ♘xc6 (14 ♘xe6!? fxe6 15 a3 ±) 14...♖xc6 15 ♘e2 ♖xc1 16 ♕xc1 ♕b6 17 ♗e5 ♖c8 18 ♕d1 ♗g4! 19 ♕d3 ♗xe2! 20 ♕xe2 ♕e6 21 ♗d4 ♘e4 22 ♖d1 ♗f6 = G.Georgadze-Korneev, Elgoibar 1997.

We now return to the position after 6...♗f5 (D):

**7 ♕b3**

White immediately attempts to exploit the most sensitive point in Black's position: the b7-pawn. White often chooses instead 7 ♘ge2 (as played by Kasparov) 7...0-0, and now:

a) 8 ♖c1 c6 (8...c5?! 9 dxc5 ♗xc5 10 ♘xd5 ± shows why White put his rook on c1) 9 ♘g3 (9 h3 ♘bd7 10 g4 ♗e4 11 ♖g1 ♗f3 12 ♖g3 ♗xe2 13 ♗xe2 ♘e4 = S.Mohr-Kotronias, Debrecen 1989) 9...♗e6 (9...♗g6?! 10 h4 h6 11 h5 ♗h7 12 ♗d3 ±) 10 ♗d3 ♖e8 11 ♕b3 ♕b6 12 ♕c2 ♘bd7 13 0-0 g6 14 h3 ♗f8 15 ♘ge2 ♖ac8 = Kasparov-Karpov, Seville Wch (12) 1987.

b) 8 ♘g3 ♗e6 9 ♗d3 c5! 10 dxc5 ♗xc5 11 0-0 ♘c6 12 ♖c1 d4! (12...♗d6 13 ♘ge2! ♖c8 14 ♗b1 ♗xf4 15 ♘xf4 ± Gelfand-Kasparov, Linares 1994) and then:

b1) 13 exd4 ♗xd4 14 ♘ge2 ♗b6 15 ♗g5 h6 16 ♗h4 ♘e5 17 ♗b1 g5 18 ♗g3 ♘c4 19 ♕c2 ♕e7 ∞ Savenko-Koniushkov, Krasnodar 1997.

b2) 13 ♘b5!? ♗b6 14 e4 (∞ Kasparov) 14...♘g4! 15 h3 ♘ge5 16 ♗xe5 ♘xe5 17 f4 ♘xd3 18 ♕xd3 f6 19 ♘a3 ½-½ Scherbakov-Koniushkov, Krasnodar 1997.

b3) 13 ♘ce4 ♗e7 14 ♘c5 ♗xc5 15 ♖xc5 dxe3 16 ♗xe3 ♘b4 17 ♗f5 ♗xa2 18 ♕xd8 ♖fxd8 19 ♖b5 ♘bd5 20 ♖xb7 ♘xe3 21 fxe3 ♖db8 22 ♖xb8+ ♖xb8 23 ♖c1 = Lautier-Ivanchuk, Moscow OL 1994.

**7...♘c6 (D)**

This is a gambit variation, which was principally developed by the well-known theoretician Borisenko and the Georgian grandmaster Ubilava.

**8 ♕xb7**

White can decline the gambit:

a) 8 g4?! ♘xg4 9 a3 (9 ♕xd5 ♕c8 ∓; 9 ♘xd5 0-0 10 ♗g2 ♗h4! 11 ♗g3 ♗e6 12 ♔f1 a5! 13 ♘h3 a4 14 ♕c4 ♘a5 15 ♕c5 b6 16 ♗xh4 bxc5 17

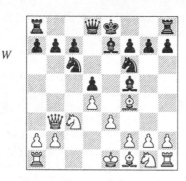

W

♗xd8 ♖axd8 18 ♘e7+ ♔h8 19 d5 ♗d7 ∓ Topalov-Kasparov, Linares 1997) 9...0-0 10 ♗g2 ♗h4 11 ♗g3 ♗xg3 12 hxg3 ♘e7 13 ♘xd5 ♘xd5 14 ♕xd5 ♕xd5 15 ♗xd5 ♖ad8 16 ♗xb7 ♖b8 17 ♗f3 ♖xb2 18 ♘e2 ♘f6! 19 ♘c3 (19 0-0 ♗e4 20 ♗xe4 ♘xe4 21 ♘f4 c5 =) 19...♖c2 20 ♘a4 ♗e4 21 ♗xe4 ♘xe4 22 0-0 c5 23 ♖ac1 ♖xc1 24 ♖xc1 cxd4 25 exd4 ♖d8 26 ♘c5 ♘xc5 27 ♖xc5 ♔f8 28 d5 ♔e7 29 ♔g2 ♔d6 30 ♖a5 ♖d7 = Aleksandrov-Az-maiparashvili, Groningen FIDE 1997.

b) 8 a3 and now:

b1) 8...♖b8 9 ♘f3 0-0 10 ♗e2 and now:

b11) 10...a6 11 h3 (11 0-0 b5 12 ♘e5 ♘a5 13 ♕d1 ♖b6 ∞ Spraggett-Yusupov, Hastings 1989/90) 11...b5 12 0-0 ± Spraggett.

b12) 10...h6 11 0-0 ♗e6! 12 ♘d2 ♗d6 13 ♗xd6 cxd6?! (13...♕xd6 ±) 14 ♗f3 ♕a5 15 ♕a2 ♘e7 16 b4 ♕c7 17 ♖fc1 ± Ki.Georgiev-Kotronias, Corfu 1991.

b2) 8...♘a5 9 ♕a4+ (9 ♕a2!? c6 {9...♗e6!?} 10 b4 ♘c4 11 ♗xc4 dxc4 12 ♕xc4 a5 13 b5 ♖c8 with compensation) 9...c6 10 ♘f3 0-0 (10...♘h5?! 11 ♗c7! ♕xc7 12 ♘xd5 ♕d8 13 ♘xe7 ♔xe7 14 b4 ♘c4 15 ♗xc4 b5 16 ♕d1 bxc4 17 ♘e5 ± Gavrikov-Ubilava, Tbilisi 1983) and now:

b21) 11 ♘e5 and now:

b211) 11...b5 12 ♕d1 ♖c8 13 ♗d3 ♗xd3 14 ♘xd3 ♘c4 15 0-0 ♖e8 16 a4 b4?! (better is 16...a6) 17 ♘e2 ♘h5 18 b3 ♘xf4 19 ♘exf4 ♘a5 20 ♖c1 ♗d6 21 g3 ± Burmakin-Koniushkov, Kstovo 1997.

b212) 11...♘d7!? 12 ♘xd7 (12 ♗e2 ♘xe5 13 ♗xe5 b5 14 ♕d1 ♘c4) 12...♗xd7 13 ♗d3! h6 (13...c5?! 14 ♕c2 ±) 14 ♕c2 (14 0-0 c5 =) 14...♘c4! =.

b22) 11 ♗e2 b5 12 ♕d1 ♘c4 13 ♕c1 a5 14 ♘e5 ♕c8 15 0-0 a4 16 ♘xc4 dxc4 17 ♗g5 ♕c7 18 ♖e1 ♖ae8 19 ♗f3 ♗d3 20 e4 ♘d7 = Vaïsser-San Segundo, Athens 1997.

**8...♘b4 9 ♗b5+**

9 ♖c1 0-0 10 a3 (10 ♘f3 transposes to note 'a21' to Black's 6th move; 10 ♕xc7 ♕xc7 11 ♗xc7 ♖ac8, Raste-nis-Ubilava, USSR 1983, 12 ♗e5 ♘e4 gives Black compensation) 10...♘c2+ 11 ♖xc2 ♗xc2 12 ♗xc7 ♕c8 13 ♗a6 ♕xb7 14 ♗xb7 ♖ab8 15 ♗xb8 ♖xb8 16 ♗a6 ♖xb2 17 ♘ge2 ♖b6 18 ♗c8 ♗xa3 19 0-0 ♗b2 = Ehlvest-Yusupov, Linares 1991.

**9...♔f8** *(D)*

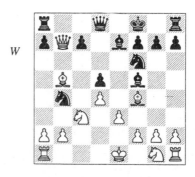

W

**10 ♔d2**

Or 10 ♖d1:

a) 10...a6 11 ♗a4 ♘d3+ 12 ♖xd3! ♗xd3 13 ♗xc7 ♕c8 14 ♕xc8+! (14 ♕b6 a5 15 ♗e5 ♘e4 ∞ Granda-San Segundo, Pamplona 1995/6) 14...♖xc8 15 ♗a5 ± intending f3, ♔d2 and ♘ge2.

b) 10...♘e4 11 ♗a4! ♘xc3 12 bxc3 ♘d3+ 13 ♖xd3 ♗xd3 14 ♗xc7 ♗a6! 15 ♕xa6 ♕xc7 16 ♘e2 ± Chernin-Detreeuw, Antwerp 1993.

c) 10...♗d6! 11 ♗xd6+ cxd6 = intending ...♖b8-a8.

**10...♘e4+!**

The best move. Black is worse after 10...a6 11 ♗a4 ♘d3 (11...c5 12 ♗c7 ♕c8 13 ♕xc8+ ♖xc8 14 ♗b6 c4 15 ♗a5 ♖b8 16 ♗xb4 ♗xb4 17 f3 ♗a5 18 ♔c1 ± H.Olafsson-Thorsteins, Akureyri 1988) 12 ♗xc7 ♕c8 13 ♕xc8+ ♖xc8 14 ♗a5 ♘xf2 15 ♖f1! ♘6e4+ 16 ♘xe4 ♘xe4+ 17 ♔e2 ♘d6 18 ♘f3 ± Salov-Timoshchenko, Irkutsk 1986.

**11 ♘xe4 ♗xe4** *(D)*

**12 ♗xc7**

12 f3 ♖b8 and now:

a) 13 ♕xa7 ♖xb5 14 fxe4 (14 a4 ♘c6 −+) 14...dxe4 15 a4 ♖c5 16 ♘e2 (16 ♖c1 ♖xc1 17 ♔xc1 g5! 18 ♗xc7 ♘d3+ 19 ♔b1 ♕d5 ∓) 16...g5! ∓.

b) 13 ♕xc7 ♕xc7 14 ♗xc7 ♖xb5 15 fxe4 dxe4 16 b3 (16 ♘e2 ♘d5 17 ♘c3 ♘xc7 18 ♘xb5 ♘xb5 19 ♖hc1 ♗d8) 16...♘d5 17 ♗g3 ♗b4+ 18 ♔e2 ♘c3+ 19 ♔f1 ♖f5+ 20 ♗f2 ♘d5 21 ♔e2 ♘c3+ = (analysis).

**12...♕c8 13 ♕xc8+ ♖xc8 14 f3 ♖xc7 15 fxe4 dxe4 16 a3 ♘d5 17 ♘h3 g5!? 18 ♗a4**

Or: 18 ♖hf1?! ♔g7 19 ♗a4 (19 ♖f5 ♖c2+! ∓) 19...♖b8 20 ♖ab1 ♔g6 21 g4 h5 22 gxh5+ ♔xh5 23 ♗d1+ ♔h4 24 ♘f2 f5 with compensation, Riazantsev-Koniushkov, Moscow 1998; 18 ♖hc1?! ♖b7 19 ♖c8+ ♔g7 20 ♖xh8 ♔xh8 21 ♗c6 ♖xb2+ 22 ♔c1 ♖xg2 23 ♗xd5 ♖xh2 24 ♘g1 ♖g2 ∓.

**18...g4! 19 ♘f2**

19 ♘f4 ♘xf4 20 exf4 ♖c4 =.

**19...f5 20 ♗b3**

20 ♖ac1 ♗d6! 21 ♗b3 ♘b6 22 ♖xc7 ♗xc7 23 ♖c1 ♗d6 24 ♗e6 ♔e7 =.

**20...♘xe3! 21 ♔xe3 ♖b7 22 ♗e6!**

22 ♗c2 ♗g5+ 23 ♔e2 ♖xb2 24 ♔d1 e3 ∓.

**22...♗g5+ 23 ♔e2 ♔e7 24 ♗xf5 ♖xb2+ 25 ♔e1 ♖f8 26 ♘xe4 ♖xf5**

½-½ Thorsteins-I.Zaitsev, Protvino 1988.

**Conclusion:** The line 4 cxd5 exd5 5 ♗f4 leads to a very sharp situation. In the end, it is a matter of taste whether to play 5...c6 or 5...♘f6, but in my opinion, Black enjoys richer possibilities after 5...♘f6 6 e3 ♗f5.

# 2 The Eingorn Variation

**1 d4 d5 2 c4 e6 3 ♘c3 ♗e7 4 ♘f3 ♘f6**

Here White has at his disposal the following continuations: 5 ♕c2 (Eingorn Variation), 5 ♗f4 and 5 ♗g5. The two bishop moves are covered in later chapters; our subject here is the queen move.

**5 ♕c2** *(D)*

**5...0-0**

This seems to be the most accurate move. Or:

a) 5...c5 6 dxc5 and now:

a1) 6...♘c6 7 e3 ♗xc5 8 a3 a5 9 b3 0-0 10 ♗b2 ♕e7 11 ♘a4! ♗a7 12 ♗d3 dxc4 13 bxc4! ± Miles-Odendahl, Philadelphia 1989.

a2) 6...d4 7 ♘b5 (7 ♘a4?! ♘c6 8 a3 e5 9 e4 ♘xe4 10 ♕xe4 ♕a5+ 11 ♗d2 ♕xa4 12 ♘xe5 ♘xe5 13 ♕xe5 0-0 14 ♗d3 ♗f6 15 ♕h5! ½-½ Miles-Greenfeld, Biel 1986; Black has compensation) and then:

a21) 7...♗xc5 8 ♗f4 e5 (8...0-0?! 9 0-0-0! ± Eingorn-Vaganian, USSR

Ch (Moscow) 1988; 8...♘a6 9 a3 ♘g4 10 ♕d2 0-0 11 b4 ♗b6 12 ♗d6 ± Miles-Noble, Auckland 1992; 8...♕a5+ 9 ♗d2 ♕b6 10 b4 ♗e7 11 a3 {11 ♘fxd4 ±} 11...e5! ∞ Eingorn-Beliavsky, USSR Ch (Minsk) 1987) 9 ♗xe5 ♗b4+ 10 ♘d2 ♘c6 11 ♗xd4! ♘xd4 12 ♘xd4 0-0 (12...♕xd4 13 ♕a4+ ±) 13 e3 ± Galliamova-Geller, Vienna (Ladies vs Veterans) 1993.

a22) 7...e5 8 ♘xe5 a6 9 ♘a3 ♗xc5 10 ♘d3 ♗xa3 11 bxa3 0-0 12 g3 ♖e8 13 ♗g2 ♗g4 14 0-0 ♗xe2 15 ♖e1 ♗xd3 16 ♖xe8+ ♕xe8 17 ♕xd3 and now Black should play 17...♘c6 18 ♗f4 ♖d8 19 c5!? ± rather than 17...♕e1+ 18 ♕f1 ♕c3 19 ♖b1 ♘c6 20 ♖b3 ±/± Dreev-Vaganian, Budapest 1996.

a3) 6...♘a6 7 g3 (7 ♗g5!? ♕a5 8 e3 ♘xc5 9 ♘d2 dxc4 10 ♘xc4 ♘d3+ 11 ♗xd3 ♕xg5 12 0-0 0-0 13 ♘e4 ± Eingorn-Smyslov, Sochi 1986) 7...0-0 8 ♗g2 dxc4 (8...♘xc5 9 0-0 dxc4 10 ♘e5 ±) 9 0-0 ♕a5 10 ♘e4 ♘xc5 11 ♘xf6+ ♗xf6 12 ♘g5 ♗xg5 13 ♗xg5 ♘a4 14 ♗d2 ♕b5 (14...♕a6!? ±) 15 ♖fc1! ♕xb2? (15...♖d8!? ±) 16 ♕xb2 ♘xb2 17 a4! ♗d7 18 a5 with a clear advantage for White, Kramnik-Short, Novgorod 1996.

b) 5...dxc4 and here:

b1) 6 e3!? a6 7 a4 ♘bd7 (7...c5 8 dxc5 ♗xc5 9 ♗xc4 ♕c7 10 ♘e4 ♘xe4 11 ♕xe4 ♘d7 12 ♗d2! ♘f6 13 ♕h4 ♗d7 14 ♖c1! ± Miles-Vaganian, Wijk aan Zee 1989) 8 ♗xc4 c5 9 dxc5 ♗xc5 10 0-0 b6 11 ♘e4! ♗b7 12 ♘xc5

♘xc5 13 b4 ♘cd7 14 ♗b2 ± Miles-Ubilava, Rome 1990.

b2) 6 e4 ♘c6 7 e5 ♘b4 (7...♘d5?! 8 ♗xc4 ♘b6 9 ♗b5 ♗d7 10 a3! ±) 8 ♕b1 ♘fd5 (8...♘d7 9 ♗xc4 c5 10 dxc5 ♕c7 11 ♗f4 {11 a3?! ♕xc5 12 ♗b3 ♘c6 ∞ Itkis-Kruppa, Nikolaev 1995} 11...♕xc5 12 ♗e2 ♘c6 13 0-0 ♘dxe5 14 ♘xe5 ♘xe5 15 ♘b5 +–) 9 ♗xc4 and then:

b21) 9...♘xc3 10 bxc3 ♘d5 11 ♗d2 c5 12 0-0 cxd4 13 cxd4 0-0 14 ♕e4 ± Lazarev-Korneev, Werfen 1993.

b22) 9...♘b6 10 ♗e2 ♗d7 11 0-0 ♗c6 12 a3 ♘4d5 13 ♘e4! a6 14 ♖e1! h6 15 ♗d2 ♕d7 16 ♕c2 ♗b5?! (Black should try 16...g5!? intending ...0-0-0 and ...♖dg8) 17 ♗d1 ♗c6 18 ♖c1 ♖d8 19 ♕b1 ♔f8 20 h4! ± Ehlvest-Yusupov, Vienna 1996.

b23) 9...c5 10 dxc5 ♕a5 11 0-0 ♕xc5 12 ♘xd5 ♘xd5 13 ♕e4 ♗d7 14 ♕g4! (14 ♗d2?! ♗b5 15 b3 0-0 16 ♖fc1 ♖fc8! = Kramnik-Ki.Georgiev, Erevan OL 1996) 14...♔f8 15 ♗d2 h5 16 ♕e4 ♗c6 17 ♕e2 ± Ki.Georgiev.

We now return to 5...0-0 (D):

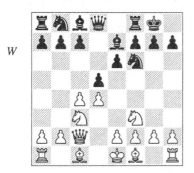

**6 ♗g5**

White can also play 6 cxd5 ♘xd5 (Black can, if he wishes, transpose to

an Exchange Variation by 6...exd5; then 7 ♗g5 c6 8 e3 ♘bd7 9 ♗d3 transposes to Line B32 of Chapter 10) 7 ♗d2 (7 e4 ♘xc3 8 bxc3 c5 =; 7 g3 ♘c6! 8 ♗g2 {8 a3!?} 8...♘db4 9 ♕b3 ♘xd4 10 ♘xd4 ♕xd4 11 ♗e3 ♕e5 12 ♖d1 c6 13 ♗f4 ♕a5 14 ♗d2 ♕a6 15 0-0 e5 ∓/∓ Korchnoi-Beliavsky, Frankfurt rpd 1998) and now:

a) 7...b6!? deserves attention: 8 g3 (8 e4!?) 8...♗b7 9 ♗g2 ♘d7 10 ♘xd5 ♗xd5 11 e4 ♗b7 12 0-0 c5 13 ♗c3 cxd4 14 ♘xd4 a6 15 ♖fd1 ♕c7 16 ♕e2 ♖ad8 17 ♖ac1 ♕b8 = Oll-Liang Jinrong, Beijing 1997.

b) 7...♘d7 8 g3 (or 8 e4 ♗b4!? {8...♘xc3 9 ♗xc3 ±} 9 ♕b3 c5 ∞) 8...♘b4!? and then:

b1) 9 ♕b1 c5 10 ♗g2 (10 dxc5 ♘xc5 ∞) 10...cxd4 11 ♘xd4 ♘e5 12 ♘b3 ♘c4 13 ♗c1 ♕b6 14 0-0 ♗d7 15 ♘d2 ♘xd2 16 ♗xd2 ♗c6 17 ♗e3 ♕c7 18 ♗xc6 ½-½ Razuvaev-Timoshchenko, Irkutsk 1986.

b2) 9 ♕d1 c5 10 dxc5 ♘xc5 11 ♗g2 a5 (11...♗d7 can be met by 12 ♘e5 ± or 12 a3 ♘d5 13 ♘xd5 ±) 12 0-0 ♕b6 (12...♗f6 13 ♗e3 ±) 13 ♗e3 ♖d8 14 ♕b1!? (14 ♕c1?! ♗d7 15 ♘e4 ♖ac8) 14...♗d7 15 ♘e4 (15 ♘g5!? ±) 15...h6 16 ♖c1 ♖ac8 17 ♘fd2 (17 ♘e5 ♗b5!? 18 a3 ♘d5 19 b4? ♘xe3 20 bxc5 ♗xc5 21 ♘xc5 ♖xc5 22 ♖xc5 ♕xc5 ∓) 17...♕b5! 18 ♘c3 ♕a6! ∞ Eingorn-Yusupov, USSR Ch (Moscow) 1988.

**6...dxc4**

Other continuations also deserve attention:

a) 6...♘bd7 7 ♖d1 dxc4 8 e4 ♘b6 9 h4 ♘fd7 (9...♗d7 10 ♘e5 ±) 10 ♗e2 ♖e8 11 ♗e3 c6 12 e5 ♘f8 13 ♘e4 ♗d7 14 0-0 f5?! (14...h6 ±) 15 exf6

gxf6 16 ♗h6 ♘g6 17 ♘c5 ♕c7 18
♗xc4 ♘xc4 19 ♕xc4 ♗f8 20 ♗xf8
♘xf8 21 ♖fe1 ± Kramnik-Beliavsky,
Dortmund 1995.

b) 6...♘a6!? and now:

b1) 7 e3 c5 8 dxc5 (8 cxd5 cxd4 9
♘xd4 ♘b4 10 ♕d2 ♘fxd5 11 ♗xe7
♕xe7 = Norri-Wong Meng Kong, Manila OL 1992) 8...♘xc5 9 0-0-0 ♘fe4
10 ♘xe4 ♘xe4 11 ♗xe7 ♕xe7 12
♗d3 ♘f6 13 cxd5 exd5 14 ♔b1 ♗g4 ∞
Rausis-Siegel, 2nd Bundesliga 1996/7.

b2) 7 a3 c5 8 dxc5 ♘xc5 9 ♖d1 b6
10 cxd5 ♘xd5! (10...exd5 11 e3 ♗b7
12 ♗e2 ♖c8 13 ♕b1 ♘e6 14 ♗h4 ±
Dolmatov-Podgaets, Kharkov 1985)
11 ♗xe7 ♕xe7 12 ♘xd5 exd5 13 e3
♕f6 14 ♘d4 ♕g5 15 ♘f3 =.

c) 6...c5 7 dxc5 dxc4 (7...♕a5 8
cxd5 exd5 9 e3 h6 10 ♗h4 ♕xc5 11
♗e2 ♘c6 12 0-0 d4 13 exd4 ♘xd4 14
♘xd4 ♕xd4 15 ♗g3 ± Borisenko-
Bondarevsky, Moscow 1950) 8 e4 and
then:

c1) 8...h6!? 9 ♗f4 ♗xc5 10 ♗xc4
♘c6 11 0-0 ♘h5 12 ♖ad1 ♕f6 13 ♗c1
♘f4 14 e5 ♘xe5 15 ♘xe5 ♕xe5 16
♖fe1 ♕b8 17 ♕e4 ♘g6 18 ♖d3 b5 19
♗xb5 ♗b7 20 ♕e2 ♘f4 21 ♗xf4
♕xf4 22 ♖d7 ½-½ Welin-Hartman,
Stockholm 1987.

c2) 8...♕a5 9 e5 ♘d5 10 ♗xc4 (10
♗xe7 ♘xe7 11 ♗xc4 ♕xc5 12 ♗d3
♘g6 13 ♗xg6 hxg6 is equal – Pach-
man) 10...♘xc3 (10...♗xc5 11 ♗xd5
exd5 12 0-0 ♗e6 13 a3 ♕c7 14 ♖fd1
♗b6 15 ♕d2 ± Popov-Chekhlov, St
Petersburg 1998) 11 0-0! ♕xc5 12
♕xc3 b6 (12...♘c6 13 ♗xe7 ♕xe7 can
be met by 14 a3 ± Kasparov-Karpov,
Seville Wch (20) 1987 or 14 ♕e3!? intending ♕e4 and ♗d3) 13 ♖fd1!? (13
♖ac1 ♗b7 = Dorfman) 13...♗b7 14

♗xe7 ♕xe7 15 ♖d6 ♘d7 16 ♖ad1 and
White is slightly better.

d) 6...h6 7 ♗xf6 ♗xf6 and now:

d1) 8 e4 dxe4 9 ♕xe4 c5 10 0-0-0
♘c6 11 d5 ♘d4 12 ♗d3 g6 = Atalik-
Stern, Budapest 1991.

d2) 8 0-0-0 ♘c6!? 9 e4 dxe4 10
♕xe4 g6 11 ♘e5 ♗g7 12 f4 ♗d7 13
g3 ♘xe5 14 dxe5 ♕e8 ∞ Janjgava-
Lputian, New York 1990.

d3) 8 ♖d1 c5 (8...g6 9 e3 c6 10
♗d3 dxc4 11 ♗xc4 ♘d7 12 h4 ♗g7
13 a3 ♕e7 14 ♗a2! ± Kramnik-Short,
Dortmund 1995) 9 dxc5 ♕a5 10 cxd5
(10 e3 dxc4 11 ♗xc4 ♕xc5 12 ♘e4
♕b4+ 13 ♖d2 ♗xb2 14 0-0 ♗a3 15
♘d6 ♕a5 16 ♖fd1 ♗b4 is unclear,
Romanishin-Stojanović, Ubeda 1997)
10...exd5 11 ♕d2 ♗xc3 12 ♕xc3
♕xc3+ 13 bxc3 and here:

d31) 13...♗e6 14 ♘d4 ♖c8 15 e4
dxe4 16 ♘xe6 fxe6 17 ♗c4 ♔f7 18
♖d4 ♖xc5!? (18...♘a6 19 ♗xa6 {19
♖d7+!?} 19...bxa6 20 ♔d2 ♖ab8 21
♖c1 ♖xc5 22 ♖xe4 ± Romanishin-
Beliavsky, Leningrad 1977) 19 ♖xe4
♖c6 20 f4 ♔f6 21 0-0 ♘d7 22 g4 ♘c5
½-½ Li Wenliang-Liang Jinrong,
Beijing 1996.

d32) 13...♘a6 14 e3 ♘xc5 15 ♖d5
b6 16 ♖d4 ♗b7 17 ♗c4 ♖ac8 18 0-0
(18 ♘e5 ♗xg2 19 ♖g1 ♗h3 20 ♘g6
♖fe8 21 ♘f4 ♗e6 = San Segundo-Van
der Sterren, Linares Z 1995) 18...♘e4
19 ♘e5! ♖c7 20 ♖c1 b5 21 ♗b3 ♘xc3
22 ♔f1 ± Van der Sterren.

We now return to 6...dxc4 (D):

**7 e4**

Also possible is the modest 7 e3 c5
8 dxc5 (8 ♗xc4 cxd4 9 ♘xd4 ♗d7 10
0-0 ♘c6 11 ♖fd1 ♘xd4 12 ♖xd4 ♕c7
=) 8...♕a5 9 ♗xc4 ♕xc5 10 ♗d3 h6
11 ♗h4 (11 ♗xf6 ♗xf6 12 ♘e4?!

W

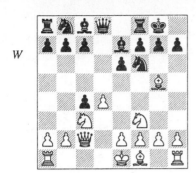

♕b4+ ∓) 11...b6!? (11...♘c6 12 a3 ♗d7 13 0-0 ♘e5 14 ♘xe5 ♕xe5 15 ♗g3 ♕a5 16 b4 ± ½-½ Dautov-Goldin, Baden-Baden 1990) 12 ♘e4 (12 a3 ♗b7 13 b4 ♕c8 =; 12 ♕e2!? ♗b7 13 0-0 ♕h5! 14 e4 ♘bd7 =) 12...♘xe4 13 ♗xe7 ♕xe7 14 ♗xe4 ♗b7 15 ♖c1 ♗xe4 16 ♕xe4 ♘a6 = analysis.

**7...♘c6 8 ♖d1 b5!**

Black has a development advantage and begins tactical play. Worse seems 8...♘b4 9 ♕b1 (9 ♕d2!? b5 10 a3 ♘d3+ 11 ♗xd3 cxd3 12 ♕xd3 ♖b8 13 b4 ± Savchenko-A.Shneider, Enakievo 1997) 9...♘d3+ 10 ♗xd3 cxd3 11 ♕xd3 b6 12 e5 ♘d5 13 ♘xd5 exd5 14 ♗xe7 ♕xe7 15 ♖c1!? (15 0-0 ♗g4 16 ♖c1 ♗xf3 17 ♕xf3 c5 18 dxc5 ♕xe5 ± Torre-Kurajica, Novi Sad 1984) 15...♗g4 16 ♘d2 intending 0-0 and f4-f5 ±.

**9 ♘xb5**

9 ♗xf6 is interesting: 9...♘b4 10 ♕b1 ♗xf6 11 a3 ♘c6 12 ♘xb5 (12 e5 ♗e7 13 ♘xb5 ♘a5 14 ♘c3 ♗b7 15 ♗e2 c5 =) 12...a6 13 ♘c3 ♗xd4 – analysis.

**9...♘b4 10 ♕xc4**

10 ♕b1 c6 11 ♘a3 ♘d3+ 12 ♗xd3 cxd3 and now:

a) 13 ♕xd3 ♕a5+ 14 ♗d2 ♕a6 15 ♕xa6 ♗xa6 16 e5 ♗xa3 17 bxa3 ♘d5 =.

b) 13 ♗xf6 ♕a5+ 14 ♘d2 ♗xf6 15 ♕xd3 (15 e5 ♗e7 16 ♘ac4 ♕d5 with compensation; 15 ♘ac4 ♕g5) 15...♗a6 with compensation – analysis.

**10...♘xe4 11 ♗xe7 ♕xe7 12 a3 c6!?**

12...♘d5 13 ♗d3 ♘d6 14 ♕c2 ♘xb5 15 ♗xb5 ♖b8?! 16 ♗d3 ± ♘f4? (better is 16...h6 ±) 17 ♗xh7+ ♔h8 18 g3 g6 19 gxf4 ♔xh7 20 ♖g1 e5?! 21 dxe5 ♗f5 22 ♕c3 f6 23 ♘h4 and White wins, Khenkin-G.Georgadze, San Marino 1998.

**13 axb4**

Or:

a) 13 ♘c3? ♘c2+ 14 ♔e2 a5 15 ♕xc6 ♗a6+ 16 ♘b5 ♘xa3! and Black wins.

b) 13 ♕xb4 ♕xb4+ 14 axb4 cxb5 15 ♗xb5 ♖b8 16 ♗c6 ♘d6 17 d5 ♖d8 =.

**13...cxb5 14 ♕xb5 ♗d7**

Black has compensation (analysis).

**Conclusion:** The Eingorn Variation is one of the most interesting and unexplored lines of the Queen's Gambit. It leads to very tense and interesting positions, while there is a great deal of scope for original analysis and new ideas. Thus we can expect this system to be developed extensively in the future.

# 3 5 ♗f4

**1 d4 d5 2 c4 e6 3 ♘c3 ♗e7 4 ♘f3 ♘f6 5 ♗f4** (D)

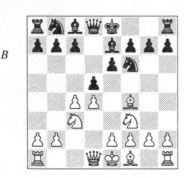

This is one of the most complex, topical and popular lines for White.

**5...0-0 6 e3 c5 7 dxc5 ♗xc5**

This is the basic starting position of this variation. White has several continuations at his disposal:

| | |
|---|---|
| **A: 8 ♗e2** | 24 |
| **B: 8 cxd5** | 26 |
| **C: 8 a3** | 28 |
| **D: 8 ♕c2** | 31 |

## A)

**8 ♗e2 dxc4 9 ♗xc4** (D)

**9...a6**

An interesting ending arises after 9...♕xd1+ 10 ♖xd1:

a) 10...♗b4!? and then:

a1) 11 ♘d4?! a6 12 f3 ♘bd7 13 ♘c2 ♗xc3+ 14 bxc3 b5 15 ♗b3 ♗b7 16 ♗d6 ♖fc8 17 ♖d3 a5! is slightly better for Black, Spraggett-Ubilava, Spain 1997.

a2) Better is 11 0-0!? ♗xc3 12 bxc3 ♗d7 (12...b6 13 ♗d6 ♖e8 14 ♘e5 ♗b7 15 ♗b5 ±) 13 ♘e5 ♗a4 with an unclear position.

b) 10...♘c6!? 11 0-0 b6 (11...♗d7 12 ♘b5! ±) 12 e4 (12 ♘g5!? ♗b7 13 ♘ge4 ♗e7 14 ♘d6 ♗xd6 15 ♗xd6 ♖fc8 16 ♗e2 ♘a5! 17 ♗e5 ♘d5! = Tregubov-Goldin, St Petersburg 1998) 12...♗b7 13 e5 ♘a5! 14 exf6 ♘xc4 15 b3 ♗b4 16 ♘b5 ♘a3 ∞ Ibragimov-Lputian, Vienna 1996.

c) 10...a6 (Black prepares to fianchetto his light-squared bishop) and now:

c1) 11 0-0 b5 12 ♗b3 ♗b7 13 ♘e5 ♘c6 14 ♘d7 ♘xd7 15 ♖xd7 ♘a5 16 ♗c2 ♗c6 17 ♖dd1 ♘c4 18 b3 ♘a3 19 ♗e4 ♖fc8 = Granda-Benko, Aruba 1992.

c2) 11 ♗d3!? ♘bd7 (11...b5 12 ♘e4!) 12 0-0 (12 ♖c1 b6 13 ♘e4 ♗b7 14 ♘xc5 ♘xc5 15 ♗e2 ♖fc8 16 0-0 ♘d5 17 ♗g3 ♘a4 18 ♗e5 f6 19 b3 ♘ac3 20 ♗xc3 ♘xc3 21 ♗c4 ♖xc4 =

Donner-Bcnko, Wijk aan Zee 1972)
12...b5 and then:

c21) 13 ♘e5 ♘xe5 14 ♗xe5 ♗b7
15 ♗xf6 gxf6 16 ♗e4 ♖ab8! (and not
16...♗xe4?! 17 ♘xe4 ♗e7 18 ♖d7 ±)
17 ♗xb7 (17 ♖d7 ♗c8 18 ♖d2 f5)
17...♖xb7 18 ♘e4 ♗e7 19 g4 ♖c8 =
analysis.

c22) 13 ♘e4! ♗b7 14 ♘xc5 ♘xc5
15 ♗e2 ♘a4 16 ♗e5! (16 ♖b1?! ♗e4;
16 ♖d2 ♘e4 17 ♖d7 {17 ♖c2 ♖fc8 18
♖fc1 ♘xb2} 17...♗d5 18 b3 ♘ac3 ∓)
16...♘e4 (intending ...f6 and ...e5;
16...♖fc8!? is best answered by 17
♗d3!? ± rather than 17 ♘d2 ♘d7) 17
♘d2 f6 18 ♘xe4 ♗xe4 19 ♗d4! (19
b3 fxe5 20 bxa4 ♗d5 21 axb5 axb5 22
♗xb5 ♖xa2 =; 19 ♗d6 ♘xb2 20 ♗xf8
♘xd1 21 ♗b4 ♘b2 ∓) 19...e5 20 b3
exd4 21 bxa4 (21 ♖xd4 ♘c3) 21...dxe3
(21...bxa4? 22 ♖xd4 +−) 22 axb5
exf2+ 23 ♖xf2 axb5 24 ♗xb5 ± (analysis).

c3) 11 ♘e5! (White tries to disrupt
the development of Black's queenside)
11...♘bd7 12 ♗e2 (another idea is 12
♗d3!?) 12...♘xe5 (12...♗b4!?) 13
♗xe5 b5 14 ♗f3 ♖a7 15 ♔e2 (15
♗xf6 gxf6 16 ♘e4 ♗e7 17 g4 ♗b7 18
♔e2 ♗d5 19 b3 ♖c8 = Nimzowitsch-
Ståhlberg, Gothenburg 1934) and then:

c31) 15...♗b7!? 16 ♗xb7 (16 ♗xf6
gxf6 17 ♗xb7 ♖xb7 18 ♘e4 ♗e7 19
g4 ♖c8 =) 16...♖xb7 17 ♗d6! ♗xd6
18 ♖xd6 ±.

c32) 15...♗d7 16 ♖c1 b4 17 ♘d5!
♗b5+ 18 ♔d2 ♘d7 19 ♗d4 ♗xd4 20
♘e7+ ♔h8 21 exd4 ♘b6 22 ♘c6 ♖d7
23 b3! with a slight advantage for
White, Malaniuk-Arlandi, Forli 1992.

We now return to 9...a6 (D):
**10 ♕e2 b5 11 ♗d3 ♗b7 12 0-0
♘bd7 13 ♖fd1**

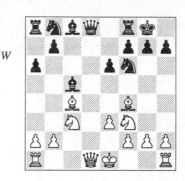

A drawback of 13 e4?! is the weakening of the square f4, and Black can
exploit this immediately: 13...♘h5! 14
♗g5 (14 ♗d2 ♕c7 15 g3 ♖ad8 16 ♗e3
♗xe3 17 ♕xe3 ♕c5! ∓ Smyslov-Kasparov, Vilnius Ct (4) 1984) 14...♕b8!
(14...♗e7!?) 15 ♖ad1 h6 16 ♗c1 ♘f4
17 ♗xf4 ♕xf4 18 ♗xb5 axb5 19
♖xd7 ♗c6 20 ♖dd1 b4 21 ♕c4 ♖a5!
22 ♘d4 ♗b7 ∓ Hertneck-Short, Garmisch rpd 1994.

13 ♖ac1 ♗e7 (13...♕e7!? 14 ♗g5
♖fc8, intending ...♕e8, with an unclear position) 14 ♖fd1 ♕b6 15 a3
♘c5 16 ♗c2 ♖fd8 17 ♘e5 ½-½
Gulko-Pigusov, Biel IZ 1993.

**13...♕b6**

13...h6!? deserves serious attention:
14 ♗g3 (14 e4 ♘h5 15 ♗e3 ♕c7)
14...♗b4 15 ♘e5 (15 a4!?) 15...♕e7 16
♘xd7 ♘xd7 17 a3 ♗xc3 18 ♗d6 ♕h4
19 ♗xf8 (19 bxc3 ½-½ M.Gurevich-
Yusupov, Munich 1992) 19...♗e5 20
f4 ♖xf8 21 fxe5 ♘xe5 with compensation.

**14 ♗g3**

If 14 ♖ac1, then 14...♖ac8 15 ♘g5
♖fd8 16 ♘ge4 ♗e7 17 ♗d6 ♔f8! 18
♗xe7+ ♔xe7 19 ♘xf6 ♘xf6 20 b4
♖c7 21 ♕b2 ♖cd7 = Kiriakov-Ruste-
mov, Elista 1997.

14 a4!? seems interesting: 14...b4 15 ♘b1 ♖fe8 (15...♕c6!? intending ...e5-e4) 16 ♗g3 e5 17 ♗c4 h6 18 a5 ♕a7 19 ♘bd2 e4 (19...♗c6!? intending ...♕b7 ∞) 20 ♘e1 ♗f8 21 ♘b3 ♘e5 22 ♗xe5 ♖xe5 23 ♖d4 (23 ♘c2 is best met by 23...♖ae8 ∞ rather than 23...♕b8? 24 ♖d4 ± Cifuentes-Van der Sterren, Dutch Ch (Eindhoven) 1992) 23...♖ae8 24 ♘c2 ♗c8 25 ♕d2 ♕b8 26 ♖a4 ♖h5 27 g3 ♗g4 28 ♘xb4 ♗f3 29 ♗f1 ♕e5 30 ♗g2? ♗xg2 31 ♔xg2 ♕f5 32 h4 (Chekhov-Gorelov, Moscow 1995) and now 32...♕b5 followed by 33...♖b8 wins material.

**14...♗b4!?**

A very interesting idea, rather than 14...♗e7 15 a4 b4 16 a5 ♕d8 (16...♕c6? 17 ♘a4 ♖fc8 18 e4! ± Zsu.Polgar-Geller, Aruba (Ladies vs Veterans) 1992; 16...♕c5 17 ♘b1 ♕h5 18 ♘bd2 ♘c5 19 ♗c4 ♖fc8 20 ♘d4 ♕g6 21 f3 ± M.Gurevich-Geller, Helsinki 1992) 17 ♘b1 ♘h5 18 ♘bd2 ♘xg3 19 hxg3 ♘c5 20 ♘c4 ♕e8! = Tregubov (not 20...♘xd3?! 21 ♘b6! ± Tregubov-Van der Sterren, Wijk aan Zee 1995).

**15 ♖ac1**

Or: 15 ♘e5 ♖fd8; 15 a4 ♗xc3 16 bxc3 ♘c5; 15 e4 ♗xc3 16 bxc3 ♘h5! 17 e5 (17 a4 ♘xg3 18 hxg3 ♘c5 19 axb5 axb5 =) 17...♘xg3 18 hxg3 ♖fd8 = 19 ♗xh7+? ♔xh7 20 ♘g5+ ♔g8 (20...♔g6 −+) 21 ♕h5 ♘xe5 22 ♕h7+ ♔f8 23 ♕h8+ ♔e7 24 ♕xg7 ♕c6 −+.

**15...♖ac8 16 ♘e5 ♖fd8**

The position is equal (analysis).

**B)**

**8 cxd5 ♘xd5 9 ♘xd5 exd5** (D)

Now White can acquiesce to the loss of castling rights or spend a tempo preserving them:

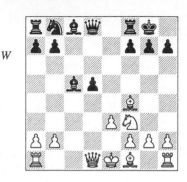

**B1: 10 ♗d3** 26
**B2: 10 a3** 27

**B1)**

**10 ♗d3 ♗b4+ 11 ♔e2**

White can also play 11 ♔f1 ♗d6 (11...♘c6!? 12 h4 ♗d6 13 ♗xd6 ♕xd6 14 h5 ♕f6 15 ♖h4 ♕xb2 ∞ Adianto-Mikhalevski, Biel 1998) 12 ♗g3 ♘c6 13 ♗c2 ♗e7 14 h4 ♗f6 15 ♕d2 d4 16 ♖d1 ♗g4 17 h5 ♖e8 ∞ ½-½ Vaiser-Speelman, Sochi 1982.

**11...♘c6**

11...♗d6 12 ♗xd6 ♕xd6 13 ♕a4 ♘c6 14 ♖hd1 ♘e5 15 ♘xe5 ♕xe5 16 ♕h4 g6 17 ♖d2 d4 18 e4 ♖e8 19 ♔f1 ♗e6 20 f4 ♕a5 21 ♕f2 is slightly better for White, Smyslov-Beliavsky, Moscow 1981.

**12 ♕c2 g6**

12...h6!? is also fully possible: 13 ♖hd1 (13 a3 ♗d6 =; 13 h3 ♗e6 14 ♖hd1 ♖c8 15 ♕a4 ♕f6 =) 13...♕f6 14 ♔f1 (14 a3 ♗e7 15 ♕c3 ♗e6 = Tukmakov-Geller, USSR Ch (Tbilisi) 1978) 14...♗a5 15 ♗e2 ♗b6 16 ♕d2 ♖d8 17 ♘d4 ♘xd4 18 exd4 ♗f5 19 ♗e5 ♕g6 = Quinteros-Najdorf, Mar del Plata 1982.

**13 a3**

Or:

a) 13 h3 ♗d6 14 ♗xd6 ♕xd6 15 a3 d4 =.

b) 13 ♘e5 ♘xe5 14 ♗xe5 ♕g5 15 ♗g3 ♗g4+ 16 ♔f1 ♖ac8 (16...♕e7!? 17 h3 ♗e6 =) 17 ♕a4 ♗c5 18 ♕f4 ♕xf4 (18...♕h5 19 h3, Djurić-Abramović, Novi Sad 1985, 19...♗d7 ∞ 20 ♗h4?! f6!) 19 ♗xf4 d4 =.

c) 13 ♖hd1 ♗g4 14 ♔f1 (14 ♗e4? dxe4! 15 ♖xd8 ♖axd8 16 ♕xe4 ♖fe8 17 ♕c4 ♖d4 −+; 14 ♕a4 ♕e7 15 ♗b5 ♖fd8 16 ♗xc6 bxc6 17 h3 ♗xf3+ 18 gxf3 ♗d6 is equal, D.Gurevich-Rechlis, Beersheba 1987) 14...♗xf3 15 gxf3 ♕f6 16 ♔g2 (16 a3 ♗a5 17 ♔g2 ♗b6 ∓ A.Petrosian-Lputian, Erevan 1982) 16...♘d4! 17 ♕a4 ♗c5 18 ♖ac1 ♘e6 19 ♗g3 d4 20 exd4 ♗xd4 21 ♗e4 ♖ad8 22 ♖c2 ♘c5 ½-½ Foisor-Oll, Tbilisi 1983.

**13...♗e7 14 h3 ♗f6 15 ♖ac1 a5 16 ♖hd1 ♗e6 17 ♔f1 a4 18 ♗b5 ♕b6 19 ♗xc6**

19 ♗xa4?? ♕a6+ −+.

**19...bxc6 20 ♗e5 ♗xe5 21 ♘xe5 ♖fc8 22 ♕c5**

22 ♘d3 ♗f5.

**22...♕xb2 23 ♘xc6 ♔g7 24 ♕d4+ ♕xd4 25 ♘xd4 ♗d7 26 ♔e1 ♖ab8 27 ♖xc8 ♖xc8 28 ♔d2 ♖b8 29 ♖c1 ♖b2+ 30 ♖c2 ♖b1**

= I.Sokolov-Van der Sterren, Rotterdam 1997. Black has counterplay due to the weakness of the a3-pawn.

**B2)**

**10 a3 ♘c6 11 ♗d3 ♗b6** *(D)*
**12 0-0**

Or: 12 h3 d4 =; 12 ♘g5 h6 13 ♗h7+ ♔h8 14 ♗c2 d4! 15 ♕h5 dxe3 16 fxe3 ♕e8 17 ♘e4 f5 18 ♕xe8 ½-½ Anikaev-Geller, Moscow 1982.

**12...♗g4**

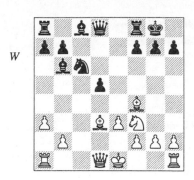

12...d4!? also deserves attention: 13 e4 ♗g4 14 h3 and now:

a) 14...♕f6 15 ♗g3 (15 hxg4!? ♕xf4 16 g5 ±) 15...♗xf3 16 ♕xf3 ♕xf3 17 gxf3 ♘a5 ∞.

b) 14...♗h5 15 g4 ♗g6 16 ♖c1:

b1) 16...♖e8 17 ♖e1 ♔h8 (17...f6!? 18 ♗c4+ ♔h8 19 ♗d5 ♕d7 intending ...♗f7 ∞) 18 e5! ♕d5 19 b4!? (19 ♗xg6 fxg6!? 20 ♕d3 ♘d8!? intending ...♘e6) 19...♘d8 (19...a5? 20 ♗c4 ♕d7 21 e6! fxe6 22 b5 ♘e7 23 ♖xe6! ± M.Gurevich-Van der Sterren, Escaldes Z 1998) 20 ♗c4 ♕d7 21 ♘h4 ♘e6 22 ♘xg6+ hxg6 23 ♗g3 ±.

b2) 16...♖c8 17 ♖e1 ♖e8 (17...♔h8 18 ♔g2 f6 19 ♘h4 ♗c7 20 ♗xc7 ♕xc7 21 ♗b5 ♕b6 = Karpov-Beliavsky, Tilburg 1993) 18 ♔g2 ♗c7 19 ♕d2 ♗xf4 20 ♕xf4 ♕e7 21 b4 f6 ∞ Piket-Kramnik, Monaco Amber rpd 1998.

**13 h3 ♗h5 14 b4**

If 14 ♗e2, then 14...♖e8 (also possible is 14...♗xf3 15 ♗xf3 d4 16 exd4 ♗xd4 17 ♕d2 ♕b6 18 ♖ad1 ♖ad8 19 b4 ♗f6 20 ♕a2 ♘d4 = Hübner-Karpov, Tilburg 1983) 15 b4 d4! (15...a6 16 ♖a2 ♕d7 17 ♘e5 ± Spassov-T.Georgadze, Bulgaria 1981) 16 exd4 ♖xe2! 17 ♕xe2 ♘xd4 18 ♕e4 f5! ∓.

**14...♖e8 15 ♖c1**

15 ♖a2 yields no advantage due to 15...d4! 16 b5 (16 e4 ♗c7 17 ♗xc7 ♕xc7 18 g4 ♗g6 19 ♕c1 ♕d6 20 ♖e1 ♘d8 21 ♘h4 ♘e6 = Tunik-Kharitonov, Gorki 1989) 16...♘e5 17 ♗xe5 ♗xf3 18 ♕xf3 ♖xe5 19 exd4 (19 e4 ♖c8 intending ...♖c3) 19...♕xd4 20 ♕xb7 ♖d8! (20...♖ae8 21 ♕f3 ♖e1 22 g3 ±) 21 ♖e2 (21 ♖d2 ♕c3 22 ♖e2 g6 23 ♖xe5 ♕xe5 24 ♕f3 ♖d6 = Tunik-Korneev, Smolensk 1991) 21...♖xe2 22 ♗xe2 ♕f4! 23 ♕f3 (½-½ Volzhin-Kharitonov, Poland 1998) 23...♕xf3 24 ♗xf3 ♖d2 =.

The sharp move 15 g4?! is dubious: 15...♗g6 16 ♗xg6 hxg6 17 b5 ♘a5 18 ♕d3 ♘c4 19 ♕b3 ♕f6 20 ♖ad1 (Chiburdanidze-Geller, Aruba (Ladies vs Veterans) 1992) 20...♘xe3! 21 ♗xe3 (21 fxe3 ♕xf4 –+) 21...♕xf3 22 ♕xd5 ♕xh3 ∓.

**15...d4!?**

Other moves are suspect: 15...a6?! 16 ♖c2! d4 17 e4 ♗c7 18 ♗xc7 ♕xc7 19 ♖c5 ± Lugovoi-Klimov, St Petersburg 1995; or 15...a5?! 16 g4! ♗g6 17 ♗xg6 hxg6 18 b5 ♘e7 (18...♘a7 19 ♕d3 ♕d7 20 ♖fd1! ± Lputian-Geller, New York 1990) 19 ♗e5! ♕d7 20 ♗d4 ♗xd4 21 ♘xd4 ♘c8! 22 ♕c2 ♖e7 23 ♕c5 and White has a slight advantage, Tunik-Kharitonov, Elista 1995.

**16 g4 ♗g6 17 ♗xg6 hxg6 18 b5 ♘e7!**

18...dxe3?! 19 bxc6 e2 20 ♕xd8 exf1♕+ 21 ♔xf1 ♖axd8 22 cxb7 ± Lima-Milos, São Paulo 1993.

**19 ♘xd4**

19 exd4 ♘d5 with compensation.

**19...♘d5 20 ♘e2 g5! 21 ♗g3 ♘xe3! 22 ♕xd8 ♖axd8 23 ♖fe1 ♘d5 24 ♔f1**

with equality, Dreev-Geller, Helsinki 1992.

**C)**

**8 a3 ♘c6** *(D)*

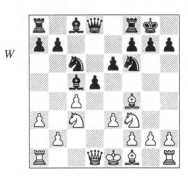

Now:

| | | |
|---|---|---|
| **C1:** | **9 ♗e2** | 28 |
| **C2:** | **9 ♖c1** | 29 |
| **C3:** | **9 b4** | 30 |

**C1)**

**9 ♗e2 dxc4 10 ♗xc4**

If 10 ♕c2, then 10...b5!? 11 ♘xb5 (11 0-0 a6 12 ♖ad1 ♕b6 13 ♘g5 h6 14 ♘ge4 ♘xe4 15 ♘xe4 e5 16 ♗g3 ♗e6 17 ♗f3 ½-½ Adorjan-Karlsson, Gjøvik 1983) 11...♕a5+ 12 ♘c3 ♘b4 13 ♕c1 ♘bd5 14 ♗xc4 ♘xf4 15 exf4 ♗xf2+ 16 ♔xf2 ♕c5+ 17 ♔g3 ♕xc4 18 ♘e5 ♕b3 ∓ Gavrikov-Lutz, Bundesliga 1995/6.

**10...♘h5**

10...♕xd1+ is also fully sufficient for equality: 11 ♖xd1 b6 (not 11...a6?! 12 ♗d3! ♖d8 13 ♘a4! ♗a7 14 ♗c7 ♖d7 {14...♖e8 15 ♘b6 ♗xb6 16 ♗xb6 e5 17 ♘g5 ±} 15 ♗b6 ♘d5 16 ♗xa7 ♖xa7 17 ♗c4 b5 18 ♗xd5 ♖xd5 19 ♖xd5 exd5 20 ♘c3 ♗e6 21 ♘d4! ♘xd4 22 exd4 ± Sakaev-Kholmov,

Moscow 1998) 12 e4 (12 ♘g5 ♗e7 13
♘ge4 ♗b7 14 ♘d6 ♘a5! 15 ♗e2
♗xd6 16 ♗xd6 ♖fc8 17 f3 ♘d5 18
♘xd5 ♗xd5 19 b4 ♘c4 = I.Sokolov-
Lputian, Wijk aan Zee 1993) 12...♖d8
13 ♖xd8+ ♘xd8 14 e5 ♘e8 15 ♔e2
♗b7 16 ♖d1 h6! 17 ♗e3 ♗xe3 18
♔xe3 ♔f8 19 g3 ♖c8 = Dreev-Vaganian, Tilburg 1993.

**11 ♗g5**

If 11 ♕xd8, then 11...♖xd8 12 ♗c7
♖d7 13 ♗e5 ♘xe5!? (13...♖d8!?;
13...b6 14 ♘e4 ♗e7 15 ♗c3 ♗b7 16
♗e2 ♖dd8 17 0-0 ♘a5 = Lobron-
Lutz, Nussloch 1996) 14 ♘xe5 ♖d8
15 0-0 ♘f6 16 ♖fd1 ♗d7 = Topalov-
Gelfand, Vienna 1996.

**11...♗e7 12 ♕xd8**

Or: 12 h4!? f6 13 ♗f4 ♘xf4 14 exf4
♕c7 15 g3 ♘e5 16 ♗e2 ♖d8 17 ♕c2
♘xf3+ 18 ♗xf3 ♖b8 19 0-0 b5 20
♖ac1 ♗f8 21 ♖fe1 b4 22 axb4 ♖xb4 23
♘a2 ♕xc2 24 ♖xc2 ♖b6 = Sakaev-
Beliavsky, Belgrade 1999; 12 ♗xe7
♕xe7 13 0-0 ♖d8 14 ♕e2 ♗d7 15 e4
(15 ♖fd1 ♗e8 =) 15...♘f4 16 ♕e3
♘g6 17 e5 ♘h4! = P.Nikolić-Ki.Geor-
giev, Dubai OL 1986.

**12...♖xd8 13 ♗xe7 ♘xe7 14 ♔e2**

14 0-0 ♗d7 15 ♖fd1 ♗c6 16 ♘e5
♘f6 =.

**14...♗d7 15 ♘e5 ♗e8 16 ♖hd1 ♘f6
17 e4 ♘c6 18 ♘xc6 ♗xc6 19 f3 ♔f8**
= M.Gurevich-Marciano, Belfort
1997.

**C2)**

**9 ♖c1 a6!** *(D)*

**10 cxd5**

Or: 10 ♗e2 dxc4 =; 10 b4 ♗e7
(10...♗a7!?; 10...♗d6!?) 11 cxd5 exd5
12 ♗e2 ♗e6 13 0-0 ♘h5 14 ♗e5 ♘xe5
15 ♘xe5 ♘f6 16 ♕d4 ♗d6 17 ♘d3

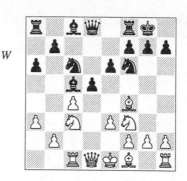

♖c8 18 ♘f4 ♖c6 = Savchenko-Sturua,
Berlin 1998.

**10...exd5 11 ♗d3**

Or:

a) 11 b4 ♗a7 12 ♗e2 d4 13 exd4
♘xd4 14 ♘xd4 ♕xd4 15 ♗e3 ♕d1+
16 ♘xd1 ♗d7 17 ♗f3 a5 18 ♗xb7
♗xe3 19 ♘xe3 ♖ab8 = Kramnik-
Ivanchuk, New York 1994.

b) 11 ♗g5 d4 12 ♘b5?! (12 exd4
♘xd4 =) 12...dxe3! 13 ♕xd8 exf2+ 14
♔e2 ♖xd8 15 ♗xf6 ♖e8+ 16 ♔d1 (16
♗e5 ♗b6 17 ♘d6 ♗g4 18 ♘xe8 ♖xe8
∓) 16...gxf6 17 ♖xc5 (17 ♘c7 ♖d8+
18 ♔e2 ♘d4+ 19 ♘xd4 ♗xd4 20 ♘xa8
♗g4+ −+) 17...♗g4! 18 ♘c3 (18 ♘c7
♖ad8+ 19 ♔c2 ♖e1 20 ♘d5 ♗f5+ 21
♔d2 b6 22 ♘xe1 bxc5 23 ♘f3 ♖xd5+
−+) 18...♘d4 19 ♗c4 ♘xf3 20 ♔c2
♗f5+! 21 ♔b3 ♘d2+ 22 ♔a2 ♗e6!
0-1 Dreev-Short, Linares 1995.

**11...♗a7**

Interesting is 11...♗g4!? 12 0-0 d4
13 ♘e2 ♗a7 14 ♘fxd4 ♗xd4 15 exd4
½-½ Horvath-Lutz, Elista OL 1998.

**12 0-0 d4 13 exd4 ♘xd4 14 ♘xd4
♕xd4 15 ♗e3 ♕h4 16 ♗xa7 ♖xa7 17
♕a4 ♕xa4 18 ♘xa4 ♗e6!**

18...b5?! 19 ♘c5 ♘d7 20 ♖fd1 is
slightly better for White, Ivanchuk-
Kasparov, Frankfurt rpd 1998.

19 ♗e2 ♖e8 20 ♖fe1 ♔f8 21 h3 b5 22 ♘c5 ♗d5

½-½ Ivanchuk-Kramnik, Linares 1999.

**C3)**
9 b4 *(D)*

A very interesting idea, which in recent years has become increasingly popular amongst top-level players.

**9...♗e7**

9...♗d6!? also deserves attention: 10 ♗xd6 (10 ♗g5 dxc4 11 ♗xc4 ♘e5 12 ♗e2 ♘xf3+ 13 ♗xf3 a5 is unclear) 10...♕xd6 11 ♗e2 (11 cxd5 exd5 12 ♗e2 ♗g4 13 0-0 {13 ♘b5 ♕e7 doesn't give White any advantage either} 13...♖ac8 =) 11...♖d8 12 0-0 dxc4!? (12...b6 13 cxd5 ♘xd5 14 ♘xd5 ♕xd5 15 ♕xd5 ♖xd5 16 ♖fd1 ♗d7 17 ♖xd5 exd5 18 ♖c1 ± Mikhalchishin-Ubilava, USSR 1981) 13 ♕xd6 (13 ♕c2 ♕e7 14 ♗xc4 ♗d7 =) 13...♖xd6 14 ♗xc4 ♖d8 15 ♖fd1 ♗d7 16 ♗e2 (16 ♘b5 a5!) 16...♔f8 (16...♗e8?! 17 ♘b5 ♘d5 18 e4! {18 ♖ac1?! a5 19 bxa5 ♖xa5 = Van Wely-Ivanchuk, Monaco 1999} 18...♘f4 19 ♗f1 ♖xd1 20 ♖xd1 a5 21 ♘c7 ±) 17 ♖ac1 ♗e8 =.

**10 cxd5**

10 h3 is inoffensive: 10...dxc4 11 ♗xc4 ♕xd1+ 12 ♖xd1 a6 13 0-0 b5 14 ♗d3 ♖d8 15 ♘e4 ♘d5 = 16 ♗g3? (Granda-Ivanchuk, Amsterdam 1996) 16...f5! 17 ♘c5 ♘dxb4! ∓.

**10...♘xd5**

Practice has also seen 10...exd5 11 ♗e2 ♗e6 12 ♘d4! (12 0-0 ♘e4 =):

a) 12...♘xd4 13 ♕xd4 ♘e4 14 0-0 ♗f6 15 ♗e5 ♘xc3 16 ♕xc3 ♖c8 17 ♕d4 ±.

b) 12...♖c8 13 0-0 a5 (13...♘xb4 14 axb4 ♖xc3 15 ♖xa7 ♕b6 16 ♘b5 ± Zsu.Polgar-Geller, Vienna 1993) 14 ♘xc6! (14 ♘xe6 fxe6 15 b5 ♘b8 16 ♕d2 ♘bd7 =) 14...♖xc6 (14...bxc6 15 ♗a6 ♖a8 16 ♗b7 ♖a7 17 ♗xc6 ±) 15 ♕d4 ± Topalov-Yusupov, Elista OL 1998.

c) 12...a5!? 13 ♘xe6 fxe6 14 b5 ♘b8 15 ♗g4 ♘xg4 16 ♕xg4 ♖f6 17 0-0 ♘d7 18 ♖fd1 ♘b6 ∞ Golod-Lputian, Belgrade 1999.

**11 ♘xd5 exd5 12 ♗d3 ♗f6 13 ♖c1 a6**

Or:

a) 13...♖e8 14 0-0 ♗g4 15 h3 ♗xf3 16 ♕xf3 ♘e5 17 ♗xe5 ♖xe5 18 ♖fd1 ±.

b) 13...♗g4!? 14 0-0 ♕e7 15 h3 (15 b5 ♘e5 =) 15...♗xf3 16 ♕xf3 ♖fd8 17 ♖fd1 (17 ♖c5 a5! 18 ♗b5 axb4 19 axb4 ♘xb4 20 ♖c7 ♕e6 21 ♖xb7 ♘a2 = Van Wely-Van der Sterren, Escaldes Z 1998) 17...g6 (17...♗b2? 18 ♖c2 ♗xa3 19 b5 ♘e5 20 ♗xh7+ ♔xh7 21 ♕h5+ ♔g8 22 ♗xe5 ±) 18 ♗b1 (18 ♖c2 a5 19 b5 {19 ♗c7?! ♖d7 20 ♗xa5 ♖d6!} 19...♘e5 20 ♗xe5 ♗xe5 =) 18...♗b2 (18...♘e5 19 ♗xe5 ♗xe5 20 ♗a2 ± Krasenkow-Karpov, Polanica Zdroj 1998) 19 ♖c2 ♗xa3 20 b5 ♘e5 (20...♘b4? 21 ♖c7 ♖d7 22 ♖xd7 ♕xd7

23 e4 +−) 21 ♗xe5 ♕xe5 22 ♗a2 ♕e7
23 ♗xd5 (23 ♖xd5 ♖ac8) 23...♖d7
24 e4 ± P.H.Nielsen-Van der Sterren,
Bundesliga 1998/9.

**14 0-0 ♖e8**

14...♗e6 15 ♗b1 ♕e7?! 16 e4 ♕d8
17 ♕d3! (17 e5 ♗e7 18 ♘d4 {18 ♕d3
g6 19 ♗h6 ♖e8 20 ♘d4? ♘xe5}
18...♘xd4 19 ♕xd4 ♕d7 20 ♕d3 g6
=) 17...dxe4 18 ♕xe4 g6 19 ♖fd1 ±
Krasenkow-Van der Sterren, Groningen FIDE 1997.

**15 ♗b1 g6 16 ♗a2 ♗e6 17 ♕d3 d4
18 ♗xe6 ♖xe6 19 exd4**

19 e4 ♕e7 20 ♘d2 ♗e5 (20...g5!?
21 ♗g3 ♖d8) 21 ♗g3 (21 ♗xe5 ♘xe5
22 ♕xd4 ♖d8 23 ♕e3 ♖d3 is equal)
21...♗xg3 22 hxg3 ♘e5 23 ♕b3? (23
♕xd4! ♖d8 24 ♕e3 ♖d3 =) 23...♖d8
24 ♖c5 d3 25 ♖fc1 ♘c6 ∓ Beliavsky-
Short, Groningen FIDE 1997.

**19...♘xd4 20 ♘xd4 ♕xd4 21
♕xd4 ♗xd4 22 ♖c7 b5**

The position is equal.

**D)**

**8 ♕c2 ♘c6 (D)**

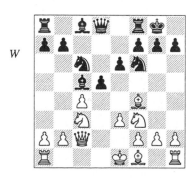

Now:

**D1)**

**9 ♖d1 ♕a5 10 a3 ♗e7 11 ♘d2**

At one time White experimented
with 11 ♖d2?!, but 11...♘e4! quickly
put players off White's position. 12
♘xe4 dxe4 13 ♕xe4 ♖d8 and now:

a) 14 ♕c2? e5 15 ♗g3 e4 16 ♕xe4
♗f5 17 ♕f4 ♖xd2 18 ♘xd2 ♖d8 19 e4
♗g4!! −+ Miles-Beliavsky, Wijk aan
Zee 1984.

b) 14 ♗e2 ♖xd2! (14...e5?! 15 b4!
♕xa3 16 ♖xd8+ ♘xd8 17 0-0 ♕xb4
18 ♘xe5 ± Meduna-Velikov, Trnava
1984) 15 ♘xd2 e5 16 ♗g3 ♗e6 17
♕c2 ♖d8 ∓.

c) 14 c5 ♖xd2 15 ♘xd2 ♕xc5 ∓
(this is better than 15...e5 16 ♗xe5
♘xe5 17 ♕xe5 ♗e6 18 ♕c3 ♕xc3 19
bxc3 ♗xc5 20 a4, with an unclear position).

**11...e5 (D)**

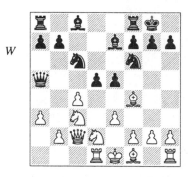

**12 ♗g5**

Or:

a) 12 ♗g3 d4 (12...♗g4?! 13 f3
♗e6 14 ♘b3 ♕d8 15 cxd5 ♗xd5,
Toth-Barbero, Switzerland 1986, 16
♘xd5! ♘xd5 17 ♕d2 ♘f6 {17...♕b6?
18 ♕xd5 +−} 18 ♕xd8 ♖fxd8 19
♖xd8+ ♖xd8 20 ♗b5 ♘d5 21 ♔e2 ±)
13 ♘b3 ♕b6 and now:

a1) 14 ♘b5!? a6 15 c5 ♕d8 (better than 15...♗xc5?! 16 ♕xc5 ♕xc5 17 ♘xc5 axb5 18 ♗xb5 ±) 16 exd4 axb5 17 dxe5 ♕e8 18 exf6 (18 ♗xb5 ♘h5 19 ♗e2 ♘xg3 20 hxg3 h6 ∓ Kaidanov-Klovans, Minsk 1986) 18...♗xf6+ 19 ♗e2 ♗e6 20 ♗d6 ♗xb3 21 ♕xb3 ♘d4 22 ♕d3 ♘xe2 23 ♕xe2 ♕xe2+ 24 ♔xe2 ♖fe8+ =.

a2) 14 exd4 ♗f5 (14...♘xd4!? 15 ♘xd4 exd4 16 ♘b5 ♗d7 17 ♘xd4 ♗c5!? 18 ♘f3 ♘g4 19 ♖d2 ♖fe8+ 20 ♔d1 ♗xf2 21 ♗xf2 ♘xf2+ 22 ♖xf2 ♗a4 23 ♕xa4 ♕xf2 with the initiative, Marianeli-Bönsch, Hungary 1989) 15 ♗d3 (not 15 ♕xf5 ♕xb3 16 dxe5 ♕xb2 17 ♘b5 ♖ad8!, when 18 exf6?? loses to 18...♗b4+ 19 axb4 ♖fe8+, while 18 ♗d3 g6 is pleasant for Black) 15...♗xd3 16 ♖xd3 ♘xd4 17 ♘xd4 exd4 18 ♘e2 ♖fd8 19 0-0 ♘e4 20 ♖fd1 ♗f6 21 b4 a5 22 c5 ♕a6 23 ♗c7 ♖dc8 24 ♗xa5 ♘xc5 25 bxc5 ♕xa5 26 ♘xd4 ♕xc5 ½-½ Glek-Averkin, USSR 1983.

b) 12 ♘b3 ♕b6 13 ♗g5 and now:

b1) 13...♗g4!? 14 f3 and here:

b11) 14...dxc4 15 ♗xc4 ♗e6 16 ♘a4!? (16 ♗xe6 fxe6 17 ♘d2 ♘d5 18 ♘c4 ♕c7 19 ♘b5 ♕d7 20 ♗xe7 ♕xe7 21 0-0 ♖ad8 = Kamsky-Short, Tilburg 1991) 16...♘b4 (16...♕c7? 17 ♗xe6 fxe6 18 ♗xf6 ♖xf6 19 0-0 ± Gulko-Yusupov, Novi Sad OL 1990) 17 ♕c3 (17 axb4? ♕xb4+ 18 ♘d2 ♖fc8 is good for Black) 17...♕c6 (17...♘a2? 18 ♕xe5! ♕c6 19 ♗xe6 ±) 18 ♗xe6 ♕xa4 19 ♗xf6 ♗xf6 20 ♗d7 ♘c6 gives Black chances of surviving.

b12) 14...♗e6!? 15 ♘a4 (15 c5?! ♕d8 16 ♗d3 d4 17 ♗xf6 ♗xf6 18 exd4 exd4 19 ♘e4 ♗h4+ 20 g3 ♗e7 21 0-0 ♕d5 22 ♘bd2 ♘e5 is very

good for Black, Yurtaev-Lputian, Tbilisi 1980) 15...♕c7! (not 15...♕a6?! 16 cxd5 ♕xa4 17 dxe6 fxe6 18 ♕c4 ±) 16 ♗xf6 dxc4! 17 ♗xc4 ♗xc4 18 ♕xc4 ♗xf6 19 ♘bc5 (19 0-0 ♗g5 20 e4 ♖ac8 =) 19...♖fd8 20 ♖xd8+ ♖xd8 21 ♘e4 ♗h4+ 22 g3 ♗e7 = Piket-Ivanchuk, Monaco Amber rpd 1997.

b2) 13...d4 14 ♗xf6 ♗xf6 15 ♘d5 ♕d8 16 ♗d3 g6 17 exd4 ♘xd4 18 ♘xd4 exd4 19 ♘xf6+ (19 0-0 ♗g7 20 ♖de1 ♗e6 21 ♘f4 ♗d7 22 ♗e4 ♖b8 23 ♘d3 ♕c7 24 b3 ♖fe8 25 ♕d2 a5! 26 ♕f4 ♕xf4 27 ♘xf4 ♗f8 28 a4 ♗b4 29 ♖e2 ♔g7 30 ♖d1 ♗c5 ½-½ Gelfand-Kramnik, Dos Hermanas 1999) 19...♕xf6 20 0-0 ♗g4! (20...♗e6!? 21 ♖fe1 ♖ac8 22 b3 ♖fd8 23 ♗e4 ♖c7 = Korchnoi-Karpov, Baguio City Wch (23) 1978) 21 ♖d2 (21 f3 ♗d7 22 ♖f2 ♖fe8 23 ♖fd2 ♖ad8 24 ♗e4 ♗c6 25 ♗xc6 bxc6 26 c5 ♖e3 27 ♕c4 ♕e5 28 ♔f2 d3 ∓ Tukmakov-Balashov, Kislovodsk 1982) 21...♖fe8 22 ♗e4 ♖e7 23 ♕d3 ♖ae8 24 f3 ♗f5 25 ♗xf5 gxf5 26 ♕xd4 ♕xd4+ 27 ♖xd4 ♖e2 28 ♖f2 ♖e1+ 29 ♖f1 ♖1e2 30 ♖d5 ♖xb2 31 ♖xf5 ♖ee2 32 ♖g5+ ♔f8 33 ♖d1 h6 34 ♖g3 ½-½ Gorelov-Andrianov, USSR 1984.

**12...d4 13 ♘b3** (D)

**13...♕d8**
13...♕b6 is possible, transposing to note 'b2' to White's 12th move.
**14 ♗e2**
Or 14 exd4 ♘xd4 15 ♘xd4 exd4 16 ♘b5 (16 ♘e2?! ♖e8 17 ♕d3 ♕c7 18 ♕xd4 ♗c5 19 ♕f4 ♘e4 20 ♖d5 ♗xf2+ 21 ♔d1 ♕xc4 −+ Kanko-Pyhälä, Finnish Ch (Espoo) 1984) and then:
a) 16...♗c5?! 17 b4! ♕e7+ 18 ♗e2 d3 19 ♕xd3 ♗xf2+ 20 ♔f1 ♕e5 21 ♗xf6 ♕xf6 22 ♕f3 ♗h4 23 g3 ♕xf3+ 24 ♗xf3 ♗f6 25 c5 ± C.Hansen-Thorsteins, Kiljava jr Wch 1984.
b) 16...♗d7!? 17 ♘xd4 ♕a5+ 18 ♕d2 ♕b6 19 ♗e3 ½-½ Ivanchuk-Vaganian, Moscow 1998. A possible continuation is 19...♗a4!? 20 b3 (20 ♖c1 ♘e4) 20...♗xb3 21 ♖b1 ♘e4 22 ♖xb3 ♘xd2 23 ♖xb6 ♘xf1 24 ♖xb7 ♘xe3 25 fxe3 ♗xa3 =.
c) 16...♗g4 17 ♖xd4 ♖e8 18 ♗e3 ♕b6 19 ♗d3 ♗c5 20 0-0 ∞ Piket-Van der Sterren, Lyons Z 1990.
**14...a5 15 ♘a4**
We have reached the main position of this variation. In addition to the text-move, White can also try:
a) 15 ♗xf6 ♗xf6 16 0-0 a4 17 ♘c5 ♕a5 18 ♘3xa4 ♗e7 19 b4 ♕a7 (19...♕c7!? with compensation) 20 ♗f3 dxe3 21 fxe3 ♗xc5 22 ♘xc5 ♕xa3 23 ♕d2 ♕xb4 24 ♕xb4 ♘xb4 25 ♘xb7 ♖a3 = Korchnoi-Hübner, Merano Ct (6) 1980/1.
b) 15 exd4 a4 16 ♘xa4 (after 16 dxe5 ♘d7 17 ♗xe7 axb3 18 ♕xh7+ {18 ♕xb3 ♕xe7 ∓} 18...♔xh7 19 ♗xd8 ♖xd8 the piece outweighs the pawns) 16...♘xd4 17 ♘xd4 exd4 18 b3 ♕a5+ 19 ♕d2 (19 ♗d2 ♗f5! 20 ♕b2 ♕e5 21 ♗b4 ♗xb4+ 22 axb4 ♖fe8 23 ♖xd4 ♗c2! 24 ♖d2 ♗xb3 25

♕xb3 ♕a1+ ∓ Portisch-Beliavsky, Moscow 1981) 19...♗xa3 20 ♕xa5 (20 0-0 ♘e4 21 ♕xa5 ♖xa5 22 ♗d2 ♘xd2 23 ♖xd2 ♗d7 24 ♖xd4 ♗xa4 25 bxa4 ♖xa4 = Bagirov-Vaganian, Telavi 1982) 20...♖xa5 21 ♗xf6 ♗b4+! 22 ♔f1 gxf6 23 ♖xd4 ♖e5! 24 g4 b5! 25 cxb5 ♗b7 26 f3 ♖fe8 27 ♗d1 ♖xb5 with compensation, Korchnoi-Karpov, Merano Wch (11) 1981.
**15...g6!** *(D)*
This appears to be the strongest continuation. One may also recommend 15...♗d7!? 16 ♘bc5 as long as Black then plays 16...♗c8! ∞ rather than 16...b6? 17 ♘xd7 ♘xd7 18 ♗xe7 ♕xe7 19 ♗f3 ± Ivanchuk-Beliavsky, USSR Ch (Moscow) 1988.
**16 ♗xf6**

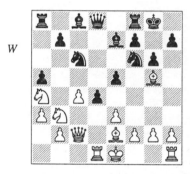

16 exd4 ♗f5 17 ♕c1 ♘xd4! (the alternative 17...exd4 18 0-0 ♖e8 is best met by 19 ♗f3!? ∞, rather than 19 ♖fe1 ♖c8 20 ♗e3? dxe3 21 ♖xd8 exf2+ 22 ♔xf2 ♗xd8 23 ♔g1 ♘e5 0-1 Hübner-Short, Tilburg 1998) 18 ♘xd4 exd4 19 0-0 ♖c8! 20 c5 d3 21 ♗xd3 ♗xd3 22 ♕e3 ♘g4! 23 ♕xe7 ♕xe7 24 ♗xe7 ♗xf1 25 ♗xf8 ♗b5 26 ♘c3 (½-½ Gutop-Vitolinš, corr. 1983) 26...♔xf8 27 ♘xb5 ♖xc5 =.

**16...♗xf6 17 c5**

White can also play 17 0-0 ♗g7! 18 c5 ♕h4! 19 e4 ♗e6 and now 20 ♗d3 f5 21 ♘d2 ♖f7 22 ♖de1 ♖af8 is unclear, A.Shneider-Kruppa, Podolsk 1989 or 20 ♘b6 ♖ad8 21 ♗c4 ♗h6 22 ♗xe6 fxe6 23 ♕d3 ♖f7 24 ♘c4 ♖df8 25 g3 ♕h5 with the initiative, Østenstad-Bönsch, Novi Sad OL 1990.

**17...♗e6!**

17...♗f5?! 18 e4 ♗e6 19 0-0 ♕e8 20 ♘b6 (20 ♘c1 ∞ Alterman-Lutz, Tel-Aviv 1999) 20...a4 21 ♘d2 ♖a5 22 ♘dc4 ♗xc4 (22...♖xc5 23 ♘xa4) 23 ♗xc4 ±.

**18 e4 ♕e8! 19 ♘b6**

If 19 0-0, then 19...♘b4! 20 axb4 ♕xa4 21 ♘xd4 ♕xc2 22 ♘xc2 ♗b3 23 ♖d6! ♗xc2 24 ♖xf6 axb4 25 ♖b6 ♗xe4 26 ♖xb4 =.

**19...a4 20 ♘d2 ♖a5 21 ♗d3!?**

21 0-0 ♗e7! 22 ♘dc4 (22 ♘xa4? d3 −+) 22...♖xc5 (22...♗xc4?! 23 ♗xc4 ♘d8 24 ♗d5 ±) 23 ♕xa4 (23 ♘xa4 d3! 24 ♗xd3 ♘d4 25 ♘xc5 ♘xc2 26 ♘xe6 fxe6 27 ♗xc2 ♗c5! 28 ♘xe5 ♖xf2! 29 ♖xf2 ♗xf2+ 30 ♔xf2 ♕c8! 31 ♗b3 ♕c5+ 32 ♔f3 ♕xe5 33 ♖d2 ♔f8 ∓ intending ...♔e7) 23...♘a5! 24 ♕xe8 ♖xe8 25 ♘xa5 ♖xa5 26 ♖c1 ♖c5 =.

**21...♗e7 22 ♘dc4**

22 ♘xa4? ♘b8 23 b3 ♗xb3 24 ♘xb3 (24 ♕xb3 ♕xa4 25 ♕xb7 ♘d7 26 ♗c4 ♗g5! ∓) 24...♖xa4 25 ♖a1 ♕c6 ∓ Alterman-Kasparov, Tel-Aviv 1998.

**22...♖xc5 23 ♘xa4**

23 ♕xa4 ♘a5!.

**23...♖b5 24 0-0**

Other moves are bad: 24 ♘d6? ♘b4! 25 ♘xe8 ♘xc2+ 26 ♗xc2 (26 ♔d2 ♘xa3 27 bxa3 ♖a5 −+) 26...♖xe8 27 b4 ♖c8 28 ♗d3 ♗xb4+ 29 ♔e2

♖a5 30 ♘b6 ♖c6 31 axb4 ♖a2+ −+; 24 b4? ♖xb4! 25 axb4 ♘xb4 26 ♕b3 b5 27 ♘ab6 ♘xd3+ 28 ♕xd3 bxc4 29 ♘xc4 ♕b5 −+.

**24...♘a5 25 b4**

25 ♘d2?! ♘b3!.

**25...♘xc4 26 ♗xc4 ♕c6 27 ♗d3**

27 ♖c1?! ♕xc4 28 ♕xc4 ♗xc4 29 ♖xc4 ♖a8 −+.

**27...♕xc2 28 ♗xc2 ♖a8**

28...♗c4!? 29 ♖fe1 ♖a8 30 ♘b2 ♗e6 ∞.

**29 ♗d3 ♖xa4 30 ♗xb5 ♖xa3 31 ♖b1 ♗g5!?**

Black has compensation.

**D2)**

**9 a3 ♕a5**

Now:

**D21: 10 ♘d2**   34
**D22: 10 0-0-0**   35

Black's best reply to 10 ♖c1 is 10...d4! 11 exd4 ♘xd4 12 ♘xd4 ♗xd4 13 ♗d3 e5 14 ♗d2 ♕d8 =.

**D21)**

**10 ♘d2** *(D)*

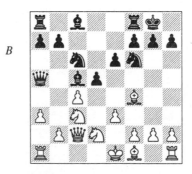

**10...♗e7**

Or 10...♗b4, and now:

a) 11 ♖c1 ♗xc3 12 ♕xc3 ♕xc3 13 ♖xc3 e5 and now 14 ♗g3 d4 15 ♖c1 ♗f5 16 c5 ♖ad8 = Gavrikov-Peshina, USSR 1981 or 14 ♗g5 d4 (14...♗e6) 15 ♖c1 dxe3 16 fxe3 ♖d8 17 ♗xf6 gxf6 18 ♗e2 ♘e7 = Grünberg-Bönsch, Hanover 1991.

b) 11 cxd5 and now:

b1) 11...♘xd5 12 ♘xd5 exd5 13 ♗d3 h6 14 ♖c1! ♗e7 15 0-0 ♗e6 16 ♘b3 ♕b6 17 ♘c5 ♗xc5 (17...♖ac8 18 ♘xe6 fxe6 19 ♕e2 ♗f6 20 ♕h5! ♘e7 21 b4 ± Kramnik-Hübner, Bundesliga 1993/4) 18 ♕xc5 ♕xb2 19 ♖b1 ♕d2 20 ♖fd1 ♕a5 21 ♖b5 ♕a4 22 ♖a1! ± Bareev-Janjgava, Debrecen Echt 1992.

b2) 11...exd5 12 ♗d3 (12 ♘b3 ♗xc3+ 13 bxc3 ♕a4 14 ♗d3 ♖e8 15 0-0 ♘e5 16 ♘d4 ♕xc2 17 ♗xc2 ♗d7 18 ♖fb1 b6 19 a4 ♘c4 = Agdestein-Gild.Garcia, New York 1994) 12...d4 13 0-0 ♗xc3 14 ♘c4 ♕h5 15 bxc3 ♘d5 16 ♗g3 (16 ♗d6 ♖d8 17 cxd4 b5 18 ♘b6 ♖xd6 19 ♘xa8 ♖h6 with the initiative) 16...dxe3 17 ♖ae1 ♗e6 18 fxe3 (18 ♘xe3 h6 19 ♘c4 ♖ad8 20 ♘d6 b6 21 ♗b5 ♘de7 22 ♕a4 {22 ♗e2 ♗g4 23 ♗d3 ♖d7 24 ♗h7+ ♔h8 25 ♗e4 ♕c5 is equal, L.B.Hansen-Lalić, Moscow OL 1994} 22...♘a5 23 ♖e5 ♕g6 ∞ Lalić) 18...♖ad8 (18...♘de7 19 ♘d6 b6 20 ♖b1 ♘d5 21 ♖b5 ♕h6 22 ♖xd5 ♗xd5 23 ♘f5 ♕g5 ∞ Nadanian-Dervishi, Panormo Z 1998) 19 ♘d6 ♘e5 20 ♗f5 ♖xd6 21 ♗xe5 ♖dd8 22 e4 ♘e7 23 ♖e3 (23 ♗d4 ♗xf5 24 exf5 ♘c6 25 ♕f2 ♘xd4 26 cxd4 ♕g5 27 ♖e5 ♖d7 = Tukmakov-Lputian, Tilburg 1994) 23...♘g6 24 ♗d4 b6 ∞.

**11 ♗g3**

11 ♘b3 ♕b6 12 cxd5 ♘xd5 13 ♘a4 (13 ♘xd5 exd5 14 ♗d3 h6 15 0-0

♗e6 16 ♖ac1 ♖ac8 = Lputian-Vaganian, Erevan 1994) 13...♕d8 14 ♖d1 (14 0-0-0!? ♕e8 15 ♗b5 ♗d7 16 ♘ac5 ♖c8 ∞ Vaganian-Arlandi, Reggio Emilia 1993/4) 14...♕e8! ∞.

**11...♗d7**

11...♕d8 deserves attention: 12 ♘f3 ♕a5 13 ♘d2 ♕b6 14 ♗e2 d4 15 ♘a4 ♕d8 16 e4 ♘d7 17 ♖d1 e5 18 b4 b6 ∞ Petrosian-Liberzon, Biel IZ 1976.

**12 ♗e2 ♕d8**

12...♖fc8 13 0-0 ♕d8 14 cxd5 ♘xd5 15 ♘de4 ±.

**13 cxd5**

13 0-0 d4!.

**13...♘xd5 14 ♘xd5 exd5 15 0-0 d4 16 e4 ♖c8 17 ♕d3 f5**

= Komarov-Beliavsky, Nikšić 1996.

**D22)**

**10 0-0-0**

Grandmaster Kaidanov's idea. White seeks a sharp battle, and in recent years the move has become extremely popular.

**10...♗e7!** *(D)*

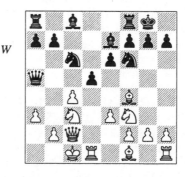

**11 g4**

White wants to gain supremacy in the centre by means of pressure on the wing. Other continuations:

a)  11 h4 a6!? *(D)* and then:

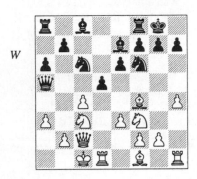

a1)  12 cxd5 exd5 13 ♘g5 ♖d8 14 ♔b1?! h6 15 ♘f3 ♗g4 16 ♗e2 ♖ac8 ∓ Van Wely-Sharif, Linares Z 1995.

a2)  12 ♔b1 dxc4! 13 ♘g5 ♕f5 14 ♕xf5 exf5 15 ♗xc4 h6 16 ♘f3 ♗e6 17 ♗a2 ♖fd8 18 ♘e5 ♘xe5 19 ♗xe5 ♖ac8 = Chernin-Chernishevich, Osterkars 1995.

a3)  12 ♘g5 ♖d8 13 cxd5 (13 ♗d3 h6 14 ♗h7+ {14 g4 is well met by 14...e5} 14...♔f8 15 ♗g6 d4! ∓; 13 ♔b1 h6 14 f3 d4 ∓ Arkhangelsky-Unzicker, Bad Liebenzell seniors Wch 1995) 13...exd5 14 e4 (14 ♗d3 h6 15 ♗h7+ ♔f8 16 ♗g6 d4 17 ♘e2? {17 ♕b3 ♘d5 ∓} 17...fxg6 18 ♕xg6 hxg5 19 hxg5 ♗f5 20 ♖h8+ ♘g8 –+) 14...♘xe4 and then:

a31)  15 ♘cxe4 dxe4 16 ♗c4 (16 ♖xd8+ ♘xd8 17 ♕xe4 ♕c5+ 18 ♗c4 ♗f5 –+) 16...♗xg5 17 hxg5 ♖xd1+ 18 ♖xd1 (18 ♕xd1 ♕c5) 18...♕f5 intending ...♗e6.

a32)  15 ♘gxe4 dxe4 16 ♖xd8+ ♕xd8 17 ♕xe4 g6 18 ♗c4 ♗f5 19 ♕e3 (19 ♕d5 ♕f8) 19...♕d4 = Gelfand-Karpov, Wijk aan Zee 1998.

b)  11 ♘d2 ♕b6 12 ♗d3 (12 g4?! d4 13 ♘a4 ♕a5 14 g5 ♘h5 15 ♘e4

♗d7 ∓ Glek-Yudasin, Tilburg 1994; 12 ♘b3 ♘a5! 13 ♘xa5 ♕xa5 14 e4 dxe4 15 ♘xe4 ♘xe4 16 ♕xe4 ♗xa3 17 bxa3 ♕c3+ 18 ♕c2 ♕a1+ 19 ♕b1 ♕c3+ 20 ♕c2 ½-½ Gabriel-Lutz, Hamburg 1997) 12...d4 13 c5 (13 ♘a4 ♕a5 14 c5 e5 15 ♘c4 ♕c7 16 ♗g3 dxe3 17 fxe3 ♗g4 18 ♖d2 ♖ad8 = Kempinski-Beliavsky, Koszalin 1998) 13...♕xc5 14 ♘b3 ♕b6 15 exd4 *(D)* and then:

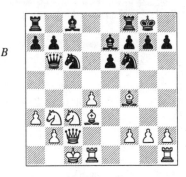

b1)  15...♘a5 16 ♘c5 ♗xc5 17 dxc5 ♘b3+ 18 ♔b1 ♘xc5 19 ♗d6 (19 ♗e5 ♘xd3 20 ♖xd3 ♘g4 21 ♗xg7 ♔xg7 22 ♖g3 e5 23 h3 ♕g6 =) 19...♖e8 (19...♘xd3 20 ♗xf8 ♘xf2 21 ♗c5! +–) 20 ♗b5 ♘cd7 21 f3 intending g4 with compensation.

b2)  15...♗d7 16 ♗e3 ♕d8 17 ♘c5 ♖c8 18 ♘xb7 (18 ♘xd7 ♕xd7 19 g4 ∞) 18...♕c7 19 ♘c5 (19 ♗a6 ♘b8 20 ♘c5 ♘xa6 21 ♘xa6 ♕b7 22 ♘c5 ♕xg2 =) 19...♘xd4 20 ♗xd4 ♗xc5 21 ♗xc5 (21 ♗xf6 gxf6 22 ♗xh7+ ♔g7 intending ...f5 and ...♗xa3) 21...♕xc5 22 ♗xh7+ ♘xh7 23 ♖xd7 ♕g5+ = 24 f4 ♕xf4+ 25 ♕d2 ♕b8 ½-½ Kempinski-Sapis, Poland 1997.

c)  11 ♔b1 ♖d8!? 12 ♘d2 dxc4 13 ♗xc4 (13 ♘xc4 ♖xd1+ 14 ♕xd1 ♕d8

=) 13...♕f5 14 ♘de4 ♖xd1+ (14...♘xe4 15 ♖xd8+ ♘xd8 16 ♘xe4 ♗d7 17 ♖d1 ♗c6 18 ♗d3 ♕a5 19 ♘d6 ± Van Wely-Van der Sterren, Bundesliga 1997/8) 15 ♖xd1 ♘xe4 16 ♘xe4 e5 17 ♗g3 ♗e6 18 f3 (18 ♗xe6 ♕xe6 19 ♘c5 ♗xc5 20 ♕xc5 f6) 18...♖c8 (or 18...h5!? 19 ♗xe6 ♕xe6 20 ♘c5 ♗xc5 21 ♕xc5 f6 ± Ekström-Arlandi, Elista OL 1998) 19 ♕b3 ♗xc4 20 ♕xc4 h5! 21 h3 (21 h4 a6 =) 21...h4 22 ♗e1 ♕g6 23 ♖d2 (23 ♖d7? ♕xg2 24 ♗xh4 ♕h1+ 25 ♔a2 ♘b4+ −+) 23...a6! (23...♖d8 24 ♖xd8+ ♗xd8 25 ♕b3! ∞ Van Wely-Van der Sterren, Wijk aan Zee 1998) 24 ♖c2 ♖d8 =.

**11...dxc4 12 ♗xc4 *(D)***

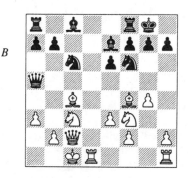

*B*

**12...e5**
12...♖d8!? also deserves attention:
a) 13 h3 ♗d7 14 e4 ♗e8 = ½-½ Bagaturov-Janjgava, Tbilisi 1996.
b) 13 ♖xd8+!? ♘xd8 (13...♗xd8 14 ♘b5!? a6 15 ♘d6 ±) 14 ♖d1 (14 ♘e5 ♘d7! 15 ♘xd7 ♗xd7 16 ♖d1 ♗e8 =) 14...♘xg4 15 ♘b5! e5! (15...♘c6 16 ♗c7 b6 17 ♕e4 +−) 16 ♗g5 (16 ♘xe5 ♘xe5 17 ♗xe5 ♗e6 ∞) and then:
b1) 16...♘c6? 17 ♗xe7 ♘xe7 18 ♕a4! ♕b6 19 ♘c7 +−.

b2) 16...♗xg5? 17 ♘xg5 g6 (or 17...♘f6 18 b4 ♕b6 19 ♘c7 +−) 18 b4! ♕b6 19 ♖d6 ♘c6 20 ♖xg6+ and White wins.
b3) 16...♘f6! 17 b4 (17 ♘c7 ♗f5! ∓) 17...♕b6 18 ♘c7 ♖b8! 19 ♗xf6 ♗xf6 (19...♕xf6!?) 20 ♘d5 ♕d6 ∓.
c) 13 ♘b5!? ♘d5! (13...e5?! 14 ♘xe5 ♘xe5 15 ♗xe5 ♗xg4 16 ♖xd8+ ♕xd8 17 ♖g1 ♗h5 18 f4 a6 19 ♘d4 ♖c8 20 ♘f5 ±) 14 ♗xd5 ♖xd5 15 ♖xd5 exd5 16 ♘c7 ♖b8 17 ♖d1 d4 ∞ analysis.
d) 13 e4 ♘xg4 14 ♖hg1 (14 ♖dg1 ♘ge5 {14...e5!?} 15 ♘xe5 ♘xe5 16 ♘d5 ♖xd5! 17 exd5 ♘xc4 18 ♕xc4 exd5 19 ♕d4 ♕c5+ 20 ♕xc5 ♗xc5 21 ♗e5 g6 with good play for Black) 14...♖xd1+ 15 ♕xd1 and now:
d1) 15...♘f6!? 16 ♗d6 (16 e5 can be met by 16...♘d5!) 16...♕d8 17 e5 ♘e8 18 ♘e4 ♗xd6 19 exd6 f5 20 ♘fg5 fxe4 21 ♕h5 ♘f6 22 ♕f7+ ♔h8 23 ♘xe6 ♕g8 24 ♕xf6! ♗xe6 (24...gxf6 25 ♖xg8+ ♔xg8 26 ♘c7+ ∞) 25 ♕xe6 ♕xe6 26 ♗xe6 ♖d8 = analysis.
d2) 15...♘xf2 16 ♕f1 ♗xa3 ∞ Shabalov-Kharitonov, Leningrad 1989.
**13 g5 exf4 14 gxf6 ♗xf6 15 ♘d5**
15 ♖d5 ♕c7 16 ♘e4 ♕e7 17 h4 g6! 18 h5 ♗f5 19 ♘xf6+ ♕xf6 20 e4 ♘e7 (20...♗g4!?) 21 ♖d4 ♗g4 22 e5 ♕c6 23 hxg6 hxg6 24 e6 ♕xf3 ∓ Agrest-Sanden, Stockholm 1991/2.
**15...♘e7! *(D)***
**16 ♘xf6+ gxf6 17 ♖hg1+**
17 ♘d4!? fxe3 18 fxe3 ♗f5! (or 18...♕e5!? 19 ♔b1 ♗f5 20 ♘xf5 ♘xf5 21 ♖d5 ♘xe3 with an equal position, Hübner-Van der Sterren, Bundesliga 1994/5) 19 ♘xf5 ♕xf5 20 ♗d3 (20 ♕c3? ♖ac8! ∓) 20...♕h3 (20...♕e5!? 21 ♗xh7+ ♔h8 22 ♕e4 is unclear) 21

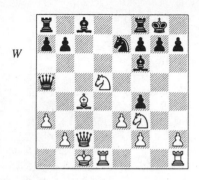

W

♔b1 ♘g6 (21...♖ac8 22 ♕a4 with compensation) 22 ♕f2 ♖ad8 23 ♖hg1 ♕e6 24 h4 ♔h8 25 h5 ♘e7 and the position is level, Dizdar-Beliavsky, Slovenian Cht (Bled) 1998.

**17...♔h8 18 ♕e4**

Or: 18 e4!? b5 19 ♗d5 ♘xd5 20 exd5 ♗d7! 21 ♔b1 b4 22 ♖d4 ♖g8 23 ♖xg8+ ♖xg8 24 ♕d2 ♗f5+ 25 ♔a2 ♖d8 26 ♕xb4 ♕xb4 27 axb4 ♖xd5 28 ♖xd5 ♗e6 29 ♔a3 ♗xd5 30 ♘d4 ♔g7 = Kramnik-Karpov, Monaco Amber blindfold 1998; 18 ♘d4!? fxe3 19 fxe3 ♗f5 20 ♘xf5 ♕xf5 21 ♗d3 ♕e5 22 ♔b1 f5 23 ♕b3 ♖ac8 24 ♗c2 b5! (24...♕f6?! 25 ♖d7 ♘c6 26 ♖f1 ± Akopian-Pigusov, Tilburg 1994) 25 ♖d7 a5 ∞.

**18...♘g6 19 ♕d4**

19 ♖d5 ♕c7 20 ♕d4 ♗e6! 21 ♖c5 ♕e7 22 ♗xe6 fxe6 gives Black a clear advantage, Shabalov-Kruppa, USSR Cht (Naberezhnye Chelny) 1988.

**19...♕b6 20 ♕xb6 axb6 21 ♖d6 ♗h3! 22 ♗d5!?** *(D)*

22 ♔b1 ♗f5+! 23 ♔a1 (23 ♔a2 ♗e4 24 ♘d4 ♘e5 25 ♗b3 fxe3 26 fxe3 ♖g8 27 ♖f1 b5! 28 ♖f4? {28 ♘xb5 ♗d3} 28...♘d3! ∓ Akopian-Kruppa, St Petersburg 1993) 23...♗e4 24 ♘d4 ♘e5 25 ♗b5 fxe3 26 fxe3 ♖g8 and Black has a slight advantage, Gelfand-Yusupov, Linares 1993.

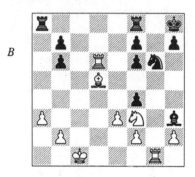

B

**22...fxe3**

22...♖ac8+ 23 ♔b1 ♖cd8 24 ♖xd8 ♖xd8 25 ♗xb7 ♗f5+ 26 ♔a1 fxe3 27 fxe3 ♖d3 = Vera-Lputian, Lucerne Wcht 1993.

**23 fxe3 ♖ac8+ 24 ♔b1 ♖cd8 25 ♖xd8 ♖xd8 26 ♗xf7 ♗f5+ 27 ♔a2 ♗e4 28 ♘d4 ♘e5 29 ♗e6 ♖e8! 30 ♗b3 ♘c6 31 ♘b5 ♗g6 32 ♖e1 ♘a5!?** = Beliavsky-Yusupov, Dortmund 1998.

**Conclusion:** By playing 5 ♗f4, White aspires to maintain his opening advantage, but Black has very rich counterchances.

# 4 The Classical QGD (with ...♘bd7)

1 d4 d5 2 c4 e6 3 ♘c3 ♗e7 4 ♘f3 ♘f6 5 ♗g5

Now we consider two approaches for Black: 5...♘bd7 and 5...h6 (Chapters 5-8). 5...0-0 does not have independent significance, since White can, by 6 ♕c2, transpose to the Eingorn Variation (Chapter 2), or, by 6 e3, reach main lines after 6...♘bd7 (this chapter) or 6...h6 (7 ♗h4 is Chapters 7 and 8; 7 ♗xf6 ♗xf6 is Line D of Chapter 5).

Our subject in this chapter is the knight move.

5...♘bd7 6 e3 0-0 *(D)*

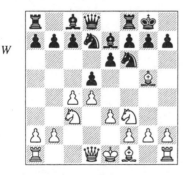

Now:
| | | |
|---|---|---|
| A: | 7 cxd5 | 39 |
| B: | 7 ♕b3 | 40 |
| C: | 7 ♗d3 | 41 |
| D: | 7 ♕c2 | 43 |
| E: | 7 ♖c1 | 48 |

A)

7 cxd5 ♘xd5

7...exd5 transposes to the Exchange Variation; then 8 ♗d3 c6 9 ♕c2 is Line B32 of Chapter 10.

8 ♗xe7 ♕xe7 9 ♗d3

White can also try:

a) 9 ♘xd5 exd5 10 ♗d3 (10 ♗e2 c6 11 0-0 ♘f6 12 ♘e5 ♘d7 =; 10 ♖c1 c6 11 ♗e2 ♘f6 12 0-0 ♗g4 13 a3 ♘e4 = Kaidanov-Kharitonov, Irkutsk 1983) 10...c6 (10...♕b4+ 11 ♕d2 ♕xd2+ 12 ♔xd2 c6 13 ♖hc1 ±) 11 0-0 ♘f6 12 ♘d2 (12 ♘e5 ♘d7 = intending to meet 13 f4 with 13...f6; 12 ♕c2 ♘e4 13 ♘d2 ♖e8 14 ♖ae1 ♗f5 =) 12...♗g4 13 ♕c2 ♗h5 14 ♖ab1 ♗g6 15 b4 a6 16 a4 ♖fe8 17 h3 ♗xd3 18 ♕xd3 ♖ad8 19 b5 axb5 20 axb5 c5 21 dxc5 ♕xc5 22 ♖fc1 ♕b6 23 ♘f3 ♖c8 24 ♘d4 g6 = Dokhoian-Ermolinsky, Aktiubinsk 1985.

b) 9 ♖c1 ♘xc3 10 ♖xc3 and now:

b1) 10...c5!? deserves attention: 11 ♗e2 (11 dxc5!?) 11...b6 12 0-0 ♗b7 13 ♕c2 ♖ac8 14 ♖c1 e5 15 dxc5 ♖xc5 ½-½ Chuchelov-Kalinichev, Novosibirsk 1989.

b2) 10...c6 11 ♗d3 e5 12 ♕c2 (12 ♕b1 h6 13 0-0 exd4 14 ♘xd4 ♘e5 15 ♗e4 ♖d8 16 h3 ½-½ Gretarsson-Kharitonov, Netherlands 1995) 12...exd4 13 ♘xd4 g6 14 0-0 c5 15 ♘f3 b6 16 e4 ♗b7 = Vilela-Ubilava, Camaguey 1987.

c) 9 ♕b3 and now:
c1) 9...♕b4!? 10 ♕xb4 ♘xb4 11
0-0-0 ♘d5 12 ♗d3 ♘xc3 13 bxc3 c5
14 ♘g5 h6 15 ♘e4 cxd4 16 cxd4 ♘b6
17 ♘c5 ♘d5 18 ♔b2 b6 ½-½ Ragozin-Kotov, Saltsjöbaden IZ 1948.
c2) 9...♘5f6!? 10 ♗e2 b6 11 0-0
♗b7 12 ♖ac1 (12 ♖fd1 ♖fd8 is equal,
Dokhoian-G.Kuzmin, Kharkov 1985)
12...♖fd8 13 ♘b5 c5 = Lin Weiguo-Nenashev, Lucerne Wcht 1993.
c3) 9...♘xc3 10 bxc3 (10 ♕xc3 c5
11 ♖d1 cxd4 12 ♖xd4 ♘f6 13 ♗e2 b6
14 0-0 ♗b7 = Lobron-Milos, Tilburg
1993) 10...b6 11 ♗e2 ♗b7 12 a4 c5 13
0-0 ♖ac8 14 a5 ♖c7 15 axb6 axb6 16
♘d2 ♖fc8 = Eingorn-Ubilava, Kharkov 1985.
**9...♘xc3 10 bxc3 c5 11 0-0 b6 12
♕c2**
Or 12 a4 ♗b7 13 a5 e5! 14 ♗b5
exd4 15 cxd4 ♘f6 (15...cxd4!? 16
♘xd4 bxa5 17 ♗xd7 ♕xd7 18 ♖xa5
♖fd8 19 h3 g6 20 ♕a1 a6 21 ♖b1 ♖ac8
= Lputian-Cifuentes, Ubeda 1996) 16
axb6 axb6 17 ♗e2 ♖fd8 ½-½ Itkis-Kharitonov, Moscow 1995.
**12...h6 13 a4 ♗b7 14 e4 ♖fc8 15
♕e2 ♘f6 16 a5 ♕d8 17 ♖ab1 cxd4 18
cxd4 ♖c3 19 a6 ♗c6 20 ♖bc1 ♖xc1
21 ♖xc1 ♖c8 22 h3 ♗a8**
= Notkin-Kharitonov, Elista 1994.

**B)**
**7 ♕b3** (D)
**7...c6**
7...c5 seems interesting: 8 cxd5
♘xd5 (8...cxd4 9 ♘xd4 ♘xd5 10 ♗xe7
♘xe7 11 ♗e2 ♘f6 12 0-0 ♕a5 13
♖fd1 ♗d7 14 ♘db5 ±) 9 ♗xe7 ♘xe7
10 dxc5 (10 ♖d1 ♕a5 {10...♕b6!?}
11 ♗e2 a6 12 0-0 b5 =) 10...♘xc5 11
♕a3 ♕b6 (11...b6 12 ♖d1 ♕c7 13

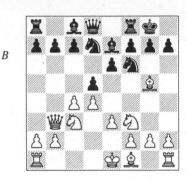

♘b5 ±) 12 ♗e2 (12 b4 ♘d7 13 ♗d3
♘c6 ∞) 12...♗d7 13 0-0 (13 b4 ♘a6)
13...a5! = analysis.
**8 ♗e2**
8 ♗d3 allows Black at least one
good reply:
a) 8...dxc4? does not work, due to
9 ♕xc4! c5 (9...a6 10 ♗c2! b5 11
♕d3! ♗b7 12 e4 ± Portisch-Lombard,
Biel IZ 1976) 10 dxc5 ♘xc5 11 ♗c2
♕a5 12 0-0 ♘cd7 13 ♖fd1 ± Akopian-San Segundo, Madrid 1997.
b) 8...a6!? 9 cxd5 cxd5?! (9...exd5!
is better) 10 0-0 b5 11 ♖fc1 ♘b6 12 a4
bxa4 13 ♘xa4 ♘xa4 14 ♕xa4 ♗d7 15
♕c2 ♖c8 16 ♕b1 ♖xc1+ 17 ♕xc1 a5
18 ♘e5 ± Akopian-Ubilava, Manila
OL 1992.
c) 8...c5! (exploiting the bishop's
position on d3, which may come under attack from a knight on c5) 9 cxd5
cxd4! 10 exd4 (10 ♘xd4 ♘c5!; 10
dxe6 ♘c5 −+) 10...♘xd5 =.
**8...♘e4**
Black must try to simplify the position. Practice has also seen:
a) 8...b6 9 0-0 ♗b7 10 cxd5! exd5
11 ♖ad1 ±/±.
b) 8...a6!? 9 a4! (9 0-0 b5 10 cxd5
cxd5 11 ♖fc1 ♗b7 12 ♕d1 h6 13 ♗f4
♖c8 = Portisch-Larsen, Linares 1981)

9...♖e8 10 0-0 ♘f8 11 ♖ad1 ♘g6 12 ♗d3 dxc4 13 ♕xc4 ♘d5 (13...♕b6?! 14 e4 ♕b4 15 ♕a2! e5? 16 ♗c4 and wins, Rauzer-Zamykhovsky, USSR Ch (Moscow) 1931) 14 ♗xe7 ♕xe7 15 a5 ± Polugaevsky.

**9 ♗xe7 ♕xe7 10 ♘xe4**

Also possible is 10 0-0 f5 11 ♖ad1 ♔h8 12 ♘e5 ♘xe5 13 dxe5 ♘xc3 14 ♕xc3 ♗d7 15 f4 ♗e8 16 ♖c1 ♖d8 17 ♖fd1 h6 18 c5 g5 with counterplay on the kingside, Bondarevsky-Konstantinopolsky, USSR Ch (Tbilisi) 1937.

**10...dxe4 11 ♘d2 e5! 12 0-0-0 ♘f6 13 h3 ♖b8 14 g4 ♖e8 15 ♖he1 h6 16 ♕c3 ♗d7 17 ♘b3 b6**

= Alekhine-Bogoljubow, Munich Wch (14) 1934.

**C)**

**7 ♗d3 dxc4 8 ♗xc4** *(D)*

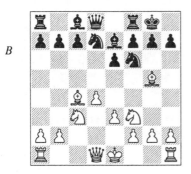

**7...c5**

8...a6 9 a4 b6 (9...c5!) 10 0-0 ♗b7 11 ♕e2 ♘d5 12 ♗xd5 exd5 13 ♗xe7 ♕xe7 14 a5! ± Gligorić.

**9 0-0 a6!**

A useful move to include, as it provokes a weakening in White's queenside. In the long run, this may provide Black with counterplay. If immediately

9...cxd4, then 10 exd4 (10 ♘xd4 ♘e5 gives equality) 10...♘b6 11 ♗b3 ♗d7 (11...♘fd5 12 ♗xe7 ♕xe7 13 ♖e1 ♖d8 14 ♖c1 ± Timman-Ree, Amsterdam 1984; 11...♘bd5 12 ♘e5 ♘d7 13 ♗xe7 ♘xe7 14 ♕e2 ♘f6 15 ♖fd1 b6 16 ♖ac1 ♗b7 17 f3 ♖c8?! 18 ♘xf7! ± Botvinnik-Batuev, Leningrad 1931) 12 ♕d3! (12 ♘e5 ♖c8 13 ♕d3 ♘fd5 14 ♗c2 g6 15 ♗h6 ♘b4 =) and here:

a) 12...♘bd5 13 ♘e5 ♗c6 14 ♖ad1 ♘b4 15 ♕h3 ♗d5 16 ♘xd5 ♘fxd5 (16...♘bxd5 17 f4! ± Botvinnik-Vidmar, Nottingham 1936) 17 ♗c1 ♖c8 ±.

b) 12...♘fd5 13 ♗e3 ♘xc3 14 bxc3 ♗a4 15 c4 ♗xb3 16 axb3 a6 17 ♖fd1 ± Polugaevsky.

**10 a4**

Preventing Black from seizing space on the queenside. Other moves:

a) 10 ♕e2 b5 11 ♗b3 ♗b7 12 ♖fd1 ♕b6 13 e4 cxd4 14 ♘xd4 ♘e5 15 ♗e3 ♗c5 16 f3 ♖fd8 = Savon-Zhukhovitsky, Moscow 1970.

b) 10 dxc5 leads to major simplifications: 10...♘xc5 11 ♕xd8 (11 ♕e2 b5 12 ♖fd1 ♕b6 13 ♗d3 ♘xd3 14 ♖xd3 ♗b7 15 ♘e5 ♖fd8 16 ♗xf6 ♗xf6 17 ♘d7 ♖xd7 18 ♖xd7 ♕c6 19 ♖xb7 =; 11 b4 ♘ce4 12 ♕xd8 ♗xd8 13 ♘xe4 ♘xe4 14 ♗xd8 ♖xd8 15 ♖fd1 ♗d7 16 ♖d4 ♗c6 = Marshall-Rubinstein, San Sebastian 1912) 11...♖xd8 12 b4 (12 ♖fd1 ♖xd1+ 13 ♖xd1 b5 14 ♗f1 ♗b7 =) 12...♘cd7 13 b5 ♘c5 14 ♖fd1 ♗d7 15 bxa6 bxa6 16 ♘e5 h6 17 ♗h4 ♖dc8 18 ♗e2 ♗e8 is also equal, Thomas-Rubinstein, Karlsbad 1929.

**10...cxd4**

10...b6 11 ♕e2 ♗b7 12 ♖fd1 ♕c7 (12...cxd4 13 exd4 ♖e8 14 ♖ac1 ♘f8

15 ♘e5 ± Petrosian-Larsen, Biel IZ 1976) 13 d5 and White has a slight advantage.

**11 exd4**

Or: 11 ♕xd4 b6 (11...♕b6!? =; 11...♕a5!?) 12 ♖fd1 ♗b7 13 ♘e5 ♘xe5 14 ♕xe5 ♕c8 15 ♖d4 ♕c6 16 f3 ♖fd8 =; 11 ♘xd4 ♕a5 12 ♗h4 ♘e5 13 ♗a2 ♗d7 14 ♗g3 ♘c6 15 ♘b3 ♕b4 16 ♕e2 ♖fd8 = Romanishin-Dokhoian, Erevan 1988.

**11...♘b6 12 ♗b3**

12 ♗d3!? ♗d7 13 ♘e5 ♗c6 14 a5 ♘bd5 ∞.

**12...♗d7** (D)

**13 a5**

Or:

a) 13 ♕d3!? ♗c6 14 ♘e5 ♘bd5 15 ♖fe1 h6 16 ♗d2! ∞ (not 16 ♗xf6 ♘xf6 17 ♘xf7 ♖xf7 18 ♗xe6 ♕d6 19 ♕g6 ♖af8 20 ♖e3 ♕xd4 21 ♖d1 ♕c5 ∓ Cvitan-V.Kovačević, Zenica 1986).

b) 13 ♘e5 ♗c6 (13...♖c8!? 14 ♕f3 ♗c6 15 ♘xc6 ♖xc6 16 ♖fd1 ♖c7 ∞) 14 ♖e1 (14 ♘xc6 bxc6 15 ♖c1 a5! =) and now:

b1) 14...♘bd5 15 ♕d3! ♘b4 16 ♕h3 ♗d5 17 ♘xd5 ♘fxd5 18 ♗d2 ♖c8 (18...♘c6 19 ♗c2 g6 20 ♗h6 ♘xd4 ∞) 19 ♘xf7!? (19 ♖ad1 ♖c7 20

♖e4 ♗f6 = Kushch-Kharitonov, Smolensk 1991) 19...♖xf7 20 ♕xe6 is unclear.

b2) 14...♘fd5! 15 ♗d2 ♗g5! =.

c) 13 ♕e2 ♗c6 14 ♖fd1 ♘bd5 (14...♗d5?! 15 ♘xd5 ♘bxd5 16 ♘e5 h6 17 ♗h4 ♖c8 18 a5 ± Spassky-Darga, Beverwijk 1967; 14...♘fd5!? 15 ♗d2 ♘b4 16 ♘e5 ♕xd4 17 ♘xf7 ♖xf7 18 ♗e3 ♕e5 19 ♗xb6 ♕xe2 20 ♘xe2 ♗d5 21 ♗xd5 ♘xd5 22 ♗d4 ♖d8 23 ♘c3 ♘xc3 24 bxc3 ½-½ Spraggett-A.Sokolov, Saint John Ct (1) 1988) 15 ♘e5 h6 16 ♗c1 ♖c8 = (16...♗b4 17 ♕d3 ♗d6 18 ♕h3 ♘xc3 19 bxc3 ♗e4 20 c4 ♕c7 21 ♗f4 ± Spraggett-Prandstetter, Taxco IZ 1985).

**13...♘bd5**

Nenashev's idea 13...♘c8!? seems interesting: 14 ♘e5 ♗c6 15 ♕d3 (15 ♖e1 ±; 15 ♗xf6?! ♗xf6 16 ♖e1 ♘e7 17 ♘xc6 bxc6 18 ♖a4 ♘f5 19 ♘e2 ♕d7 20 ♗c2 ♖ab8 ∓ Ilinsky-Nenashev, Bishkek Z 1993) 15...♘d5 16 ♘xc6 bxc6 17 ♗xe7 ♘cxe7 18 ♖fd1 ♘b4 19 ♕e2 ♘ed5 20 ♘e4 ± Lazović-Raspor, Ljubljana 1996.

**14 ♗xd5 ♘xd5 15 ♘xd5 exd5 16 ♗xe7 ♕xe7**

This position is important for the assessment of the variation. White has a good knight versus Black's lightsquared bishop, which is needed to support pawns on light squares. However, the white knight lacks an effective outpost, as Black can cover e5 by playing ...f6, while the knight will find it difficult to reach c5. On the other hand, the black bishop has the good square b5, while in some variations Black can create counterplay by ...b6. Given these circumstances, as practice shows, the game is level.

**17 ♖e1**
17 ♘e5 ♕d6 intending ...♗b5 and
...f6 =.
17 ♕b3 ♕d6 and now:
a) 18 ♖fe1 h6 (18...f6!? 19 ♖e3
♖fe8 20 ♖c1 ♗c6 21 ♖ce1 ♔f8 = Es-
lon-Hoffman, Alicante 1989) 19 ♖e5
♗e6 20 ♖ae1 b6! 21 axb6 ♖fb8 22
♖5e2 ♖xb6 23 ♕c3 ♖ab8 with equality, Kharitonov-Cherepkov, Yaroslavl
1982.
b) 18 ♖fc1 ♗b5 19 ♕a3 (19 ♖c5
♖ad8 20 ♖e1 f6 = Lintvinov-Bala-
shov, Moscow 1982) 19...♕xa3 20
♖xa3 ♖ac8 21 ♖ac3 ♖xc3 22 ♖xc3 f6
23 h4 ♖e8 24 ♖c7 h5 25 ♖xb7 ♖e2 26
♖b8+ ♔h7 27 ♖d8 ♗c4 28 ♖b8 ♗b5
29 ♖d8 ♗c4 ½-½ Eslon-A.Hoffman,
Valencia 1990.
**17...♕d6 18 ♕b3 f6 19 ♘d2 ♖fe8
20 ♘f1**
20 ♖xe8+ ♖xe8 21 ♕xb7 ♖b8 22
♕a7 ♖xb2 23 ♘f1 h6 = Timman.
**20...♗c6 21 ♕c3 ♕f4 22 ♖e3 ♖xe3
23 ♕xe3 ♕xe3 24 ♘xe3 ♔f7 25 f3
♔e6 26 ♔f2 ♖b8! 27 ♖a3 b6 28 ♖b3
♗b5 29 axb6 ♖xb6**
= Seirawan-Timman, London 1984.

**D)**
**7 ♕c2 (D)**

Rubinstein created a sensation with
this move. The main idea is that if
Black does not take active counter-
measures then White will castle queenside and launch a pawn-storm against
Black's castled position.
**7...c5!**
Teichmann's counterattack. Or:
a) 7...h6 is most aggressively met
by 8 cxd5!?:
a1) 8...hxg5 9 dxe6 fxe6 10 ♘xg5
♘b6 11 h4 c5 (11...♘bd5!? 12 ♗c4
c6) 12 h5 cxd4 13 h6 dxc3 14 ♖d1
(Siviero-Simini, Italy 1989) and after
14...♕e8 it isn't clear how White continues, as 15 ♗b5 ♕xb5 16 ♕g6 ♕xg5
gives Black too much for the queen.
a2) 8...exd5 9 ♗f4 c5 (9...c6?! 10
h3 ♖e8 11 ♗d3 ♘f8 12 0-0 gives
White a favourable form of Exchange
Variation, since the pawn on h6 proves
a weakness in many variations) 10
♗e2 (10 0-0-0!? deserves attention:
10...♕a5 11 g4 ♘b6 12 g5 hxg5 13
♘xg5 ♗d7 14 ♖g1 cxd4 15 ♖xd4 ♖fc8
16 ♗e5 ± Kiseliov-Glienke, Berlin
1994) 10...b6 11 0-0 ♗b7 12 ♖fd1
♖c8 13 dxc5 bxc5 (13...♘xc5 14 ♕f5
±) 14 a4! ♕a5?! (better is 14...a5!? 15
♘b5 ±) 15 ♘h4! ♖fd8 16 ♘f5 ♗f8 17
♘b5 ♘e8 18 ♗d6! ♘xd6 19 ♘fxd6
♖b8 20 ♘xb7 ♖xb7 21 ♖xd5 ± Kas-
parov-Portisch, Brussels 1986.
b) 7...c6 8 ♖d1 also gives White a
stable advantage:
b1) 8...♕a5 9 a3! dxc4 10 ♗xc4 e5
11 0-0 exd4 12 exd4 ♘b6 13 ♗d3 h6
14 b4! ♕xa3 15 ♖a1 ♕xb4 16 ♖fb1 ±
Suba-Ionescu, Bucharest 1981.
b2) 8...♖e8 9 a3 a6 10 h3! h6 11
♗f4 dxc4 12 ♗xc4 b5 13 ♗a2 ♗b7 14
♘e5 ♕b6 15 ♘xd7 ♘xd7 16 ♗b1 ±
Lputian-Kharitonov, Irkutsk 1983.

b3) 8...b6 9 &d3 &b7 10 0-0 c5 11 cxd5 exd5 12 ♘e5 ±.

b4) 8...a6 9 a3 b5 (9...♖e8 10 h3! ±) 10 c5 and then:

b41) 10...a5 11 &d3 h6 12 &f4 b4 13 axb4 axb4 14 ♘a4 &a6 15 &xa6 ♖xa6 16 0-0 ♕c8 17 ♘e1 ♕b7 18 b3 ♖fa8 19 ♘d3 ± Andonovski-Ramon, Santa Clara 1998.

b42) 10...♘e8 is best met by 11 h4! ±, rather than 11 &f4?! g5! 12 &g3 f5 13 ♘e5 ♘xe5 14 &xe5 ♘f6 = Henley-Kogan, USA Ch (Berkeley) 1984.

b43) 10...e5 11 dxe5 ♘e8 12 &xe7 ♕xe7 13 b4 ♘xe5 14 &e2 ♘f6 15 h3 ♘xf3+ 16 &xf3 ♕e5 17 ♕d2 ♖e8 18 0-0 &f5 19 ♕d4 a5 20 ♕xe5 ♖xe5 21 ♘e2 axb4 22 axb4 ♖a4 23 ♘d4 ± S.Ivanov-Lugovoi, St Petersburg 1997.

We now return to 7...c5 *(D)*:

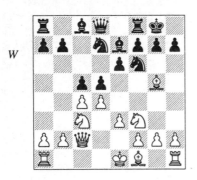

Now White has three continuations:
**D1: 8 0-0-0**     44
**D2: 8 ♖d1**     45
**D3: 8 cxd5**     46

## D1)

**8 0-0-0 ♕a5**

8...cxd4!? deserves scrutiny: 9 ♘xd4 (9 exd4 h6 10 &h4 dxc4 11

&xc4 ♘b6 12 &b3 ♘fd5 =; 9 ♖xd4 h6 10 &h4 a6! 11 cxd5 ♘xd5 12 ♘xd5 exd5 13 &xe7 ♕xe7 14 ♔b1 ♘f6 15 &d3 &e6 = Vyzhmanavin-A.Hoffman, Saragossa 1992) and now:

a) 9...dxc4 10 &xc4 a6 11 &e2 ♕c7 12 &f3 ♖e8 13 ♔b1 ♘b6 14 ♖c1 ± Browne-Bass, New York 1985.

b) 9...♕c7 10 ♘db5 ♕a5 11 cxd5 exd5 12 &f4 ±.

c) 9...♘b6 10 ♕b1 &d7 11 &xf6 &xf6 12 c5 ♘c8 13 &d3 h6 14 g4 ± Browne-I.Ivanov, USA Ch (Durango) 1992.

d) 9...a6!? 10 h4 (10 cxd5 ♘xd5 11 &xe7 ♘xe7 ∞) 10...dxc4 11 &xc4 ♕c7 12 &e2 ♖e8 13 &f4 e5 14 &g3 ♘b6 15 a3 &d6 16 ♘f3 &d7 ∞ Cvitan-A.Hoffman, Bern 1992.

**9 ♔b1**

Also possible:

a) 9 h4!? cxd4 10 ♘xd4 &b4 (10...dxc4!? 11 &xc4 ♘c5 12 f4 &d7 13 e4 ♖fe8 14 ♔b1 ♘a4 15 ♘cb5 ♖ac8 16 &xf6 gxf6 ∞ Ubilava-Kharitonov, Barnaul 1984) 11 ♘b3 ♕b6 12 cxd5 &xc3 13 ♕xc3 (13 bxc3?! exd5 14 ♖d4 ♘e5 15 f3 &d7 16 h5 ♖ac8 17 ♔d2 h6 ∓ M.Gurevich-Morović, Vršac 1985) 13...♘xd5 14 ♕d4 f6 15 &f4 ♕xd4 16 ♘xd4 ♘7b6 and ...e5 =.

b) 9 cxd5 exd5 10 dxc5 (10 h4 ♖e8 11 ♔b1 c4 12 ♘e5 &b4 13 ♘xd7 &xd7 14 &xf6 gxf6 15 g4 ♖e6 16 &g2 ♖a6 17 ♘xd5!? {17 ♖d2 ♖d8 ∞ Averkin-Pozdniakov, USSR 1970} 17...♕xa2+ 18 ♔c1 ♕a5 {18...&a5!?} 19 ♘xb4 ♕xb4 ∞) 10...&xc5 11 ♘d4 &xd4 12 ♖xd4 h6 13 &h4 a6 ∞ Gabriel-Onishchuk, Fürth 1998.

**9...dxc4 10 &xc4 cxd4 11 exd4**

11 ♖xd4!? h6 (interesting is 11...a6!? 12 ♖c1 b5 13 &d3 h6 14 &h4 &c5 15

♖f4 ♘h5 16 ♘e4 ♘xf4 17 exf4 ♗a7
18 ♘d6 ♗c5 19 ♘e4 ♗a7 = Bezman-
Grigoriants, Yalta 1996) 12 h4 ♘b6
(12...b5!? ∞) 13 ♗b3 ♗d7 14 ♕d3 e5
15 ♖xd7 ♘bxd7 16 ♕g6 ♕b6 17
♗xh6 ♘e8 18 ♕f5 ♕xh6 19 ♕xd7
♕g6+ 20 ♗c2 ♕xg2 21 ♖g1 ♕xf3 ∓
Birnbaum-Schranz, Germany 1986.

**11...b5**
A typical pawn sacrifice for the initiative. If 11...♘b6, then 12 ♗b3 ♗d7
13 ♖he1 ±.

**12 ♗xb5**
If 12 ♗xf6, then 12...♘xf6 13 ♗xb5
♖b8 gives Black compensation, e.g.
14 ♗c4 ♗b7 15 ♘d2 ♖fc8 16 f3 ♗b4
17 ♖c1 ♕b6 18 ♕d3 ♗xc3 19 ♖xc3?
♗e4 0-1 Shalov-Blass, corr. 1960.

**12...♖b8 13 ♗d3**
13 ♗a4?! ♗b4 14 ♗b3 ♗b7 15 ♗d2
♖fc8 (Black has compensation) 16
♖he1 ♘d5 17 ♖c1 ♘7f6 and Black has
a clear advantage, Shallcross-Dobson,
England 1967.

**13...♗a3 14 ♗c1 ♗b4 15 ♔a1 ♗b7
16 ♘d2 ♗xg2!**
16...♖fc8?! 17 ♘c4 ♕c7 18 ♘b5
♕d8 19 ♗f4 ♖a8 20 ♕b3 ♘d5 21
♗g3 ± Timoshchenko-Ruban, Norilsk
1987.

**17 ♖hg1 ♗d5! 18 ♘xd5 ♕xd5**
The position is unclear.

**D2)**
**8 ♖d1 (D)**
**8...cxd4**
Black often plays 8...♕a5 9 cxd5:
a) 9...exd5 10 ♗d3 h6 (10...♖e8 11
0-0 c4 12 ♗f5 g6 13 ♗h3 ♘f8 14
♗xc8 ♖axc8 15 ♘e5 ±) 11 ♗h4 cxd4
(11...♖e8 12 0-0 c4 13 ♗f5 ♘f8 14
♘e5 ± Velikov-Nenkov, Pernik 1984)
12 exd4 ♘b6 13 ♘e5 ♗e6 14 0-0

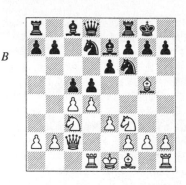

*B*

♖fe8 15 ♖fe1 ♖ac8 16 ♕e2 with a
slight advantage for White, S.Peder-
sen-Lyrberg, Lyngby 1991.
b) 9...♘xd5 10 ♗xe7 ♘xe7 11
♗d3 (11 ♗e2 seems too passive; after
11...♘f6 12 0-0 ♗d7 Black has no
problems) and now:
b1) If 11...g6, then 12 0-0 cxd4 13
♘xd4 ♘f6 (13...♘c5!?) 14 ♘e4 ♘fd5
15 a3 ♗d7 16 b4 ♕b6 17 ♘c5 ♖fd8
18 e4 ♘f4 19 ♗c4 ♗e8 20 ♕c1 ±
D.Gurevich-Kogan, Reykjavik 1982.
b2) 11...♘f6 12 0-0 cxd4 13 ♘xd4
♗d7 (13...e5?! is dubious due to 14
♘b3 ♕b6 15 ♘e4 ♘ed5 16 ♗c4 ♗e6
17 ♘bc5! ♗b4 18 ♘xf6+ gxf6 19 ♕e4
f5 20 ♕h4 ♗xc4 21 ♘d7 +− Benja-
min-Morović, New York 1987) 14
♘e4 (Black experiences no problems
after 14 ♘b3 ♕c7 15 ♕e2 ♗c6 16
♘d4 ♖fd8 = Bogoljubow-Ståhlberg,
Bad Nauheim 1936) 14...♘ed5 15
♘b3 ♕d8 (greater problems arise for
Black after 15...♕a4?! 16 ♘ec5 ♕h4
17 ♘xb7 ♖ac8 18 ♕e2 ♗c6 19 ♘7a5
♗a8 20 ♗a6 ♖b8 21 ♖d4 ± Miles-
F.Olafsson, Dubai OL 1986) 16 ♘xf6+
(16 ♘bc5?! ♖c8!) 16...♘xf6 17 ♕c5
♕b6! = Capablanca-Lasker, Havana
Wch (7) 1921.
**9 ♘xd4**

If 9 exd4, then 9...b6! (9...dxc4?! 10 ♗xc4 h6 11 ♗h4 ♘b6 12 ♗b3 ♗d7 13 0-0 ♖c8 14 ♕e2! a6 15 ♖fe1 ♗b4 16 ♘e5! ± Réti – Znosko-Borovsky, London 1922) 10 ♗e2 dxc4 11 ♗xc4 ♗b7 12 ♕e2 ♘d5 13 ♗xe7 ♘xe7 14 0-0 ♘f6 15 ♘e5 ♘ed5 = Lisitsyn-Zagoriansky, Leningrad 1938.

**9...dxc4**
Also possible is 9...♘b6!? 10 ♗e2 ♗d7 11 ♗xf6 ♗xf6 12 cxd5 ♘xd5 13 ♘xd5 exd5 14 0-0 (14 ♕c5 ♗e7!? {14...♕b6 15 ♕xb6 axb6 16 a3 ± Miles-Hellers, Biel 1989} 15 ♕xd5 ♗b4+ with compensation) 14...♕b6 15 ♗f3 ♗e6 16 ♖d2 ♖ac8 17 ♕b1 ♖c5 18 ♖fd1 g6 19 h3 ♖fc8 = Mikhal-chishin-Segueira, Lisbon 1986. Black has an isolated pawn, but his bishop-pair and full control of the c-file provide compensation.

**10 ♗xc4 ♕a5 11 ♗h4 ♘e5 12 ♗e2 ♘g6 13 ♗g3 e5**
Black tries to activate his light-squared bishop. If 13...♗d7, then 14 ♘b3 ♕b6 15 h4! ♖fc8 (15...h5 16 ♗d3 ±) 16 h5 ♘f8 17 h6 g6 18 0-0 ± Korchnoi-Osnos, USSR Ch (Leningrad) 1963.

**14 ♘b3 ♕b6 15 0-0**
Gorelov recommends 15 h4!? h5 16 0-0 ♗e6 17 ♗d3 with a slight advantage for White.

**15...♗e6 16 ♗d3 ♗d6 17 ♗f5 ♗c4 18 ♖fe1 ♖ad8 19 ♘d2**
± C.Hansen-Kveinys, Groningen 1990.

**D3)**
**8 cxd5** *(D)*
The main and most popular continuation.
**8...cxd4**

B

8...♘xd5 is not bad either. 9 ♗xe7 and now:

a) 9...♘xe7 10 dxc5 (10 0-0-0 ♕a5 11 ♗d3 h6 12 ♔b1 ♖b8 ∞) 10...♕a5 (10...♘xc5 11 ♗e2 b6 12 ♖d1 ♕e8 {12...♕c7 13 ♘b5 ±} 13 0-0 ♗b7 14 b4 ♘d7 15 ♗b5 ♘c6 16 ♘e4 +−) 11 ♗d3 h6 (11...♘f6 12 0-0 ♕xc5 13 ♖fd1 ♘c6 14 a3 ±) 12 0-0 ♕xc5 13 ♖fd1 ♘c6 14 ♘e4 ± Züger-Kelečević, Biel 1996.

b) 9...♕xe7 10 ♘xd5 exd5 and now:
b1) Possible is 11 dxc5 ♘xc5 12 ♗e2 ♗g4! (the best move; 12...♗e6 is too passive due to 13 0-0 ♖ac8 14 ♕d2 {14 ♘d4!? ♘e4 15 ♕a4 a6 16 ♖ad1 ♖fd8 17 a3 ♖d6 18 ♖c1 ± Szabo-Korensky, Sochi 1973} 14...♘e4 15 ♕d4 ♕c5 16 ♗d3 ♕xd4 17 ♘xd4 ♘c5 18 ♖fd1 a6 19 f3 ± E.Vladimirov-A.Hoffman, Salamanca 1991, when White has a stable advantage in the ending) and then:
b11) 13 ♘d4 ♘e6 (13...♗xe2!? 14 ♕xe2 ♘e6 15 ♕d2 ♕f6 =) 14 ♗xg4 (14 ♘xe6 fxe6 15 ♗xg4 ♕b4+ =) 14...♘xd4 15 ♕a4 ♘c6 16 0-0 ♖fd8 17 ♖fd1 ♖d6 ½-½ Polugaevsky-Geller, Portorož 1973.
b12) 13 0-0 ♖ac8 14 ♖ac1 (14 ♕d1 ♖fd8 15 ♖c1 ♕f6 16 ♘d4 ♗xe2

17 ♕xe2 ♘e6 =) 14...♕f6! 15 ♕d2 ♘e4 16 ♕d4! (16 ♕xd5? ♖xc1 17 ♖xc1 ♕xb2 ∓) 16...♗xf3 17 ♕xf6 (17 ♗xf3 ♕xd4 18 exd4 ♘f6! 19 ♖fe1 ♖fe8 =) 17...♘xf6 18 ♗xf3 ♖fd8 19 ♖fd1 ♔f8 20 ♔f1 ♔e7! ½-½ Lilienthal-Lasker, Moscow 1936.

b2) 11 ♗d3 g6 12 dxc5 ♘xc5 (D) and then:

b21) 13 ♖c1 ♘xd3+ 14 ♕xd3 ♗f5! and here:

b211) 15 ♕e2 ♗g4 16 0-0 d4 =.

b212) 15 ♕xd5 ♖fd8 16 ♕c5 (16 ♕a5 ♗d3; 16 ♕e5 ♕xe5 17 ♘xe5 ♖ac8 with compensation) 16...♖ac8! 17 ♕xe7 ♖xc1+ 18 ♔e2 ♖c2+ =.

b213) 15 ♕d4 ♗e4 16 0-0 ♗xf3 17 gxf3 ♕g5+ 18 ♔h1 ♕f5 19 ♔g2 ♕g5+ 20 ♔g4 ♕e5 21 ♖c3 f5 22 ♕g5 d4 is equal, P.Nikolić-Morović, Tunis IZ 1985.

b214) 15 ♕d1 ♖ac8 16 0-0 ♖xc1 17 ♕xc1 ♖c8 18 ♕a1 ♕b4 19 ♘d4 ♗d7 20 h3 a5 21 ♖d1 b6 = Hübner-Balashov, Munich 1979.

b22) 13 0-0 ♗g4 (13...♗e6 14 ♖ac1 ♖ac8 15 ♘d4 ±; 13...♗d7 14 ♖ac1 ♖ac8 15 ♕d2 b6 16 ♗e2 ♖fd8 17 b4! ♘e4 18 ♕d4 ♗e8 19 a3 ♖c7 20 ♗d3 ± A.Kuzmin-Ubilava, Benasque 1997)

14 ♘d4 ♖ac8 (14...♖fc8 15 ♖ac1 ♗d7 16 ♕d2 ♕f6 {16...♘e6 17 ♗e2 ♕f6 18 ♘f3 ♖xc1 19 ♖xc1 ♖c8 20 ♖d1 ± I.Ivanov-Morović, New York 1988} 17 ♖fd1 ♕b6 18 ♖c3 ± Shirov-Piket, Dos Hermanas 1995) and here:

b221) 15 ♖fc1 ♖fe8 16 ♕d2 a6 17 ♖c2 ♘e6 18 ♖xc8 ♖xc8 19 ♗e2 ♗xe2 20 ♘xe2 ♕d6 21 ♖d1 ♖d8 22 h3 ♕b6 = Levitina-Chiburdanidze, Volgograd 1984.

b222) 15 ♕d2 ♘e4 (15...♘xd3?! 16 ♕xd3 ♕b4 17 h3 ♗e6 18 ♕e2 ♖fe8 19 a3! ♕b6 20 ♕d2 ♖c7 21 ♖ac1 ±) 16 ♕a5 ♘c5 17 ♗e2 b6 18 ♕a3 ♗xe2 19 ♘xe2 ♕b7 20 ♖fd1 ♖fd8 21 ♖ac1 ♘e6 = Lilienthal-Kan, USSR Ch (Tbilisi) 1937.

b223) 15 ♖ac1 ♕g5 (15...♘xd3?! 16 ♕xd3 ♕b4 17 ♕b1! ♔g7 18 h3 ♗d7 19 ♖xc8 ♖xc8 20 ♖c1 ±; 15...a6 16 ♗e2 ♘e4 17 ♕d3 ♗d7 18 ♗f3 ♕b4 19 ♕b3 ± Salov-A.Sokolov, USSR Ch (Moscow) 1988) 16 ♗e2 and now:

b2231) 16...a6 17 ♖fd1 ♖fd8 18 ♗xg4 ♕xg4 19 h3 ♕e4 20 ♘e2 ♕xc2 21 ♖xc2 ♘a4 22 ♖cd2 ♘b6 23 b3 ± Gagarin-Grigoriants, Moscow 1998.

b2232) 16...♘e6 17 ♕xc8 ♖xc8 18 ♖xc8+ ♔g7 19 f4 ♕h4 20 ♘xe6+ ♗xe6 21 ♖c3 ± Hort-Balashov, Moscow 1981.

b2233) 16...♘e4 17 ♕d3 ♗xe2 18 ♕xe2 a6 19 ♖c2 ♘d6 20 ♖fc1 ♖c4 21 b3 ♖xc2 22 ♖xc2 ♖c8 23 ♖xc8+ ♘xc8 24 ♕c2 ♕d8 25 ♕c5 ♘e7 26 h3 h5 27 g4 hxg4 28 hxg4 b6 29 ♕c3 ♕d7 30 f3 ♕d6 31 ♔g2 ♕c5 = Savchenko-Moroz, Enakievo 1997.

**9 ♘xd4 ♘xd5 10 ♗xe7 (D)**
**10...♘xe7**
Black is worse after 10...♕xe7?! 11 ♘xd5 exd5 12 ♗d3 (12 ♗e2!? ♘e5 13

B

0-0 ♗d7 ±) 12...♕b4+ 13 ♕d2 ♘e5
(13...♘c5 14 ♗b5! ♕xd2+ 15 ♔xd2
a6 16 ♗d3 ♗e6 17 ♖ac1 ± Flohr-
Capablanca, Moscow 1935) 14 ♗e2
♕xd2+ (14...♕b6 15 b3 ♘c6 16 ♖d1
♗e6 17 0-0 ♖ac8 18 ♕b2 ± Fine-Ståhlberg, Gothenburg 1937) 15 ♔xd2 ♗d7
16 ♖ac1 ♖fc8 17 b3 ♔f8 18 f4! ♘c6
19 ♗f3 (19 ♗b5 ♔e7 20 ♗xc6 bxc6!
21 ♖c5 a5! 22 ♖hc1 ♔d6 23 ♖1c3
♖a6 = Alekhine-Capablanca, Buenos
Aires Wch (8) 1927) 19...♘xd4 20 exd4
♗c6 21 ♖c5 ♖d8 22 b4 and White is
slightly better – Alekhine.

**11 ♗e2**
Or:
a) 11 ♗d3 yields no advantage due
to 11...♘f6 (11...♘g6?! 12 0-0-0! ±)
12 0-0 ♗d7 13 ♖fd1 ♕b6 14 ♖ac1 (14
♘e4 ♘ed5 =; 14 ♘f3 ♖fd8 15 ♘e5
♗e8 16 h3 ♖ac8 17 ♘g4 ♘xg4 18
hxg4 h6 = Tataev-Shestakov, Belgorod
1989) 14...♖ac8 15 ♕b3 ♕xb3 16
♘xb3 b6 17 ♘d4 ♘fd5 18 ♘xd5
♘xd5 19 ♗e4 ♘f6 20 ♗b7 ♖xc1 21
♖xc1 ♖d8 22 ♔f1 ♔f8 23 ♔e2 ♔e7 24
♗a6 ♘e8 = Novikov-Gorelov, Pavlodar 1987.
b) 11 0-0-0!? deserves serious attention: 11...♕a5 12 g4 (12 ♘b3 ♕b6
∞) 12...♘f6 13 ♘b3 and now:

b1) 13...♕c7 14 g5 ♘fd5 15 ♘xd5
♕xc2+ 16 ♔xc2 ♘xd5 (16...exd5!?)
17 ♗g2 ♘b4+ (17...♗d7 18 ♗xd5
exd5 19 ♘d4 f6 20 gxf6 ♖xf6 21 f4 ±)
18 ♔b1 ♖b8 (18...e5 19 a3 ♘c6 20
♘c5 ±) 19 a3 ♘a6 20 ♘a5 ± Ruzhale-
Khurtsidze, Groningen 1996.
b2) 13...♕b6 14 g5 ♘fd5 ∞.
**11...♘f6 12 0-0**
White also obtains no advantage by
12 ♕b3 a6 (12...♕a5!? 13 0-0 ♗d7 =)
13 0-0 ♕a5 14 ♗f3 e5 15 ♘c2 ♖b8 =
Kiseliov-Arbakov, Moscow 1987.
**12...♗d7 13 ♕b3!**
This gives Black the greatest problems. To equality lead 13 ♗f3 ♕b6!
(also possible is 13...e5 14 ♘b3 ♕b6
15 ♖fd1 ♖fd8 =) 14 ♕b3 ♕xb3 15
♘xb3 ♗c6 = and 13 ♖fd1 ♕b6!?
(13...♖c8 14 ♕b3 ♕a5 15 ♘db5 ♗c6
16 ♕a3 ♕xa3 17 ♘xa3 ♘ed5 = Peev-
Ziatdinov, Belgrade 1990) 14 ♕b3
♕xb3 15 ♘xb3 ♖fd8 =.
**13...♕a5 14 ♖fd1 ♖ab8!?**
Worse is 14...♖ac8 15 ♖ac1 b6 16
♘db5 ♘ed5 17 ♘xd5 ♘xd5 18 ♖xc8
(18 e4 ♘f4 19 ♗f1 ♖xc1 20 ♖xc1
♗xb5 21 ♗xb5 ♖d8 = Hort-Castro,
Nice OL 1974) 18...♖xc8 19 e4 ♘f4
20 ♗f1 ±.
**15 a3**
15 ♖ac1 b5!; 15 a4!? intending
♕a3.
**15...♘ed5 16 ♘xd5 ♘xd5 17 ♗b5**
**♗xb5 18 ♕xb5 ♕xb5 19 ♘xb5 a6 20**
**♘d4 ♖fc8**
= P.Cramling-Portisch, Roquebrune
(Ladies vs Veterans) 1998.

**E)**
**7 ♖c1 (D)**
Now Black has several continuations:

E1: 7...h6    49
E2: 7...dxc4    49
E3: 7...b6    51
E4: 7...a6    52
E5: 7...c6    55

**E1)**
**7...h6 8 ♗xf6**
In my view, the most logical continuation.
**8...♘xf6 9 c5!**
This was the idea behind White's eighth move: he blocks the queenside.
**9...c6 10 ♗d3 ♘d7 11 b4 f5**
If 11...♕c7, then 12 e4! dxe4 13 ♗xe4 a5 14 a3 axb4 15 axb4 ♘f6 16 0-0 ♖a3 17 ♗b1 ♗d7 18 ♘e5 ♖d8 19 ♘a4 ♖a8 20 ♘b6 ± Lputian-Kharitonov, Sochi 1987.
**12 0-0 ♕c7 13 b5 e5 14 ♘xe5 ♘xe5 15 dxe5 ♕xe5 16 ♕a4 ♕c7 17 ♘e2 ♗d7 18 ♖c2**
± Gelfand-Kharitonov, Sverdlovsk 1987.

**E2)**
**7...dxc4**
This system of defence deserves serious attention.
**8 ♗xc4 (D)**
**8...a6**

This is a useful move to insert, since after 8...c5 White obtains additional possibilities. 9 0-0 a6 and now:
a) 10 ♘e5!? ♘xe5 11 dxe5 ♘d7 12 ♗xe7 ♕xe7 13 f4 b5 14 ♗d3 ♗b7 15 ♗e4 ± Gligorić-Guimard, Havana 1962.
b) 10 ♗d3!? cxd4 (10...b5 11 a4 ±) 11 ♘xd4 ♘e5 12 ♗b1 ♗d7 13 ♕c2 g6 14 ♖fd1 ± Yuferov-Vasiliev, Moscow 1990.
c) 10 ♗e2 cxd4 11 ♘xd4 ♕b6 12 ♕c2 ♖e8 13 ♖fd1 ♘f8 14 ♘f3 ♘8d7 15 ♘d2 ± Nenashev-Peregudov, Akmola 1993.
**9 a4**
If 9 0-0, then 9...b5 10 ♗d3 (10 ♗e2 ♗b7 11 a3 c5 12 dxc5 ♘xc5 = Czerwonski-Kveinys, Katowice 1991) 10...♗b7 11 ♕e2 c5 12 ♖fd1 cxd4 13 ♘xd4 b4 14 ♗xf6 (14 ♘b1?! ♕a5 15 ♗h4 ♘e5 16 ♗c2 ♘g6 17 ♗g3 ♖ac8 18 ♗b3 h5 ∓ Stone-Gild.Garcia, New York 1989) 14...♘xf6 15 ♘a4 ♕a5 16 b3 ♖ac8 and Black has a slight advantage, Schuster-A.Hoffman, Buenos Aires 1995.
**9...c5 10 0-0 cxd4 11 exd4**
In return for the isolated pawn, White obtains possibilities of developing his initiative. Or:

a) 11 ♘xd4 ♕b6! 12 ♕b3 ♕a5 13 ♘f3 ♘b6 14 e4 h6 15 ♗h4 ♕b4 16 ♕xb4 ♗xb4 17 ♘a2 ♗e7 18 e5 ♘fd5 19 ♗xe7 ♘xe7 20 ♗b3 ♘c6 21 ♖fd1 ♗d7 22 ♖d6 ♖fd8 23 ♖cd1 ♗e8 = Loginov-Kharitonov, Pavlodar 1987.

b) 11 ♕xd4!? ♕a5! (11...♘b6 12 ♗b3 ♕xd4 13 ♘xd4 ♖d8 14 ♖fd1 ♔f8 15 e4 ♗d7 16 a5 ♘c8 17 e5 ♘e8 18 ♘e4 ± Eingorn-Dokhoian, Pamplona 1991/2) and then:

b1) 12 ♖fd1 h6 (12...b6!? 13 ♗f4 ♗c5 14 ♕d3 ♗b7 15 ♘d4 ♗e7 =) 13 ♗h4 b6 14 ♗e2 ♗b7 15 ♘d2 ♖fd8 16 ♘b3 ♕f5 17 ♕d3 ♕xd3 18 ♖xd3 ♘e5 = I.Farago-Rausis, 2nd Bundesliga 1996/7.

b2) 12 e4 ♗c5 13 ♕d3 (13 ♕d2 ♗b4 14 ♕e2 ♘g4 15 ♗f4 ♘ge5 16 ♘xe5 ♘xe5 17 ♖fd1 ♘xc4 18 ♕xc4 ♗xc3 19 bxc3 e5 = Tempone-A.Hoffman, Argentine Ch 1995) 13...♗b4 14 ♗xf6 ♘xf6 15 e5 ♖d8 16 ♕c2 ♗xc3 17 ♕xc3 ♕xc3 18 ♖xc3 ♘e4 19 ♖e3 ♘c5 20 a5 ♗d7 21 ♖c1 ♖ac8 = Izeta-San Segundo, Elgoibar 1994.

**11...♘b6** (D)

W

**12 ♗b3**

The alternative 12 ♗d3!? deserves attention: 12...♗d7 13 ♘e5 ♗c6 14 ♘xc6 bxc6 15 ♘e4 and now Black should play 15...♕xd4! ∞ rather than 15...♘xe4?! 16 ♗xe7 ♕xe7 17 ♗xe4 ♕b4 18 ♖xc6 ♖ad8 19 ♕c2 and White has a slight advantage, Janjgava-Kharitonov, Pavlodar 1987.

**12...♗d7 13 ♘e5**

13 a5 promises little after 13...♘bd5 14 ♘xd5 (or 14 ♗xd5 ♘xd5 15 ♘xd5 ♗xg5 16 ♘xg5 ♕xg5 17 ♘b6 ♖ad8 18 ♖c5 ♕f6 19 ♖e1 ♗c6 20 ♖ce5 ♖d6 21 ♘c4 ♖d5 ∓ Petursson-A.Sokolov, Reykjavik 1988) 14...♘xd5 15 ♗xd5 (15 ♗xe7 ♘xe7 16 ♖c5 ♖c8 17 ♖xc8 ♕xc8 18 ♕d2 ♖d8 19 ♘e5 ♗e8 = Spangenberg-A.Hoffman, Argentine Ch (Buenos Aires) 1998) 15...♗xg5 16 ♘xg5 exd5 17 ♕d2 f6 18 ♘f3 ♗c6 = Cvitan-Ubilava, Tbilisi 1986.

**13...♗c6 14 ♕d3**

This seems to be the strongest continuation. The capture on c6 would be hasty: 14 ♘xc6 bxc6 15 ♘e2 (15 ♕d3 ♘bd5 16 ♘xd5 ♘xd5 17 ♗d2 ♕d7 18 a5 ♘c7 19 ♖c4 ½-½ Levitt-Goldin, Polanica Zdroj 1988) 15...♕d7 16 a5 (16 ♕d3 a5 17 ♖fd1 ♘bd5 18 ♗c4 ♘b4 19 ♕h3 ♘fd5 ½-½ Cebalo-A.Hoffman, Biel open 1993) 16...♘bd5 17 ♗a4 ♖fc8 18 ♖c4 ♘e4 19 ♗xe7 ♘xe7 20 ♗c2 ♘d6 with equality, Portisch-A.Hoffman, Biel 1992.

**14...♘fd5!**

Black tries to relieve his game. 14...♘bd5 is worse due to 15 ♕h3 g6 16 ♖fe1 ♕d6 17 ♖cd1! ♘h5 18 ♗xd5 ♗xg5 19 ♗xc6 bxc6 20 ♘e4 ♕d8 21 ♘xc6 ♕d5 22 ♘e5 with a clear advantage for White, Naumkin-Dokhoian, Vilnius 1988.

**15 ♗c2**

Or 15 ♘xc6 bxc6 16 ♗c2 g6 17 ♗xe7 (17 ♗h6 ♗g5! =) 17...♕xe7 18 a5 ♘b4 19 ♕e2 ♘d7 20 ♕c4 ♖fb8 21 ♗e4 ♖a7 leading to an equal position, Spangenberg-San Segundo, Buenos Aires 1995.

**15...g6 16 ♗h6 ♗g5! 17 ♗xf8 ♗xc1 18 ♗a3 ♗h6 19 ♘xc6 bxc6 20 g3**

If 20 a5, then 20...♘f4 intending ...♘c4.

**20...a5! 21 ♘e4 ♗g7 22 ♖d1 ♘d7 23 ♗b3 ♕b6 24 ♗c4 ♘b4**

with an equal position, Garcia Palermo-A.Hoffman, Elgoibar 1991.

**E3)**

**7...b6 8 cxd5 exd5 9 ♕a4** *(D)*

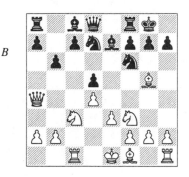

*B*

White tries to exploit the weak light squares in Black's queenside.

**9...c5**

9...♗b7?! 10 ♗a6! ♗xa6 11 ♕xa6 c5 (if 11...c6, then 12 0-0 ♘e4?! {better is 12...♕c8} 13 ♗xe7 ♕xe7 14 ♕b7 ♖fc8 15 ♘xd5 ♕d6 16 ♖xc6! 1-0 Marshall-Kline, New York 1913) 12 0-0 and now:

a) 12...c4 13 ♘e5! ♘xe5 14 dxe5 ♘e4 15 ♘xe4 ♗xg5 16 ♖fd1 ♖e8 17 f4 ♗h6 18 ♘d6 ♖xe5 19 fxe5 ♗xe3+ 20 ♔h1 ♗xc1 21 ♕b7 ♗xb2 22 ♕xf7+ ♔h8 23 ♕xd5 ♕b8 24 ♘f7+ ♔g8 25 ♖f1 ♗a3 26 ♘g5+ ♔h8 27

♕e4 g6 28 ♖f7 ♕g8 29 ♕b7 1-0 Lukacs-Ermenkov, Kecskemet 1977.

b) 12...♕c8 13 ♕xc8 ♖axc8 14 dxc5! bxc5 15 ♖fd1 ♘b6 16 ♗xf6 ♗xf6 17 ♘xd5 ♘xd5 18 ♖xd5 ♗xb2 19 ♖cxc5 ± Gheorghiu-Brunner, Mendrisio 1989.

c) 12...h6 13 ♗h4 ♕c8 14 ♕xc8 ♖axc8 15 ♘e5! g5? (a better continuation is 15...♖fd8 16 ♖fd1 ♔f8 ±) 16 ♘xd7 ♘xd7 17 ♘xd5! ♗d6 18 ♗g3 +— Goglidze-Menchik, Moscow 1935.

d) 12...♖e8 13 ♖fd1 ♕c8 (13...h6 14 ♗xf6 ♘xf6 15 dxc5 bxc5 16 ♖c2! ♗d6 17 ♖cd2 ♖e6 18 ♕a4 ± Duras-Marshall, Breslau 1912; 13...cxd4 14 ♘xd4 ♘c5 15 ♕f1 ♕d7 16 ♘de2 and White has a clear advantage, L.Meyer-Å.Olsen, Danish League 1997/8) 14 ♕xc8 ♖axc8 15 dxc5! ♖xc5 16 ♘d4 ± Duras-von Balla, Breslau 1912.

**10 ♗a6**

If 10 ♕c6, then 10...♖b8 11 ♘xd5 ♘xd5 12 ♕xd5 ♗b7 13 ♗xe7 ♕xe7 with sufficient compensation for the pawn.

**10...cxd4**

10...h6!? deserves serious attention: 11 ♗xf6!? (11 ♗h4 cxd4 12 exd4 ♘h5! 13 ♗g3 ♗xa6 14 ♕xa6 ♗g5 15 ♖d1 ♖e8+ 16 ♔f1 ♘df6 17 ♘xg5 hxg5 18 f3 b5! ∞ Gelfand-Short, Brussels 1991) 11...♘xf6 12 0-0 ± Short.

**11 exd4 ♗xa6**

11...♘g4?! is dubious due to 12 ♗f4 ±.

**12 ♕xa6 ♕c8 13 ♕a4**

After 13 ♕b5 ♕b7 14 0-0 a6 15 ♕b3 ♗d6 16 ♖fe1 ♖fe8 the game is equal.

**13...♕b7 14 0-0 ♖ac8 15 ♘e5 ♖fd8 16 ♖fe1 h6 17 ♗h4 ♘f8 18 ♘g4 ♘8h7 19 ♘e3**

White is slightly better, Makary-chev-Sturua, Frunze 1985.

**E4)**
   **7...a6** *(D)*

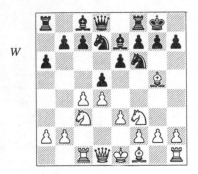

**8 cxd5**
Other continuations also deserve attention:

a) 8 a4!? and now:

a1) 8...b6!? 9 cxd5 (9 ♗d3 ♗b7 10 0-0 c5 11 ♕e2 ♘e4 12 ♗xe7 ♕xe7 13 ♖fd1 ♖fd8 = Klein-Tartakower, Paris (3) 1935) 9...exd5 10 ♗d3 ♗b7 11 0-0 c5 12 ♗f5 ♖e8 13 ♕c2 g6 14 ♗h3 ♘e4 15 ♗xe7 ♕xe7 16 ♖fd1 ♘df6 17 g3 ♗c8 = Adorjan-Portisch, Hungary 1993.

a2) 8...c6 9 ♗d3 dxc4 10 ♗xc4 ♘d5 11 ♗xe7 (interesting is 11 ♗f4!? ♘xf4 12 exf4 ♘b6 13 ♗d3 ♘d5 14 g3 ± Euwe-Sergeant, Hastings 1945) 11...♕xe7 12 0-0 ♘xc3 (12...♘5f6 13 e4 b5 14 ♗a2 b4 15 e5 bxc3 16 exf6 ♘xf6 17 ♖xc3 ♖b8 18 ♕c2 ± Leven-fish-Riumin, USSR Ch (Leningrad) 1934) 13 ♖xc3 (also fully possible is 13 bxc3!? e5 14 ♕c2 exd4 15 cxd4 ♘f6 16 ♗d3 ♗e6 17 ♘g5 h6 18 ♘xe6 ♕xe6 19 ♖b1 ♕e7 20 a5 ± Bondarev-sky-Pachman, Moscow 1946) 13...e5

14 ♘xe5 ♘xe5 15 dxe5 ♕xe5 16 f4 ♕e4 (16...♕a5?! 17 ♕c2 ♗e6 18 ♗xe6 fxe6 19 ♕b3 ♖f7 20 ♖d1 ± F.Olafs-son-Najdorf, Reykjavik 1976) 17 a5 ±.

b) 8 a3 h6 9 ♗h4 dxc4 10 ♗xc4 and then:

b1) 10...c5 is bad due to 11 ♗e2!:
b11) 11...b5 12 ♗xf6 ♘xf6 (or 12...♗xf6 13 ♘e4 ±) 13 dxc5 ♗xc5 14 ♘xb5 ±.
b12) 11...cxd4 12 ♘xd4 ♘b6 13 ♗g3 ♘bd5 14 ♘xd5 ♘xd5 15 e4! (15 0-0 ♗f6 ∞ Capablanca-Alekhine, Bue-nos Aires Wch (20) 1927) 15...♘f6 (15...e5 16 exd5! {16 ♗xe5?! ♘e3!} 16...exd4 17 ♕xd4 ♗f6 18 ♕d2 ±) 16 ♗c7 ♕e8 17 ♗f3 ±.

b2) 10...b5 and then:
b21) 11 ♗a2 ♗b7 12 0-0 c5 13 ♕e2 b4 (13...♘e4!?) 14 axb4 cxb4 15 ♘a4 ♕a5 16 ♗b3 ♖ac8 = Mikenas-Fairhurst, Folkestone OL 1933.

b22) 11 ♗e2 ♗b7 12 0-0 (12 b4 a5 13 ♕b3 axb4 14 axb4 g5! 15 ♗g3 ♘d5 16 ♘xd5 ♗xd5 ∓) 12...c5 13 dxc5 ♘xc5 and now rather than 14 ♗xf6 ♗xf6 15 ♘xb5 ♕xd1 16 ♖fxd1 (16 ♗xd1 ♘d3!) 16...♘b3 17 ♖c7 ♗xf3 18 ♗xf3 axb5 19 ♗xa8 ♖xa8 ∓ or 14 ♘d4 ♖c8 15 b4 (15 ♗f3!? ♕b6 16 ♕e2 intending ♖fd1) 15...♘cd7! 16 ♗g3 (16 ♗f3 ♕b6!) 16...♘b6 17 ♕b3 ♘fd5! 18 ♗f3 ♖c4! ∓ Capa-blanca-Alekhine, Buenos Aires Wch (21) 1927, White should play 14 ♕xd8 ♖fxd8 15 ♖fd1 with an equal position.

c) 8 b3 h6 9 ♗h4 ♗b4 10 ♗d3 c5 11 0-0 and now:

c1) 11...cxd4!? 12 exd4 ♕a5 13 ♕c2 dxc4 14 bxc4 b5 15 c5 ♗b7 16 ♗e4 ♘xe4 17 ♘xe4 ♗xe4 (17...♗d5 18 ♖b1 ♕a3 19 ♘d6 ± Zviagintsev-

Kharitonov, Elista 1995) 18 ♕xe4 ♕xa2∞19 ♗e7 ♖fe8 20 d5 ♗a3 21 d6 ♗xc1 22 ♖xc1 ♕d5 23 ♖xd5 exd5 24 c6 ♖xe7 25 dxe7 ♘f6 26 ♘e5 ♘e8 0-1 Kragelj-Lazović, Ljubljana 1996.

c2) 11...♕a5 12 ♕c2 ♗a3 13 ♖b1 ♗b4 14 ♖fc1 ♗a3 = Kharitonov.

d) 8 c5!? c6 (D) (8...♘e4 9 ♘xe4 dxe4 10 ♗xe7 ♕xe7 11 ♘d2 ♘f6 12 ♘c4 ♗d7 13 ♘e5 ± Karpov-O.Jakobsen, Malta OL 1980) and now:

d1) 9 b4 a5! 10 a3 (10 b5 e5!) 10...axb4 11 axb4 b6 12 ♗f4 bxc5 13 bxc5 ♖a3 14 ♕d2 (14 ♗d3 ♕a5 15 ♕d2 ♗a6! 16 ♗xa6 ♕xa6 ∓ Alekhine-Henneberger, Bern 1925) 14...♕a5 15 ♘b1! (15 ♗e2 ♘xc5! 16 dxc5 ♗xc5 17 ♘e5 ♖xc3! 18 ♖xc3 ♗b4 −+) 15...♘e4 ∓.

d2) 9 ♗e2 c5 10 0-0 h6 11 ♗h4 ♘e4 (11...e4?! 12 ♘d2 ♘h7 13 ♗g3 ♘g5 14 b4 ♘e6 15 f3 ±; 11...exd4 12 exd4 g5 13 ♗g3 ♘h5 14 ♗d3 ♘xg3 15 fxg3 ♗f6 16 ♗b1 ♖e8 is unclear, Farago-Portisch, Hungary 1996) 12 ♗xe7 ♕xe7 13 ♘a4 (13 ♘xe4 dxe4 14 ♘xe5 ♘xe5 15 dxe5 ♖d8?! {15...♕xe5 is slightly better for White} 16 ♕b3 ♖d2 17 ♖fe1 ♕xe5 18 ♖cd1 ♗e6 19 ♕xb7 ♖ad8 20 ♕xc6 ♕xb2 21 ♖xd2??

{a blunder; 21 ♕xa6 ±} 21...♕xd2 22 ♔f1 ♕xe2+!! 0-1 Gligorić-Z.Vuković, Yugoslav Cht (Nikšić) 1996) 13...♘g5 14 ♘xg5 hxg5 15 dxe5 ♕xe5 16 ♕d4 ± Tatai-Mantovani, Italian Ch (Chianciano) 1989.

d3) 9 ♗d3 and then:

d31) 9...♖e8 10 ♗f4!? ♘h5 11 0-0 g6 12 h3 ♘xf4 13 exf4 ♗f8 14 ♕c2 ♗g7 15 ♖fe1 ± Zsu.Polgar-Lechtynski, Trenčianske Teplice 1985.

d32) 9...b6 10 cxb6 c5 (10...♕xb6 11 0-0! ♕xb2 12 ♘a4 ♕b7 13 ♘e5 c5 14 ♘xd7 ♗xd7 15 ♘xc5 ♗xc5 16 ♗xf6 ± Hort-Portisch, Madrid 1973) 11 0-0 ♗b7 (11...c4 12 ♗c2 ♘xb6 13 ♘e5 ♗b7 14 f4 ♖b8 {14...♘fd7 15 ♕h5 ±} 15 f5! ± Portisch-Petrosian, Palma de Mallorca Ct (10) 1974) 12 ♗b1 (12 ♕e2 ♖e8 13 ♗b1 cxd4 14 exd4 ♕xb6 = Christiansen-Csom, Lucerne OL 1982) 12...cxd4 13 exd4 ♘xb6 14 ♘e5 ♖c8 (14...♘fd7 15 ♗xe7 ♕xe7 16 ♘a4 ♖ab8 17 ♘xb6!? ♘xb6 18 ♖c3! ± Eingorn) 15 ♖e1 ♘bd7 16 ♕b3 ♗a8 17 ♕a4 ♖b8 18 ♖e2 ± Gavrikov-Balashov, USSR Ch (Riga) 1985.

d33) 9...e5 (Black frees his game) 10 dxe5 ♘e8 and then:

d331) 11 ♗xe7 ♕xe7 12 b4 (12 ♕c2 h6 13 0-0 ♘xe5 14 ♘xe5 ♕xe5 15 e4 ♘f6 =) 12...♘xe5 13 ♘xe5 ♕xe5 14 0-0 ♘f6 15 h3 ♗f5 =.

d332) Interesting is 11 h4!? ♘xc5 12 ♗b1 ♘e6 13 ♕c2 (13 ♘d4 g6 14 ♗h6 ♘8g7 15 h5 ♗g5 = Korchnoi-Agdestein, Tilburg 1989) 13...g6 14 ♗h6 ♘8g7 15 h5 ♖e8 16 hxg6 fxg6 17 ♖d1 ♕a5 ∞ Lipinsky-Kharitonov, Berlin 1997.

d333) 11 ♗f4 ♘xc5 12 ♗b1 ♗g4 (12...♘e6 also seems interesting: 13

♕c2 g6 14 ♗h6 ♘8g7 15 0-0 {15 ♖d1 ♖e8 16 ♗xg7 ♔xg7 17 0-0 ♕b6 18 a3 ♗d7 19 ♖d2 ♖ad8 = Tukmakov-Balashov, Dortmund 1987} 15...f6 16 exf6 ♖xf6 17 e4 d4 18 ♖fd1 ♖xf3 19 gxf3 ♗g5 ∞ Levitt-Borges, Polanica Zdroj 1988) 13 h3 (White obtains no advantage by 13 ♕c2 g6 14 ♘d4 ♘e6 15 ♗h6 ♘8g7 16 0-0 ♖e8 17 ♕d2 ♘xd4 18 exd4 ♗f5 19 ♗xg7 ♗xb1 = Reshevsky-Lombardy, USA Ch (Oberlin) 1975) 13...♗h5 14 g4 ♗g6 15 ♗f5 (intending h4-h5) 15...♘c7 16 h4 h5 17 ♘d4 ♘7e6 18 ♔f1 ∞ Vaganian-Speelman, London 1984.

**8...exd5 9 ♗d3 c6** *(D)*

We have arrived at a position akin to the Exchange Variation, with the difference that Black has weakened the dark squares on his queenside, in particular b6 and c5.

**10 0-0 ♖e8**

Alekhine's idea 10...♘e8 seems interesting: 11 ♗f4! (11 ♗xe7 ♕xe7 12 e4 dxe4 13 ♘xe4 ♘df6! 14 ♕c2 ♘xe4 15 ♗xe4 ♘f6 = Capablanca-Alekhine, Buenos Aires Wch (23) 1927) 11...♗d6 12 ♕c2 (12 ♘g5!? ♘df6 13 ♗e5 ±) 12...♗xf4 (12...h6 13 ♗g3 ±) 13 exf4 ♘df6 14 ♘e5 ♘d6 15 ♘e2 g6

16 ♘g3 ♘fe8 17 f5 ♘g7 18 fxg6 fxg6 19 ♖ce1 ± Podgaets-Danielian, Moscow 1992.

**11 ♕c2**

Practice has also seen 11 ♗b1!? ♘f8 12 ♘e5 ♘6d7 (12...♘e4 13 ♗f4 f6 14 ♘d3 ♗d6 15 f3 ♗xf4 16 ♘xf4 ♘d6 17 e4 dxe4 18 fxe4 ♘e6 19 ♘fe2 ±) 13 ♗f4 ♘xe5 14 ♗xe5 ♗d6 15 ♗xd6 ♕xd6 16 a3 ♖e7 17 ♘a4 ♗e6 18 ♘c5 ± Gligorić-Ivkov, Bugojno 1978.

**11...♘f8**

11...h6 and now:

a) 12 ♗h4 ♘e4 13 ♗xe7 ♕xe7 14 ♖fe1 (14 ♗xe4 dxe4 15 ♘d2 ♘f6 16 ♖fe1 ♗f5 17 f4 ♖ad8 18 ♘b3 h5 19 h3 h4 20 ♕f2 ½-½ Lerner-Eingorn, USSR Ch (Odessa) 1989) 14...♘df6 15 ♘e5 ♗f5 16 ♘a4 ♗h7 17 ♘c5 ♘xc5 18 ♗xh7+ ♘xh7 19 ♕xc5 = Dorfman-C.Hansen, Helsinki 1986.

b) 12 ♗f4!? ♘f8 (12...♘h5? 13 ♘xd5! +−) 13 h3 ♗d6 14 ♗xd6 ♕xd6 15 ♖fe1 ♗e6 16 ♘a4 ± Grünfeld-Yates, Scarborough 1930.

**12 h3**

12 ♖fe1!? ♗e6 (12...♗g4 13 ♘d2 ♘6d7 14 ♗f4 ♗g5 15 h3 ♗h5 16 ♗h2 ♗g6 17 ♗xg6 hxg6 18 ♕b3 ♕b6 19 ♘a4 ♕xb3 20 ♘xb3 ± Rubinstein-Takacs, Budapest 1926) 13 a3 (13 ♘a4 ♘6d7 14 ♗xe7 ♕xe7 15 ♘c5 ♘xc5 16 ♕xc5 ± Capablanca-Alekhine, Buenos Aires Wch (25) 1927) 13...♘h5 14 ♗xe7 ♕xe7 15 ♘a4 ♖ad8 16 ♘c5 ♗c8 17 b4 ± Andersson-A.Sokolov, Reykjavik 1988.

**12...♗e6**

Or:

a) 12...♘e4 13 ♗f4 and now:

a1) 13...♘xc3 14 bxc3 ♗d6 15 ♗xd6 ♕xd6 16 c4 dxc4 (16...b5 17 cxd5 cxd5 18 ♕c5 ±) 17 ♗xc4 ♗e6 18

♘d2 ♕e7 19 ♖b1 ♖ab8 20 ♘b3 ♕g5 21 ♘c5! ± Grünfeld-Bernstein, Karlsbad 1923.

a2) 13...f5 14 ♘e5 ♘d7 15 ♘xc6!? (15 f3 ±) 15...bxc6 16 ♘xd5 cxd5 (16...♖a7!?) 17 ♗c7 wins the queen for probably inadequate compensation.

a3) 13...♘g5 14 ♘xg5 ♗xg5 15 ♗h2 ♗e7 16 ♘a4 ± Benjamin-Ziatdinov, New York 1995.

b) 12...♘h5 13 ♗xe7 ♕xe7 14 ♘a4 g6 15 ♘c5 ♘g7 16 ♕b3 ♘fe6 17 ♖fe1 ♘xc5 18 dxc5 ♗f5 19 ♗f1 ♘e6 20 ♕c3 ♘g5 21 ♘d4 ♕d7 22 f3 ± Lugovoi-Gavrilov, Smolensk 1992.

**13 ♗xf6**

White gains nothing by 13 ♘e5 ♘6d7 14 ♗xe7 ♖xe7 15 ♘a4 ♕c7 16 ♘xd7 ♗xd7 17 ♕c5 ♗e8 18 ♘b6 ♖d8 19 ♗f5 g6 20 ♗g4 f5 21 ♗f3 ♗f7 22 ♕b4 ♖ee8 23 ♘a4 ♘e6 = Beliavsky-Hort, Tunis IZ 1985 or 13 a3 ♘6d7 14 ♗f4 ♘g6 15 ♗h2 ♘df8 16 ♕b3 ♗c8 17 e4 dxe4 18 ♘xe4 ♘e6 = Timoshchenko-C.Hansen, Helsinki 1986.

**13...♗xf6 14 ♘a4 ♗e7 15 ♘c5 ♗xc5 16 dxc5 ♕f6 17 ♕c3 ♕h6 18 ♕b4 ♖e7 19 ♖fd1 ♘g6**

The chances are roughly equal, Piket-I.Sokolov, Amsterdam 1994.

**E5)**

**7...c6 (D)**

This is the main line. Now:

**E51: 8 ♕c2**     55
**E52: 8 ♗d3**     58

With the former, White plays a waiting game – the so-called 'battle for tempi'. The latter is more direct, and tends to lead to more forcing play.

**E51)**

**8 ♕c2 a6**

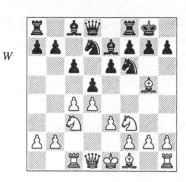

This good idea was originated by Janowski and developed by Rubinstein. In addition to the text-move, Black has other defensive possibilities:

a) 8...c5 9 cxd5! exd5 10 ♗xf6! ♘xf6 11 dxc5 ♕a5 12 ♘d4 ♕xc5 13 ♗d3 ♗d7 14 0-0 ♖fe8 (14...♖fc8 15 ♗f5 ♖c7 16 ♗xd7 ♖xd7 17 ♕a4 ♕c4 18 ♖fd1 ± Réti-Yates, Karlsbad 1923) 15 ♗f5 ♖ad8 16 ♖fd1 ± Grünfeld-Yates, Karlsbad 1929.

b) 8...h6 9 ♗f4! and here:

b1) 9...♘e4 10 ♗d3!? (10 ♘xe4 dxe4 11 ♕xe4 ♗b4+ 12 ♔d1! is also good for White) 10...f5 11 h4 intending g3 and ♘e5 ±.

b2) 9...♘h5 10 ♗e5! g6 (10...♘xe5 11 dxe5 ±) 11 ♗d3 ♕e8 12 0-0 f5 13 a3 ♘df6 14 b4 ± Novikov-Van der Zee, Cattolica 1993.

b3) 9...♖e8 10 ♗d3 dxc4 11 ♗xc4 b5 12 ♗d3 a6 13 a4! ♗b7 14 0-0 ♖c8 15 ♕b3 ♕b6 16 ♘e5 ♖ed8? 17 ♘g6! ♗f8 18 ♘xf8 ♘xf8 19 ♘e4 ♘xe4 20 ♗xe4 ♘d7 21 ♗d6! ± Alekhine-Teichmann, Karlsbad 1923.

c) 8...♖e8 (a useful waiting move) 9 ♗d3 dxc4 10 ♗xc4 ♘d5 (10...b5 11 ♗d3 a6 12 ♘e5! ♗b7 13 ♘xd7 ♕xd7 14 ♗xf6 ♗xf6 15 ♗xh7+ ♔h8 16 ♗e4

± Rubinstein-Capablanca, St Petersburg 1914) 11 ♗xe7 (11 ♘e4!? f5? 12 ♗xe7 ♖xe7 13 ♘ed2 ± Alekhine-Yates, London 1922) and then:

c1) 11...♕xe7 12 ♘e4! ♘5f6 13 ♘g3 ♕b4+ (13...e5? is very strongly met by 14 ♘g5) 14 ♕d2 ♕xd2+ 15 ♔xd2 b6 16 e4! ± intending e5 and ♘e4.

c2) 11...♖xe7 12 0-0 ♘f8 (alternatively, 12...♘xc3 13 ♕xc3 b6 ±) 13 ♖fd1 ♗d7 14 e4 ± Capablanca-Lasker, Havana Wch (11) 1921.

d) 8...♘e4 9 ♗xe7 (also interesting is 9 ♗f4 f5 10 h3 {10 h4 ♘df6 intending ...♘g4 ∞} 10...♘df6 11 ♗d3 ♗d7 12 0-0 ♗e8 13 ♘e5 ♘d7 14 f3 ♘xe5 15 ♗xe5 ± Pinter-Prandstetter, Taxco IZ 1985) 9...♕xe7 *(D)* and now:

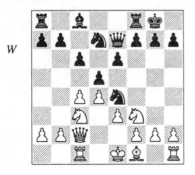

d1) 10 a3 leads only to equality: 10...♘xc3 11 ♕xc3 dxc4 (11...♖e8 12 ♖d1 dxc4 13 ♗xc4 b6 14 0-0 ♗b7 15 e4 c5 = Fine-Ståhlberg, Stockholm OL 1937) 12 ♗xc4 b6 13 ♗e2 ♗b7 14 0-0 ♖fc8 15 b4 a5 16 ♘d2 axb4 17 axb4 c5 18 dxc5 bxc5 19 b5 ♘b6 20 ♘c4 ♕g5 21 f3 ♘xc4 22 ♗xc4 ♗d5 ½-½ Keene-Prandstetter, Skara Echt 1980.

d2) 10 ♘xe4 dxe4 11 ♕xe4 ♕b4+ 12 ♘d2 ♕xb2 13 ♖b1 (13 ♖d1?! ♕xa2 14 ♗d3 ♘f6 15 ♕f3 ♕a3 16 e4 e5 ∓; 13 ♕b1 ♕xb1 14 ♖xb1 e5 15 ♗d3 exd4 16 exd4 ♖e8+ 17 ♔d1 c5 18 d5 ♘e5 19 ♖e1 ♗g4+ 20 ♔c2 ♘xd3 21 ♔xd3 ♗f5+ 22 ♘e4 ♖e7 = Tarrasch-Bogoljubow, Baden-Baden 1925) and here:

d21) 13...♕xa2 14 ♗d3 ♘f6 (or 14...g6 15 h4 ♕a5 16 h5 ♕f5 17 hxg6 ♕xg6 18 ♕h4 ♕xd3 19 ♖b3 ♕c2 20 e4 ♖e8 21 ♕g5+ 1-0 Ftačnik-Ree, Lucerne OL 1982) 15 ♕h4 (15 ♕e5!?) 15...♕a5 16 g4 h6 17 ♖g1 with the initiative.

d22) 13...♕a3 14 ♗e2 ♕e7 15 f4 c5 16 0-0 ♖b8 17 f5 ♘f6 18 ♕f4 ♗d7 19 e4 exf5 20 e5 cxd4 21 exf6 ♕xe2 22 ♖f3 ∞ Ftačnik-Franzen, Czechoslovakia 1984.

d3) 10 ♗d3 ♘xc3 and now:

d31) 11 ♕xc3 dxc4 12 ♗xc4 (12 ♕xc4 e5 =) 12...b6 13 0-0 ♗b7 14 b4 (14 ♖fd1 c5 =) 14...a5 15 ♖b1 (15 a3 =) 15...axb4 16 ♖xb4 ♖fc8 17 ♘d2 c5 ∓ Rubinstein-Becker, Karlsbad 1929.

d32) 11 bxc3 dxc4 (11...h6 12 cxd5 exd5 13 0-0 ♘f6 14 c4 dxc4 15 ♗xc4 ♗e6 16 ♘e5 ♗xc4 17 ♕xc4 ♖fe8 18 ♖c2 and White's activity grants him an edge, Timman-Prandstetter, Taxco IZ 1985) 12 ♗xc4 b6 13 0-0 ♗b7 14 e4! (not 14 ♗d3 g6 15 ♘d2 c5 = Grünfeld-Wolf, Mährisch Ostrau 1923) 14...c5 15 d5 exd5 16 ♗xd5 ± Smejkal-Prandstetter, Trenčianske Teplice 1985.

We now return to 8...a6 *(D)*:

**9 cxd5**

Or:

a) On 9 a4 Black can simply reply 9...♘e4! =.

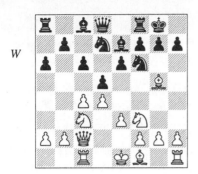

W

b) 9 c5 also yields nothing due to 9...e5 10 dxe5 ♘e8 (10...♘g4?! 11 ♗f4! ±) 11 ♗xe7 ♕xe7 12 ♗d3 h6 13 0-0 ♘xe5 14 ♘xe5 ♕xe5 15 e4 ♘f6 16 f4 ♕d4+ 17 ♔h1 dxe4 18 ♘xe4 ♘xe4 19 ♗xe4 ♖e8 20 ♗f3 ♕f6 21 ♕b3 ♖e7 = Rivas-Toth, Rome 1984.

c) 9 ♗d3 h6 and then:

c1) 10 ♗h4 dxc4 11 ♗xc4 b5 12 ♗d3 c5 ∓ Alekhine.

c2) 10 ♗xf6 ♗xf6 11 0-0 b5 12 cxd5 cxd5 13 a4 b4 14 ♘e2 ♗b7 15 ♕c7 ♖b8 = Magerramov-Kharitonov, Podolsk 1992.

c3) 10 cxd5 ♘xd5 (10...hxg5 11 dxe6 fxe6 12 ♘xg5 ♘b6 ∞ Magerramov-Ziatdinov, Berlin 1993) 11 ♗xe7 ♕xe7 12 a3 ♘5f6 13 0-0 c5 14 ♘e4 cxd4 15 ♘xd4 ♘xe4 16 ♗xe4 ♘f6 17 ♗f3 e5 = Savchenko-Kharitonov, Russian Army Ch (Zavoronki) 1995.

d) Fully possible is 9 a3!? h6 (9...b5 10 c5 ♘h5 11 ♗xe7 {11 h4!? f5 12 ♗d3 ♘hf6 13 ♘e2 ± Capablanca-Ragozin, Semmering 1937} 11...♕xe7 12 ♗d3 g6 13 ♘e2 e5 14 dxe5 ♘xe5 15 ♘xe5 ♕xe5 16 ♕c3 ± Andersson-Arlandi, Rome 1985) and here:

d1) Very interesting is 10 cxd5!? hxg5 (10...exd5 11 ♗h4 ±; 10...♘xd5 11 ♗xe7 ♕xe7 12 ♗c4 ♖e8 13 ♘e4

e5 14 ♗xd5 cxd5 15 ♘c3 ♕d6 16 ♕b3 ± Yusupov-Van der Sterren, Amsterdam 1982) 11 dxe6 fxe6 12 ♘xg5 ♘b6 ∞.

d2) 10 ♗h4 ♖e8 and then:

d21) 11 cxd5 exd5 12 ♗d3 ♘h5 13 ♗xe7 ♖xe7 14 0-0 ♘hf6 15 h3 ♘e8 16 ♘e2 ♘d6 17 ♘g3 ♘f8 18 ♘e5 f6! = Alekhine-Capablanca, Buenos Aires Wch (14) 1927.

d22) 11 ♗g3 dxc4 12 ♗xc4 b5 13 ♗a2 c5 14 dxc5 ♘xc5 15 ♖d1 (15 0-0 ♕d3 =) 15...♕b6 16 b4 (16 0-0 ♗b7 17 b4 ♘ce4 ∓) 16...♘cd7 17 ♗b1 ♘f8 18 ♘e4 ♘xe4 19 ♗c7 ♕a7 ∓ Vuković-Kmoch, Debrecen 1925.

d23) 11 ♗d3 dxc4 12 ♗xc4 b5 13 ♗a2 c5 14 0-0 (14 dxc5 ♘xc5 15 0-0 ♕d3! =; 14 ♖d1 cxd4 15 ♘xd4 ♕b6 16 ♗b1 ♗b7 17 0-0 {17 ♘dxb5 ♕c6 18 ♘d4 ♕xg2 ∓} 17...♖ac8 18 ♕d2 ♘e5 ∓ Grünfeld-Alekhine, Karlsbad 1923) 14...cxd4 15 exd4 ♗b7 16 ♘e5 (16 ♖fd1 ♕b6 17 ♘e5 ♘xe5 18 dxe5 ♕c6! 19 f3 ♘g4! is slightly better for Black) 16...♘xe5 (16...♘f8 17 ♖fd1 ± Réti-Teichmann, Karlsbad 1923) 17 dxe5 ♘d5 18 ♗xe7 ♖xe7 19 ♖fd1 ♖d7 20 ♘e4 ♘f4 =.

We now return to the position after 9 cxd5 (D):

B

**9...exd5**

Or:

a) 9...cxd5 can be met by 10 ♗d3 h6 11 ♗f4 (11 ♗h4 b5 12 a4 b4 13 ♘b1 ♗b7 14 ♗g3?! ♖c8 15 ♗c7? ♕e8 ∓ Engel-Maroczy, Bad Sliac 1932) 11...b5 12 a4 b4 13 ♘a2! ♗b7 14 0-0 ♕b6 15 ♗c7 ♕a7 16 ♗a5 ± Averbakh.

b) 9...♘xd5 10 ♗xe7 ♕xe7 and then:

b1) 11 ♗e2 ♖e8 12 0-0 ♘xc3 13 ♕xc3 e5 14 ♖fd1 exd4 15 ♘xd4 ♘f6 16 ♗f3 (16 h3 ♘e4!) 16...♗g4 17 ♗xg4 ♘xg4 18 ♘f5 ♕f6 19 ♕xf6 ♘xf6 ½-½ Alekhine-Capablanca, Buenos Aires Wch (2) 1927.

b2) 11 ♗c4 ♘xc3 12 ♕xc3 c5 (12...♖e8 13 ♖d1!) 13 dxc5 ♘xc5 (13...♕xc5? 14 ♗b3! b6 15 ♕d2 ♕h5 16 ♗d1! ± Alekhine-Vidmar, Hastings 1936) 14 ♗d5! (14 ♗e2 ♘e4 15 ♕d4 ♘f6 16 0-0 ±) 14...exd5 (14...♘a4 15 ♕d4! ♘xb2 16 ♗e4! {16 ♗b3 ♕b4+} 16...♕a3 17 0-0 ±) 15 ♕xc5 ±.

**10 ♗d3 ♖e8 11 0-0 ♘f8 12 ♘e5 ♘g4**

Black tries to free his position.

**13 ♗xe7 ♕xe7 14 ♘xg4 ♗xg4 15 ♖ce1**

White prepares play in the centre and on the kingside.

**15...♖ad8**

Or: 15...♕d6 16 f4 f6 17 f5 ♗h5 18 ♕f2 ♖e7 19 ♕f4 ± Novikov-Lengyel, Cappelle la Grande 1995; 15...♗e6!? 16 a3 ♖ad8 17 f4 f6 18 f5 ♗f7 ∞.

**16 f4 ♗h5**

Or 16...♗c8:

a) 17 f5 ♘d7! (17...f6?! 18 g4 ♔h8 19 ♕f2 c5 20 ♗c2 c4 21 ♕g2 ♕d7 22 h4 ± Korchnoi-Lutikov, Sverdlovsk 1957) 18 ♕f2 (18 ♖f4?! ♘f6 19 g4 h6

20 ♕f2 c5 ∞ Lapienis-Kimelfeld, Riga 1968) 18...♘f6 19 ♘a4 ♕d6 20 h3 ♖e7 21 ♕f4 and White has a slight advantage, Magerramov-Balashov, Uzhgorod 1988.

b) 17 a3 h6 18 ♕f2 ♘d7 19 f5! ♘f6 20 ♘a4! ♕d6 21 ♕f4! ♕xf4 22 ♖xf4 ♘d7 23 b4 ± Psakhis-Csom, Hungary 1986.

**17 f5 f6 18 a3 ♗f7 19 b4**

±. White has a space advantage.

## E52)

**8 ♗d3** *(D)*

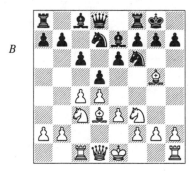

**8...dxc4**

Black can also insert 8...h6, upon which may follow 9 ♗h4 dxc4 10 ♗xc4, and now:

a) 10...♘d5 11 ♗g3 (11 ♗xe7 ♕xe7 12 0-0 ♘xc3 13 ♖xc3 transposes to the Lasker Defence – Line C of Chapter 7) 11...♘xc3 (11...♘7b6 12 ♗d3 ♘xc3 13 bxc3 ♗a3 14 ♖c2 ♗d7 15 ♘e5 ± Steinitz-Showalter, New York 1894) 12 bxc3 and now:

a1) 12...♕a5 13 0-0 b5 (13...♘b6 14 ♗b3 ♗a3 15 ♖c2 c5 16 ♘e5 cxd4 17 cxd4 ♗e7 18 ♕f3 ♘d5 19 ♖fc1 ± Tartakower – Znosko-Borovsky, Paris 1925) 14 ♗d3 ♕xa2 15 ♖a1 ♕b2 16

♘d2 ± F.Olafsson-Gerusel, Bad Lau-
terberg 1977.
　　a2) 12...b6 13 0-0 ♗b7 14 ♕e2 ♘f6
(14...c5!? seems interesting: 15 ♖fd1
♘f6!? 16 dxc5 ♕c8 17 cxb6 axb6 18
♗e5 ♗a6 with compensation, Ionov-
Shulskis, Vilnius 1997) 15 ♖fd1 ♘e4
(15...♕c8 16 e4 ♖d8 17 e5 ♘h7 18
♘d2 c5 19 ♘e4 ♘g5 20 f3 ± Furman-
Jimenez, Harrachov 1966) 16 ♗f4
♕c8 17 ♘e5 c5 18 ♗b5 ♘f6 19 c4
♖d8 20 ♗g3 ± Lputian-Bischoff,
Altensteig 1989.
　　b) 10...b5 11 ♗d3 a6 (11...♗b7 12
0-0 ♖c8 13 ♕e2! b4 14 ♘a4 ♕a5 15
b3 c5 16 ♘e5 ± Tal-Nei, USSR 1981)
12 a4 and now:
　　b1) 12...♗b7 13 0-0 ♖c8 14 ♕e2
♖e8 15 ♖fd1 ± Ribli-Handoko, Surakarta 1982.
　　b2) 12...b4 13 ♗xf6 gxf6 (13...♘xf6
14 ♘e4 ±) 14 ♘e4 f5 15 ♘g3 c5 16 e4
cxd4 17 exf5 e5 18 ♖c6! ♘f6 19 ♕c1
♔h7 20 ♘xe5 ♗b7 21 ♖c7 ♗xg2 22
♖g1 ♗d6 23 ♘h5 ♕xc7 24 ♘xf6+
♔g7 25 ♘h5+ 1-0 Ribli-Hennings,
Leipzig 1973.
　　b3) 12...bxa4 13 ♘xa4 ♕a5+ 14
♘d2 ♗b4 (14...c5 15 ♗xf6 ±) 15 ♘c3
and then:
　　b31) 15...♘d5 16 0-0 ♗xc3 17 ♘c4
♕b4 18 bxc3 ♘xc3 19 ♕c2 is slightly
better for White, Ståhlberg-Foltys,
Munich 1936.
　　b32) 15...♗b7 16 0-0 c5 17 ♘b3
♕d8 18 ♘a2! ♖c8 19 ♕e2 ♕b6 20
♘xb4 cxb4 21 ♖a1 ♖a8 22 ♘a5 ±
Hort-Rossetto, Skopje OL 1972.
　　b33) 15...c5 16 ♘b3 (16 ♘c4 ♕c7?!
17 0-0 ♗b7 18 ♘a2! Vyzhmanavin-
Djurić, Cappelle la Grande 1994)
16...♕d8 (16...♕b6 17 0-0 cxd4 18
♘a4 ♕d8 19 ♗e4 ♖b8 20 ♘xd4 ♗b7

21 ♗xb7 ♖xb7 22 ♘c6 ± Levitina-
Gaprindashvili, Lvov 1983) 17 0-0
cxd4 18 ♘xd4 ♗b7 19 ♗e4 ♕b8 20
♘c6! ♗xc6 21 ♗xc6 ♖a7 22 ♗g3 ♘e5
23 ♕d4! (23 ♕e2 ♗d6! is unclear,
G.Agzamov-T.Georgadze, Tashkent
1984; 23 ♘e4 ♗e7 24 ♕d4 ♘xc6 25
♖xc6 ♕b5! 26 ♕xa7 {26 ♖xe6 ♖d7}
26...♕xc6 =) 23...♗d6 24 ♘e4! (24
♖fd1?! ♗c7 = Pinter-Martin, Linz
1984) 24...♘xc6 (24...♘xe4 25 ♗xe4
♖d8 26 ♖cd1 ♖ad7 27 ♕a4 ♘g4 28
♗f3 ♘f6 29 ♗c6 ♗xg3 30 ♗xd7
♗xh2+ 31 ♔h1 ♗e5 32 ♗c6 ♖xd1 33
♖xd1 ♕xb2 34 ♔g1 ± Morović-Ill-
escas, Spain 1995) 25 ♘xf6+ gxf6 26
♖xc6 ♗e5 27 ♕g4+! (27 ♗xe5 fxe5
28 ♕h4 ♔h7 29 ♕e4+ ♔g7 30 f4 exf4
31 ♖xf4 ♕xb2 ±) 27...♔h7 28 ♕e4+
♔g7 29 f4 ± Kamsky-Salov, Sanghi
Nagar FIDE Ct (3) 1995.
　　**9 ♗xc4 (D)**

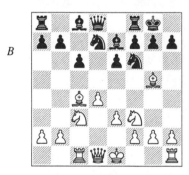

B

　　**9...♘d5**
　　Also possible is 9...b5 10 ♗d3 a6
(10...♗b7 11 e4 a6 12 e5 ±; 10...b4 11
♘e4 ♗b7 12 0-0 c5 13 ♗xf6 gxf6 14
dxc5 ♖c8 15 ♘d4 ± Euwe-Maroczy,
Netherlands 1933):
　　a) 11 a4 yields no advantage due to
11...bxa4 12 ♘xa4 ♕a5+ 13 ♘c3 c5

14 ♖a1 ♕b4 15 0-0 ♗b7 16 ♕e2 cxd4 17 exd4 ♗xf3 18 ♕xf3 ♕xd4 19 ♗xa6 ♕b6 20 ♗b5 ♖xa1 21 ♖xa1 ♘e5 22 ♕e2 ♘g6 23 ♗e3 ♕b8 = Vidmar-Em.Lasker, Nottingham 1936.

b) 11 e4 h6 (11...c5 12 e5 ♘d5 13 ♗xe7 ♕xe7 {13...♘xe7? 14 ♗xh7+ +−} 14 ♘xd5 exd5 15 dxc5 ±) 12 ♗f4! (12 ♗h4?! ♘xe4! 13 ♗xe4 ♗xh4 14 ♗xc6 ♖a7 15 0-0 ♘b6 16 ♘e4 ♗e7 17 ♘e5 ♖c7 18 ♕d3 ♘c4 19 ♘xc4 ♖xc6 20 ♘e5 ♖xc1 21 ♖xc1 ♗b7 ∓ Euwe-Alekhine, Amsterdam Wch (28) 1935) 12...♗b7 (12...c5 13 e5 ±) 13 e5! ♘d5 14 ♘xd5 cxd5 15 0-0 ♖e8 16 ♗e3 ♖c8 17 ♖xc8 ♗xc8 18 ♗b1 ♘f8 19 ♘d2 ± Gligorić-Ståhlberg, Belgrade 1949.

**10 ♗xe7 ♕xe7**

White has two paths:

**E521: 11 ♘e4    60**
**E522: 11 0-0    61**

The former avoids simplifications.

Black easily equalizes following 11 ♕c2 ♘xc3 12 ♕xc3 b6 13 0-0 ♗b7 14 ♕d3 ♖fd8 15 ♕e2 c5 = Vidmar-Capablanca, Hastings 1929/30.

**E521)**
**11 ♘e4** *(D)*

**11...♘5f6!**

The best move. Others:

a) Black obtains an inferior ending after 11...♕b4+ 12 ♕d2 ♕xd2+ 13 ♔xd2 ♖d8 14 ♖hd1 ♘5f6 15 ♘xf6+ ♘xf6 16 ♗b3! (preventing ...b6 and ...♗b7) 16...♔f8 (16...c5 17 ♔e1! cxd4 18 ♖xd4 ♖xd4 19 ♘xd4 ± intending ♖c7) 17 ♔e2 ♔e7 18 ♘e5 ♗d7 19 f3 ± Alekhine-Capablanca, Buenos Aires Wch (6) 1927.

b) Black sometimes plays 11...e5 12 dxe5 ♘xe5 13 ♘xe5 ♕xe5 14 ♗xd5 cxd5 15 ♘c3:

b1) 15...♗e6 16 0-0 (16 ♕d4 ♕xd4 17 exd4 ♖fc8 ±) 16...♖fd8 17 ♕d3 ± (with the point 17...d4?! 18 ♖fd1 ±) Farago-Mariano, Bratto 1997.

b2) 15...♖d8 16 ♕d4 ♕xd4 17 exd4 ♗e6 18 ♔d2 ♖ac8 19 ♘b5 ± Cherepkov-Korelov, Sochi 1969.

c) Black can also adopt a plan with the fianchetto of the light-squared bishop: 11...b6 12 0-0 ♗b7 13 ♘g3 c5 14 e4 ♘f4 (14...♘5f6 15 ♖e1 cxd4 16 ♗b5! ♖fc8 17 ♕xd4 ♖c5 18 ♗xd7 ♘xd7 19 b4 ♖xc1 20 ♖xc1 ♖c8 21 ♖xc8+ ♗xc8 22 ♕c3 ± Alekhine-Maroczy, San Remo 1930) 15 ♗b5 ♖fd8 16 ♕a4 ♘f6 17 e5 ♘6d5 18 dxc5 a6 19 ♗e2 bxc5 20 a3 ± Portisch-Ljubojević, Milan 1975.

**12 ♘g3** *(D)*

Or 12 ♘xf6+ ♕xf6 13 0-0 e5 (13...c5?! 14 dxc5 ♘xc5 15 b4! ±), and now:

a) 14 dxe5 ♘xe5 15 ♘xe5 ♕xe5 16 ♕b3 ♕e7 17 ♖fd1 ♗e6 with equality, Bondarevsky-Makogonov, Leningrad 1938.

b) 14 d5!? e4 15 dxc6 bxc6 16 ♘d2 ♕g6 17 ♗e2 ∞ Farago-Campora, Lucerne Wcht 1985.

c) 14 e4!? exd4 15 ♕xd4 ♕xd4 16 ♘xd4 ♘e5 17 ♗b3 ♖d8 18 ♖fd1 ♗d7 = Petrosian-Portisch, Santa Monica 1966.

d) 14 ♗b3 exd4 15 ♕xd4 ♕xd4 16 ♘xd4 ♘f6! (16...♖d8 17 ♖cd1 ♘e5 18 f4 ♘g6 19 h3 ± Korchnoi-Hübner, Biel 1986) 17 f3 ♗d7 18 e4 ♖fe8 19 ♖fd1 ♖ad8 20 ♔f2 ♔f8 = Hertneck-Hübner, Garmisch 1994.

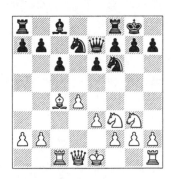

**12...e5**
Or:

a) White is better after 12...b6 13 0-0 c5 14 e4 ♖d8 (14...cxd4 15 e5 ±; 14...♗b7 15 d5 exd5 16 exd5 ±) 15 e5 ♘g4 16 h3 ♘h6 17 d5 exd5 18 ♕xd5 ♖b8 19 e6 ♗b7 20 ♘f5 ♕xe6 21 ♕xe6 fxe6 22 ♗xe6+ ♔f8 23 ♘xh6 gxh6 24 ♖fe1 ± Yermolinsky-G.Orlov, USA Ch (Modesto) 1995.

b) Black can simplify to an ending with 12...♕b4+ 13 ♕d2 ♕xd2+ 14 ♔xd2:

b1) 14...c5!? 15 ♗b5 (15 dxc5 ♘xc5 16 ♔e2 ♗d7 17 ♘e5 ♖fd8 18 b4 ♘ce4 19 ♘xe4 ♘xe4 20 ♖hd1 ♗a4 21 ♖xd8+ ♖xd8 22 ♗d3 ♘d6 23 ♖c7 ♖c8 = Taimanov) 15...cxd4 16 ♘xd4 ♘b6 17 f4 ♖d8 18 ♔e2 ♗d7 = Alekhine-Ståhlberg, Buenos Aires 1939.

b2) 14...♖d8 15 ♔e2 b6 16 ♖hd1 ♗b7 17 ♖d2 ♔f8 18 ♖cd1 ♔e7 19 e4 h6 = Alekhine-Capablanca, Buenos Aires Wch (18) 1927.

c) 12...♖d8 also seems interesting: 13 0-0 c5 14 e4 (14 ♕e2 cxd4 15 ♘xd4 ♘b6 16 ♗b3 ♗d7 17 ♖c7 ♖ab8 18 ♖fc1 ♘bd5 19 ♖7c2 ♘b4 20 ♖c7 ♘c6 = A.Shneider-Kharitonov, Jurmala 1983) 14...cxd4 15 e5 ♘e8 16 ♖e1 ♘f8 17 ♘xd4 ♘g6 18 ♕d2 b6! = Ivanchuk-Ehlvest, Erevan OL 1996.

**13 0-0 exd4 14 ♘f5**
Alekhine recommended 14 exd4 ♘b6 15 ♗b3 ♗g4 (15...♖e8!? 16 ♖e1 ♕f8 ∞) 16 ♖e1 ♕d6 17 h3 ♗xf3 18 ♕xf3 with the initiative, but modern practice considers otherwise: 18...g6 19 ♖e5 ♘bd7 20 ♘e4 ♘xe4 21 ♖xe4 ♘f6 22 ♖e5 ♔g7 23 ♕e3 ♖ad8 24 ♖e7 ♖d7 25 ♖e1 ♘d5 = Høi-U.Hansen, Copenhagen 1993.

**14...♕d8 15 ♘5xd4**
Other continuations promise nothing: 15 ♕xd4 ♘b6 =; 15 exd4 ♘b6 =; 15 ♘3xd4 ♘e5 16 ♗b3 ♗xf5 17 ♘xf5 g6! 18 ♘d4 (18 ♕d6 ♖e8! =; 18 ♘d6 ♕e7 =) 18...♕e7 19 ♕c2 ♖ac8 = Lilienthal-Renter, Pärnu 1947.

**15...♘b6 16 ♗d3**
16 ♗b3 ♗g4 17 ♕c2 ♕e7 18 h3 ♗xf3 =.

**16...♕e7 17 ♕c2 ♗g4 18 a3 ♖ad8 19 ♖fe1 ♘bd7! 20 ♘g5 h6 21 ♘h7 ♖fe8**
= Topalov-Yermolinsky, Erevan OL 1996.

**E522)**
**11 0-0 ♘xc3 12 ♖xc3** *(D)*
**12...e5**
Black can also play 12...b6, upon which may follow 13 ♕c2 ♗b7 (13...c5

14 dxc5 ♘xc5 15 b4 ♘d7 {15...♘a6 16 a3 ♗b7 17 ♗d3 g6 18 ♖c1 ♖ad8 19 ♘e5 ± Capablanca-H.Steiner, Budapest 1928} 16 ♗d3 ♘f6 17 a3 ♗d7 18 ♖c7 ♖fc8 19 ♗a6! ±) 14 ♗d3 f5 (14...h6 15 ♗e4 ±; 14...♘f6 15 ♘e5 ±), when White should probably play 15 ♕e2 ±, rather than 15 e4!? c5 16 d5 ∞.

**13 dxe5**
The main continuation, but White can also play:

a) 13 ♗b3!? exd4 14 exd4 ♘f6 15 ♖e1 (15 ♖e3 ♕d6 16 h3 ♗d7 17 ♖fe1 ♘d5 18 ♖e5 f6 19 ♗xd5+ cxd5 20 ♖e7 ♖fe8 21 ♖xe8+ ♖xe8 22 ♖xe8+ ♗xe8 23 ♕c2 ♗c6 24 ♕c5 ♕f4! = Ubilava-Kharitonov, Sevastopol 1986) 15...♕d6 16 ♘e5! (16 ♖ce3 ♗g4! 17 h3 ♗xf3 18 ♖xf3 ♖ad8 19 ♖d3 ♖d7 is equal) 16...♘d5 (16...♗e6 17 ♗xe6 fxe6 18 ♕b3 ♖ab8 19 ♖ce3 ♘d5 20 ♖e4 ± Khenkin-Shulskis, Poland 1998; 16...♗f5 17 ♖f3 ♗g4 {17...♗g6!?} 18 ♖xf6! ♕xe5 19 dxe5 ♗xd1 20 ♗xf7+ ♖xf7 21 ♖xf7 ♔xf7 22 ♖xd1 ♔e6 23 f4 ± Karpov-Campora, Spain 1997) 17 ♖g3 ♗f5 18 ♕f3 ♗g6 19 h4!? ∞.

b) 13 ♕b1 exd4 (13...e4 14 ♘d2 ♘f6 15 b4 ♘d5 16 ♗xd5 cxd5 17 ♕b3 ♗e6 18 ♖fc1 ± Najdorf-Guimard,

Mar del Plata 1946) 14 exd4 ♘b6 (or 14...♘f6 15 ♖e1 ♕d6 16 h3 ♗d7 17 ♖ce3 ♖ae8 18 ♖e5 h6 19 a3 ±) 15 ♗b3 ♕f6 16 ♖e3 (16 ♖e1 ♗e6 17 ♗xe6 fxe6 18 ♕e4 {18 ♖ce3 ♖ae8 is equal} 18...♖ae8 19 ♖b3 ♖e7 =) 16...♗g4 17 ♕e4 ♗xf3 18 ♖xf3 ♖ae8 19 ♕d3 (19 ♕xe8 ♖xe8 20 ♖xf6 gxf6 21 f3 ♖e2 22 ♖f2 ½-½ Knežević-Nikolac, Bahrain 1990) 19...♕d6 20 ♖h3 g6 21 ♕d2 ♕f6 22 ♖f3 ♕g7 23 h4 ♖e4 = Ståhlberg-Gligorić, Split 1949.

c) 13 ♕c2 exd4 (13...e4 14 ♘d2 ♘f6 15 ♖c1 ♗g4 16 b4! a6 17 ♕b1 ♖ad8 18 a4 ♕d6 19 b5 ± Vidmar-Fine, Warsaw OL 1935) 14 exd4 (D) (14 ♘xd4 ♘f6 15 a3 c5 16 ♘e2 b6 =) and now:

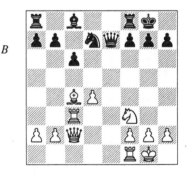

c1) 14...♘f6 15 ♖e1 ♕d6 (but not 15...♕d8?! 16 h3 ♘d5 17 ♗xd5 ♕xd5 18 ♖e5 ♕d6 19 ♘g5 g6 20 ♖f3 ♕xd4 {20...f6? 21 ♕b3+ ♔g7 22 ♖e8 a5 23 ♖xc8 1-0 Lputian-Balashov, Erevan 1986} 21 ♖e4 ♕d5 22 ♘xf7 ±) and now:

c11) 16 h3 ♗d7 17 ♖ce3 ♖ae8 18 ♘e5 (18 ♖e5!?) 18...♗e6 19 ♗xe6 ♖xe6 20 ♘xf7 ♖xe3 21 ♘xd6 ♖xe1+ 22 ♔h2 ♖e7 23 ♕b3+ ♘d5 with an unclear position.

c12) 16 ♕b3 b5! 17 ♗d3 (17
♗xf7+? ♖xf7 18 ♘g5 ♕d5 wins for
Black) 17...♗e6 18 ♕c2 ♗d5 19 ♘e5
♖fe8 20 ♖c1 h6 21 ♘xc6 b4 22 ♖c5
♗xc6 23 ♖xc6 ♕xd4! =.

c13) 16 ♘g5 and then:

c131) 16...♕xd4 17 ♖f3 +−.

c132) 16...♕f4 17 ♘xf7 b5 18 ♗b3
♖xf7 19 ♖e7 ♘d5 20 ♗xd5 cxd5 21
♖xf7 +−.

c133) 16...g6 17 ♕b3 ♕c7 (alternatively, 17...♘d5 18 ♘e4 ♕d8 19
♗xd5 cxd5 20 ♕xd5 ±) 18 ♖ce3! ♘g4
19 ♗xf7+ ♖xf7 (19...♔g7 20 ♖h3 ±)
20 ♖e8+ ♔g7 21 g3! +−.

c134) 16...h6 17 ♘xf7 ♖xf7 18
♕g6! ♕d7 (18...♕f8 19 ♖f3 ♘d5 20
♖xf7 ♕xf7 21 ♖e8+ +− Alekhine-
Karlson, Örebro 1935) 19 ♖f3 ♔f8
(19...♘d5 20 ♖xf7 ♕xf7 21 ♖e8++−)
20 ♖xf6! gxf6 (20...♖xf6 21 ♕h7 +−)
21 ♕xh6+ ♔g8 22 ♖e3 +−.

c135) 16...♗g4! 17 ♖ce3 (17 ♕b3
♗h5 18 ♕xb7 ♖ab8 19 ♕xa7 ♖xb2 20
♕c5 {20 ♕a3!? ∞} 20...♕f4 21 ♘h3
♕d2 22 ♖ce3 ♗g4! with compensation) 17...♗h5 18 ♖e6 ♕f4 (18...♗g6
19 ♖xd6 ♗xc2 20 ♖e7 ±) 19 ♖xf6
♕xg5 20 ♖f5 ♗g6 (20...♕h6 21 ♖fe5
±) 21 ♖xg5 ♗xc2 22 d5! ♖ac8 23
♖ge5 ± Grau-Vaitonis, Stockholm OL
1937.

c2) 14...♘b6 and then:

c21) 15 ♗d3 g6 =.

c22) 15 ♗b3 ♗e6! 16 ♖e1 (16 ♕e4
♖ae8 17 ♖e1 ♕f6 =) 16...♗xb3 17
♖xb3 ♕d6 18 ♕c5 ♖ad8 19 ♕a5 ♕b8
=.

c23) 15 ♖e3 and now:

c231) 15...♕f6 16 ♗b3 (16 ♗d3
g6 = intending ...♗e6 and ...♘d5)
16...♗g4 17 ♖fe1! ♖ad8 18 ♕c5 ♕d6
19 h3 ♗xf3 20 ♖xf3 ♕xc5 21 dxc5

♘c8 (21...♘d7 22 ♖e7 ♘xc5 23
♗xf7+ ♔h8 24 b4 ± Gligorić-Drimer,
Hastings 1969/70) 22 ♖e4 g6 23 ♖ef4
♖d7 24 ♖f6 ± Gligorić.

c232) 15...♕d8 16 ♗b3 ♘d5 (after
16...♗g4 17 ♘e5 ♗e6 18 ♗xe6 fxe6
19 ♘f3 White is slightly better) 17
♖e5 f6 18 ♗xd5+ cxd5 19 ♖e3 ♗g4
=.

c24) 15 ♖e1 ♕d8 16 ♗b3 ♘d5 17
♗xd5 ♕xd5 18 ♖e5 (18 ♖c5 ♕d6! 19
♕e4 {19 ♖ce5 h6 =} 19...h6 20 ♕e7
♕xe7 21 ♖xe7 ♖d8 =) 18...♕d6 19
♕e4 (19 ♖ce3 h6 20 ♕c3 {20 ♖e7
♖b8 =} 20...♗e6 21 h3 ♖ad8 = Pirc-
Gligorić, Yugoslavia 1951) 19...f6 20
♖e7 ♗d7 21 ♕e2 ♖fe8 22 ♖ce3 ♔f8
=.

**13...♘xe5 14 ♘xe5 ♕xe5** (D)

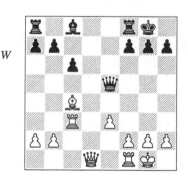

**15 f4**

The rapid advance of the f-pawn
provides the sternest test of Black's resources. Other moves:

a) 15 h3 ♗f5 =.

b) If 15 ♕b3, then 15...♕e7 16
♖d1 ♗f5 17 e4 ♗g6 18 f3 ♖fd8 19
♖cd3 b5 20 ♖xd8+ ♖xd8 21 ♗e2
♖xd1+ 22 ♕xd1 f5 with an equal position, Grünfeld-Bogoljubow, Karlsbad 1929.

c) 15 ♕c2 ♗f5 16 ♗d3 ♗xd3 17 ♖xd3 ♖ad8 = A.Zaitsev-Cirić, Sochi 1965.

**15...♕e4**

Or:

a) On 15...♕a5?! Taimanov gave 16 f5 ♗xf5 17 ♕h5 g6 18 ♕g5 ♔g7 19 e4 f6 20 ♕f4 ♗d7 21 ♕d6 ±.

b) After 15...♕e7?! 16 f5 White obtains a strong attack, e.g. 16...b5 17 ♗b3 b4 18 f6 gxf6 19 ♖xc6 ♕xe3+ 20 ♔h1 ♗b7 21 ♖cxf6 ±.

c) 15...♕f6!? is an alternative: c1) 16 e4 ♗e6 (16...♖d8!? 17 ♖d3 ♗g4! 18 e5! ♗xd1 19 exf6 ♗c2! 20 ♖g3 g6 =) 17 e5 ♕e7 18 ♗d3 f5! 19 ♕a4! a6 20 ♗c4 ♖ad8 = Capablanca-Lasker, Moscow 1936.

c2) 16 f5 b5 and here: c21) 17 ♗d3 b4 (17...♗b7!? 18 ♕f3 ♖ad8! 19 ♗xb5 ♖d2 20 ♗xc6 ♖xb2 ∞ Capablanca) 18 ♖c5 ♖e8 19 ♕c1 ♗b7 20 ♖c4 a5 21 ♕ff4 ♖ad8 22 ♗f1 ♖e5 23 ♖c5 ∞ Ståhlberg-Eliskases, Saltsjöbaden IZ 1952.

c22) 17 ♗b3 b4 (17...♖d8 18 ♕h5 ±) 18 ♖c5 ♗a6 (18...♕xb2 19 f6! +–) 19 ♖f4 ♖ad8 20 ♕c1 ♖d6 21 ♖xb4 ♖fd8 22 ♖f4 ± Bronstein-Gereben, Moscow-Budapest 1949.

**16 ♗b3**

Or:

a) The pawn sacrifice 16 ♗d3?! is unjustified in view of 16...♕xe3+ 17 ♔h1 ♕e7 18 f5 ♕f6:

a1) 19 ♗b1 b6! 20 ♖h3 ♗a6 21 ♖e1 ♖ad8 ∓.

a2) 19 ♕h5 h6 20 ♗c4 b5! ∓ Lilienthal-I.Rabinovich, USSR Ch (Tbilisi) 1937.

a3) 19 ♗e4!? ♖e8! (19...♖d8 20 ♖d3 ♖xd3 21 ♕xd3 b6 22 ♖d1 ♗b7 23 b4 with compensation) 20 ♖d3 h6

21 ♖d6 ♕e5 22 ♗c2 b6 23 f6 ♗a6 and Black has a slight advantage, Chekhover-Huber, corr. 1932.

b) 16 ♕e2!? appears interesting. 16...♗f5 *(D)* and now:

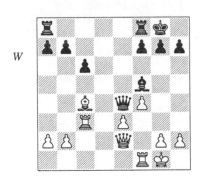

W

b1) 17 g4?! ♗e6 18 ♗d3 ♕b4 19 a3 (19 f5 ♗xa2 ∓) 19...♕b6 20 f5 ♗d5 21 f6 g6 22 ♕f2 ♖fe8 23 ♗b1 ♖e6 24 b4 (24 ♕f4 ♔h8 {24...♕xb2! 25 ♖c2 ♕xa3! and wins} 25 ♗xg6 ♕xb2 26 ♖c2 ♕b3 ∓ Euwe-H.Steiner, Hastings 1945/6) 24...♖ae8 25 ♖e1 ♕d4! 26 exd4 ♖xe1+ 27 ♕f1 ♖8e2 28 ♖c2 ♖e4 ∓ Möller-Mastrojeni, corr. 1990-2.

b2) 17 ♗d3 ♕d5 (17...♕e6?! 18 e4 ♖fe8 19 ♖e1 ♕d6 20 ♕f2 ♗e6 21 e5 ♕b4 22 a3 ♕b6 23 f5 ± Garcia Gonzales-Toth, Thessaloniki OL 1984) 18 e4 ♕d4+ 19 ♕f2 (19 ♔h1 ♖fe8 20 ♖c4 ♕d7 =) 19...♕xf2+ 20 ♔xf2 ♗d7 21 ♖d1 ♖fd8! (21...♖ad8?! is dubious due to 22 ♖a3! a6 23 ♗c4 {23 ♗xa6!? bxa6 24 ♖ad3 ♖b8 25 ♖xd7 ♖xb2+ 26 ♖1d2 ± Ganem-Thompson, corr. 1987} 23...♗e6 24 ♖xd8 ♖xd8 25 ♗xe6 fxe6 26 ♔e3 c5 27 ♖c3 b6 28 ♖a3 ♖a8 29 ♖d3 ± Hertneck-Sonntag, Bundesliga 1985/6) 22 ♗c4 ♗e8 23 ♖cd3 (23 ♖xd8 ♖xd8 24 ♖d3 ½-½ Franco-Campora, Spain 1992) 23...♖xd3 24

♖xd3 b5 25 ♗b3 ♔f8 26 e5 c5 is equal.

**16...♗f5 (D)**

The most accurate continuation. 16...♕g6 is strongly met by 17 e4! ♕xe4 (17...♗g4 18 ♕e1 ♖ad8 19 ♖g3 ♕h5 20 ♕c3 ±) 18 f5 ♕h4 (18...♕e5 19 f6 ♗f5 20 fxg7 ♔xg7 21 ♕d2 ±; 18...b6 19 f6 ♗a6 20 fxg7 ♔xg7 21 ♗c2 ♕e5 22 ♕g4+ ♔h8 23 ♗xh7! ± Gligorić) 19 ♖d3 ♕f6 20 ♕h5 b6 21 g4 h6 22 ♖fd1 ± Napolitano-Grob, Lausanne 1938.

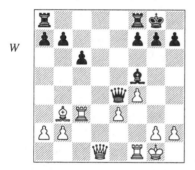

W

**17 ♕h5**

The line once recommended by Capablanca, 17 ♗c2 ♕e6 18 ♗xf5 ♕xf5 19 ♕b3 ♕d7 20 ♖d3, yields no advantage either due to 20...♕c7 21 ♖fd1 ♖ad8! 22 ♖xd8 ♖xd8 23 ♖xd8+ ♕xd8 24 ♕xb7 ♕d1+ 25 ♔f2 ♕d2+ 26 ♔f3 ♕d1+ 27 ♔g3 ♕e1+ =.

**17...g6 18 ♕h6**

18 ♕h4 is harmless, owing to 18...♖ad8 19 ♗c2 ♕d5 20 ♖d1 ♕a5 21 ♖xd8 ♕xd8 22 ♕xd8 ♖xd8 23 ♗xf5 gxf5 24 ♖c2 ♔g7 25 ♔f2 ♔f6 ½-½ Keres-Nei, Tallinn 1975.

**18...♖ad8 19 ♗c2 ♕d5 20 e4 ♗xe4 21 ♖h3 (D)**

21 f5?! is risky due to 21...♕d4+ 22 ♖f2 ♗xf5 23 ♗xf5 ♖fe8! 24 g4 (24 ♗d3 ♖e1+ 25 ♗f1 ♖xf1+ wins for Black) 24...gxf5 25 ♕g5+ ♕g7 26 ♕xf5 ♖e5, when Black has a clear advantage.

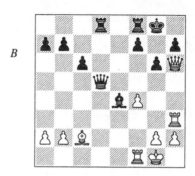

B

**21...♕c5+ 22 ♖f2 ♖fe8 23 ♕xh7+ ♔f8 24 ♕h6+ ♔e7 25 ♖c3 ♕d4 26 h3**

26 ♕g5+ ♔d7 27 ♕c5 ♕xc5 is equal.

**26...♖d5 27 ♕h4+ ♔d7 28 ♗b3 ♖f5**

The game is unclear.

**Conclusion:** The system involving ...♘bd7 was extremely popular in the 1920s and 1930s. Nowadays it has largely fallen into disuse, with its place in the limelight taken by the Tartakower and Lasker variations. However, deep investigation of the variation shows that it is very solid and that it contains many unexplored possibilities.

# 5  5 ♗g5 h6 6 ♗xf6

**1 d4 d5 2 c4 e6 3 ♘c3 ♗e7 4 ♘f3 ♘f6 5 ♗g5 h6 6 ♗xf6**

This is one of the most popular systems in modern practice. In particular it was explored extensively in the matches between Kasparov and Karpov.

**6...♗xf6** *(D)*

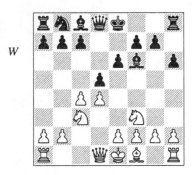

White now has several continuations:

| | |
|---|---|
| **A: 7 e4** | 66 |
| **B: 7 ♕d2** | 67 |
| **C: 7 ♕b3** | 68 |
| **D: 7 e3** | 69 |

The exchange 7 cxd5 exd5 permits Black free development:

a) 8 e3 0-0 9 ♗d3 (9 ♗e2 ♗e6 10 0-0 ♘d7 11 ♖c1 c5 12 dxc5 ♘xc5 13 ♘d4 ♕b6 = Nei-Geller, Cappelle la Grande 1993) 9...c5 10 dxc5 ♗xc3+ 11 bxc3 ♘d7 12 ♖c1 ♘xc5 13 ♗b1 b6 14 0-0 ♗a6 15 ♖e1 ♖e8 = Pfleger-Gligorić, Plovdiv Echt 1983.

b) 8 g3 0-0 9 ♗g2 c6 10 0-0 ♗e7 11 ♕c2 ♗e6 12 e3 ♘d7 13 ♘e2 g6 14 ♘f4 ♗f5 15 ♕e2 ♖e8 16 ♖fd1 ♘f6 17 ♘d3 ♗d6 = Timman-Kavalek, Bugojno 1982.

## A)

**7 e4 dxe4 8 ♘xe4 ♘c6**

Black exerts pressure on White's centre.

**9 ♘xf6+**

White has also tried 9 d5 ♘c5 10 ♘xf6+ (10 ♗e2 0-0 11 ♕b3 exd5 12 cxd5 c6 ∓ Romanishin-Geller, USSR Ch (Tbilisi) 1978) 10...♕xf6 11 ♘xe5 ♕xe5+ 12 ♕e2 ♕f6 13 g3 0-0 14 ♗g2 ♖e8 15 0-0 ♗d7 16 ♕c2 exd5 17 cxd5 ♖ac8 18 ♖fe1 ½-½ Nikolić-Tal, Wijk aan Zee 1982.

**9...♕xf6 10 ♕d2**

10 ♕d3 0-0 (also possible is 10...b6 11 ♕e4 ♗b7 12 ♘e5 0-0-0 13 ♘xc6 ♖d6 14 ♘xa7+ ♔b8 15 ♕e5 ♔xa7 16 0-0-0 ♖hd8 ½-½ Ghitescu-Geller, Palma de Mallorca 1989) 11 ♕e4 ♗d7 12 ♗d3 g6 13 0-0 ♘b4 (13...♖fd8 14 ♖ad1 ♖ab8 15 ♕e3 ♔g7 16 ♖fe1 ± Beliavsky-T.Georgadze, USSR Ch (Tbilisi) 1978) 14 ♘e5 ♗c6 =.

**10...♗d7**

10...0-0 is also possible:

a) 11 ♕e3 ♘b4! (11...♖d8 12 0-0-0 b6 13 ♗d3 ♗b7 14 ♗e4 ♘a5 15 ♗xb7 ♘xb7 16 ♕e5 ♕g6 ∞ Bondarevsky-Chekhover, Kiev 1940) 12 ♕b3 c5 13 dxc5 ♘a6 14 0-0-0 ♘xc5 = Matulović-Ivkov, Sousse IZ 1967.

b) 11 ♕c3 e5! (11...b6?! 12 ♗d3 ♗b7 13 ♗e4 ♖fd8 14 ♖d1 ± Goldenov-Kasparian, USSR Ch (Moscow) 1952) 12 dxe5 ♖e8 13 0-0-0 ♘xe5 14 ♘xe5 ♖xe5 15 ♖d8+ ♕xd8 16 ♕xe5 ♗e6 17 ♗e2 ♕d7 (intending ...♕a4) 18 b3 ♖d8 19 ♖d1 ♕e7 20 f4 ♖xd1+ 21 ♗xd1 ♔f8 = P.Nikolić-Rukavina, Vrbas 1982.

**11 ♕e3**

11 ♕c3 0-0-0 12 b4?! e5! 13 d5 ♘d4 14 ♘d2 ♗f5 15 ♖c1 g5 16 ♗d3 ♕g6 17 ♗xf5+ ♕xf5 18 f3 g4 ∓ Wendelius-Hultunen, corr. 1989.

**11...0-0-0 12 ♗e2 ♖he8 13 0-0 ♔b8 14 ♘e5 ♘xe5 15 dxe5 ♕g5**

½-½ B.Vladimirov-Kholmov, Leningrad 1967.

**B)**

**7 ♕d2** *(D)*

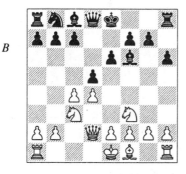

White's aim is to play e2-e4 in one move.

**7...dxc4!**

After 7...b6 8 0-0-0! ♗b7 9 cxd5 exd5 10 ♔b1 ♘d7 11 e3 ♘f8 12 ♘e5 a6 13 f4 White has an advantage.

Or 7...0-0 8 e4! and now:

a) 8...dxe4 9 ♘xe4 b6 10 0-0-0 ♗b7 11 ♕e3 c5 (11...♘d7 12 h4 c5 13

d5 exd5 14 cxd5 ± Ro.Hernandez-J.C.Diaz, Havana 1985) 12 d5 exd5 13 cxd5 ♗d4 14 ♘xd4 ♕xd5 15 ♘b5 ♕xe4 16 ♕xe4 ♗xe4 17 ♘c7 ± Lerner-Bangiev, USSR 1982.

b) 8...c5 9 cxd5 cxd4 10 ♘xd4 exd5 11 exd5 ♘c6 12 ♘c2 ♖e8+ 13 ♘e3 ♘d4 14 ♗d3 ♘f5 15 ♗xf5 ♗xf5 16 0-0 ♗d7 with compensation, Tukmakov-Speelman, Moscow 1985.

**8 e4 c5 9 d5**

9 e5 can be met by 9...cxd4 10 exf6 dxc3 11 ♕xd8+ ♔xd8 12 fxg7 ♖g8 13 bxc3 (or 13 ♗xc4 ♖xg7) 13...♖xg7 14 g3 b6 15 ♗g2 ♗b7 ∓ analysis.

**9...exd5 10 e5**

Other continuations are worse. For example: 10 exd5 0-0 11 ♗xc4 ♖e8+ 12 ♗e2 ♗g4 13 0-0 ♗xf3! 14 ♗xf3 ♘c6! intending ...♘d4; 10 ♕xd5 ♕b6 11 ♗xc4 ♗e6 12 ♕d3 ♕xb2 −+; or 10 ♘xd5 ♘c6 11 ♗xc4 ♗g4 12 ♘xf6+ ♕xf6 ∓ (analysis).

**10...♗g5 11 ♕xd5**

11 ♘xg5!? deserves serious attention: 11...hxg5 12 ♕xd5 (but not 12 ♘xd5 ♖h4! 13 f4 gxf4 14 ♗xc4 ♘c6 15 0-0 ♗e6 −+) 12...♕b6!? with unclear play.

**11...♘c6**

11...♗e6?! is dubious due to 12 ♕xb7 ♘d7 13 ♕e4 ♘b6 14 ♖d1 ♕c8 15 ♘xg5 hxg5 16 ♗e2 g4 17 0-0 0-0 18 ♖d6 ± P.Nikolić-Wedberg, Lugano 1987.

**12 ♗xc4**

But not 12 ♕xc5 ♗e6 13 ♗xc4? in view of 13...♗e7 14 ♕b5 a6 15 ♕xb7 ♘a5, when Black wins a piece.

**12...0-0** *(D)*

**13 0-0**

On 13 ♕xc5 there is the unpleasant reply 13...♗g4!, and in the case of 13

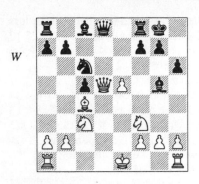

W

♕e4 ♖e8 Black develops counterplay against the e5-pawn.

**13...♕xd5 14 ♗xd5**

14 ♘xd5 is worse due to 14...♗e6 threatening ...♘c6-a5.

**14...♘b4! 15 ♗e4**

15 ♗c4 is strongly answered by 15...♗f5!, while 15 ♘xg5 is answered by 15...♘xd5 (15...hxg5 16 ♗e4! intending to meet 16...f5 with 17 exf6 ±) 16 ♘xd5 hxg5 17 f4 (17 ♖fd1 ♗e6 18 ♘c7 ♖ad8 is slightly better for Black) 17...gxf4 and now:

a) 18 ♘e7+ ♔h7 19 ♖xf4 (19 ♘xc8 ♖axc8 20 ♖xf4 ♔g8 ∓ Hafner-Shestoperova, corr. 1985) 19...g6 20 ♖c1 (but not 20 ♖f6 ♔g7 21 ♖af1 ♗d7 22 e6?! ♗xe6 23 ♘xg6 ♖fe8!) 20...b6 21 b4 ♗e6! (21...cxb4?! 22 ♘xc8 ♖axc8 23 ♖xc8 ♖xc8 24 ♖xf7+ and 25 ♖xa7 ±) 22 bxc5 ♖fe8 23 ♘c6 ♗xa2 =.

b) 18 ♖xf4 ♖d8! 19 ♘c7 ♖b8 20 ♖af1 ♖d7 21 ♘b5 ♖e7 22 ♘xa7 ♗d7 23 a4 ♖a8 24 ♘b5 ♗xb5 (24...g5!? 25 ♖e4 ∞) 25 axb5 ♖a5 26 b6 ♖b5 = Karpov-Kasparov, Moscow Wch (21) 1984/5.

**15...f5!**

But not 15...♖b8 16 a3 ♘a6 17 ♘xg5 hxg5 18 ♘b5 ♗d7 19 ♘d6 b5

20 f4 gxf4 21 ♖xf4 with a slight advantage for White, Beliavsky-H.Olafsson, Thessaloniki OL 1984.

**16 ♗d5+**

16 exf6 can be met by 16...♗xf6!, and 16 ♗b1 by 16...♗e6. In both cases Black has good play.

**16...♘xd5 17 ♘xd5 ♗d8 18 ♖fd1 ♖e8 19 ♖ac1 b6 20 b4 cxb4 21 ♘xb4 ♗b7 22 ♘c6 ♗g5! 23 ♘xg5 hxg5 24 ♖d7 ♗xc6 25 ♖xc6 ♖ad8**

with equality, Ubilava-Dorfman, Tashkent 1984.

**C)**

**7 ♕b3** *(D)*

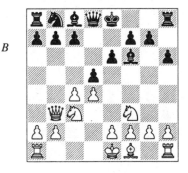

B

This aggressive but slightly loosening move is best met with active counterplay.

**7...dxc4**

Also possible are:

a) 7...c5!? 8 dxc5 dxc4 9 ♕xc4 0-0 10 ♖c1 (or 10 e3 ♕a5 11 ♘d4 ♘a6 12 ♘b3 ♕c7 13 ♗d3 ♗e7 14 ♘b5 ♕e5 15 ♕d4 ♘xc5 16 ♘xc5 ½-½ Gligorić-A.Petrosian, Erevan 1989) 10...♗d7 11 g3 (or 11 e3 ♕e7 12 ♗d3 ♗c6 13 e4 ♘d7 14 b4 b6 15 b5 ♗d5! ∓ Malaniuk-Kruppa, Kiev 1986) 11...♕a5 12 ♗g2 ♗b5 13 ♕b3 ♗c6 14 0-0 ♘a6

= Lerner-Beliavsky, USSR Ch (Kiev) 1986.

b) 7...c6 also seems interesting: 8 0-0-0 (the most critical reply; 8 ♖d1 can be met by 8...0-0 9 e4 dxe4 10 ♘xe4 ♗e7 11 ♗e2 ♕a5+ 12 ♖d2 ♘d7 13 0-0 e5 = Lerner-M.Gurevich, USSR Ch (Kiev) 1986) and then:

b1) 8...♘d7 9 e4 0-0 (9...dxe4 10 ♘xe4 0-0 11 g4 ±; 9...dxc4 10 ♗xc4 0-0 11 e5 ♗e7 12 ♗d3 b5 13 ♗c2 ♗b7 14 ♘e4 intending ♕d3 ± Ftačnik) 10 cxd5 cxd5 11 h4 ♘b6 12 e5 ♗e7 13 ♗d3 ♗d7 14 ♔b1 ∞ Levenfish-Makogonov, USSR Ch (Moscow) 1940.

b2) 8...dxc4 9 ♕xc4 b5 10 ♕b3 a5 11 e4 a4 12 ♕c2 ♘d7 (also possible is 12...♘a6!? 13 ♔b1 0-0 14 h4 a3 15 b3 ♘b4 16 ♕d2 ♗b7 17 ♕e3 ♕a5 ∞ P.Cramling-Gurieli, Groningen wom Ct 1997; 12...a3!? 13 b3 ♘a6 14 e5 ♘b4 15 ♕e4 ♗e7 ∞ von Herman-Klovans, Berlin 1998) 13 d5 ∞ Timman-Yusupov, Tilburg Ct (6) 1986.

**8 ♕xc4 0-0**

8...a6!?, intending ...b5 and ...♗b7, is very interesting: 9 ♘e4 ♗e7 10 ♖c1 0-0 11 e3 ♗d7! 12 ♘e5 (12 ♗d3 ♗b5 13 ♕c2 c6 14 0-0 ♗xd3 15 ♕xd3 ♘d7 = Lerner-Van der Sterren, Tallinn 1987) 12...♗d6 13 ♘xd7 ♘xd7 14 ♗e2 ♘f6 15 ♘c5 ♗xc5 16 ♕xc5 c6 17 0-0 ♕d5 18 ♕a3 ♖ad8 19 ♗f3 ♕d6 20 ♕a5 ♖fe8 = Yusupov-Lputian, Kazan 1997.

**9 g3**

If 9 ♖d1?! then 9...a6! 10 e3 b5 11 ♕b3 ♘d7 12 ♗d3 c5 13 ♗b1 ♕b6 ∓ Rashkovsky-Lputian, USSR Ch (Kiev) 1986.

9 e4!? seems interesting: 9...a6 (9...b6!? 10 e5 ♗e7 11 0-0-0 ♗b7 12 ♗d3 ♕d7 13 ♗e4 ♗xe4 14 ♘xe4 ♕c6

= Timman-Beliavsky, Frankfurt rpd 1998) 10 e5 ♗e7 11 ♗d3 (11 ♕e2 c5 12 dxc5 ♗xc5 13 ♕e4 ♕b6 =) 11...b5 12 ♕b3 c5 13 ♗e4 ♖a7 14 dxc5 ♗xc5 15 0-0 ♕b6 16 ♖ad1 ♘d7 17 ♗b1 ♖c7 18 ♕c2 and now 18...f5 and 18...g6!? are both unclear (analysis).

**9...♘d7 10 ♗g2**

10 ♖d1!? deserves attention: 10...b6 (10...a6?! 11 ♗g2 b5 12 ♕c6 ±; 10...c5 11 dxc5 ♕e7 12 b4 a5 13 a3 ∞) 11 ♗g2 ♗b7 12 0-0 with a slight advantage for White.

**10...e5 11 d5 ♘b6 12 ♕b3 e4!?**

12...♗f5?! 13 ♘d2 ♖b8 14 0-0 c6 15 e4 ♗d7 16 ♖fd1 ± Uhlmann-Hjartarson, Leningrad 1984.

**13 ♘xe4 ♘xd5 14 0-0 c6 15 ♖ad1 ♕e7**

The game is equal. Play might continue 16 ♘xf6+ ♘xf6 17 ♘d4 c5 18 ♘b5 ♕xe2 19 ♖fe1 ♕g4 (19...♕h5!?) 20 ♘d6 ♖b8 21 ♕a3 ♕b4 22 ♕xa7 ♗g4 ∞ (analysis).

**D)**

**7 e3 0-0** *(D)*

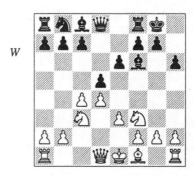

This is the main position of the variation. White has several continuations:

D1: 8 cxd5      70
D2: 8 ♕b3      70
D3: 8 ♕d2      72
D4: 8 ♕c2      76
D5: 8 ♖c1      78

**D1)**
**8 cxd5 exd5 9 ♗d3**
White can also play:
a) 9 ♕d2 ♗f5 10 ♗d3 ♕d7 11 0-0
♘c6 12 ♖ac1 ♗xd3 13 ♕xd3 ♘e7 =
Spiridonov-Lalev, Varna 1983.
b) 9 ♕c2 ♘c6 10 ♗e2 ♘e7 11 b4
(11 0-0 ♗f5 =) 11...♗f5 12 ♕b3 a6 13
0-0 c6 = Uhlmann-Spasov, Warsaw
1983.
c) 9 ♗e2 c6 10 0-0 ♗e7! (Black
hinders the b4 advance while transfer-
ring his bishop to a more convenient
location) 11 a3 (alternatively, 11 ♖b1
♗d6 {11...a5!?} 12 b4 a6 13 a4 ♕e7
14 b5 a5 15 ♘e1 ♘d7 16 ♘d3 ♘f6 17
♗f3 ♗f5 = Kodinets-Lugovoi, Moscow 1998) 11...♘d7 12 b4 a6 13 ♕b3
♗d6 14 a4 ♕e7 15 b5 a5! = Bönsch-
Vaganian, Tallinn 1983.
d) 9 b4 (preventing ...c5 and seizing space) 9...c6 and now:
d1) 10 ♗e2 ♗e6 11 0-0 (11 ♕b3
♕d6 12 0-0 ♘d7 13 ♖fd1 b5 14 a4 a6
15 ♘e1 ♗f5 16 a5 ♗d8 17 ♖ac1 ♗c7
18 g3 ♘f6 = Blocker-Mikhalchishin,
Mexico 1980) 11...♘d7 and then:
d11) 12 ♖c1 ♖c8 (also possible is
12...♕e7 13 ♕b3 ♖fc8 14 a4 a5 15
bxa5 ♖cb8 = Nesterov-Geller, Tiras-
pol 1994) 13 ♘a4 b5 14 ♘c5 ♘xc5
½-½ Ubilava-Azmaiparashvili, San
Sebastian 1991.
d12) 12 ♕b3 a6 13 a4 ♕e7 14 ♘e1
a5 15 ♘d3 axb4 16 ♘xb4 ♖a5 17
♖fb1 ♕d6 18 ♘d3 ♖b8 = Seirawan-
Lutz, Wijk aan Zee 1995.

d2) 10 ♗d3 ♗g4 (10...♗e6 = Beliavsky) 11 0-0 ♕d6 12 ♖b1 ♘d7 13 h3
♗h5 14 b5 ♗d8! 15 bxc6 bxc6 16 ♖b7
♗c7 17 g4 ♗g6 18 e4 dxe4 19 ♘xe4
♕f4 20 ♘g3 ♘f6 21 ♗xg6 fxg6 22
♘h4 ♕g5 23 ♘f3 ½-½ Razuvaev-
Yusupov, Ashkhabad 1978.
**9...c5 10 dxc5 ♗xc3+ 11 bxc3 ♕a5**
Also possible is 11...♘d7 12 0-0 (or
12 ♖c1 ♘xc5 13 ♗b1 b6 14 0-0 ♗a6
15 ♖e1 ♖e8 16 ♕d4 ♖c8 = Pfleger-
Gligorić, Plovdiv Echt 1983) 12...♘xc5
13 ♗c2 ♗e6 14 ♘d4 ♖c8 = Gufeld-
Lein, USSR 1967.
**12 0-0 ♕xc5 13 ♖c1**
Or 13 ♕b3 b6 14 h3 ♗b7 15 ♖fd1
♖c8 16 ♕a4 ½-½ Dydyshko-Filip,
Bangalore 1981.
**13...♘c6 14 c4 ♗e6**
= Cortlever-Kurajica, Wijk aan Zee
1970.

**D2)**
**8 ♕b3** *(D)*

B

**8...c6**
A solid reply. However, 8...c5!? is
also possible:
a) 9 dxc5 and now:
a1) 9...♘a6!? 10 cxd5 ♘xc5 11
♕a3 (11 ♕b4!?) 11...♕b6 12 ♗e2

♖d8 13 0-0 exd5 14 ♖fd1 ♗e6 15 ♘d4 ♖ac8 16 ♖ac1 ♘e4 = Farago-Geller, Amsterdam 1987.

a2) 9...♘d7!? 10 cxd5 ♕a5 11 ♖c1 exd5 12 ♕a3 ♕xa3 13 bxa3 ♖d8 (the only move; 13...♘xc5 14 ♘xd5 ±) 14 ♘xd5 ♗b2 15 ♖d1 ♗xa3 16 ♗c4 ♗xc5 (16...♔f8! =) 17 ♘c7 ♖b8 18 ♘e5 ♘xe5 19 ♖xd8+ ♔h7 20 ♗d3+ g6 21 ♖d5 ♘xd3+ 22 ♖xd3 ♗f5 offers compensation, P.Nikolić-Portisch, Reykjavik 1988.

a3) 9...♕a5 10 cxd5 exd5 11 ♗e2 (11 ♖c1 ♘c6 12 ♗e2 d4 13 exd4 ♗xd4 14 0-0 ♗xc5 15 ♖fd1 ♖b8 16 ♘e4 ♗e6 17 ♗c4 ♗xc4 18 ♕xc4 ♗e7 19 ♖d5 ♕b6 20 ♖b5 ♕d8 21 h3 a6 22 ♖d5 ♕b6 23 b3 ♖bd8 = Dreev-Kotronias, Moscow 1989) 11...♘d7 12 0-0 ♘xc5 13 ♕xd5 ♗e6 14 ♕h5 ♕b4 15 ♘d4 ♗xd4 16 exd4 ♕xd4 17 ♖fd1 ♕b4 18 ♗f3 ♖ac8 19 ♖ab1 b6 20 ♕e5 ♘d7 21 ♕e3 ♘f6 22 ♖d4 ♖c4 23 a3 ♕c5 is equal, Szabo-Flesch, Budapest 1963.

b) 9 cxd5 cxd4 10 ♘xd4 and then:

b1) 10...♗xd4 11 exd4 ♕h4 12 dxe6 fxe6! (12...♕xd4 13 ♕d5 ♕xd5 14 ♘xd5 ♘c6 15 ♘c7 ♖b8 16 ♗c4 ♗xe6 17 ♘xe6 ♖fe8 18 0-0-0 fxe6 19 ♖he1 ± Kožul-Mikhalchishin, Ljubljana 1997) 13 0-0-0 ♕xf2 14 ♗c4 ♘c6 15 ♗xe6+ ♗xe6 16 ♕xe6+ ♔h8 with compensation – Mikhalchishin.

b2) 10...exd5 11 ♗e2 (11 ♕xd5 ♕b6 with compensation) 11...♘c6 12 ♖d1 ♗xd4 13 exd4 ♕h4 14 ♕a4 ♗g4 15 ♗xg4 ♕xg4 16 0-0 ♖ad8 17 h3 ♕d7 ½-½ Christiansen-Portisch, Reggio Emilia 1987/8.

**9 ♖d1** (D)

White also has sharper continuations at his disposal:

a) 9 ♗d3 ♘d7 10 0-0 dxc4 11 ♕xc4 c5 12 ♗c2 cxd4 13 exd4 ♘b6 14 ♕d3 g6 = analysis.

b) 9 h4 g6 10 g4 ♗g7 ∞.

c) 9 g4 ♘d7 (9...g6!?) 10 h4 g6 11 g5 hxg5 12 hxg5 ♗g7 13 0-0-0 ♕e7 14 cxd5 exd5 15 ♗d3 ♖d8 16 ♖h4 b5 17 ♔b1 ♗b7 18 ♖dh1 a6 19 ♖1h3 c5 20 ♕d1 ♕d6 21 ♕h1 ♔f8 22 ♖h7 c4 ∞ analysis.

d) 9 0-0-0 ♘d7 and then:

d1) 10 e4 dxc4 11 ♗xc4 e5! (or 11...b5 12 ♗e2 ∞) 12 d5 (12 dxe5 ♗xe5 intending to meet 13 ♘xe5 by 13...♕g5+) 12...♘c5 13 ♕c2 ♕b6 14 h3 a5 15 ♔b1 ♗d7 is equal, Filip-Zita, Prague 1963.

d2) 10 h4 g6 11 e4 (11 h5 g5 12 e4 dxc4 13 ♗xc4 b5 14 ♗e2 ∞) 11...♘b6! 12 e5 (12 c5 dxe4; 12 g4 ♗g7 13 g5 h5 14 e5 ∞) 12...♗g7 13 h5 g5 14 ♗d3 f5 15 exf6 ♕xf6 ∞ analysis.

d3) 10 g4 ♗h4! 11 ♕c2 ♕e7 12 ♗d3 dxc4 13 ♗xc4 e5 14 ♗b3 exd4 15 exd4 ♘b6 16 ♖hg1 ♗e6 = Ro.Hernandez-Spassky, Tallinn 1975.

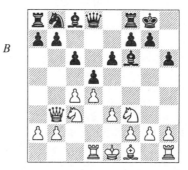

**9...♘d7**

Other moves also deserve attention:

a) 9...♕b6!? 10 ♕c2 dxc4 11 ♗xc4 c5 12 ♘e4 ♗e7 13 dxc5 ♗xc5 14 0-0

♗e7 15 ♗e2 ♗d7 16 ♘e5 ♖c8 17
♕d3 ♗e8 18 ♘c4 ♕c7 19 ♘ed6 ♖d8
20 ♘xe8 ♖xe8 21 ♗f3 ♖d8 22 ♕b3
♘c6 = Kasparov-Timman, Amsterdam 1988.

b) 9...a5!? 10 ♕c2 (10 a3 a4 11
♕c2 ♕a5 12 ♗e2 ♘d7 13 0-0 ♘b6 =
Yusupov-Vaganian, Rotterdam 1989)
10...b6 11 ♗e2 ♗b7 12 0-0 g6 13 e4
♘a6! ∞ I.Farago-Glimbrant, Dieren
1990.

**10 ♗d3**

White gains nothing by 10 ♗e2 b6
11 0-0 ♗b7 12 e4 dxe4 13 ♘xe4 c5!
14 ♘d6 ♕c7 15 ♘xb7 ♕xb7 16 ♘e5
♗xe5 17 ♗f3 ♕c7 18 ♗xa8 cxd4 19
♕f3 ♗xh2+ 20 ♔h1 ♗e5 = (analysis)
or 10 ♕c2 b6 11 e4 dxe4 12 ♕xe4
♗b7 13 ♗d3 g6 14 ♘e5 ♗g7 15 0-0
♕c7 = Dreev-Beliavsky, USSR Ch
(Odessa) 1989.

**10...♕b6**

Black is worse after 10...♖b8 11 0-0
(11 ♕c2 dxc4 12 ♗xc4 b5!? 13 ♗e2
♕a5! = Nikolić-Vaganian, Lucerne
Wcht 1989) 11...b5 12 cxb5 cxb5 13
♖c1 (13 ♘e2!? intending ♗b1 and
♘f4) 13...a6 14 ♘e2 e5 15 dxe5 ♘xe5
16 ♘fd4! ± Yusupov-Bönsch, Baden-
Baden 1992.

However, 10...b6 deserves attention: 11 0-0 (11 cxd5 cxd5 12 e4 dxe4
13 ♗xe4 ♖b8 14 0-0 b5! = Kasparov-
Karpov, Moscow Wch (3) 1985)
11...♗b7 12 ♖fe1 ♗e7 (12...♖e8 13
♗b1 ♖c8 14 cxd5 exd5 15 e4 ♘f8 16
e5 ♗e7 17 ♕c2 ♖c7 18 a3 ♗c8 19 h3
g6 20 ♕d2 ♔g7 21 ♘h2 ± Yusupov-
Short, Barcelona 1989) 13 e4 dxc4 14
♗xc4 b5 15 ♗d3 ♕b6 16 e5 ♖fd8 17
♗e4 ♖ac8 18 h4 a6 19 ♕c2 ♘f8 20 h5
♖d7! ∞ Yusupov-Spraggett, Quebec
Ct (1) 1989.

11 ♕c2 dxc4 12 ♗xc4 c5 13 0-0
cxd4 14 exd4 ♕c7!

But not 14...♕a5 15 ♘e4 ♗e7 16 d5
exd5 17 ♖xd5 ♕c7 18 ♖h5 ± Hulak-
Sr.Cvetković, Yugoslavia 1984.

**15 ♘b5**

15 ♗b3 b6 16 d5 exd5 (16...♘e5!?)
17 ♘xd5 ♕xc2 =.

**15...♕c6 16 ♕e2**

16 d5!? deserves attention: 16...exd5
17 ♖xd5 ♔h8 18 b4 ∞.

**16...a6 17 ♘c3 b5 18 ♗b3 ♗b7 19
d5 exd5 20 ♘xd5**

20 ♗xd5 ♕b6 =.

**20...♖fe8**

= analysis.

**D3)**

**8 ♕d2** (D)

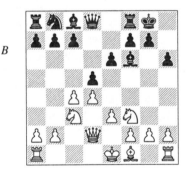

**8...dxc4**

Other continuations are also possible:

a) 8...c6 and now:

a1) 9 h4 g6 10 g4 ♗g7 (a typical
device in this type of position: Black
takes the sting out of White's kingside
pawn-storm) 11 g5 (11 h5 g5) 11...h5
12 ♘e5 (12 0-0-0 ♕a5 13 ♔b1 dxc4 14
♕c2 {14 ♗xc4 b5 ∓} 14...b5 15 ♘e5
♗xe5 16 dxe5 ♘a6 17 ♗g2 ♖b8 ∓

Klauser-Hort, Biel 1991) 12...c5! 13 f4 cxd4 14 exd4 ♘c6 = Spassky-S.Cvetković, Lugano 1984.

a2) 9 ♖d1 and then:

a21) 9...b6!? 10 cxd5 (10 ♗d3 ♗a6 11 b3!?∞) 10...cxd5 11 ♗d3 ♗a6 12 0-0 ♗xd3 13 ♕xd3 ♘c6 14 ♖c1 ♕d7 15 ♖fd1 ♕b7 = Smyslov-Beliavsky, Lvov 1978.

a22) 9...♘d7 10 ♗d3 (10 ♗e2 b6 11 0-0 ♗b7 12 cxd5 cxd5 13 ♖c1 ♕e7 14 ♖c2 a6 15 a4 ♕d6 16 ♖fc1 ♖ac8 17 ♘a2 ♗e7 18 ♘e1 ♘b8 = A.Shneider-Vaganian, Telavi 1982) 10...a6!? 11 0-0 b5 12 cxd5 cxd5 13 ♗b1 ♗b7 14 ♘e2 ♕e7 15 ♘f4 g6 16 ♖c1 ♖fc8 17 ♘d3 ♕d6 18 ♖xc8+ ♖xc8 19 ♖c1 = Agzamov-Klovans, Moscow 1979.

a3) 9 0-0-0 ♘d7 and then:

a31) 10 g4 g6 11 h4 ♗g7 12 g5 h5 (12...hxg5!? 13 hxg5 b5!? 14 cxb5 cxb5 15 ♗xb5 ♖b8 16 ♗xd7 ♗xd7 17 ♘e5 ♕c7 18 f4 ♗a4 19 ♖dg1 ♖fc8 20 ♖g3 ♕a5 21 ♘d3 ♗b3 with compensation, Psakhis-Bönsch, Lvov 1984) 13 e4 and then:

a311) 13...dxc4!? 14 e5 (14 ♗xc4 b5! 15 ♗b3 a6 16 ♗e3 {16 ♕f4 ♗b7 17 e5 c5 18 d5 c4 19 ♗c2 ♘c5 ∓ Borges-S.Gonzalez, Cuba 1990} 16...♕c7 17 ♔b1 ∓) 14...b5 15 ♘e4 ♕c7 ∞ Borges.

a312) 13...b5!? 14 cxb5 dxe4 15 ♘xe4 cxb5 16 ♗d3 (16 ♗xb5 ♗b7 {16...♕b6!?} 17 ♖he1 ♘b6 with compensation) 16...♗b7 17 ♖he1 ♘b6 18 ♔b1 ♖c8 19 ♕e2 ♘c4 ∓ Karpeshov-Korneev, Moscow 1998.

a32) 10 e4 dxc4 11 ♗xc4 c5 12 e5 cxd4 13 ♕xd4 ♗e7 14 ♕e4 ♕a5 15 ♗d3 g6 16 ♕f4 ♔g7 17 h4 ♘c5 18 ♗c2 ♗d7 19 ♘h2 ♗c6 20 ♘g4 ♖h8 21 ♘f6 ♖ad8 with an equal position,

Fayard-Spassky, French Ch (Montpellier) 1991.

a33) 10 h4 g6 11 h5 (11 e4 ♗g7 12 cxd5 exd5 13 exd5 cxd5 14 h5 g5 15 ♗d3 ♘f6 16 ♘xg5 ♖e8! 17 ♘f3 ♘e4 with compensation, Tukmakov-Klovans, USSR 1983) 11...g5 12 ♔b1 ♗g7 13 ♗d3 dxc4 14 ♗xc4 and here:

a331) 14...c5!? 15 ♕c2 (15 dxc5!? ♕c7 16 b4 ♘e5 17 ♘b5 ♕b8 18 ♘d6 ♘xf3 19 gxf3 a5 with compensation – Alterman) 15...cxd4 16 ♘xd4 ♕e7 17 f4 ♘b6 ∞ Alterman-Liang Jinrong, Beijing 1997.

a332) 14...♕e7 15 ♕c2 b6 16 ♘h2 ♗b7 17 f4 b5 18 ♗d3 b4 19 ♘a4 gxf4 20 exf4 c5! ∞ P.Cramling-Hort, France 1998.

b) 8...♘c6 9 ♖c1 (9 cxd5 exd5 10 ♗e2 ♗f5 {10...a6!? 11 0-0 ♖e8 12 ♖fc1 ♗e7 13 ♕d1 ♘a7 14 ♘e5 c6 15 ♗h5 ♖f8 16 a4 ½-½ Nikolić-Speelman, Hastings 1989/90} 11 0-0 ♘e7 12 b4 c6 13 ♖fc1 a6 14 a4 ♕d6 = Kasparov-Karpov, Moscow 1981; 9 ♖d1 dxc4 10 ♗xc4 e5 11 d5 ♘e7 12 0-0 ♗g4 = Knaak-Brameyer, E.German Ch (Erfurt) 1973) 9...a6 *(D)* (an important defensive idea: Black is in no hurry to commit himself to ...dxc4 or ...e5) and then:

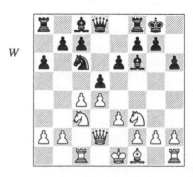

W

b1) 10 h3 dxc4 11 ♗xc4 e5 12 d5 ♘a7 13 0-0 ♘b5 14 ♘xb5 axb5 15 ♗b3 e4 16 ♘d4 ♗e5 17 ♕c2 ♕e8 18 f4 ♗d6 19 ♕e2 ½-½ Timman-H.Olafsson, Reykjavik 1987.

b2) 10 cxd5 exd5 11 ♗d3 (11 g3 ♘e7 12 ♗g2 c6 13 0-0 ♘f5 14 ♘a4 ♘d6 = Lerner-Geller, USSR Ch (Moscow) 1983; 11 ♗e2 ♖e8 12 0-0 ♕d6 13 ♘a4 b6 14 ♖fd1 ♗b7 = Neivelt-Kishniov, Moscow 1981) 11...♘e7!? (11...♗g4 12 0-0 ♕d7 13 ♘e1 ♘e7 14 ♕c2 ♗f5 15 ♗xf5 ♘xf5 16 ♘d3 ± Rogozenko-Grishchak, Lvov 1995) 12 ♕c2 (12 0-0 ♗f5 =) 12...g6 13 0-0 ♗f5 =.

b3) 10 ♗e2 dxc4 11 ♗xc4 e5 12 d5 ♘a7 (12...♘e7?! 13 ♘e4 ♘f5 14 ♗e2 {14 ♗b3!?} 14...♘d6 15 ♘xf6+ ♕xf6 16 0-0 e4 17 ♘d4 ♖e8 18 ♖xc7 ♕g5 19 ♖fc1 ♗h3 20 ♗f1 ♗g4 21 ♕b4! ± Karpov-T.Georgadze, Hanover 1984) 13 ♕c2 (13 ♗e2 ♗f5!; 13 ♘e4 ♗f5 14 ♘c5?! b6! 15 ♘xa6 c5! 16 dxc6 ♘xc6 17 ♗b5 e4 18 ♕xd8 ♖fxd8 with a dangerous initiative for Black, Lerner-Vaganian, USSR Ch (Moscow) 1983) and now:

b31) 13...♗g4 14 ♘d2 ♘b5 15 ♗xb5 axb5 16 ♘xb5 ♖xa2 17 ♘e4! ± Mirallès-Gi.Garcia, Novi Sad OL 1990.

b32) 13...♗d7 14 ♗d3 (14 ♘e4 ♗f5! 15 ♘xf6+ ♕xf6 16 ♗d3 ♗xd3 17 ♕xd3 c6 18 ♕e4 ♖fe8 ½-½ Eingorn-A.Petrosian, USSR Ch (Riga) 1985; 14 0-0 ♘b5 15 ♘e4 ♘d6 16 ♗d3 ♗b5 = Gabriel-Bönsch, Bad Homburg 1996) 14...♘b5 15 ♘e4 ♘d6 16 ♕xc7 ♖c8 17 ♕xd8 ♖xc1+ 18 ♔d2 ♗xd8 19 ♖xc1 ♘xe4+ 20 ♗xe4 ±.

b33) 13...♖e8 is best met by 14 ♗d3! ± rather than 14 0-0 ♗d7 15 ♘e4 ♗f5 16 ♘fd2 ♗e7 17 ♕b3 b5 18 ♗d3 c6 19 dxc6 ♖c8 = Groszpeter-Renet, Novi Sad OL 1990.

b34) 13...♘b5!? (D) and here:

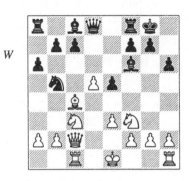

b341) 14 ♗xb5 axb5 15 a3 (15 ♘xb5?! c6! 16 dxc6 bxc6 17 ♘c3 ♗a6 with compensation) should be met by 15...c6! = rather than 15...c5 16 ♘xb5 b6 17 e4 ♗a6 18 a4 ♕d7 19 0-0 ♗xb5 20 axb5 ♕xb5 21 ♖a1 ± Eingorn-Lputian, USSR Ch (Riga) 1985.

b342) 14 ♘xb5 axb5 15 ♗b3 and here:

b3421) 15...♗g4?! 16 ♘d2! (16 0-0 ♖c8 17 ♕e4 ♗xf3 18 ♕xf3 ♗e7 19 ♖fd1 ♗d6 20 ♕e2 b4 = Basin-Klovans, Kostroma 1985) and now:

b34211) 16...♗e7? is bad due to 17 f3! ♗d7 18 ♕xc7 ♖c8 19 ♕xd8 ♖xc1+ 20 ♔e2 +–.

b34212) 16...c5 can be met by 17 dxc6 bxc6 18 0-0 c5 19 f3! ±.

b34213) 16...♖c8 17 ♕d3 ♗d7 (not 17...c6?! 18 d6! ± Zsu.Polgar-Chiburdanidze, St Petersburg wom Ct (3) 1995) 18 ♘e4 ± Chernin-Lputian, USSR Ch (Riga) 1985.

b3422) 15...e4!? and then:

b34221) 16 ♕xe4 ♗xb2 17 ♖c2 ♗a3 18 0-0 ♗d6 (18...♖e8!? 19 ♕d3?!

c5!) 19 ♘d4 ♗d7 20 ♕d3 ♕e8 ∞
Chernin-A.Petrosian, USSR Ch (Riga)
1985.
　b34222) 16 ♘d4 ♗xd4 17 exd4 c6
18 dxc6 ♕xd4 19 0-0 (19 c7 ♗d7! intending ...♗c6) 19...bxc6 20 ♕xc6
♗d7 (20...♖a7!? 21 ♖fd1 {21 ♕xb5?
♗a6; 21 ♕c3 ♕xc3 22 ♖xc3 b4!}
21...♕xb2 22 ♕xb5 ♗e6 =) 21 ♕d5
♕xd5 22 ♗xd5 ♖a6! 23 ♖fd1 (23 a3
b4! 24 axb4 ♖b8 25 ♖fd1 ♗e6 26
♗xe4 ♖ab6 =; 23 ♖c5 ♖c8 24 ♖xc8+
♗xc8 25 ♖c1 ♗e6 26 ♗xe6 fxe6 27
a3 ♖d6 =) 23...♗e6 = Karpov-Kasparov, Moscow Wch (19) 1984/5.
　**9 ♗xc4 (D)**

　**9...c5**
　9...♘d7 is also possible:
　a) 10 ♘e4 ♗e7 11 0-0 c5 12 ♖ac1
(12 ♖fd1!?) 12...cxd4 13 ♘xd4 ♘f6 =
Van der Sterren-Ki.Georgiev, Amsterdam 1985.
　b) 10 h4 e5 (10...c5!?) 11 0-0-0
exd4 12 exd4 ♘b6 13 ♗b3 c6 14 ♕d3
♘d5 15 ♘e5 ± Epishin-Faibisovich,
USSR 1985.
　c) 10 0-0-0 g6 (10...c5!? 11 h4 a6
intending ...b5 ∞) 11 h4 ♗g7 12 ♔b1
a6 13 ♗b3 ♕e7 14 ♖c1 b6 15 d5 (15
♘a4!?; 15 ♘e2 c5 16 ♘f4 ♗b7 17 d5

exd5 18 ♗xd5 ♗xd5 19 ♕xd5 ♘f6 20
♕c4 ♕e4+ 21 ♖c2 ♖fd8 ∓ Sadler-Van
der Sterren, Linares Z 1995) 15...♘c5
=.
　d) 10 0-0 c5 and then:
　d1) 11 ♖ad1 cxd4!? (11...a6 12 a4
cxd4 13 exd4 ♕a5 14 ♕e2 ♘b6 15
♗b3 ♕b4 16 ♗c2 ♖d8 is equal, Mos-
kalenko-Kruppa, Kiev 1986) 12 exd4
♘b6 13 ♗b3 ♗d7.
　d2) 11 ♖fd1 cxd4 12 ♘xd4 ♘b6
and then:
　d21) 13 ♗b3 ♗d7 14 ♘e4 ♗xd4!
15 ♕xd4 ♗c6 16 ♘d6 (16 ♕e5 ♕h4!
=) 16...♕e7 17 e4 ♖ad8 = Beliavsky-
Portisch, Tilburg 1984.
　d22) 13 ♗e2 ♗d7 14 ♗f3 (14 ♕c2
♕e7 =) and now:
　d221) 14...♕b8!? deserves serious
attention: 15 ♖ac1 (15 ♘e4 ♗e7 16 g3
♖d8 17 ♕e2 ♗a4 18 b3 ♗e8 19 ♗g2
♘d5 = Orlov-Kruppa, Podolsk 1989)
15...♖d8 16 ♕e2 a6 17 h3 ♗e8 18 ♘b3
♖xd1+ 19 ♕xd1 ♘a4 20 ♘xa4 ♗xa4
21 ♕d2 ♗xb3 22 axb3 ½-½ Alter-
man-Kruppa, Lvov 1988.
　d222) 14...♖b8 15 ♘e4 ♗xd4 16
♕xd4 ♗a4! (16...♗c6?! 17 ♕c5 and
now 17...♕c7 18 ♘d6 ± or 17...♗d5
18 ♘c3 ±) 17 ♕xd8 (or 17 b3 ♕xd4
18 ♖xd4 ♗c6 19 ♖ad1 ½-½ Grosz-
peter-L.Lengyel, Hungarian Ch 1987)
♖fxd8 18 ♖xd8+ ♖xd8 19 ♘c5 and
White is a little better, Karpov-Kasparov, Moscow Wch (6) 1985.
　**10 dxc5 ♘d7 11 ♘e4 ♗e7 12 c6**
　White returns the pawn in order to
damage Black's pawn-structure. In return, Black obtains an open b-file,
which in tandem with the strong dark-
squared bishop seems to be sufficient
compensation. 12 ♖d1 yields nothing
due to 12...♕c7 13 b4 a5 14 a3 axb4

15 axb4 b6 16 ♘d6 ♖d8! 17 ♘b5 ♕b7 18 ♘d6 with a draw by repetition, Hillarp Persson-McDonald, Hampstead 1998.

**12...bxc6 13 0-0 ♘f6 14 ♕c2 ♗b7**
Fully possible is 14...♘xe4 15 ♕xe4 ♗f6 16 ♖ad1 ♕c7 17 b3 ♗b7 18 ♗d3 g6 19 ♕a4 a5 20 ♘d2 ♖fd8 21 ♗e4 ♗a6 22 ♘c4 ♗b5 23 ♕a3 a4 24 ♕c1 axb3 ½-½ Tukmakov-A.Petrosian, USSR Ch (Riga) 1985.

**15 ♘ed2 c5 16 ♖fd1 ♕c7**
with equality, Korchnoi-Short, Amsterdam 1991.

**D4)**
**8 ♕c2 (D)**

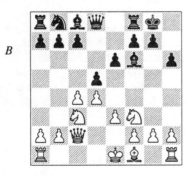

*B*

**8...♘a6!?**
This move was introduced by Kasparov. However, as practice has shown, after 8...c5!? Black can reckon on equality. 9 dxc5 dxc4 and now:
a) 10 ♘e4 and here:
a1) 10...♘d7 11 c6 ♘b6 (11...♕a5+ 12 ♘fd2 c3 13 ♘xc3 ♗xc3 14 ♕xc3 ♕xc3 15 bxc3 bxc6 16 ♘e4 is slightly better for White, Timman-Van der Wiel, Amsterdam 1987) 12 ♖d1 ♕e7 13 ♘xf6+ ♕xf6 ½-½ Browne-Spraggett, Taxco IZ 1985.

a2) 10...♘a6 11 ♘fd2 (11 ♗xc4 ♘xc5 12 ♘xf6+ ♕xf6 13 0-0 ♗d7 14 b4 ♘a4 15 ♖fd1 ♘b6 = analysis) 11...♗e7 12 ♕xc4 f5 13 ♘g3 ♘xc5 14 ♗e2 b5 15 ♕c2 ♗b7 16 0-0 ♖c8 = Åkesson-Schüssler, Malmö 1986.
b) 10 ♗xc4 and then:
b1) 10...♕a5 11 0-0 ♗xc3 (alternatively, 11...♕xc5?! 12 ♘e4 ♕e7 13 ♘xf6+ ♕xf6 14 ♖fd1 ±) 12 ♕xc3 ♕xc3 (12...♕xc5 13 b4 ♕e7 14 ♖fd1 a6 ± Levin-Polovodin, Smolensk 1984) 13 bxc3 ♘d7 14 c6 bxc6 15 ♖ab1 ♘b6 16 ♗e2 c5 17 ♖fc1! and then:
b11) 17...♗b7?! 18 ♔f1 ♗d5 (or 18...♗c6!? 19 ♘e5 ♗a4 20 ♗b5 ♗xb5+ 21 ♖xb5 ♖fc8 22 ♘d3 c4 23 ♘b2 ± Geller) 19 ♖b5! ± Karpov-Kasparov, Moscow Wch (27) 1984/5.
b12) 17...♗d7! 18 ♔f1 ♖fd8 19 ♖b3! (19 ♗b5 ♗xb5+ 20 ♖xb5 ♖ac8 21 ♖a5 ♖c7 =) 19...♖ac8 20 ♖a3 ♖c7 21 c4 ♗a4 22 ♖b1 ♗e8 23 ♖a5 ♔f8 = Novikov-Sturua, Lvov 1985.
b2) 10...♘d7 11 c6 (11 ♘e4 can be met by 11...♘xc5! =; 11 0-0 ♘xc5 12 ♖ac1 ♗d7 13 b4 ♗xc3 14 ♕xc3 ♘e4 15 ♕b2 ♕b6 16 ♖fd1 ♖fd8 =) 11...♘e5 12 ♘xe5 ♗xe5 and then:
b21) 13 ♕e4 ♕a5 14 0-0 bxc6 (Pogorelov-Barsov, Prague 1988) 15 ♕xc6 ♖b8 16 ♗b3 and now 16...♗b7 and 16...♖b4!? both give Black compensation – Barsov.
b22) 13 ♗e2 bxc6 (13...♕c7!? 14 f4 ♗f6 15 ♘e4 ♗e7 16 0-0 bxc6 17 ♖ac1 ♕b6 18 ♖f3 ♖d8 19 ♘d2 c5 20 ♘c4 ♕c7 21 ♗d3 ♗b7 = Levitt-King, London 1988) 14 0-0 ♖b8 15 ♖ac1 c5 16 b3 ♗b7 17 f4 ♗xc3 18 ♕xc3 ♖c8 19 ♗f3 (½-½ Van Wely-Dautov, Belgium 1992) 19...♗xf3 20 ♖xf3 ♕d5 21 ♕c2 ♖fd8 22 ♖ff1 ♕d2 = Dautov.

We now return to 8...♘a6 *(D)*:

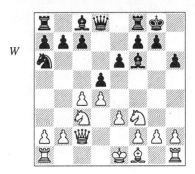

**9 a3**

Other continuations are possible:

a) 9 ♕d2 dxc4 10 ♗xc4 c5 11 ♘e4 cxd4 12 ♘xf6+ ♕xf6 13 ♕xd4 ♕xd4 14 ♘xd4 ♘c5 = Neverov-Rantanen, Tbilisi 1985.

b) 9 c5!? b6! (9...♘b4 10 ♕b3 ♘c6 11 ♗b5! ±) 10 c6 (10 ♕a4 ♘b8 11 cxb6 cxb6 =) 10...♘b8 11 ♕a4 (11 ♘e2!? ♕d6 12 ♖c1 ♖e8 13 a3 ♗a6 14 ♘f4 e5 15 dxe5 ♗xe5 16 ♗xa6 ♘xa6 17 ♘xe5 ♕xe5 18 0-0 ♘c5 =) 11...♕d6 12 ♗b5 a6 13 0-0 ♖a7 (13...♗e7!? intending ...♕b4) 14 ♖fc1 axb5 15 ♕xa7 ♘xc6 16 ♘xb5 ♘xa7 17 ♘xd6 cxd6 18 ♖c7 ♘b5 19 ♖c6 ♗d7 20 ♖xb6 ♖a8 intending ...♗d8 ∞ (analysis).

c) 9 cxd5 ♘b4 and here:

c1) 10 ♕d2 ♘xd5 and then 11 ♖c1 c5 12 ♘xd5 ♕xd5 13 ♖xc5 ♕xa2 14 ♗d3 b6 15 ♖c7 ♗a6 = or 11 ♘e4 ♗e7 12 a3 b6 13 ♘e5 (13 ♖c1 ♗b7 14 ♗d3 f5 intending ...c5) 13...♗b7 14 ♗b5 ♘f6 = analysis.

c2) 10 ♕b3 ♘xd5 11 ♖c1 (11 ♗c4 ♘xc3 12 bxc3 b6 13 0-0 ♗b7 is equal, Nikolić-Ki.Georgiev, Iraklion 1985) 11...♘xc3 12 ♕xc3 (12 ♖xc3 b6 13 ♗b5 c5 14 ♗c6 cxd4 15 exd4 ♖b8 16 0-0 = analysis) 12...c6 (12...♗d7!? 13 ♕xc7 and now rather than 13...♖c8 14 ♕xd8 ♖xc1+ 15 ♔d2 ♖xd8 16 ♔xc1 ♖c8+ 17 ♔d2 ±/± Black should play 13...♕e7 with compensation) 13 ♗e2 ♗d7 14 0-0 ±/= Tal-Balashov, Erevan 1986.

d) 9 ♖d1 c5 10 dxc5 (10 cxd5?! ♘b4! 11 ♕b3 ♘xd5 12 ♗e2 {12 ♘xd5 exd5 13 dxc5 ♕a5+ with compensation; 12 dxc5 ♕a5 =; 12 ♗c4!?} 12...♘xc3 13 bxc3 cxd4 14 cxd4 b6 = analysis) 10...♕a5 11 cxd5 ♘xc5 and then:

d1) 12 a3 ♘a4! ∓.

d2) 12 d6 ♗d7 intending ...♖ac8 with compensation.

d3) 12 ♗e2 is met by 12...♘a4!.

d4) 12 ♗c4 b5!.

d5) 12 dxe6 ♗xe6! (12...♗xc3+?! 13 ♕xc3 ♕xc3+ 14 bxc3 ♗xe6 15 c4 ♗g4 16 ♗e2 ♖fd8 17 ♖xd8+ ♖xd8 18 ♘d4 ± Granda-Robbiano, Peru 1995) 13 ♘d4 ♗d5 14 ♕d2 (14 ♕f5 ♗e4 15 ♕f4 ♖ad8 16 ♗c4 ♘a4 gives Black the initiative) 14...♗c6 15 a3 (15 ♘xc6 bxc6 16 ♗e2 ♖fd8 17 ♕c2 ♘a4 18 0-0 ♗xc3 19 ♖xd8+ ♖xd8 20 bxc3 ♘xc3 21 ♗f3 c5 22 ♖c1 ♘xa2 23 ♕xc5?? ♖d1+! −+; 15 f3 ♖ad8 16 ♗e2 ♖fe8 17 0-0 ♕b6 18 ♗c4 ♕b4 19 ♘xc6 bxc6 20 ♕e2 ♗xc3 ∓) 15...♘a4 16 ♘xc6 bxc6 17 b4 ♗xc3 18 bxa5 ♖ab8 = analysis.

d6) 12 ♕d2 ♖d8 13 ♘d4 (13 ♗e2 ♗xc3 14 ♕xc3 ♕xc3+ 15 bxc3 exd5 16 c4 ♗e6 17 ♘d4 dxc4 18 ♘xe6 ♖xd1+ 19 ♔xd1 fxe6 20 ♗xc4 b5! =) 13...exd5 14 ♗e2 ♕b6 (14...♘e6 15 ♘b3 ♗xc3 16 ♕xc3! ♕xc3+ 17 bxc3 ±) 15 0-0 ♘e4 16 ♕c2 ♘xc3 17 ♕xc3 ♗f5!? (17...♗e6 18 ♕c2 ± Karpov-Kasparov, Moscow Wch (4) 1985) 18

♕d2 ♗e4 19 ♗g4 and now 19...♖e8 =
or 19...a5!? intending ...a4 =.
  d7) 12 ♘d4 exd5 and now:
    d71) 13 a3?! ♘e6! 14 ♘db5? (14
♗e2 ♘xd4 15 exd4 ♗e6 =; 14 ♘b3
♗xc3+ 15 ♕xc3 ♕xc3+ 16 bxc3 ♘c7
=) 14...a6 15 b4?! (White must play 15
♘d4 ♘xd4 16 exd4 ♗g4!) 15...♕d8
16 ♖xd5 ♗d7! 17 ♕d2 (17 ♘d6 ♗c6
18 ♖d1 ♘d4 −+) 17...axb5 18 ♖xd7
(18 ♘e4 ♖xa3 19 ♖xd7 ♖a1+ 20 ♔e2
♕c8 ∓) 18...♕xd7! 19 ♕xd7 ♗xc3+
20 ♔e2 ♖fd8 21 ♕xb7 ♘g5!! 22 e4
♖xa3 23 ♕xb5 ♖a2+ 24 ♔e3 ♗d2+
0-1 Piket-Sturua, Debrecen Echt 1992.
  d72) 13 ♗d3 ♘xd3+ (13...♗g4 14
♖d2 ♖ac8 15 0-0 ♖fd8 16 ♗f5! ♗xf5
17 ♕xf5 ♖d7 18 ♖fd1 ± Van Wely-
Galdunts, Krumbach 1991) 14 ♕xd3
♗e6 15 0-0 ♖fd8 16 ♕b5 (16 ♖d2!?)
16...♕xb5 17 ♘cxb5 ♖ac8! 18 ♖c1 a6
19 ♘c7 ♗xd4 20 exd4 ♗d7! = Van
Wely-Pigusov, Vienna 1991.
  We now return to 9 a3 *(D)*:

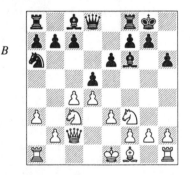

**9...c5!?**
  Or 9...dxc4 10 ♗xc4 c5, and now:
    a) 11 ♖d1 cxd4 12 ♘xd4 ♗d7 13
♗a2! ♕e7 14 h4 ♗xd4 (14...♗xh4 15
♕e4 ♗f6 16 ♘f5! exf5 17 ♕xe7 ♗xe7
18 ♖xd7 ∞) 15 ♖xd4 ♖fd8 16 0-0 ♗c6

17 ♖fd1 ♖xd4 18 ♖xd4 ♖d8 19 ♗b1!
is slightly better for White, Ribli-Beliavsky, Reggio Emilia 1986/7.
    b) 11 0-0 cxd4 12 exd4 ♗d7 13
♖ad1 ♕c7 14 ♕e2 (14 ♗a2!?) 14...♗c6
15 d5 (15 ♘e5!?) 15...exd5 16 ♘xd5
♗xd5 17 ♗xd5 ♕b6 18 b3 ♘c5 19
♕c4 ♖ac8 20 ♖fe1 ♖c7 21 g3 ♘e6 22
♕e4 ♖e7 23 ♕g4 ♖fe8 24 a4 ½-½
Ribli-Beliavsky, Reggio Emilia 1987/8.
  **10 cxd5**
    10 ♖d1 ♕a5 11 cxd5 exd5 12 ♗e2
♗e6 13 0-0 ♖ac8 14 ♕d2 c4 is unclear.
  **10...cxd4 11 ♘xd4 ♗xd4 12 exd4
♘c7 13 dxe6**
    13 ♗c4?! exd5 14 ♗e2 ♕g5 15 ♗f3
♗g4 16 ♗xg4 ♕xg4 17 0-0 ♕xd4 18
♖ad1 ♕c4 19 ♕f5 ♖ad8 ∓ Grigorov-
Magomedov, Pavlodar 1991.
  **13...♘xe6**
    13...♗xe6!? intending ...♘d5 is un-
clear.
  **14 0-0-0 ♘xd4 15 ♕e4 ♘b3+ 16
♔c2 ♕b6 17 ♘d5 ♘c5 18 ♘xb6
♘xe4 19 ♘xa8 ♘xf2**
    The game is unclear. Black's idea is
20 ♘c7 ♗f5+ (20...♘xh1!? ∞) 21 ♗d3
♘xd3 22 ♖xd3 (22 ♘d5?? ♘f2+ 23
♔b3 ♗e6 −+) 22...♖c8 23 ♖c1! ♖d8
24 ♖d1 ♖c8 =.

**D5)**
  **8 ♖c1 *(D)***
  This is the most popular line. Black
has two replies at his disposal:
  **D51: 8...a6**
  **D52: 8...c6**
  The former is the favourite continu-
ation of Short and Vaganian.

**D51)**
  **8...a6 9 a3**

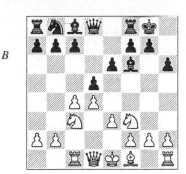

B

White also waits. Practice has seen other continuations too:

a) 9 cxd5 exd5 10 ♗d3 (10 ♗e2 c6 11 0-0 ♘d7 12 ♘e1 ♗e7 13 ♘d3 ♗d6 14 ♗f3 ♖e8 = Piket-Campora, Lugano 1987) 10...♖e8 11 0-0 c6 12 ♕b3 ♘d7 13 ♖fe1 ♘b6 14 h3 ♗e6 15 ♘e2 ♖b8 16 ♘f4 ♘d7 17 ♘xe6 ♖xe6 18 ♗f5 ♖e7 = G.Georgadze-Goldin, Uzhgorod 1987.

b) 9 ♗d3 dxc4 10 ♗xc4 ♘d7 11 ♘e4!? (11 0-0 b5 12 ♗e2 ♗b7 13 ♕c2 c5 = Mikhalchishin-Lputian, Lvov 1986) 11...b6 (11...c5 12 ♘xf6+ ♕xf6 13 0-0, Speelman-Xu Jun, Subotica IZ 1987, 13...b6!? 14 ♕a4 ♕e7!? is equal – Speelman) 12 0-0 ♗b7 13 ♗d3 ♗e7 14 ♕e2 c5 15 ♖fd1 cxd4 16 exd4 ♘f6 17 ♘xf6+ ♗xf6 18 ♗e4 ♕e7 19 ♖c3 ♖ac8 ½-½ Andersson-Short, Wijk aan Zee 1987.

c) 9 ♕c2 c6 (9...♘c6!? 10 a3 ♖e8 11 ♗e2 dxc4 12 ♗xc4 e5 13 d5 ♘e7 14 0-0 ♘f5 15 ♘e4 ♘d6 16 ♗d3 ♘xe4 17 ♗xe4 ♖e7 18 ♕b3 ± Lagunov-Vaganian, Frankfurt rpd 1998) 10 ♗d3 b5 11 c5 ♘d7 12 e4 (12 0-0?! e5! =) 12...e5 13 exd5 exd4 14 ♘e2 (14 ♘e4 is unclear) 14...♕a5+ 15 ♕d2 b4 16 ♘fxd4? ♘xc5 17 ♗b1 cxd5 18 0-0 ♕b6 19 ♖fd1 ♗b7 is much better for

Black, I.Sokolov-Short, Groningen 1996.

**9...c6 10 ♗d3**

10 e4 gives White nothing in view of 10...dxe4 11 ♘xe4 c5! 12 ♘xc5 ♘c6 13 b4 ♘xd4 14 ♗d3 a5! 15 0-0 axb4 16 axb4 ♖a3 = Mikhalchishin-Sabura, Karvina 1987.

**10...♘d7**

The advance 10...b5 is premature: 11 cxb5 cxb5 12 ♗b1!? ♘d7 13 ♕c2 g6 14 h4 h5 15 g4! ± Rashkovsky-Barsov, USSR 1987.

**11 0-0 b5**

The alternative 11...dxc4 deserves attention: 12 ♗xc4 b5 (12...c5!?) 13 ♗e2 (13 ♗a2 c5 14 ♘e4 c4 15 ♘xf6+ ♘xf6 16 b3 cxb3 17 ♗xb3 ♗b7 18 ♘e5 ♖c8 and Black has a slight advantage, Ftačnik-Ki.Georgiev, Varna 1987) 13...c5 14 dxc5 ♘xc5 15 ♕c2 ♗b7 16 ♖fd1 ♕e7 17 b4 ♘d7 18 ♘e4 ± Ki.Georgiev.

**12 cxd5 cxd5 13 ♘e2**

13 ♗b1 yields nothing due to 13...♗b7 14 a4 bxa4 15 ♘xa4 ♖c8 16 ♕d3 g6 17 b4 ♗c6 18 ♕b3 ♗xa4 19 ♕xa4 ♘b8 20 ♗d3 ½-½ Portisch-Short, Brussels 1986.

Or 13 e4 dxe4 14 ♗xe4 (14 ♘xe4 ♗b7 15 ♖e1 ♘b6 16 ♗b1 ♗xe4 17 ♖xe4 ♖c8 18 ♖xc8 ♕xc8 19 ♖e1 ♖d8 20 ♕d3 g6 ∓ Matamoros-Garcia Gonzales, Camaguey 1987) 14...♖b8 15 ♕e2 b4 16 axb4 ♖xb4 17 ♘a2 ♖b8 18 ♖fd1 ♕b6 19 ♖c2 ♖d8 20 ♘c3 a5 ∓ Gligorić-Vaganian, Panormo Z 1998.

**13...♗b7 14 ♗b1 ♖e8**

14...g6!? 15 ♘f4 ♖c8 16 ♕d3 ♕e7 17 h4! h5 18 ♘xh5! (18 ♘xg6!? fxg6 19 ♕xg6+ ♕g7 20 ♕xh5 ♖fd8! 21 ♘g5! ♘f8 22 ♖xc8 ♖xc8 23 f4 ♗c6! ∞ Browne-Vaganian, Saint John 1988)

18...♗xh4 19 ♘xh4 ♕xh4 20 ♘f4 and White is slightly better.

**15 ♕d3**

15 ♕c2!? g6 (15...♘f8 16 ♘e5!? ±) 16 ♕c7 ♖b8 ∞.

**15...g6 16 ♖fe1 ♖c8**

Now Karpov-Short, Brussels 1987 continued 17 ♖xc8 ♕xc8 18 h4 e5 19 dxe5 ♘xe5 20 ♘xe5 ♖xe5 ∞.

**D52)**

**8...c6 9 ♗d3 ♘d7** *(D)*

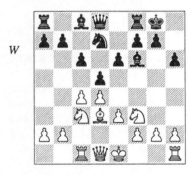

**10 0-0**

White can also play 10 cxd5 exd5 11 b4 (11 0-0 ♗e7 12 ♗b1 ♖e8 13 ♕d3 g6 14 ♖ce1 ♘f8 15 ♕d2 ♔g7 16 ♘e5 f6 17 ♘d3 ♗f5 18 ♘f4 ♗xb1 19 ♖xb1 ♗d6 = Petrosian-Beliavsky, Moscow 1981), and then:

a) 11...♗e7!? seems interesting: 12 b5 ♗a3 13 ♖c2 ♗d6 14 0-0 ♘f6 15 bxc6 bxc6 and here:

a1) 16 ♘a4 ♘e4 17 ♘e5 ♕e8 18 f3 c5 19 fxe4 cxd4 (19...♕xa4? 20 ♘xf7! +−) 20 ♘g4!? dxe4 21 ♗c4 ♗xg4 22 ♕xg4 ♕xa4 23 ♖xf7! (23 ♕xe4 ♖ae8 24 ♕f5 dxe3 25 ♗xf7+ ♔h8 26 ♗xe8 ♕d4! ∓/∓ Cebalo-Van der Sterren, Munich 1989) 23...♖xf7 24 ♗xf7+ ♔xf7 25 ♕f5+ ♔e7 (only move) 26

♕xe4+ ♔d7 27 ♕b7+ ♔e6 28 ♕e4+ ♔d7 ½-½ Tal-Geller, USSR Ch (Tbilisi) 1978.

a2) 16 e4 dxe4 17 ♘xe4 ♖e8 18 ♖e1 ♘xe4 19 ♖xe4 ♗d7 = Lputian-K.Grigorian, Erevan 1980.

b) 11...a6 and now:

b1) 12 0-0 ♗e7 13 ♕b3 ♗d6 14 a4 (14 ♘a4 ♖e8 15 ♘c5 ♘f6 ∞ Rajna-Bönsch, Polanica Zdroj 1987) 14...♘f6 15 ♖fe1 (15 b5 a5 16 ♘e2 ♗d7 17 ♘g3 g6 18 ♖fd1 ♕e7 = Cebalo-Campora, Bern 1987) 15...♗e6 16 ♕b2 ♕e7 = Rajković-Abramov, Subotica 1984.

b2) 12 a4 (White continues his general plan: a queenside minority attack) 12...a5 13 b5 ♗e7 (13...♘b6 14 0-0 ♗g4 15 ♕b3 ± Gligorić-Benko, Palma de Mallorca 1968) 14 0-0 ♖e8 15 ♕b3 ♖b8 16 e4 dxe4 17 ♗xe4 ♘f6 = Tukmakov-Dolmatov, USSR 1981.

**10...dxc4 11 ♗xc4**

We have reached the main position of this variation. Black should undermine White's centre and activate his dark-squared bishop. He can try to do so by:

**D521: 11...c5** 80
**D522: 11...e5** 81

Routine development is worse: 11...b6 12 e4! ♗b7 13 e5 ♗e7 14 ♕e2 b5 15 ♗d3 c5 16 ♘xb5 cxd4 17 ♗e4 ± Karpov-Spassky, Lucerne Wcht 1985.

**D521)**

**11...c5** *(D)*

**12 ♕e2**

The straightforward 12 ♘e4 gives White nothing: 12...cxd4 13 ♘xd4 (13 ♘xf6+ ♕xf6 14 ♕xd4 ♕xd4 15 ♘xd4 ♘b6 and 16...♗d7 =) 13...♘b6 14

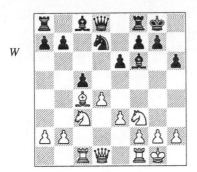

W

♘xf6+ ♕xf6 15 ♗b3 e5 16 ♘b5 ♗d7
17 ♘c3 ♖ad8 18 ♕h5 ♗c6 19 ♖cd1
♖xd1 20 ♖xd1 ♕g5 21 ♕xg5 hxg5 22
f3 ♖c8 23 ♘e4 ♗xe4 24 fxe4 ♔f8 25
♔f2 ½-½ A.Shneider-Faibisovich,
Groningen 1991.

Or 12 dxc5 ♘xc5 13 b4 ♗xc3 14
♖xc3 ♘e4 15 ♖d3 ♕e7 16 ♖d4 ♘f6
(intending ...e5) 17 ♘e5 ♕xb4 18
♗xe6 ♕e7 19 ♗xf7+ ♖xf7 20 ♖d8+
♖f8 21 ♖xf8+ ♕xf8 22 ♕b3+ ♔h7 23
♕c2+ ½-½ A.Petrosian-M.Gurevich,
Baku 1988.

**12...a6**

Black tries extend the diagonal for
the light-squared bishop. Worse is
12...cxd4 13 exd4 ♘b6 14 ♗d3 intending to meet 14...♗d7 with 15 ♕e4
followed by ♖fd1, ♗e4 and ♘e5.

**13 ♖fd1 cxd4**

This is forced; instead 13...b5? fails
to 14 dxc5! ♕e7 (14...♕c7 15 ♗d3)
15 c6 ♘b8 16 ♗b3 ±.

**14 ♘xd4**

Here this is stronger than 14 exd4,
which only superficially gives White a
menacing position. It turns out that after 14...b5 15 ♗b3 ♕b6! Black man-
ages to deploy his forces effectively,
while the thrust 16 d5 just liquidates to
Black's benefit: 16...♘c5 17 ♕e3 ♖b8!

18 dxe6 ♘xb3! 19 exf7+ ♔xf7 20
♕xb6 ♖xb6 21 axb3 ♗e6.

**14...♕e7**

Black must solve his development
problems carefully. 14...b5 is risky in
view of 15 ♗xe6 (15 ♗b3 ♕b6 16
♘e4 ♗b7 =; 15 ♕f3 ♖a7 16 ♘c6 ♗b7
=) 15...fxe6 16 ♘xe6. If 14...♗xd4 15
♖xd4 b5 16 ♗b3 ♕e7, then 17 ♘e4
♘f6 18 ♘xf6+ ♕xf6 19 ♕d2 ±.

**15 ♘e4 ♗e5 16 ♕h5!?**

White gets no advantage from 16
♘f3 (16 f4 ♗b8 intending ...♘f6)
16...♗b8 17 ♕d2! b5 18 ♗e2 ♘f6 19
♘xf6+ (19 ♘c5 e5 20 ♕c2 ♗d6! 21
b4 ♗g4 22 h3 {22 ♘h4 ♖xc5 23 bxc5
♗xe2 24 ♕xe2 g6 25 ♘f3 ♖ac8}
22...♗xf3 23 ♗xf3 ♖ac8 is unclear)
19...♕xf6 20 ♕d4 (Kasparov-Karpov,
London/Leningrad Wch (12) 1986)
20...e5!? 21 ♕e4 (21 ♕b4!?) 21...♖a7
and now 22 ♖c6 ♗f5! 23 ♕d5 ♕e7 or
22 ♗d3 g6 23 ♖c6 ♕g7! with an unclear position – Kasparov.

**16...♖d8 17 ♗f1 ♗b8 18 ♕a5 b6
19 ♕c3 ♗b7 20 ♘c6 ♗xc6 21 ♕xc6**

± Kasparov-H.Olafsson, Dubai OL
1986.

**D522)**
  **11...e5** *(D)*

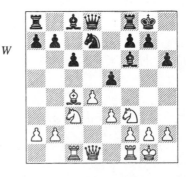

W

**12 h3**

This move was introduced into practice by Kasparov, and presents Black with the greatest problems. Other continuations yield no advantage:

a) 12 ♘e4 exd4 13 ♘xf6+ ♘xf6 and here:

a1) 14 ♘xd4 ♕e7 15 ♕b3 (15 ♗b3 c5 16 ♘b5 ♖d8 17 ♕c2 b6 18 a4 ♗b7 19 ♖fe1 ♕e5 20 ♕e2 ½-½ Bukhman-An.Bykhovsky, Tallinn 1965; 15 ♕e2 c5 16 ♘b5 ♗d7 17 ♘c3 ♗c6 = Terekhov-Rustemov, St Petersburg 1996) 15...c5 (also not bad is 15...♗g4 16 f3 c5 17 ♘e2 ♗d7 18 a4 ♕e8 19 ♖a1 ♖b8 20 e4 b5 21 axb5 ♗xb5 22 ♖xa7 ♗xc4 23 ♕xc4 ♖xb2 = Vaganian-Ivkov, Sochi 1980) 16 ♘e2 b6 (16...♖b8!? 17 a4 ♗d7 18 ♘f4 ♗c6 19 f3 ♖fd8 20 ♖fd1 ♗e8 21 e4 a6 ½-½ Adler-Geller, Bern 1988) 17 ♘f4 ♖d8 18 ♖fd1 ♗b7 19 f3 ♔f8 20 e4 ♗c6 = Dementiev-Klovans, USSR 1970.

a2) 14 ♕xd4 ♕xd4 (also possible is 14...♗g4 15 ♕f4 ♗xf3 16 ♕xf3 ♕d2 17 ♕e2 ♖ad8 18 ♖fd1 ♕xe2 19 ♗xe2 ♖fe8 = Dorfman-Lputian, USSR 1984) 15 ♘xd4 ♖e8 16 ♖fd1 (16 ♖fe1 ♗d7 17 f3 ♖ad8 18 ♔f2 ♗c8 19 ♖ed1 ♘d5 20 e4 ♘c7 21 b4 ♖d6 22 ♘b3 ♖ed8 23 ♖xd6 ♖xd6 24 ♔e3 ♖d8 25 ♖c2 ♔f8 = Portisch-Spassky, Linares 1990) 16...♗d7 17 ♔f1 ♔f8 18 a3 (18 ♔e2 ♖e5 19 h3 c5 20 ♘b5 ½-½ Petrosian-Spassky, Moscow 1979) 18...♖e5 19 ♗e2 a5 20 ♘f3 ♖d5 = Andersson-Spassky, Nikšić 1983.

b) 12 ♗b3 exd4 13 exd4 ♖e8 (13...♘b6?! 14 ♘e5 ±) and then:

b1) 14 ♖e1 ♖xe1+ 15 ♕xe1 ♘f8 16 ♘e4 ♗e6 17 ♕b4 ♗xb3 18 axb3 ♖b8 with equality, Tal-Beliavsky, Lvov 1981.

b2) 14 ♕d2 ♘f8! 15 d5 (15 ♖fe1 ♖xe1+ 16 ♖xe1 ♗e6 is level) 15...♗f5 (15...♗d7!? 16 ♖fd1 ♕b6 ∞) 16 ♕f4 ♗g6 17 dxc6 bxc6 18 ♖fd1 ♕a5 19 ♕a4 ♕b6 20 ♖d6 ♖ac8 21 ♕c4 ♕c7 22 ♖dd1 ♘e6 = Portisch-Spassky, Bugojno 1986.

b3) 14 h3 ♘f8 15 d5 (15 ♖e1 ♖xe1+ 16 ♕xe1 ♗e6 =) and now:

b31) 15...♗xc3 is not bad: 16 ♖xc3 cxd5 17 ♕xd5 (17 ♗xd5 is interesting, since 17...♗e6? loses a pawn after 18 ♗xb7 ♖b8 19 ♗c6) 17...♕xd5 18 ♗xd5 ♖b8 19 ♖d1 (19 ♖c7 ♗e6 =) 19...♗e6 20 ♗xe6 ♘xe6 21 ♖d7 ♖ed8 22 ♖cd3 ♖xd7 23 ♖xd7 ♘c5 24 ♖c7 ♘e6 with equality, Adamski-Cvitan, Valjevo 1984.

b32) 15...♗d7 16 ♖e1 (or 16 ♕d2 ♖c8 17 dxc6 ♗xc6 18 ♘d5 ♘e6 19 ♖fe1 ♗xd5 20 ♖xc8 ♕xc8 21 ♗xd5 ♘c7 = Smejkal-Andersson, Reggio Emilia 1985/6) 16...♖xe1+ 17 ♕xe1 cxd5 18 ♖d1 ♗xc3 19 ♕xc3 ♗e6 20 ♗xd5 ♖c8 21 ♕b3 ½-½ Ribli-Karpov, London 1984.

**12...exd4 13 exd4** (D)

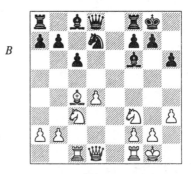

**13...♘b6**

Other continuations have been tried in practice:

a) 13...c5 14 ♗b3 (a cunning move, clearing the c-file and preparing ♘d5; if immediately 14 ♘d5 then 14...♗xd4 15 ♘xd4 cxd4 16 ♕xd4 ♘b6 with equality, or else 14 ♘e4 cxd4 15 ♘xf6+ ♘xf6 16 ♕b3 ♕b6 17 ♖fd1 ♗d7 18 ♖xd4 ♕xb3 19 ♗xb3 ♖ac8 = Tukmakov-Abramović, Bor 1983) 14...cxd4 (14...b6?! 15 ♗d5 ♖b8 16 ♘e4 ±) 15 ♘d5! b6 (15...♘b6 16 ♘xf6+ ♕xf6 17 ♕xd4 ♕xd4 18 ♘xd4 ±/±; 15...♘e5 16 ♘xd4 ♗d7 17 ♖c7! ±; 15...d3 16 ♕xd3 ♗xb2 17 ♖c7! ±) and here:

a1) 16 ♘xf6+!? ♕xf6 (16...♘xf6 17 ♘xd4 ♗d7 {17...♗b7 18 ♘f5} 18 ♕f3 ♖c8 19 ♕f4! ± Nikolić-Korchnoi, Reggio Emilia 1987/8) 17 ♕xd4 ♕xd4 18 ♘xd4 ♘c5 19 ♗d5 ♗a6 20 ♖fd1 ♖ae8 21 b4 ♘d3 22 ♖c7 ♘xb4 23 ♗b3 ♗c8 24 ♖xa7 ♖d8 25 a3 ♖xd4 26 ♖xd4 ♘c6 27 ♖dd7 ♘xa7 28 ♖xa7 ♗e6 = Rashkovsky-Pigusov, Tashkent 1986.

a2) 16 ♘xd4 ♗xd4 (16...♘c5 17 ♘c6 ♕d6 18 ♕f3 is risky for Black, as also is 16...♗b7 17 ♘c6 ♗xc6 18 ♖xc6 with the point that 18...♗xb2? is met by 19 ♖d6) 17 ♕xd4 ♘c5 18 ♗c4 with a slight advantage for White, Kasparov-Karpov, London/Leningrad Wch (10) 1986.

b) 13...♖e8 14 ♕b3 ♖f8 (14...♖e7!? 15 ♖fe1 b5 16 ♗f1 ♖xe1 17 ♖xe1 ♘b6 18 ♘e4 ♗e6 19 ♕c2 ♗d5 20 ♗d3 ♖c8 21 b3 ♗xe4 22 ♗xe4 ♕d6 = Wang Yaoyao-Liang Jinrong, Beijing 1995) 15 ♕c2 ♖e8 16 ♖fe1 (16 ♕g6 ♖e7 17 ♖fe1 ♘f8 18 ♕h5?! ♖xe1+ 19 ♖xe1 ♗e6 20 ♗xe6 ♘xe6 21 ♘e5?!, Dlugy-Abramović, New York 1988, 21...g6! ∓ 22 ♕xh6? {22 ♘xg6? ♗g7} 22...♗g5) 16...♘f8 17 ♖xe8 (17 ♕b3!?

♘e6 18 ♖cd1 ±) 17...♕xe8 18 ♖e1 ♗e6 19 d5 cxd5 20 ♘xd5 ♕d8 21 ♕b3 ♖b8 22 a4 b6 23 ♖d1 ♖b7 24 ♖d2 ♖d7 = Paunović-Abramović, Yugoslavia 1988.

14 ♗b3 (D)

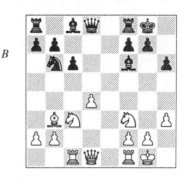

**14...♖e8**

Also possible is 14...♗f5 15 ♖e1 a5:

a) 16 ♘e5 ♗xe5 17 ♖xe5 ♗h7!? (alternatively, 17...♗g6 18 ♕g4 ♔h8 19 a3 a4 20 ♗a2 ♘d7 21 ♖e3 ♘f6 22 ♕d1! b5 23 d5! cxd5 24 ♘xd5 ♖b8 25 ♘e7!, Browne-Barsov, Windsor 1991, 25...♗e4!? 26 ♕xd8 ♖bxd8 27 ♖ce1 ♗a8! 28 ♖e5 ♖b8 ±) 18 a3 ♕d6 19 ♕e2 a4 20 ♗a2 ♕xd4 21 ♖d1 ♕f4 22 ♖e7 ♖ab8 23 ♕d2 ♕xd2 24 ♖xd2 ♗f5 = (analysis).

b) 16 a3 ♖e8 (16...♕d7?! 17 ♘e5 ♗xe5 18 ♖xe5 ♖fe8 19 ♕e2 ± Karpov-Beliavsky, CSKA-Trud 1986) and then:

b1) 17 ♖xe8+ ♕xe8 18 ♕d2 and here:

b11) 18...♘d7?! 19 ♕f4! ♗g6 (or 19...♗e6 20 ♗xe6 ♕xe6 21 ♕c7 ♕b3 22 ♘e4! ♕xb2 23 ♖e1! ♘f8 24 ♘xf6+ gxf6 25 ♕f4 ±) 20 h4! ♕d8 21 ♘a4! h5 22 ♖e1 b5 23 ♘c3 ♕b8 24 ♕e3!? ±

Kasparov-Karpov, London/Leningrad Wch (22) 1986.

b12) 18...♕d7 19 ♖e1 ♖e8 20 ♖xe8+ ♕xe8 21 ♕f4 ♗e6! 22 ♗xe6 ♕xe6 and now:

b121) 23 ♕b8+ ♕c8 24 ♕a7 ♘c4 25 ♕c5 (25 b3 ♘xa3 26 ♕xa5 ♗e7 = Gurevich-Van der Sterren, Baku 1986) 25...♕e6 26 d5 cxd5 27 ♘xd5 ♘xb2 28 ♕xa5 ♘c4 29 ♕a8+ ♔h7 30 ♕xb7 ♘xa3 31 ♕b3 ♗e7 = Ftačnik-H.Olafsson, New York 1987.

b122) 23 ♕c7 ♘c4 24 ♕b8+ (24 ♕xb7 ♗xd4! 25 ♘xd4 ♕e1+ 26 ♔h2 ♕e5+ 27 g3 ♕xd4 28 ♔g2 ♕c5 29 ♕b8+ ♔h7 30 ♕b3 g6 31 ♕c2 ♔g7 =) 24...♔h7 25 ♕xb7 ♗xd4! 26 ♘xd4 ♕e1+ 27 ♔h2 ♕e5+ 28 g3 ♕xd4 29 ♕xf7 ♘xb2 30 ♕f5+ ♔h8 31 ♘e2 ♕d2! =.

b123) 23 ♘e4 ♗e7 24 ♕b8+ (24 ♘c5 ♗xc5 25 dxc5 ♘d7 =) 24...♕c8 25 ♕a7 (25 ♕e5 ♘d5 26 ♘c3 ♘xc3 27 bxc3 ♗xa3 28 ♕xa5 ♗d6 = Laketić-Upton, Cattolica 1993) 25...♘c4 26 ♘c5! ♕f5! 27 ♕b8+ ♔h7 28 ♘xb7 (only move) 28...♕b1+ 29 ♔h2 ♕xb2 30 ♕c7 ♕xa3 31 ♕xc6 ♕b4 32 ♘c5 = Lagunov.

b2) 17 g4 ♗g6 (17...♖xe1+!? 18 ♕xe1 ♗g6 19 ♘e4 {19 ♘e5!? is another idea} 19...a4 20 ♗a2 ♗xd4 21 ♖d1 ♗xe4 22 ♘xd4 ♗d5 23 ♘f5 ♕f6 24 ♕b4 ∞ Zakharevich-Krogius, St Petersburg 1994) 18 ♖xe8+ ♕xe8 19 ♕d2 and then:

b21) 19...a4 20 ♗a2 ♕d7 21 ♖e1 ♖d8 22 ♕f4 transposes to line 'b23'.

b22) 19...♖d8 20 ♖e1!? ♕d7 21 ♕f4 ♗d3 22 ♘e5 gives White a substantial advantage.

b23) 19...♕d7 20 ♕f4 a4 21 ♗a2 ♖d8 22 ♖e1 ♔h7 (22...♕d6 23 ♕e3

♔h7 24 ♖d1 ♕c7 {24...♘d5!?} 25 ♘e4 ± Savchenko-Klovans, Riga 1988) 23 h4 h5 24 gxh5 ♗xh5 25 ♘e5 ♕xd4!? (25...♗xe5 26 ♖xe5 ♕g4+ 27 ♕xg4 ♗xg4 28 ♗xf7 ± Vyzhmanavin-Aseev, Irkutsk 1986) 26 ♗b1+ ♔g8 27 ♕f5 was given as +− by Aseev, but 27...♗xe5 just looks very unclear.

**15 ♖e1** (D)

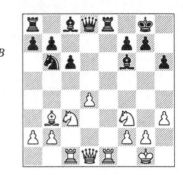

**15...♗f5** (D)

The exchange on e1 deserves serious attention: 15...♖xe1+ 16 ♕xe1 and now:

a) 16...♗d7 17 ♕e4 ♕e7 18 ♕f4 ♖e8 19 ♖e1 ♗e6!? (other ideas are 19...♕d8!? and 19...♕f8!?) 20 ♗xe6 fxe6 21 ♕g4 with a slight advantage for White, Speelman-Benko, Volmac-Spartacus 1987.

b) 16...♗f5 and then:

b1) 17 g4 ♗d3 18 ♘e5 ♗xe5 19 dxe5 c5 20 ♕e3 c4 21 ♗d1 ♕e7 22 ♗e2 ♗xe2 23 ♕xe2 ♖e8 24 ♖e1 ½-½ Bacrot-Siegel, France 1998.

b2) 17 ♕e2 a5 18 ♘e5 ♗xe5 19 ♕xe5 ♗g6 =.

b3) 17 ♕e3!? ♕e7 18 ♕f4 ♗g5 19 ♘xg5 ♕xg5 20 ♕xg5 hxg5 21 ♖e1 ♔f8 22 ♖e5 g6 23 g4 ♗d3 24 d5 (24 ♖xg5!?, with the point 24...♖d8 25

♖a5 a6 26 d5 ±, is best met by 24...f6 25 ♖a5!? ∞) 24...♖e8 = Schandorff-Wong Meng Kong, Manila OL 1992.
   b4) 17 ♘e4 ♗xe4! (17...♘d5 18 ♗xd5 cxd5 19 ♘xf6+ ♕xf6 20 ♕e5! ♕xe5 21 dxe5 ±) 18 ♕xe4 ♘d5 19 ♗xd5 cxd5 20 ♕f5 ♕b6 21 ♖c8+ (21 ♕xd5 ♖d8 22 ♕e4 ♕xb2 23 ♖c7 ♗xd4 24 ♘xd4 ♕xd4 =) 21...♖xc8 22 ♕xc8+ ♔h7 23 ♕f5+ ♔g8 24 ♕xd5 ♕xb2 25 g4 ♕b6 26 ♕e4 ♔f8 = Shabalov-Klovans, USSR 1987.

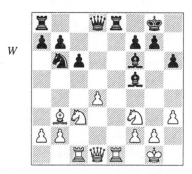

**16 g4**
White has also played 16 ♖xe8+ ♕xe8 17 ♕d2 ♕d7 18 ♖e1:
   a) 18...♖d8 19 ♕f4 ♘d5 (19...♗g6 20 ♕g3 ♗h5 21 ♘e4 ♗xd4 22 ♘xd4 ♕xd4 23 ♕h4 ♗g6 24 ♖d1 ± Gavrikov-Beliavsky, Minsk 1983) 20 ♘xd5 cxd5 21 ♘e5 ♗xe5 22 ♖xe5 ♗e6 23 ♕e3 ♔f8 24 ♕d3 and White has a slight advantage, Kasparov-Karpov, Moscow Wch (23) 1985.
   b) 18...a5! 19 ♕f4 (for 19 a3, see note 'b12' to Black's 14th move) 19...g5! 20 ♘e4 gxf4! 21 ♘xf6+ ♔f8 22 ♘xd7+ ♘xd7 23 ♘e5 ♘xe5 (also

possible is 23...♖e8 24 ♘xd7+ ♗xd7 25 ♖xe8+ ♔xe8 26 ♔f1 ♗f5 27 ♔e2 ♗e4 28 g3 fxg3 29 fxg3 ♔e7 = Farago-Pigusov, Dordrecht 1987) 24 ♖xe5 ♗g6 25 d5 a4 26 ♗c4 ♖a5 27 b4 axb3 28 ♗xb3 cxd5 29 ♖xd5 ½-½ Piket-Ioseliani, Spijkenisse 1987.
   **16...♗e6 17 ♗xe6 ♖xe6 18 ♖xe6 fxe6 19 ♕e2 ♕e7 20 ♖e1** *(D)*

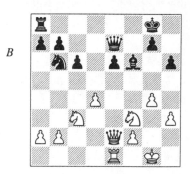

**20...♖e8**
20...♖d8 21 ♕e4 ♕d6 22 ♕xe6+ ♕xe6 23 ♖xe6 ♗xd4 24 ♘xd4 ♖xd4 25 ♖e8+ ♔h7 26 ♖b8 (Savchenko-Rotshtein, USSR 1988) 26...♘a4! 27 ♖xb7 ♘xc3 28 bxc3 ♖a4 29 ♖b2 ± Savchenko.
   **21 ♕c2 ♕f7 22 ♘e4 ♖d8**
   The game is equal. Gelfand-Kramnik, Dortmund 1997 continued 23 ♘c5 ♗xd4 24 ♘xd4 ♖xd4 25 ♘xe6 ♖d6 26 ♕e4 ♖d5 27 f4 ♘d7 28 ♘d8 ♕f6 29 ♕e8+ ♔h7 30 ♕e4+ ♔g8 31 ♕e8+ ♔h7 32 ♕e4+ ½-½.

**Conclusion:** 6 ♗xf6 leads to very sharp and interesting positions, where Black has good counterchances.

# 6  5 ♗g5 h6 6 ♗h4 0-0 without 7 e3

1 d4 d5 2 c4 e6 3 ♘c3 ♗e7 4 ♘f3 ♘f6
5 ♗g5 h6 6 ♗h4 0-0 *(D)*

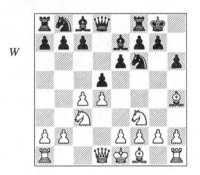

In this position, the main line is considered to be 7 e3, which is discussed in Chapters 7 and 8. White also has these continuations at his disposal:
**A: 7 ♕c2**
**B: 7 ♖c1**
**C: 7 cxd5**
However, as we shall see, these moves do not present Black with any particular problems.

## A)
**7 ♕c2 c5!**
The most precise route to equality.
**8 dxc5 dxc4**
8...♘c6 9 e3 ♕a5 10 a3 ♗d7 11 ♖d1 ♕xc5 12 ♗e2 ♖fc8 13 ♕b1 ♗e8 14 cxd5 and White is slightly better, Lerner-Gulko, Moscow 1986.

**9 e3**
Interesting is 9 e4 ♘fd7 (9...♕a5!? 10 e5 ♘d5 11 ♗xe7 ♘xe7 12 ♗xc4 ♕xc5 13 ♕e4 ♗d7 14 ♗d3 ♘g6 ∞ analysis) 10 ♗xe7 (10 ♗g3 ♕a5 11 ♗xc4 ♕xc5 12 ♗e2 a6 13 0-0 b5 14 a3 ♗b7 15 ♖ac1 b4 16 axb4 ♕xb4 17 ♖fd1 ♘c5 18 ♖d4 ♕b3 = Lauber-Vaganian, Bundesliga 1998/9) 10...♕xe7 11 ♗xc4 ♕xc5 12 ♕e2 a6 13 0-0 b5 14 ♗b3 ♗b7 15 ♖ac1 ♖c8! 16 a3 ♘c6 17 ♖fd1 ♘de5 18 ♘xe5 ♘xe5 19 ♕d2 ♕b6 20 ♕d4 ♕xd4 21 ♖xd4 g5! = Lauber-Vaganian, Bundesliga 1996/7.

**9...♕a5 10 ♗xc4 ♕xc5 11 ♗d3 ♘c6**
11...♘bd7?! 12 a3 (12 0-0 b6 13 ♖ac1 ♗b7 14 ♕e2 ♕h5 =) 12...b6 13 b4 (13 ♘e4 ♕xc2 14 ♗xc2 ♗b7 =; 13 0-0 ♗b7 14 ♕e2 ♕h5 =) 13...♕h5? 14 h3! (Black's idea was 14 ♗g3? ♗b7 15 ♗e2 ♖ac8!! 16 ♘e5 ♕f5! 17 ♗d3 ♕xe5 18 ♗xe5 ♘xe5 ∓) is very good for White, since both the black queen and the a8-rook are in grave danger:
a) 14...♘e5 15 ♘xe5 ♕xh4 (after 15...♕xe5 16 ♗g3 ♕g5 17 h4 ♕h5 18 ♗e2 White will trap the a8-rook) 16 ♘f3! ♕h5 17 0-0-0 (or 17 ♖h2) followed by g4 wins material.
b) 14...♗b7 15 g4 ♗xf3, giving up queen for rook and knight, might be necessary.
**12 a3 ♗d7 13 b4**

Now:
a) 13...♛b6 14 ♘a4 ♛d8 15 0-0 ± Petrosian-Lerner, USSR Ch (Moscow) 1983.
b) 13...♛h5 intending 14...♘e5 = (Petrosian).

**B)**
**7 ♖c1** *(D)*

**7...dxc4!**
The modern move, first employed by Karpov against Korchnoi in their match at Merano in 1981. Previously Black had preferred 7...b6!? 8 cxd5 ♘xd5 9 ♗xe7 ♛xe7 10 ♘xd5 exd5:
a) It is worth mentioning that 11 ♛c2 ♗a6! 12 e3 ♗xf1 13 ♔xf1 c5 14 dxc5 bxc5 (14...♖c8!?) 15 ♛xc5 ♛b7 gives Black compensation, Ermolinsky-Podgaets, USSR 1981.
b) 11 g3 (here we see the idea behind White's 7 ♖c1: by fianchettoing the bishop, he creates very unpleasant pressure, forcing Black to act very carefully) 11...♖e8 and then:
b1) 12 ♖c3 ♘a6 (12...c5!? 13 dxc5 bxc5 14 ♛xd5 ♗b7 15 ♛d2 ♘c6 with compensation, Seirawan-Geller, Linares 1983) 13 ♛a4 b5! 14 ♛a5? (14 ♛c2!?) 14...♛e4 15 ♔d2 ♖e6 16 b3 b4

and Black has a distinct advantage, Seirawan-Karpov, Hamburg 1982.
b2) 12 ♗g2 ♗a6 and here:
b21) 13 ♘e5 ♘d7! 14 f4 (14 ♖xc7 ♖ac8! 15 ♖xd7 ♛b4+ 16 ♔f1 ♛xd4 ∓ Uhlmann-Veresov, 1969) 14...♘xe5 15 dxe5 ♗b7 16 0-0 ♖ed8 17 b4 c6 18 ♛b3 ♖ac8 19 ♖fd1 ♗a6 20 ♛b2 ♗b5 = Uhlmann-Kurajica, Sarajevo 1981.
b22) 13 e3 c5 14 ♛a4 ♖c8 15 ♘e5 ♛e6 16 ♖c3 cxd4! (16...♖d8 17 h4 ♛d6 18 a3 ♛e7 19 h5 ♗b7 20 0-0 ♘a6 21 ♖fc1 ♘c7 22 b4 c4? 23 ♖xc4! dxc4 24 ♗xb7 +– Smyslov-Portisch, Tilburg 1984) 17 ♛xd4 ♘d7 18 ♗xd5 ♛xe5 19 ♗xa8 ♖xa8 20 ♛xd7 ♛e4 21 ♖g1 ♛b1+ 22 ♛d1 ♛xb2 23 ♛d2 ♛a1+ 24 ♖c1 ♛f6 25 ♛d4 ♛f3 26 ♛d1 ♛f6 27 ♛d4 ♛f3 ½-½ Yusupov-Short, Madrid 1995.

**8 e3**
8 e4 does not yield an advantage: 8...♘c6! 9 e5 (9 ♗xc4 ♘xe4 10 ♗xe7 ♘xc3 11 ♗xd8 ♘xd1 12 ♗xc7 ♘xb2 13 ♗b5 a6 14 ♗e2 ♘b4 15 ♔d2 ♘d5 ∓) 9...♘d5 10 ♗xe7 ♘cxe7 11 ♗xc4 ♘xc3 12 bxc3 b6 13 ♛e2 ♗b7 14 ♗a6 ♗d5 15 0-0 c5 16 dxc5 bxc5 17 ♗c4 ♗c6 18 ♗b5 ♛c7 with an equal position, Tukmakov-Beliavsky, Tilburg 1984.

**8...c5 9 ♗xc4**
9 dxc5 ♛xd1+ 10 ♔xd1 ♖d8+ 11 ♔c2 ♗xc5 = Agdestein-Andersson, Næstved 1985.

**9...cxd4 10 ♘xd4**
Or 10 exd4 ♘c6 11 0-0 ♘h5! 12 ♗xe7 ♘xe7:
a) 13 ♗b3 ♘f6 14 ♘e5 ♗d7 15 ♛e2 ♖c8 16 ♘e4?! (better is 16 ♖fd1, with equality) 16...♘xe4 17 ♛xe4 ♗c6 ∓ Korchnoi-Karpov, Merano Wch (9) 1981.

b) 13 d5 exd5 14 ♘xd5 ♘xd5 15 ♕xd5 (15 ♗xd5 ♘f4 =) 15...♕xd5 16 ♗xd5 ♘f4 17 ♗c4 ♗e6! 18 g3 ♖ac8 19 ♘e5 ♖xc4 20 ♖xc4 ♘e2+ 21 ♔g2 ♗d5+ 22 f3 ♗xc4 23 ♘xc4 ♖c8 ½-½ Uhlmann-Kurajica, Sarajevo 1982.

c) 13 ♖e1 ♘f6 14 ♘e5 and now:

c1) 14...♗d7 15 ♕b3 (15 d5 exd5 16 ♘xd5 ♘exd5 17 ♗xd5 ♘xd5 18 ♕xd5 ♗e6 19 ♕xb7 ♕a5 20 a3 ♖ab8 21 ♕f3 ♖xb2 22 ♘c6 ♕g5 23 ♘xa7 ♖b3 = Browne-Chandler, Surakarta 1982) 15...♖b8 16 ♖cd1 b5 17 ♘xd7 ♘xd7 18 ♗d3 ♘f6 19 ♗b1 a6 20 ♘e4 ♘ed5 = Christiansen-Karpov, London 1982.

c2) 14...♕b6 15 ♖c2 ♖d8 16 ♖d2 ♗d7 17 ♗b3 ♗e8 = Piket-Van der Sterren, Netherlands 1993.

**10...♗d7** (D)

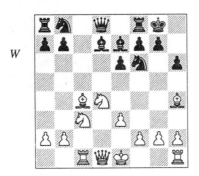

**11 0-0**

Or:

a) 11 ♗e2 ♘c6 12 ♘b3 ♘d5 13 ♗xe7 ♘cxe7 14 ♘xd5 ♘xd5 15 ♕d4 ♗c6 16 ♗f3 ♘e7 with a balanced position, Korchnoi-Karpov, Merano Wch (17) 1981.

b) 11 ♗g3 and now:

b1) 11...a6!? 12 e4 ♘c6 13 ♘b3 b5! (13...♕b6 14 e5 ♘h7 15 0-0 ♖fd8 16 ♕e2 ♗e8 17 ♔h1! ♘d4 18 ♘xd4 ♖xd4 19 f3! ± Karpov-Beliavsky, Dortmund 1995) 14 ♗d3 and now:

b11) 14...b4 15 ♘a4 ♘e5 16 ♗xe5 ♗xa4 17 ♕e2 ♕b6 (17...♗b5!?) 18 ♗d4 ♕b8 19 e5 ♘d5 20 ♕e4 g6 21 h4! ♖c8 22 ♖d1! (22 ♔d2 ♗b5 23 ♗b1 ♖xc1 24 ♖xc1 ♕d8 ∞ Ivanchuk-Gelfand, Dortmund 1997) 22...♗xb3 23 axb3 ♗c5 24 h5 ♗xd4 25 ♕xd4 g5 26 g3 ±.

b12) 14...e5!? 15 ♘d5 (15 0-0 ♗e6 16 ♗h4 ♖c8 =) 15...♘b4! 16 ♘xe7+ ♕xe7 17 ♗b1 ♗e6! 18 ♗xe5 ♘xe4! 19 ♗xe4 ♗xb3 20 ♕xb3 ♕xe5 21 ♕xb4 ♖ae8 = Ivanchuk.

b2) 11...♘c6 12 ♘db5 (12 ♘b3 ♘a5 =) and then:

b21) 12...e5!? 13 a4 a6 14 ♘a3 ♗xa3 15 bxa3 ♕e7 16 ♗h4 g5 17 ♗g3 ♗e6 18 ♗xe6 ♕xe6 19 0-0 ♖fd8 20 ♕c2 ♖ac8 21 ♕b1 ♖d7 22 h4 ♔g7 23 ♘a2 ♖dc7 = Korchnoi-Short, Groningen FIDE 1997.

b22) 12...a6 13 ♘d6 b5 (13...♕b6 14 ♗e2 ♗xd6 15 ♗xd6 ♖fd8 16 ♗g3 ♗e8 17 ♕c2 ♘b4 18 ♕b1 a5 19 0-0 ♗c6 20 ♖fd1 ♘bd5 21 ♗e5 ♘xc3 ½-½ Komarov-Goldin, Kazan 1997) 14 ♗e2 ♕b6 (14...e5!? 15 ♗f3 ♕b6 16 ♘de4 ♗e6 17 ♘xf6+ ♗xf6 18 ♘d5 ♗xd5 19 ♕xd5 ♕a5+ 20 ♔e2 ♘b4 21 ♕b3 ♖ad8 22 ♖cd1 ♘xa2 23 ♖xd8 ♖xd8 24 ♗d5 ♕c7 25 ♕xa2 ♕c2+ 26 ♔f3 ♕f5+ 27 ♔e2 ♕c2+ ½-½ Van Wely-Van der Sterren, Bundesliga 1998/9) 15 a4 b4 and here:

b221) 16 ♘b1 ♘a5 17 ♘xf7 ♗c6! 18 ♘e5 ♗xg2 19 ♖g1 ♖ad8 20 ♘d2 ♘e4 21 ♗d3 ♘xd2 22 ♖xg2 ♕b7? (22...♘db3! ∞) 23 ♖g1! (23 ♕g4! ♖f5 24 ♕g6! wins) 23...♘ab3 24 ♕g4 ♖xd3 25 ♕xe6+ ♔h7 26 ♕g6+ ♔h8 is unclear, Piket-Van der Sterren, Antwerp 1997.

b222) 16 ♘c4 ♕a7 17 ♘b1 ♖fd8 18 ♗f3 ♗e8 19 ♘bd2 a5 20 0-0 ♖ac8 21 ♕e2 ♘b8 = Piket.

**11...♘c6** *(D)*

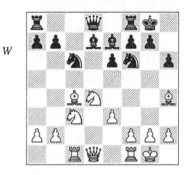

**12 ♘f3**

White does not obtain an advantage by 12 ♘b3 ♖c8 13 ♗e2 ♘d5! (this manoeuvre leads to equality):

a) 14 ♗g3 ♘xc3 (14...♘cb4!?) 15 ♖xc3 ♘b4 16 ♖xc8 ♕xc8 17 a3 ♘c6 18 ♕c2 e5 19 ♕c3 ♗e6 20 ♖c1 ♕d8 21 ♘c5 ♗xc5 22 ♕xc5 ♕d2 23 ♕c2 ♖d8 = Dorfman-Van der Sterren, Brussels 1993.

b) 14 ♗xe7 ♘cxe7 15 ♘xd5 ♘xd5 16 ♖xc8 ♕xc8 17 ♕d4 b6 (fully possible is also 17...♕b8 18 ♗f3 ♘f6 19 ♘c5 ♗b5 20 ♖d1 b6 21 ♘e4 ♘xe4 22 ♗xe4 ♖c8 = ½-½ Kasparov-Karpov, Moscow Wch (23) 1984/5) 18 ♖c1 ♕b8 19 e4 ♘f4 20 ♗f1 ♖d8 ½-½ Korchnoi-Short, Brussels 1986.

**12...♖c8**

The direct freeing try 12...♘h5!? is interesting: 13 ♗xe7 ♕xe7 14 ♘e4 ♖fd8 15 ♕d6 ♗e8 16 ♕xe7 ♘xe7 17 ♘d4 ♘c6 18 ♘b3 ♘f6 19 ♘xf6+ gxf6 20 ♗e2 ♖ac8 21 ♖fd1 ♔f8 with

equality, Li Wenliang-Bönsch, Beijing 1995.

It is also worth considering the alternative 12...♕b6!? 13 ♘a4 (13 a3 ♘a5 14 ♗xf6 ♗xf6 15 ♕xd7 ♘xc4 16 ♘e4 ♘xb2 17 ♘xf6+ gxf6 18 ♖b1 ♖fd8 19 ♕e7 ♔g7 20 a4 ♖e8 21 ♕a3 ♘c4 22 ♕c3 {22 ♖xb6 ♘xa3 23 ♖xb7 =} 22...♕a6 23 ♖b4 ♖ac8 and Black is slightly better, Uhlmann-Bönsch, Berlin 1989) 13...♕c7 14 ♗e2 ♖fd8 15 a3 ♗e8 16 ♕c2 ♖ac8 with equality, Kharitonov-Beliavsky, USSR Ch (Moscow) 1988.

**13 a3**

13 ♕e2 ♕a5 =; 13 ♗g3!?.

**13...♘h5**

13...a6?! 14 ♗a2 b5 15 ♗b1! g6 16 e4! b4 17 axb4 ♘xb4 18 ♕e2 (18 ♘e5?! ♗e8 19 ♕f3 ♘d7 20 ♗g3 ♘xe5 21 ♗xe5 ♘c6 22 ♗f4 ♗g5 = Uhlmann-Van der Sterren, Tallinn 1987) 18...♘h5 19 ♗xe7 ♕xe7 20 ♕e3 and White has a clear advantage.

**14 ♗xe7 ♕xe7**

14...♘xe7?! gives White additional possibilities: 15 ♘e4 ♗c6 16 ♘fd2! g6 17 ♕e2 ♕a5 18 ♗d3 ♘d5 19 ♘c4 ♕c7 20 b4 ± Greenfeld-Bany, Polanica Zdroj 1987.

**15 ♘e4**

Or: 15 ♗a2 ♖fd8 16 ♕e2 ♗e8 =; 15 e4 ♖fd8 16 ♕e2 ♕c5 17 ♗a2 ♘e5 18 ♘xe5 ♕xe5 19 ♕e3 ♗c6 20 ♖fd1 a6 21 g3 ♘f6 = Uhlmann-Jackelen, Porz 1990.

**15...♖fd8 16 ♕d6 ♗e8 17 ♕xe7 ♘xe7**

The position is equal.

**C)**

**7 cxd5 ♘xd5 8 ♗xe7 ♕xe7 9 ♕b3** *(D)*

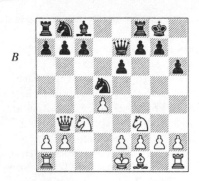

B

**9...Rd8**

9...Nxc3 is also fully possible. 10 Qxc3 b6 11 Rc1 and now:

a) 11...Ba6!? 12 g3 (12 Qxc7 Nd7 13 Qc3 Rfc8 14 Qd2 Rxc1+ 15 Qxc1 Rc8 16 Qd2 Nf6 gives Black excellent compensation) 12...Nd7 13 Bg2 Rac8 14 Nd2?! (better is 14 Qd2 c5 15 0-0 Rfd8 with an equal position) 14...c5 15 Qa3? cxd4! 16 Rxc8 Rxc8 17 b4 Qxb4! 0-1 Sliwa-Bondarevsky, Hastings 1960/1.

b) 11...c6!? 12 e3 Bb7 13 Be2 Nd7 14 0-0 c5 15 dxc5 Nxc5 16 b4 Na6! (16...Ne4 17 Qc7 Qxc7 18 Rxc7 Bd5 19 Ba6 Nf6 20 Ne5 Bxa2 21 e4 with compensation, M.Gurevich-Hjartarson, Groningen PCA qual 1993) 17 a3 Rac8 18 Qb3 Nb8 19 Qa4 a6 20 Nd4 Rc7 =.

c) 11...Nd7 12 e3 (12 Qxc7 Ba6 with compensation) 12...Bb7 13 Bb5 c6 14 Be2 c5 15 0-0 Rfc8 16 Rfd1 cxd4 17 Qxd4 Rxc1 18 Rxc1 Rc8 = M.Gurevich-Marciano, French Cht 1995.

**10 Rc1 Nf6**

10...b6 11 Nxd5 exd5 12 e3 c5 13 Qa3 Nd7 14 Bb5 ±.

**11 e4!?**

11 e3 b6 12 Be2 Bb7 13 0-0 Nbd7 14 Rfd1 c5 = Kharitonov-Pigusov, Tashkent 1987.

**11...Nc6! 12 e5 Nh7!** *(D)*

W

Intending ...Ng5.

**13 d5 Na5!**

13...exd5 14 Nxd5 ±; 13...Nxe5 14 Nxe5 exd5 15 f4 ±.

**14 Qa4 b6 15 b4!**

Or: 15 Nb5 exd5 16 Rxc7 (16 Nxc7 Rb8! intending ...Ng5) 16...Bd7!; 15 dxe6 Bxe6 16 b4 Nc4 15 Nd4 Qg5!.

**15...Nb7 16 Bb5!?**

16 Nd4 Qg5! 17 Nce2 Qxe5 18 Nc6 Bd7 19 Nxe5 Bxa4 20 Rxc7 Rxd5 –+.

**16...exd5 17 Bc6 Ng5 18 Nxg5 Qxe5+ 19 Nge4 dxe4 20 0-0 f5!**

20...e3 21 fxe3 Qxe3+ 22 Kh1 with compensation.

**21 Qb5! Qxb5 22 Nxb5 a5 23 Nxc7 Rb8 24 Na6 Ra8**

The position is equal (analysis).

# 7 The Lasker Defence

1 d4 d5 2 c4 e6 3 ♘c3 ♗e7 4 ♘f3 ♘f6
5 ♗g5 h6 6 ♗h4 0-0 7 e3 ♘e4 *(D)*

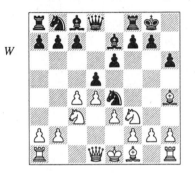

W

This move characterizes the Lasker Defence. Black seeks to ease his defence by means of exchanges. This line has been rejuvenated since the Karpov-Yusupov Candidates match (London 1989), where Yusupov as Black employed a variety of new ideas and very much succeeded in making the case for the variation.

**8 ♗xe7**

White can avoid the exchange of bishops by 8 ♗g3, upon which may follow 8...c5 9 ♗d3 ♘xg3 10 hxg3 cxd4 11 exd4 dxc4 12 ♗xc4 ♘c6! (12...a6!?) 13 ♕d3 (13 0-0 ♗f6; 13 ♕d2 ♗f6 14 ♖d1 b6 15 0-0 ♗b7 = intending to meet 16 d5 with 16...♘a5) 13...♘b4 14 ♕e4 ♗d7 15 ♘e5 ♗c6 16 ♘xc6 bxc6 with an equal position, Kouatly-Marciano, French Ch (Méribel) 1998.

**8...♕xe7**

White has several continuations at his disposal:

A: 9 ♘xe4     91
B: 9 cxd5     92
C: 9 ♖c1     93
D: 9 ♕c2     96

Or: 9 ♗d3 ♘xc3 10 bxc3 dxc4 11 ♗xc4 c5 12 0-0 b6 13 ♕e2 ♗b7 14 e4 (14 ♘e5 ♘c6 15 f4 ♖ac8 16 ♖f2 ♖c7 17 ♖af1 cxd4 18 cxd4 ♕a3 19 ♘xc6 ♖xc6 20 d5 exd5 21 ♗xd5 ♗a6 22 ♕b2 ♕xb2 23 ♖xb2 ♖c3 = Ståhlberg-Reinhardt, Mar del Plata 1946) 14...♘c6 15 ♖ad1 ♖ad8 = P.Cramling-Krogius, Genoa 1989.

**A)**
**9 ♘xe4 dxe4 10 ♘d2** *(D)*

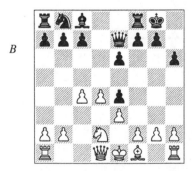

B

**10...f5**
10...e5!? deserves serious attention: 11 d5 (11 ♘xe4? exd4 12 ♕xd4?! ♖d8 −+; 11 dxe5 ♕xe5 12 ♕c2 ♗f5 13 c5 ♘d7 14 ♖c1 b6 15 b4 a5 16 ♘c4 ♕e7

with counterplay for Black, Ftačnik-Bönsch, Bundesliga 1995/6; 11 ♕b3 exd4 12 exd4 ♘c6 13 d5 ♘d4 14 ♕c3 c5 =) 11...f5 (11...♗f5!? 12 ♗e2 c6 ∞) 12 ♕c2 ♘d7 13 0-0-0 ♘c5 ∞.

**11 ♕c2**
Other continuations have also been played:

a) 11 c5 e5 12 ♕b3+ ♔h8 13 ♘c4 exd4 14 exd4 ♘c6 15 0-0-0 should be met by 15...♖b8!? intending ...b5 ∞, rather than 15...b5?! 16 ♕xb5 ♗d7 17 d5 ♖ab8 18 ♕a4 ♘b4 19 c6 ± Spassky-Lutikov, Moscow 1961.

b) 11 ♖c1 ♘d7 12 ♕c2 c6 13 c5 e5 14 ♗c4+ ♔h8 15 0-0 ♘f6 16 ♖fe1 ♖d8 17 ♕c3 exd4 18 exd4 ♗e6 = Bogoljubow-Eliskases, Mannheim 1939.

**11...c5 12 dxc5 ♘d7 13 ♗e2 ♘xc5 14 0-0 a5**
= Popchev-Bednarski, Berlin 1988.

**B)**
**9 cxd5 ♘xc3 10 bxc3 exd5** *(D)*
10...♕a3?! 11 ♕c1! ♕xc1+ 12 ♖xc1 exd5 13 c4 ±.

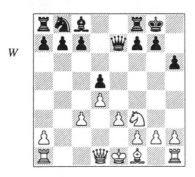

W

**11 ♕b3**
Also possible are:

a) 11 ♗e2 c5 12 0-0 ♘c6 13 dxc5 ♕xc5 14 ♕b3 b6 15 ♖fd1 (15 ♘d4

♗b7 16 ♖fd1 ♘e5 17 ♖ac1 ♖ac8 =) 15...♗e6 16 ♘d4 ♖ac8 17 ♕b2 ♘e5 = Kiseliov-Egiazarian, Moscow 1996.

b) 11 ♗d3 c5 12 0-0 ♘c6 13 h3 (13 dxc5 ♕xc5 14 ♕b3 ♗g4 15 ♘d4 ♘e5 16 ♗c2 b6 17 h3 ♗d7 = Hort-Donner, Havana 1971; 13 ♖b1 ♗e6 14 dxc5 ♖ab8 15 ♕a4 ♕xc5 16 ♖fc1 ♖fc8 17 ♘d4 ♗d7 = Eingorn-Li Wenliang, Lucerne Wcht 1993) 13...♗e6 14 ♖e1 ♖fd8 15 ♖b1 ♖ac8 16 e4 dxe4 (alternatively, 16...cxd4 17 exd5 ♖xd5 18 ♗c4 ♖d6 19 cxd4 ♕d7 20 ♗xe6 fxe6 21 ♕b3 b6 22 ♖e4 ± Uhlmann-Averbakh, Polanica Zdroj 1975) 17 ♗xe4 cxd4 18 cxd4 (18 ♘xd4 ♘xd4 19 cxd4 {19 ♖xb7? ♘f5 −+} 19...b6 20 d5 ♕f6 =) 18...♕c7 =.

**11...♖d8 12 c4**
White wants to achieve a pawn majority in the centre. He can also play 12 ♗d3 c5 13 ♕a3 b6 14 0-0 ♘d7 15 ♖fe1 ♗b7 16 ♖ab1 (16 ♗f5 ♘f6 17 ♘e5 ♖e8 18 ♕a4 ♘e4 19 ♕c2 ♕f6 20 ♗xe4 dxe4 21 a4 ½-½ Ljubojević-Andersson, Tilburg 1984) 16...♕e6 = Ftačnik-Inkiov, Banja Luka 1983.

**12...dxc4 13 ♗xc4 ♘c6 14 ♕c3**
Or 14 ♗e2!? b6 15 0-0 ♗b7 16 ♖ac1 ♘a5 17 ♕b2 ♖ac8, and now:

a) 18 ♖c3!? c5 19 ♕a3 ♔f8! 20 dxc5 ♖xc5 (20...♗xf3 21 ♗xf3 ♖xc5 22 ♖xc5 ♕xc5 23 ♕xc5+ bxc5 24 ♖b1 ± analysis) 21 ♖xc5 ♕xc5 22 ♕xc5+ bxc5 23 ♖c1 (23 ♖b1 ♗d5 24 ♖b5 ♗c4! 25 ♗xc4 ♘xc4 26 g3 ♖c8 = analysis) 23...♖c8 24 ♘e5!? (24 ♖c3 ♗d5 25 ♘d2 c4 26 e4 ♗e6 27 f4 f6 28 ♔f2 ♘c6 ½-½ Ivkov-Krogius, Belgrade tt 1998) 24...♔e7 25 f3 ♔d6!? 26 f4! ± (analysis).

b) 18 h3 c5 19 dxc5 ♗xf3!? (or 19...♖xc5 20 ♖xc5 ♕xc5 21 ♖c1 ♕e7

22 ♘d4 ♕g5 23 ♗g4 ± Kramnik-Lutz, Bundesliga 1993/4) 20 ♗xf3 ♖xc5 21 ♖xc5 ♕xc5 22 ♖c1 ♘c4 23 ♕c3 can be answered by 23...♖c8 = or 23...b5 = (analysis).

**14...♗g4 15 0-0 ♗xf3 16 gxf3**

White has obtained a powerful pawn-centre and the possibility of play on the g-file. However, Black has sufficient counterplay.

**16...♕f6!**

16...♕h4?! is dubious: 17 ♔h1 ♖d6 18 ♖g1! ♘e7 19 ♖g4! ♕h5 20 ♖ag1 ♖g6 21 ♕b4! ± Beliavsky-Vaganian, Reggio Emilia 1995/6.

**17 ♗e2**

17 f4!? seems interesting: 17...♘e7! 18 ♖ac1 (18 ♗d3 ♖ac8 =) 18...♕g6+! (18...♖ac8?! 19 h3 ♖d6 20 ♔h2 ♘f5 21 ♗e2 g6 22 ♕a5 ± Shabrin-Gorelov, USSR Club Ch (Pavlodar) 1991) 19 ♔h1 ♕h5 20 f3 ♘f5 21 ♖f2 ♖d6!? intending ...♖e8 and ...♖g6 ∞ (analysis).

**17...♖ac8 18 ♔h1**

18 ♖ab1 b6 19 f4 (19 ♗a6 ♕xf3 20 ♗xc8 ♖xc8 21 ♖fc1 ♘e7 with compensation; 19 ♖fc1 ♘e7 20 ♔h1 ♖d5 ∓ Karpov-Yusupov, London Ct (6) 1989) 19...♘e7 20 ♗a6 ♕g6+ 21 ♔h1 ♘d5 22 ♕d3 ♕xd3 23 ♗xd3 c5 24 ♗a6 ♖c7 = Kobaliya-Korneev, Krasnodar 1998.

**18...♘e7 19 ♖ac1 ♖d5**

This unclear position needs to be tried in practice.

**C)**

**9 ♖c1 c6 (D)**

**10 ♗d3**

It has long been known that no advantage is given by 10 ♘xe4 dxe4 11 ♘d2 f5 12 c5 ♘d7 13 ♘c4 e5 14 ♘d6 exd4 (14...♘f6!? 15 ♗c4+ ♔h7 16

W

0-0 exd4 17 ♕xd4 ♘g4 =) 15 ♗c4+ ♔h8 16 ♕xd4 ♘e5 17 0-0 ♖b8 18 ♗e2 ♗d7 19 ♖fd1 ♕f6 20 ♘c4 ♘xc4 21 ♗xc4 ♗e8 22 ♕d6 ♕xd6 23 ♖xd6 ♗f7 = Capablanca-Rubinstein, Budapest 1929.

Practice has also seen 10 ♕c2 ♘xc3 11 ♕xc3 ♘d7:

a) 12 ♗d3 dxc4 13 ♗xc4 b6 14 0-0 ♗b7 15 e4 (15 ♗e2 ♖fc8 =) 15...c5 16 ♕e3 cxd4 17 ♘xd4 ♖ac8 = Taimanov-Khavsky, USSR 1971.

b) 12 cxd5 exd5 13 ♗d3 ♘f6 14 0-0 ♘e4 15 ♗xe4 dxe4 16 ♘d2 ♗g4 = Chuchelov-Korneev, Germany 1991/2.

c) 12 a3 dxc4 13 ♗xc4 b6 14 0-0 ♗b7 and here:

c1) 15 ♖fd1 c5! 16 dxc5 ♘xc5 17 ♕e5 (17 ♘d4 ♖ac8 18 b4 ♘e4 = Smyslov-Unzicker, Bad Wörishofen 1992; 17 b4 ♘e4 18 ♕e5 ♖ac8 =) 17...♖ac8 18 b4 ♘d7 19 ♕f4 ♖fd8 20 h3 ♘f6 = I.Sokolov-Timman, Erevan OL 1996.

c2) 15 e4 c5 16 ♕e3 ♖fd8 17 ♖fd1 cxd4 18 ♘xd4 ♘e5 19 ♗e2 ♖ac8 20 f3 ♘c6 = Gavrikov-Janjgava, Geneva 1991.

**10...♘xc3 11 ♖xc3**

11 bxc3 ♘d7 12 0-0 e5 13 dxe5 dxc4 14 ♗xc4 ♘xe5 15 ♘xe5 ♕xe5

16 ♕d4 ♕e7 ½-½ Petrosian-Keres, Sarajevo 1972.

**11...dxc4** *(D)*

On 11...♘d7 White's best reply is 12 cxd5! (12 0-0 e5! ∞ intending to meet 13 dxe5 with 13...dxc4 =) 12...exd5 13 0-0 ♖e8 (13...♘f6 14 ♕b1 ♘e4 15 ♗xe4 dxe4 16 ♘d2 ♖e8 17 ♖c5! f6 18 b4 ♗d7 19 ♖fc1 a6 20 a4 ♖ad8 21 ♘c4 ± Van Scheltinga-Donner, Birmingham 1951) 14 ♕b1 (supporting b4 and freeing the c1-square for the king's rook) 14...♘f6 15 b4 ♘e4 16 ♗xe4 dxe4 17 ♘d2 ♗e6 18 ♖fc1 ♗d5 19 b5 ♖ad8 20 bxc6 (20 a4 h5! 21 ♖1c2 h4 ∞ P.Nikolić-Yusupov, Horgen 1994) 20...bxc6 21 ♖c5! ± intending ♘c4-e5.

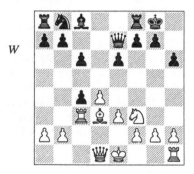

W

**12 ♗xc4**

12 ♖xc4 also deserves consideration. 12...♘d7 and now:

a) 13 0-0 e5 14 dxe5 (14 ♕c2 exd4 15 exd4 ♘f6 16 ♖c5 ♘d5 17 a3 ♗e6 18 b4 ♖fd8 19 ♖e1 ♕f6 = Pinter-Sturua, Manila OL 1992) 14...♘xe5 15 ♖e4 ♘xf3+ 16 ♕xf3 ♗e6 17 ♗c4 ♖ad8 18 ♗xe6 fxe6 19 ♕e2 (19 ♕g4 ♖f6 20 ♖d1 ♖d5 = Andersson-Pfleger, Amsterdam 1978) 19...♖d5 20 ♖d1 (20 h3 ♖fd8 21 b4 ♖d2 22 ♕c4 ♖8d5 23 a4

♕d6 = Christiansen-Andersson, Szirak IZ 1987) 20...♕f6 21 ♖ed4 ♖fd8 22 ♕c4 a5 = Ionov-Yusupov, Oviedo rpd 1993.

b) 13 ♗b1 e5 14 ♕c2 f5 15 dxe5 (15 0-0 e4 16 ♘d2 ♘b6 17 ♖c5 ♗e6 18 a4 ♗d5 19 a5 ♘d7 20 ♖c3 ♕b4 21 ♖a3 ♖ac8 22 ♗a2 ♘f6 = Keres-Mikenas, USSR Ch (Moscow) 1957) 15...♘xe5 16 ♘xe5 ♕xe5 17 0-0 ♗e6 18 ♖d4 ♖ad8 (18...c5!? 19 ♖d2 ♖ad8 20 ♖fd1 ♖xd2 21 ♕xd2 ♖f7 22 ♕d8+ {22 ♕d6?? ♖d7 –+} 22...♔h7 =) 19 ♖fd1 ♖d5 20 ♖xd5 ♗xd5 21 ♕d2 (21 ♖d4 ♗e4 22 ♕b3+ ♗d5 = intending to meet 23 ♕xb7? with 23...f4) 21...♖f6 22 ♕d4 ♕e8 23 f3 b6 24 e4 fxe4 25 fxe4 ♖e6 26 ♗d3 ♗xe4 27 ♗c4 ♗d5 = Bukić-A.Zaitsev, Debrecen 1971.

**12...♘d7 13 0-0 b6** *(D)*

Another plan is 13...e5 14 ♗b3:

a) 14...exd4 15 exd4 ♘f6 16 ♖e1 ♕d6 (16...♗e6 17 ♗xe6 fxe6 18 ♘e5 ±) 17 ♘e5 ♘d5 (17...♗f5?! 18 ♘xf7 ♖xf7 19 ♗xf7+ ♔xf7 20 ♕b3+ ♔f8 21 ♕xb7 ♖b8 22 ♕xa7 ♖xb2 23 ♖xc6! ♖xa2 24 ♕b7 ♖b2 25 ♕xg7+ ♔xg7 26 ♖xd6 +– Piket-Pleister, Hilversum 1990; 17...♗e6 18 ♗xe6 fxe6 19 ♖g3 ♖ad8 20 ♕b3 ±) 18 ♖g3 ♗e6 (18...♗f5 19 ♕h5! ♗h7 20 ♕g4 g5 21 h4 ± Karpov-Yusupov, London Ct (8) 1989) 19 ♕h5 ♔h8 20 ♖f3 ♕c7 21 ♗c2 with the initiative.

b) 14...♖e8 and here:

b1) 15 d5 leads to exchanges and equality: 15...cxd5 16 ♕xd5 ♘f6 17 ♕c5 (17 ♕b5 b6 18 ♖fc1 ♗d7 19 ♕a6 ♘e4! 20 ♖c7 ♘c5 = 21 ♖1xc5?! bxc5 22 ♘xe5 {22 ♗a4 ♖ed8} 22...♕xe5 23 ♖xd7 ♖e7 24 ♕b7 ♖ae8 25 ♕xa7?? ♕f5 –+) 17...♘e4 18 ♕xe7 ♖xe7 19

罩c2 (19 罩cc1 &g4 =; 19 罩c4 ⑤g5 20 ⑤xg5 hxg5 21 罩fc1 &e6 22 罩c7 罩xc7 23 罩xc7 &xb3 24 axb3 罩d8 = Izeta-Janjgava, San Sebastian 1991) 19...⑤g5 20 ⑤xg5 hxg5 21 罩d1 &f5 22 罩c3 ♔f8 = P.Nikolić-Yusupov, Belgrade 1989.

b2) 15 ♕c2 and now:

b21) 15...e4 16 ⑤d2 ⑤f6 17 罩c5 &e6 (17...♕d8 18 罩e5 罩xe5 19 dxe5 ⑤g4 20 ⑤xe4 ⑤xe5 21 ♕c5 ± Vyzhmanavin-Klovans, Bern 1993) 18 &xe6 ♕xe6 19 b4 ⑤d5 20 罩b1 a6 21 a4 ±.

b22) 15...exd4 16 ⑤xd4! ⑤f6 17 f3 c5 (17...&d7!? 18 e4 罩ad8 ±) 18 罩xc5 ♕xe3+ 19 ♕f2 ±.

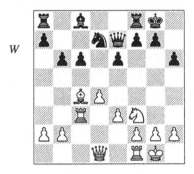

**14 &d3**
The most popular move. Other continuations also deserve attention:

a) 14 ♕c2 &b7 15 &d3 c5 16 &h7+ ♔h8 17 &e4 &xe4 18 ♕xe4 ⑤f6 with equality, Chekhov-Przewoznik, Polish Ch (Bydgoszcz) 1990.

b) 14 ♕d3 罩d8! 15 罩fc1 &b7 16 ♕e4 罩ac8 17 &b3 (17 &d3 ⑤f6 18 ♕h4 c5 =) 17...&a8 18 ♕f4 c5 19 罩3c2 b5 20 dxc5 &xf3 21 ♕xf3 ⑤xc5 = Epishin-C.Hansen, Malmö 1994.

c) 14 ♕e2 and now:

c1) 14...a5!? 15 罩fc1 &b7 16 h3 (16 a3 罩fd8 17 h3 a4 18 罩d1 c5 19 &b5 罩a5 = Epishin-Vaganian, Erevan 1996) 16...c5 17 &b5 e5 18 dxe5 ⑤xe5 19 ⑤xe5 ♕xe5 20 罩d3 ± Epishin-Vaganian, Reggio Emilia 1995/6.

c2) 14...&b7 15 &a6 &xa6 16 ♕xa6 c5 17 罩fc1 (17 ♕a3 e5 18 dxc5 ⑤xc5 19 b4 ⑤e4 20 罩c4 ⑤g5 with equality, P.Cramling-Pigusov, Spanish Cht (Cala Galdana) 1994) 17...e5 18 ♕b7 (18 dxc5 ⑤xc5 19 ♕b5 罩fe8 20 b4 a6 21 ♕c4 ⑤a4 22 罩3c2 b5 = Zarubin-Korneev, Russian Club Cup (Maikop) 1998) 18...♕d6 19 罩c4 罩fb8 20 ♕e4 exd4 21 exd4 罩e8 = Gulko-Yusupov, Reykjavik 1990.

**14...c5 15 &e4**
White has also played 15 &b5!? 罩d8 (15...cxd4?! 16 ⑤xd4 ⑤c5 17 &c6 &b7 18 ♕f3 &xc6 19 ⑤xc6 ♕b7 20 ⑤e5 ♕xf3 21 gxf3 ± Polugaevsky-Andersson, Reggio Emilia 1991) 16 &c6 (16 ♕e2 &b7 17 &xd7 cxd4 =; 16 ♕c2 &b7 17 &e2 e5 =), and now:

a) 16...&a6!? 17 &xa8 (17 罩e1 罩ac8 18 ♕a4 ⑤b8 19 &e4 cxd4 20 exd4 罩xc3 21 bxc3 ♕c7 ½-½ Vyzhmanavin-Janjgava, Manila OL 1992) 17...&xf1 18 &c6 (18 ♔xf1 罩xa8 19 ♕c2 a5 20 ♕e4 罩c8 21 ♕b7 ♕d8 is equal, Dautov-Ekström, Geneva 1997) 18...&a6 19 ♕c2 ♕d6 20 &xd7 ♕xd7 21 h3 cxd4 22 ⑤xd4 罩c8 = Vyzhmanavin-Li Wenliang, Beijing 1991.

b) 16...罩b8 17 ♕c2 cxd4! (better than 17...&b7?! 18 &xb7 罩xb7 19 dxc5 ⑤xc5 20 b4 ⑤a6 21 a3 罩c7 22 h3 罩xc3 23 ♕xc3 ⑤c7 24 ⑤d4 ⑤d5 25 ♕c4 ♕b7 26 罩c1 a6 27 ♕c6 ± Polugaevsky-Rashkovsky, USSR Ch (Moscow) 1973) 18 ⑤xd4 e5 19 ⑤f5 ♕f6 20 罩d1 ⑤c5! 21 罩xd8+ ♕xd8 22

&g3 &e6 23 b4 &c8! 24 &f3 &a6 25 a3 &xc3 26 ♕xc3 ♕c7 27 ♕d2 &b8 with equality, Smyslov-Kasparov, Vilnius Ct (6) 1984.

**15...&b8 16 ♕a4**

16 ♕c2 a5 17 &c1 &b7 18 &xb7 &xb7 19 dxc5 &xc5 20 &e5 ♕f6 21 &d3 &d8 = Khalifman-Yusupov, Bundesliga 1992/3.

**16...a5**

16...&b7 17 &xb7 &xb7 18 ♕c2 a5 (18...&c8 19 &c1 &bc7 20 b4 ± Kramnik-Kasparov, Las Palmas 1996) 19 a3 &e8 20 &d1 &bb8 21 h3 (21 dxc5 &xc5 22 b4 axb4 23 axb4 &a6 24 b5 &c5 25 &e5 &a8 26 &c6 ♕f6 =) 21...&bd8 (21...e5 22 dxe5 &xe5 23 &xe5 ♕xe5 24 &cd3 ±) 22 &cd3 &c8 (22...cxd4 23 &xd4 &c5 24 b4 axb4 25 axb4 &a6 26 ♕c4! ±) 23 d5 exd5 (23...e5 24 d6 ♕e6 25 e4 intending &d5 ±) 24 &xd5 &f6 25 &e5! ♕c7 26 &xe8+ &xe8 27 a4! ± Karpov-Yusupov, Dortmund 1997.

**17 &fc1**

17 a3 e5 =.

**17...e5 18 &c6 cxd4 19 exd4 exd4 20 ♕xd4 &c5 21 ♕e5 ♕xe5 22 &xe5 &e6**

½-½ Chuchelov-Winants, Brussels 1998.

**D)**

**9 ♕c2 (D)**

**9...c6**

Also possible is 9...&xc3 10 ♕xc3 dxc4 11 &xc4 b6:

a) 12 &c1 &b7 13 &e2 &d7 14 0-0 &fc8 15 b4 (15 &fd1 c5 16 ♕a3 &c7 17 &c3 &ac8 18 &dc1 &f6 19 dxc5 &e4 20 &3c2 &xc5 = Tal-Averkin, Sochi 1982) 15...c5 16 dxc5 (16 bxc5 bxc5 17 ♕a3 &f8 18 dxc5 &xc5 =

Taimanov-Vasiukov, Leningrad 1974) 16...bxc5 17 b5 a6 18 a4 axb5 19 &xb5 &b6 20 &a1 c4 21 ♕d4 &c5 22 &fd1 &xf3 23 gxf3 c3 = Lisik-Korneev, Podolsk 1992.

b) 12 d5!? exd5 13 &xd5 c6 14 &c4 &a6! (14...&b7?! 15 &e5 b5 16 &b3 ♕c7 17 a4 &d7 18 &g6 &fe8 19 axb5 &ac8 20 0-0 c5 21 &f4 c4 22 &c2 ± Lobron-Yusupov, Munich 1993; 14...c5!? 15 ♕e5! &c6 16 ♕xe7 &xe7 17 0-0-0! ±) 15 &xa6 &xa6 16 0-0 c5 17 &fd1 &ad8!? 18 &e5 ♕e6 = (analysis).

c) 12 0-0 &b7 13 &e2 and then:

c1) 13...&c8 14 b4 &d7 15 &fc1! (15 &fd1 &f6 16 ♕b3 &d5 17 &c4 &xf3 18 gxf3 c6 = Lutz-Yusupov, Munich 1993) 15...c5 16 dxc5 bxc5 17 b5 a6 (17...&b6 18 &d2 &d5 19 ♕a5! ±) 18 a4 axb5 (18...c4 19 bxa6 &xa6 20 &d2!? {20 a5 &c5 21 &d2 &e5 22 f4 &g6 23 &xc4 &h4 ± Psakhis-Yusupov, Baden-Baden 1992} 20...&b6 21 a5 &d5 22 ♕e5 f6 23 ♕d4 e5 24 ♕g4 ±) 19 &xb5 &c6 20 &xc6 &xc6 21 a5 ± Zsu.Polgar-Chiburdanidze, St Petersburg wom Ct (5) 1995.

c2) 13...c5 14 dxc5 &c8 15 b4 (15 &d4?! &xc5 16 ♕a3 &c6 17 &xc6 &xc6 = Karpov-Yusupov, London Ct

(4) 1989) 15...bxc5 16 b5 (16 bxc5
♘d7 17 ♖fe1 ♘xc5 18 ♖ab1 ♘e4 19
♕b2 ♗d5 = Epishin-Lputian, New
York 1990) 16...a6 and here:
c21) 17 ♖fd1!? axb5 18 ♗xb5
♗xf3!? 19 gxf3 c4 20 a4 ♕g5+ 21
♔h1 ♕h5 22 e4 ♘c6 23 ♖g1 (23 f4
♕c5 24 ♖g1 ♘d4 25 ♖ad1 e5 26 fxe5
{26 ♕g3 ♕f8!} 26...♘e2 ∓) 23...e5
intending ...♘d4 – analysis.
c22) 17 ♖fb1 ♘d7 18 a4 axb5 19
♗xb5 ♗xf3 20 gxf3 c4 21 ♔h1 ♖c5
22 ♖g1 ♕f6 23 ♕xf6 ♘xf6 24 ♖ac1
♘d5 = Romanishin-Ovseevich, Donetsk Z 1998.
c23) 17 a4 axb5 18 axb5 ♘d7 19
♖fc1 ♘b6 20 ♘d2 ±.
We now return to 9...c6 (D):

W

**10 ♗d3**
10 ♘xe4 deserves scrutiny: 10...dxe4
11 ♕xe4 ♕b4+ 12 ♘d2 ♕xb2 13 ♖b1
(13 ♕b1 ♕c3 14 ♕c1 ♕xc1+ 15 ♖xc1
♘d7 16 ♗e2 c5 17 dxc5 ♘xc5 18 ♘b3
b6 = Trifunović-Najdorf, Yugoslavia
1949) 13...♕xa2 14 ♗d3 f5 and now:
a) 15 ♕h4? c5 (15...♕a5 16 g4 e5
17 gxf5 exd4 ∞) 16 d5 (16 dxc5 ♕a3
17 ♔e2 ♘d7 ∓; 16 ♔e2 cxd4 17 ♖a1
♕b2 18 ♖hb1 ♕c3 19 ♘e4 fxe4 20
♕xe4 dxe3 –+) 16...♘d7 (16...e5!?) 17

dxe6 ♘e5 and now:
a1) 18 e7 ♘xd3+ 19 ♔e2 ♖e8 20
♔xd3 ♕a6 ∓.
a2) 18 ♗xf5!? ♖xf5 19 ♕d8+ ♔h7
20 e7 ♗d7! 21 0-0 (21 ♕xa8 ♘d3+
–+) 21...♖xd8 22 exd8♕ ♕xd2 ∓ 23
♖bd1 ♕e2 24 ♖xd7 ♖g5! –+.
b) 15 ♕e5 ♕a3 16 ♔e2 ♕e7 17 c5
♘d7 18 ♕c7 e5 19 ♘f3 exd4 20 ♘xd4
♕e5 21 ♕xe5 ♘xe5 22 f4 ♘xd3 23
♔xd3 b6 ∞.
**10...♘xc3 11 ♕xc3 dxc4 12 ♗xc4**
12 ♕xc4 ♘d7 13 0-0 e5 =.
**12...♘d7 13 0-0 b6 14 e4**
Or: 14 b4 ♗b7 15 ♗e2 a5! 16 a3
axb4 17 axb4 c5 18 bxc5 bxc5 19 ♖xa8
♖xa8 20 ♖a1 = Ro.Hernandez-An-
dersson, Rome 1986; 14 ♖fd1 ♗b7 15
♖ac1 ♖fc8 16 ♗d3 c5 17 ♕a3 ♔f8 =
Averbakh-Kotov, Saltsjöbaden IZ 1952.
**14...♗b7 15 ♖fe1**
15 ♖ad1 c5 16 d5 exd5 17 exd5
♕d6 18 ♘h4 ♘e5 19 ♘f5 ♕f6 20 ♘e3
♖ad8 21 ♗e2 a6 22 a4 ♘d7 = Den-
ker-Vidmar, Groningen 1946.
**15...c5 16 d5**
16 ♕a3 ♕f6 17 ♗b5 ♖fd8 = Aver-
bakh-Ravinsky, Moscow 1952.
**16...exd5 17 exd5 ♕f6**
17...♕d6 18 ♘h4! g6 19 ♕e3 ♔g7
20 ♕e7 ±.
**18 ♕xf6**
18 ♘e5 ♘xe5 19 ♖xe5 ♖ad8 =; 18
♗b5!? ♖fd8 19 ♖ad1 ∞.
**18...♘xf6 19 ♖ad1 ♖ad8 20 ♖e7
♗xd5 21 ♗xd5 ♖xd5 22 ♖xd5 ♘xd5
23 ♖xa7 ♖e8 24 g3 ♖e7**
= Szabo-Portisch, Sarajevo 1963.

**Conclusion:** The Lasker Defence
is one of Black's most reliable variations. It is very hard for White to break
through Black's defensive barrier.

# 8 The Tartakower Defence

1 d4 d5 2 c4 e6 3 ♘c3 ♗e7 4 ♘f3 ♘f6
5 ♗g5 h6 6 ♗h4 0-0 7 e3 b6 *(D)*

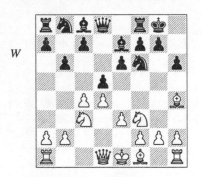

W

In this variation there arise very intricate positions. It became popular mainly as a result of its use by such players as Spassky, Geller, Karpov, Kasparov, Beliavsky, Short and others. Its theory was developed in particular in the matches between Karpov and Kasparov.

White now has several major continuations:

A: 8 ♖b1      98
B: 8 ♕b3      99
C: 8 ♕c2      101
D: 8 ♖c1      105
E: 8 cxd5     111
F: 8 ♗d3      117
G: 8 ♗e2      123

Or 8 ♕d2 ♘bd7 9 cxd5 exd5 10 ♗b5 ♗b7 11 ♗xd7 ♕xd7 12 ♘e5 ♕e6 13 0-0 ♘e4 = Šahović-Sr.Cvetković, Yugoslavia 1984.

## A)

**8 ♖b1**

This is Eingorn's move. It has some interesting points, but Black's resources are fully adequate.

**8...♘bd7**

8...a5!? 9 ♗e2 ♗b7 10 0-0 ♘bd7 11 ♖c1 c5 12 dxc5 bxc5 ∞ Levitt-Arlandi, Catania 1994.

Also interesting is 8...♘e4!? 9 ♗xe7 ♕xe7 10 cxd5 ♘xc3 11 bxc3 exd5 12 c4 ♗e6 (12...dxc4?! 13 ♗xc4 ♗b7 14 ♘e5 ♘c6 15 ♘g6 ♕g5 16 ♘xf8 ♕xg2 17 ♕h5! ♘d8 18 ♔e2 ♔xf8 19 ♖hg1 ♕e4 20 ♗d3 ♕e6 21 ♖bc1 ± Hodgson-Parker, Dublin Z 1993) 13 ♕b3 ♘c6 14 cxd5 ♘a5 15 ♕b5 a6 16 ♕b4 ♕xb4+ 17 ♖xb4 ♗xd5 18 ♖b2 ♖fc8 ∞ G.Buckley-Parker, British Ch (Nottingham) 1996.

**9 cxd5 ♘xd5**

9...exd5!?.

**10 ♗xe7 ♕xe7 11 ♘xd5**

11 ♗c4 ♘xc3 12 bxc3 ♗b7 13 a4 c5 ∞.

**11...exd5 12 ♗e2**

12 b4 c5 13 ♗b5 (13 bxc5 bxc5 14 ♗b5 ♖b8 intending 15...c4 ∞) 13...♖b8 ∞.

**12...♘f6 13 b4**

13 ♕a4?! ♗d7 14 ♕b3?! (14 ♗b5 =) 14...c5 15 ♕a3 ♖fe8 16 ♖c1?! (16 dxc5 bxc5 17 ♖c1 ∞) 16...c4 ∓ Tukmakov-Lputian, Lucerne Wcht 1993.

**13...♗f5 14 ♖b3**

14 ♖b2 c5 15 bxc5 bxc5 16 dxc5 ♕xc5 17 0-0 ♖fb8 =.

**14...a5 15 b5 a4 16 ♖b2 ♕a3 17 ♕c1 ♘e4 18 ♘e5 ♘c3**
The game is unclear.

**B)**
   **8 ♕b3** *(D)*

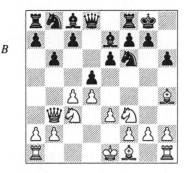

**8...♗b7**
Practice has also seen 8...dxc4 9 ♗xc4 ♗b7:

a) If 10 0-0, then 10...♘c6! 11 ♗e2 ♘a5 12 ♕c2 ♘d5! 13 ♗g3 (13 ♗xe7 ♕xe7 14 ♘xd5 ♗xd5 {14...exd5!?} 15 e4 ♗b7 16 ♖ac1 ♖ac8 intending ...c5 =) 13...c5 14 dxc5 ♗xc5 15 ♖fd1 ♕e7 = Maiorov-Kveinys, USSR 1989.

b) White should play the active 10 ♘e5!:

b1) 10...♘bd7 11 0-0 (after 11 ♘xf7 ♖xf7 12 ♗xe6 ♕e8 the position is unclear) 11...♘xe5 12 dxe5 ♘d5 (12...♘g4 13 ♗g3 ±; 12...♘d7 13 ♗g3 ♘c5 14 ♕c2 ±) 13 ♗xe7 ♘xe7 14 ♖ad1 ±.

b2) 10...♘fd7 11 ♘xf7 ♔xf7 (not 11...♖xf7? 12 ♗xe6 ♗xh4 13 ♗xf7+ ♔h8 14 ♗d5 +− Shirov-Beliavsky, Belgrade 1995) 12 ♗xe6+ ♔e8 13 ♕c2 (13 ♗g3!? with compensation – Shirov) 13...♗xh4 14 ♕g6+ ♔e7 15 ♗d5 ♖xf2! 16 ♕e6+ ♔f8 17 ♕g8+

♔e7 18 ♕xd8+ ♔xd8 19 ♗xb7 ♖xg2+ 20 ♔d1 ♖xb2 21 ♗xa8 ∞ Shirov.

**9 ♗xf6 ♗xf6 10 cxd5**
White achieves nothing by 10 ♖d1 c6! 11 e4 (now 11 cxd5 can be met by 11...cxd5 12 ♗e2 ♘c6 ∓) 11...♘d7:

a) 12 e5 ♗e7 13 cxd5 exd5 (or 13...cxd5!? 14 ♗d3 a6 {intending ...b5} 15 a4 ♘b8 intending ...♘c6, ...♖c8 and ...♘a5 ∞) 14 ♗e2 ♖e8 =.

b) 12 cxd5 exd5 13 exd5 ♖e8+ 14 ♗e2 cxd5 15 0-0 (if 15 ♘xd5, then 15...♗xd5 16 ♕xd5 ♕e7 17 ♖d2 ♖ad8 = intending ...♘e5) 15...♘f8 16 ♖fe1 ♘e6 and now 17 ♗b5? ♖e7 18 ♖e3 ♕d6 19 g3 a6 20 ♗f1 b5 ∓ gave Black the better chances in Damljanović-Yusupov, Belgrade 1989. According to Yusupov, White can maintain equality by 17 ♗f1 a6 18 a4 =.

**10...exd5 11 ♖d1 ♖e8** *(D)*
Black is worse after 11...c6 12 ♗d3 ♘a6 (12...♖c8 13 0-0 ♗g4 14 ♘e2 ♕e7 15 ♗b1 ♖c8 16 h3 ♗xf3 17 gxf3 ♘d7 18 ♘f4 ♘f8 19 ♖d2 ♖d8 20 ♖c1 ♖d6 21 ♗f5 ♗g5 22 ♘g2! ± Karpov-Beliavsky, Yugoslav Cht (Nikšić) 1996) 13 0-0 ♘c7 14 e4 ♘e6 15 e5 ♗e7 16 ♗b1 ♖e8 17 ♕c2 g6 18 ♕d2 ♗f8 19 ♖fe1 ± Dlugy-H.Olafsson, Moscow 1989.

However, 11...♕d6 deserves serious attention: 12 ♗d3 c5 13 dxc5 (13 ♗b1 ♘d7 14 0-0 ♖fd8! 15 dxc5 ♘xc5 16 ♕a3 ♕f8! = Basin-Gelfand, 1984) 13...♕xc5 (but not 13...♗xc3+?! 14 ♕xc3 bxc5 15 0-0 ♘d7 16 ♗b1 ♖fd8 17 ♖c1 ♖ac8 18 ♖fd1 ♘f8 19 ♕e5 ♘e6 20 ♗f5 ± Komarov-Gelfand, 1984; White has definite pressure) 14 0-0 ♘d7 15 ♖c1 ♖fd8 = Sturua-Klovans, 1985.

**12 ♗d3**

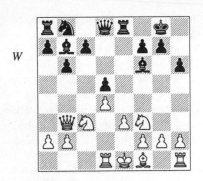

W

This line tends to be rather equal. Otherwise:

a) 12 g3!? (White fianchettoes the bishop so as to maximize the pressure on the d5-pawn) 12...c5! 13 ♗g2 c4 14 ♕c2 ♞a6! 15 0-0 ♞c7 16 ♞e5 (16 b3 b5 17 bxc4 dxc4! ∞) 16...♗xe5 17 dxe5 ♖xe5 18 ♞xd5 ♞xd5 19 e4 ♖c8 20 exd5 ♕d6 ∞ Dokhoian.

b) 12 a3!? is a useful move, by which White avoids obstructing the d-file, thus seeking to hinder the counterattack with ...c5. Then:

b1) 12...c6 13 ♗d3 ♞d7 14 0-0 g6 15 ♖fe1 (15 e4 c5! 16 exd5 cxd4 17 ♞e4 ♞c5! 18 ♞xc5 ♗xd5) 15...♞f8 16 ♗b1 (16 e4 ♞e6 17 e5 ♗g7 =) 16...♞e6 17 ♗a2! ♕c7! 18 ♕a4 (18 e4 ∞) 18...♖ad8 = Korchnoi-Kasparov, London Ct (10) 1983.

b2) 12...♖e7!? and now:

b21) 13 ♗e2 c6 14 0-0 ♞a6! and now 15 ♖d2 ♞c7 16 ♖e1 ♞e8!, intending ...♞d6, ...♕e8 and ...♖d8 ∓, Khenkin-Geller, USSR 1984 or 15 ♕a2 ♞c7 16 ♖d2 ♞e8! 17 ♖c1 ♞d6 18 ♞e1 ♕e8, intending ...♖d8 ∓, Witt-Geller, Baden-Baden 1985.

b22) 13 ♗d3 c5 14 dxc5 bxc5 15 0-0 (intending ♗c4) 15...♕b6!? (15...d4 16 ♞e4 ♗xe4 17 ♗xe4 ♖xe4 18 ♕b7

♞c6! {the only move} 19 ♕xc6 ♕e8! 20 ♕xe8+ ♖axe8 21 exd4 ♗xd4 22 ♞xd4 ♖xd4 23 ♖xd4 cxd4 24 ♖d1 ♖e2 = I.Nowak and Wl.Schmidt) 16 ♕c2 ♞d7 17 ♗f5 ♗xc3 (17...d4!? ∞ Wl.Schmidt-Bönsch, Dresden 1985) 18 ♕xc3 ♞f6 19 b4 cxb4 20 axb4 ♖c7 =.

b3) 12...c5!? (an interesting reply despite White's last move) 13 dxc5 ♞d7 14 ♞xd5 (14 cxb6 ♞c5 with compensation) 14...♞xc5 15 ♕a2 ♗xb2! and then:

b31) 16 ♗c4?! b5!.

b32) 16 ♕xb2 ♗xd5 17 ♗e2 (17 ♗b5 ♖e6 18 0-0 ♖d6 19 ♕e5 ♞e4 intending ...♗b7 =) 17...♖e6 (17...♖e7!?) 18 0-0 ♖d6 19 ♕e5 ♖d7 20 ♞d4 ♕g5! with an equal position, Psakhis-Beliavsky, Burevestnik-Trud 1984.

b33) 16 ♗b5 ♖e6 17 ♞f4 ♗c3+ 18 ♔e2 ♕f6! (18...♖d6?! 19 ♗c4 ♗a6 20 ♗xa6 ♞xa6 21 ♖xd6 ♕xd6 22 ♖d1 ±) 19 ♞xe6 fxe6, intending ...♖f8, gives Black compensation, Bischoff-Razuvaev, Dortmund 1985.

We now return to the position after 12 ♗d3 (D):

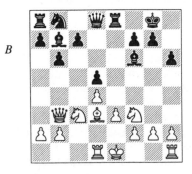

B

**12...c5**
12...♞c6 is also good:

a) 13 ♘xd5 ♗xd4 =.

b) 13 ♗b1 ♘a5 14 ♕c2 g6 15 h4 h5 16 g4 hxg4 17 h5 gxf3 18 hxg6 ♖e7 (18...♕d7!?; 18...♖xe3+ 19 fxe3 ♗h4+ 20 ♔d2 ♘c4+ 21 ♔c1 ♕g5 ∞ Lputian-Geller, USSR 1979) 19 g7 (Movsesian-A.Kuzmin, 1985) 19...♔xg7 20 ♕h7+ ♔f8 21 ♖g1 ♖e8 22 ♗g6 ♕d7 23 ♗h5 ♕e6 24 ♗g4 ♕d6 = Karpov.

c) 13 0-0 ♘a5 14 ♕c2 c5 (alternatively, 14...♕e7!? 15 ♖fe1 c5 16 dxc5 ♕xc5! 17 ♘b5 ♕xc2 18 ♗xc2 ♖ed8 19 ♘bd4 ♘c4 = Gheorghiu-Liberzon, Baden-Baden 1980) 15 dxc5 bxc5 16 ♘a4 c4 17 ♗e2 ♖b8 = K.Grigorian-Geller, USSR Ch (Leningrad) 1977.

**13 dxc5 ♘d7 14 c6**

14 cxb6 allows Black compensation after either 14...♘c5 or 14...d4.

**14...♗xc6 15 0-0 ♘c5 16 ♕c2**

16 ♕a3 a5 17 ♘e2 ♕d6 (another idea is 17...♘xd3!? ∞) 18 ♘ed4 ♗b7 19 ♗b5 ♖ed8 ∞ Bagirov-Beliavsky, Moscow tt 1981.

**16...♖c8 17 ♗b5**

17 ♗h7+ ♔h8 18 ♗f5 ♘e6! 19 ♕b3 (19 ♘d4? ♘xd4 20 exd4 ♖c7 ∓ Beliavsky-Kramnik, Belgrade 1997) 19...♗xc3 20 bxc3 ♕f6 = Gulko-Radashkevich, USSR 1971.

**17...♘e4 18 ♗xc6 ♖xc6 19 ♕a4 ♘xc3 20 bxc3**

20 ♕xc6 ♘xd1 21 ♖xd1 ♗xb2 22 ♖xd5 ♕c8 =/∓.

**20...♖c5**

The game is equal: 21 ♕xa7 ♗xc3 =; or 21 c4 ½-½ D.Gurevich-Portisch, New York 1984.

## C)

**8 ♕c2**

White tries to generate queenside play; this continuation achieved some

popularity in the early 1980s, but interest has since declined.

**8...♗b7** *(D)*

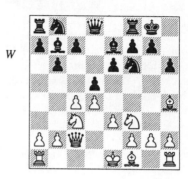

W

Now:
C1: **9 ♖d1**          101
C2: **9 ♗xf6**          102

The direct 9 0-0-0 has been tried: 9...♘bd7 10 ♖g1 ♘e4 (10...c5 11 g4 ♘e4 12 ♗xe7 ♕xe7 13 g5 cxd4 14 exd4 ♘xg5 15 ♘xg5 hxg5 16 ♖d3 ∞ Spassky-Drimer, Reykjavik U-26 Wcht 1957) 11 ♗xe7 ♕xe7 12 ♘xe4 dxe4 13 ♘d2 f5 14 g4 ♕h4 ∞ Skembris-Kovacs, Rome 1983.

## C1)

**9 ♖d1 ♘bd7**

9...♘e4 deserves serious attention:

a) 10 ♗xe7 ♕xe7 and now after 11 ♗d3 ♘xc3 12 bxc3 dxc4 13 ♗xc4 c5 14 0-0 ♘c6 Black has free and easy development. Or 11 ♘xe4 dxe4 12 ♘d2 f5 with the initiative.

b) 10 ♗g3 ♘d7 11 ♗d3 (11 cxd5 exd5 12 ♘xe4 dxe4 13 ♗xc7?! ♕e8 intending to meet 14 ♘d2 {14 ♘e5 ♗b4+} with 14...♖c8) 11...♘xg3 12 hxg3 c5!? ∞ (not 12...♘f6 13 e4 ± Romanishin-Chandler, Sochi 1982).

**10 cxd5 ♘xd5**

Also possible is 10...exd5 11 ♗d3 c5 12 0-0 ♘e8 (12...a6!? 13 ♗f5 c4 14 a4 ♘e8 15 ♗xe7 ♕xe7 16 ♗xd7?! ♕xd7 17 b3 ♘d6 18 bxc4 ♘xc4 19 ♕b3 ♖ac8 20 ♘e5 ♕d6 = Ubilava-Vasiukov, USSR 1982) 13 ♗g3 c4 14 ♗h7+ ♔h8 15 ♗f5 ♘df6 16 b3 ♘d6 (16...cxb3 17 ♕xb3 ±) 17 ♗xd6 ♗xd6 18 bxc4 dxc4 19 e4 ∞ ♗b4 20 d5 and now not 20...♕e7?? 21 e5! ♗xc3 22 d6 +− Ree-Beliavsky, Lucerne OL 1982, but 20...♖e8!? 21 ♖d4!? (21 e5 ♗xc3 22 ♕xc3 ♘xd5 23 ♕xc4 ♕c7 =; 21 ♖fe1 b5 ∞) 21...♗c5 22 ♖xc4 ♗a6 23 ♖xc5 ♗xf1 (23...bxc5 24 ♖d1 ∞) 24 ♖c6 ♗a6 25 e5! ∞.

**11 ♗g3**

White cannot reckon on achieving anything by exchanging. For example: 11 ♗xe7 ♕xe7 12 ♘xd5 ♗xd5 13 e4 (13 ♕xc7 ♖fc8 with the initiative) 13...♗b7 intending ...c5 =.

**11...c5**

Black should not delay this planned advance. If 11...♖c8, then, according to Karpov, White has the better chances after 12 ♗b5! c6 13 ♘xd5 ±.

**12 ♗b5**

Harmless is 12 ♘xd5 exd5 13 dxc5 bxc5 14 ♗e2 ♕a5+ with the initiative, Romanishin-Geller, USSR 1981.

Interesting play results after 12 dxc5 ♖c8 (12...♘xc5 leads to complex play: 13 ♗c4 ♖c8 14 0-0 ♗f6 15 ♘b5 ♗a6 16 e4 ♘b7 17 ♕e2 ♘a5 ∞ Romanishin-Geller, USSR Ch (Moscow) 1983; 12...♗xc5 13 ♗b5 ♘7f6 14 e4 ♘b4 15 ♕b1 ♕c8 16 a3 ♘c6 17 b4 ♗e7 18 ♖c1 a6 should be answered by 19 ♗e2! ±, but not 19 ♗xc6 ♕xc6! 20 ♘d5 ♕e8 21 ♘c7 ♕a4 22 ♘xa8 ♖xa8 23 e5 ♘d5 24 ♕b2 a5

with compensation, Lputian-M.Gurevich, USSR Ch (Riga) 1985) 13 ♗b5 (not 13 e4? ♘xc3 14 bxc3 ♖xc5 15 ♘e5 ♘xe5 16 ♖xd8 ♖xd8 17 ♗xe5 ♗xe5 ∓ Romanishin-Beliavsky, USSR Ch (Moscow) 1983; 13 ♘xd5 exd5 14 ♗b5 a6 15 ♗d3 bxc5 16 0-0 ♘f6 17 ♗f5 ♖a8 18 ♗e5 ♕b6 19 ♖d3 a5 is equal, Lputian-Pigusov, Irkutsk 1982) 13...♘xc5 14 0-0 ♗f6 =.

**12...cxd4 13 ♖xd4 ♗c5**

13...♗f6!? deserves attention.

**14 ♖d1 ♘7f6 15 e4 a6 16 ♗c4 ♘b4 17 ♕e2 ♕c8 18 0-0 b5**

= Ki.Georgiev-T.Georgadze, Lvov 1984.

**C2)**

**9 ♗xf6 ♗xf6 10 cxd5 exd5** *(D)*

**11 0-0-0**

Another aggressive idea is 11 g4 c5 12 0-0-0 ♘c6 13 h4 cxd4 (interesting is 13...g6 14 g5 hxg5 15 hxg5 ♗g7 16 ♖h4 cxd4 17 exd4 ♖c8 18 ♔b1 ♖e8 19 ♗h3 ♖c7 20 ♕d2 ♖ce7 ∞ P.Cramling-Geller, Aruba (Ladies vs Veterans) 1992) 14 exd4, and now:

a) A sharp battle arises after the moves 14...♗c8 15 g5 hxg5 16 hxg5 ♗xg5+:

a1) 17 Nxg5!? Qxg5+ 18 Kb1 should be met by 18...g6!? ∞, rather than 18...Bf5? 19 Bd3 Nb4 20 Bxf5 Nxc2 21 Bh7+ Kh8 22 Bxc2+ Kg8 23 Rdg1! Qd8 24 Bh7+ Kh8 25 Rh5! Re8 (25...g6 26 Bxg6+ Kg7 27 Be4+ Kf6 28 Rf5+ Ke6 29 Re5+ +−) 26 Be4+! Kg8 27 Rgh1! Kf8 28 Nxd5 f5 29 Rxf5+ Kg8 30 Bc2 Re6 31 Bb3 Rh6 32 Rxh6 +−.

a2) 17 Kb1 g6 18 Nxg5 Qxg5 19 f4!? Qxf4 20 Nxd5 Qf5 (the only move; 20...Qd6 21 Qxc6 +−) 21 Bd3 Qxd5 and here:

a21) 22 Bxg6 Qxa2+! 23 Kxa2 (23 Kc1 Qa1+ 24 Kd2 Qa5+) 23...Nb4+ 24 Kb1 Nxc2 25 Be4 (25 Bxc2 Kg7!) 25...Bg4 26 Rdg1 Be3 27 Bxa8 Rxa8 28 Rg3 Rd8! intending ...Rd4.

a22) 22 Qh2 Kg7 23 Qh6+ (23 Rdf1? can be answered by 23...f5!? or 23...Bh3!) 23...Kf6 (forced) 24 Qxf8 Qxa2+!! 25 Kxa2 (25 Kc1 Qa1+ 26 Bb1?? Qxb1+ −+) 25...Be6+ 26 Ka3 (½-½ Malyshev-Semionov, USSR 1987) 26...Rxf8 27 Be4 (27 d5 Bxd5 28 Rhf1+ Kg7 29 Bxg6 fxg6 30 Rxf8 Kxf8 31 Rxd5 Kf7 =) 27...Ne7 28 d5 Bf5 29 Bf3 Rd8 with counterplay.

b) 14...g6 15 g5 (White achieves nothing in the event of 15 h5 g5 16 Qf5 Nb4 17 Ne5 Bc8 18 Qf3 Bxe5 19 dxe5 Qc7 20 Kb1 Qxe5 21 Bg2 Ba6 22 a3 d4 with equality, Agdestein-H.Olafsson, Nordic Ch playoff (Gjøvik) (1) 1985) 15...hxg5 16 hxg5 Bxg5+ (also possible is 16...Bg7 17 Rh4 Re8 18 Bh3 b5 19 Kb1 Bc8 20 Bxc8 Rxc8 21 Qd2 Qd7 22 Ka1 b4 23 Na4 Nxd4 24 Rxd4 Qxa4 25 Rxb4 Qc6 = P.Cramling-Vaganian, Biel 1994) 17 Kb1 Bf6 (17...Kg7 18 a3 Bf6 19 Rg1 Rh8 20 Bd3 Rh6 21

Ne2! Qd6 22 Qd2 with compensation, Tisdall-H.Olafsson, Espoo Z 1989) 18 Bd3 Nb4 19 Bxg6! Nxc2 20 Bh7+ and now:

b1) 20...Kg7 21 Rdg1+ Bg5 22 Nxg5 Kf6 23 Rh6+ Ke7 24 Bxc2 Qd7 25 Re1+ Kd8 26 Re5! Kc7 27 Bf5 Qd8 28 Be6!! gave White the initiative in Bellon-Ki.Georgiev, Terrassa 1990.

b2) Instead, 20...Kh8!? is fully possible. After 21 Bxc2+ Kg8 22 Rdg1+ Bg7, White should opt for 23 Bh7+ =, since 23 Rh7?! is dubious: 23...Qf6 24 Ne5 Rfe8 25 Ng4 Qxd4 26 Nh6+ Kf8 27 Nf5 Qxf2 28 Rhxg7 (28 Rgxg7 Re1+ 29 Nd1 Rxd1+! 30 Bxd1 Qxf5+ −+) 28...Re1+ 29 Rxe1 Qxe1+ 30 Nd1 Bc8 −+.

We now return to 11 0-0-0 (D):

B

**11...c5**

Dubious is 11...Nd7?! (delaying Black's counterattack) 12 h4 c5 13 g4 cxd4 14 exd4 Be7 (14...Qc7 15 Kb1 Qf4 16 Be2 Be7 17 g5 h5 18 Ng1! g6 19 Nh3 Qd6 20 f4 a6 21 f5 Rfe8 22 Rdf1 Nf8 23 Nf4 Bd8 24 Bd3 +− Zsu.Polgar-Lau, Polanica Zdroj 1991) 15 g5 h5 16 Bh3 g6 17 Qb3 ± Borisenko-Shishov, USSR 1964.

However, 11...♘c6!? deserves serious attention: 12 h4 (12 a3 is too sluggish: 12...♘e7 13 h4 c5 14 g4 g6 15 g5 hxg5 16 hxg5 ♗g7 17 ♗h3 ♕d6 18 ♔b1 ♗c8 ∓ Polugaevsky-Bannik, USSR Ch (Moscow) 1961) 12...♗c8 (interesting is 12...♘b4!? 13 ♕d2 {13 ♕f5 ♕c8! =} 13...c5 14 g4, Borisenko-Ilivitsky, Sverdlovsk 1957, when 14...♕c8! looks rather strong: 15 g5 cxd4!) 13 a3 (White employed an interesting idea in Banikas-A.Shneider, Cappelle la Grande 1998: 13 ♘g5!? ♗xg5 14 hxg5 ♕xg5 15 ♗e2 ♘e7 16 g4! ♗xg4 17 ♖dg1 ♗f5 18 ♖xg5 ♗xc2 19 ♖e5 ♘c6 20 ♖xd5 ♗g6 21 ♖d7 with compensation) 13...♘e7 14 e4 dxe4 15 ♘xe4 ♘d5 16 ♗c4 ♗g4 17 ♖de1 ♗xf3 (Cvitan-Sr.Cvetković, Opatija 1984) 18 ♗xd5 ♗xe4 ∓.

**12 dxc5 ♘d7!**

Black offers a pawn sacrifice that White can hardly accept. 12...bxc5?! is dubious in view of 13 ♘xd5 ♗xd5 14 ♗c4 ♘d7 15 ♖xd5 ♖b8 16 b3 ♕e7 (16...♕c7 17 ♔d1 ♖fc8 18 ♘d2! ±) 17 h4! ♘b6 18 ♖e5! ♕c7 19 ♖e4 ± Lapienis-A.Petrosian, USSR 1979.

**13 c6**

After 13 cxb6 ♕xb6 Black's initiative at least counterbalances White's minimal material advantage.

13 ♘xd5!? leads to very sharp play: 13...♘xc5 14 ♗c4 (14 ♕f5 is met by the strong retort 14...♕c8! 15 ♘xf6+ gxf6 16 ♕xc8 ♖axc8 17 ♔b1 ♘e4 with the better game for Black) 14...b5! and now:

a) 15 ♗xb5 ♗xd5 16 ♗c4 runs into an effective reply, involving a queen sacrifice – 16...♗e4! 17 ♖xd8 ♖fxd8 18 ♕e2 ♖ac8, and Black's attack is unstoppable.

b) Also after 15 ♗b3 ♖c8 (15...a5!?) 16 ♔b1 ♘xb3 17 ♕xb3 ♖c5 Black ousts the knight from d5 and obtains excellent play, e.g. 18 e4 ♖e8 19 ♖he1 ♖xe4.

c) 15 ♘xf6+ ♕xf6 16 ♗d5 ♖ac8 17 ♔b1 ♘a4 18 ♕e2 ♗xd5 19 ♖xd5 ♖c4! 20 ♖d4 (20 ♖xb5?! ♖fc8 21 ♘e5 ♕a6! 22 ♘xc4 ♕xb5 23 ♖c1 ♖xc4! 24 ♖xc4 ♘c3+ –+; 20 ♘d4?! ♕g6+ ∓) 20...♖fc8 and here:

c1) 21 ♕d3 ♘c5! 22 ♕e2 (22 ♖xc4 ♘xd3 23 ♖xc8+ ♔h7 24 ♖c2 ♕g6) 22...♕g6+ 23 ♔a1 and now Black forces mate: 23...♖c1+! 24 ♖xc1 ♘b3+ 25 axb3 ♖xc1+ 26 ♔a2 ♕b1+ 27 ♔a3 a5 28 ♖d8+ ♔h7 29 ♘g5+ (29 ♕d3+ ♕xd3 30 ♖xd3 ♖a1#) 29...♔g6 30 ♖d6+ f6.

c2) 21 ♖hd1 ♖c2! (21...♕g6+? 22 ♕d3 ♕xg2 23 ♕f5! ± Kasparov-I.Zaitsev, Baku 1980) 22 ♕xc2 ♖xc2 23 ♔xc2 ♕g6+ (23...♕e6!?) 24 ♔d2 ♘xb2 25 ♖c1 ♕xg2 26 ♔e2 ♘c4 =/∓.

**13...♗xc6 14 ♘d4 ♗b7 15 g4**

White is worse after 15 ♔b1 a6! 16 g4 b5 17 ♗g2 ♖c8 18 ♕f5 ♘e5 ∓ P.Nikolić-Lputian, Sarajevo 1983 or 15 ♗e2 a6! 16 ♔b1 b5 17 ♗f3 ♖c8 18 ♕d2 ♘c5 19 ♘de2 ♘e4 20 ♘xe4 dxe4 21 ♗g4 ♕xd2 22 ♖xd2 ♖fd8 23 ♖hd1 ♖xd2 24 ♖xd2 ♖d8 is slightly better for Black, Lputian-A.Petrosian, Erevan 1980.

**15...♘e5 16 ♗e2 ♘c6!**

Black wants to exchange off the lynchpin of White's position: the d4-knight. Dubious is 16...♖c8?! 17 h4! ♗xh4 18 f4 ♘g6 19 ♗d3 ± Zaichik-Lputian, Jurmala 1983.

**17 ♕d2 ♘xd4 18 exd4 ♖e8**

Black is slightly better. 19 ♔b1 a6 20 f4 b5 21 ♗f3 ♖c8 22 ♕g2 ♖e3 23

♕f2 ♕e7 24 ♘e2 ♖e8 25 ♖d2 a5 26 ♖hd1 b4 27 ♘g3 g6 ∓ Ubilava-Kharitonov, Jurmala 1983.

## D)

**8 ♖c1 ♗b7** *(D)*

W

Now:
**D1: 9 ♗e2**          105
**D2: 9 ♗xf6**        107

Instead 9 ♗d3 ♘bd7 10 0-0 transposes to Line F23.

9 a3 is harmless owing to 9...♘bd7 10 cxd5 exd5 11 ♗e2 (11 b4!? c5! =) 11...c5 12 0-0 ♘e4 with an equal position, Andersson-Short, Thessaloniki OL 1988.

## D1)

**9 ♗e2 dxc4**

The most accurate reply. 9...♘bd7 allows a poisonous plan introduced by Karpov: 10 cxd5 exd5 11 0-0 c5 12 ♕a4!? a6 (12...♘e4 13 ♗xe7 ♕xe7 14 ♗a6 gives White a slight advantage) 13 dxc5 bxc5 14 ♖fd1 ♕b6 15 ♕b3. Black now has a choice:
a) Either go in for complications by 15...♕a7 16 ♗g3 ♖ad8 (16...♖ac8 17 ♘e5 ♖fd8 18 ♗f3 is slightly better

for White, Chekhov-Bönsch, Potsdam 1985) 17 ♘e1 (intending 18 ♗f3) 17...d4 18 exd4 cxd4 19 ♘a4 ♖c8 (19...♗d5!?) 20 ♖xc8 ♖xc8 21 ♗c4 ♖f8 22 ♕d3! ± Karpov-Kasparov, Moscow Wch (31) 1984/5.
b) Or else defend a somewhat worse ending by 15...♕xb3 16 axb3 (after the exchange of queens White's pressure on Black's hanging pawns is intensified):
b1) 16...♖fd8 17 ♘e1 g5 (17...♘b6 18 ♗f3 ♖ac8 {18...♖d7? 19 ♘d3 g5 20 ♗g3 ♖c8 21 ♘e5 ♖dd8 22 ♘c4! ± Lputian-Dorfman, Tashkent 1984} 19 ♘d3 ♗a8 20 ♖a1 d4 21 ♗xa8 ♖xa8 22 exd4 cxd4 23 ♘e2 ±) 18 ♗g3 ± Efimov-G.Georgadze, Tbilisi 1987.
b2) 16...♖fe8 17 ♗g3 ♗f8 18 ♘e1 ♖e6 19 ♗f3 ♘b6 20 h3 ± Eingorn-Lputian, USSR Ch (Lvov) 1984.
c) 15...♖fd8 has also been tried and found wanting: 16 ♗g3! ♖ac8! 17 ♘e5 ♕xb3 18 axb3 ♘b6 (18...♘f8 19 ♗f3 ± Gavrikov-King, Palma de Mallorca 1989) 19 ♗f3 ± Yusupov-Short, Linares 1992.

**10 ♗xc4 ♘bd7 11 0-0 c5** *(D)*

11...♘e4?! is dubious in view of 12 ♘xe4 ♗xh4 13 d5! ± Gheorghiu-Sofrigin, Lenk 1990.

W

**12 ♕e2**

The main move; practice has also seen:

a) 12 dxc5 ♘xc5 13 ♕e2 a6 14 ♖fd1 ♕e8 and then:

a1) 15 a3 ♘fe4! 16 ♘xe4 ♘xe4 17 ♗xe7 ♕xe7 18 ♘d4 (18 ♘e5 b5 19 ♖d7 ♕c5 20 ♘g6 bxc4 21 ♘e7+ {21 ♘xf8 ♗d5 −+} 21...♔h8 22 ♖xb7 ♘d6 23 b4 ♕g5 ∓ Tal) 18...♖fc8 ½-½ Korchnoi-Karpov, Baguio City Wch (1) 1978.

a2) 15 ♘e5 b5! 16 ♘xb5 and then:

a21) 16...axb5? 17 ♗xb5 ♗a6 18 ♖xc5 ♗xc5 19 ♗xa6! ♕a4 20 ♗xf6 gxf6 (20...♕xa6 21 ♕g4 +−; 20...♖xa6 21 b3! ♕xa2 22 ♕g4 g6 23 ♘xg6 +−) 21 ♗b5 ♕xa2 22 ♘d7 ± Kasparov-Karpov, Moscow Wch (26) 1984/5.

a22) 16...♕b8! 17 ♗g3 axb5 18 ♘c6 (18 ♘xf7 ♕a7; 18 ♘g6 fxg6 19 ♗xb8 bxc4 20 ♗g3 ♗d5) 18...♗xc6 19 ♗xb8 bxc4 20 ♗d6 ♗xd6 21 ♖xd6 ♗d5 and Black has three pieces for the queen, which is more than enough.

b) 12 ♗g3 is very interesting: White preserves his bishop from exchange following ...♘e4 and transfers it to an active diagonal. 12...a6 and now:

b1) 13 d5 (Gheorghiu) is very interesting: 13...exd5 14 ♗xd5 ♘xd5 (14...♕c8 15 e4 ± Gheorghiu) 15 ♘xd5 ♗xd5 16 ♕xd5 ♖a7 17 ♖fd1 ♕a8 18 ♕f5 ♘f6 19 ♘e5 b5 20 b3 ♖e8 (not 20...♕e4? 21 ♕xe4 ♘xe4 22 ♘c6 ♖b7 23 ♘xe7+ ♖xe7 24 ♗d6 ♘xd6 25 ♖xd6 ± Gheorghiu-Donev, Liechtenstein 1991) 21 ♗h4 (21 f3!? intending e4 ∞) 21...♕e4 22 ♕xe4 ♘xe4 23 ♗xe7 ♖axe7 24 ♘d7 c4! 25 bxc4 b4 with compensation, Akopian-Kotronias, Khalkidhiki 1992.

b2) 13 a4 cxd4 14 ♘xd4 ♘c5 15 f3 ♘d5 16 ♗xd5 exd5. Black has an isolated pawn on d5, but in compensation he has the bishop-pair and there are many weaknesses in White's position (e3 and a4 for instance). The game is close to equality. 17 ♘f5 ♖e8 18 ♘xe7+ ♕xe7 19 b4 (19 ♖e1 ♖ad8 20 ♖c2 ♘b3 21 ♗f2 ½-½ Gavrikov-Portisch, Reggio Emilia 1991/2) 19...♘e6 20 ♘xd5 ♗xd5 21 ♕xd5 ♕xb4 22 ♕c6 b5 23 axb5 axb5 24 ♖b1 ♕d2 25 ♗f2 (25 ♕b6 ♖eb8! 26 ♕xb8+ {26 ♗xb8 ♖a2} 26...♖xb8 27 ♗xb8 ♕xe3+ ∓) 25...b4 26 ♖fd1 (26 ♕c4 ♖a2 is unclear) 26...♕e2 27 ♖e1 ♕d2 28 ♖ed1 ½-½ Portisch-Arlandi, Reggio Emilia 1991/2.

We now return to 12 ♕e2 (D):

**12...a6**

Alekhine's recommendation. Other moves:

a) 12...♘e4 is weaker: 13 ♘xe4 ♗xh4 (after 13...♗xe4 14 ♗xe7 ♕xe7 15 ♗a6 White controls important squares on the queenside) 14 ♘c3! ♗e7 (14...♗f6 15 ♖fd1 ♕e7 16 ♗a6 ♖ab8 17 ♗xb7 ♖xb7 18 ♘e4! ± Alekhine-Bogoljubow, Bad Nauheim 1937; 14...cxd4 15 exd4 ♗g5 16 ♖cd1 ♘f6

17 ♘xg5 hxg5 18 f4! ± Ki.Georgiev-Lputian, Sarajevo 1985) 15 ♖fd1 ♕c7 16 d5 ± Portisch-Spassky, Linares 1981.

b) 12...cxd4!? deserves attention: 13 exd4 (13 ♘xd4 a6 14 ♖fd1 ♕e8 15 a4 ♘c5 transposes to the note to White's 15th move) 13...♘h5 (an important relieving move) 14 ♗g3 ♘df6!? 15 ♖fd1 ♗d6 and here:

b1) 16 d5!? ♘xg3 17 hxg3 exd5 (17...e5 18 ♗a6 ±) 18 ♘xd5 ♖e8 19 ♕c2 (19 ♕d3 ♘xd5 20 ♗xd5 ♗xd5 21 ♕xd5 ♗c5 =) 19...♖c8 ∞.

b2) 16 ♘e5 ♖c8 17 ♗a6 (17 ♘xf7? ♖xf7 18 ♕xe6 ♖xc4 ∓) 17...♕c7! 18 ♘b5 ♕xc1 19 ♗xb7 ♗b8 (the only move) 20 ♗xc8 ♕xc8 21 ♘c3 ♕b7 is equal, Ftačnik-Beliavsky, Wijk aan Zee 1985.

**13 a4 cxd4 14 ♘xd4**

14 exd4 gives White nothing due to 14...♘h5! 15 ♗xe7 ♕xe7 16 d5 ♘f4 17 ♕e3 ♕f6 18 ♘e4 ♕f5 19 ♘g3 ♕f6 20 ♘e4 ♕f5 ½-½ Kasparov-Karpov, Moscow Wch (34) 1984/5.

**14...♘c5 15 f3**

Placing the important central square e4 under control and freeing a convenient retreat-square for the h4-bishop. In Yusupov-Karpov, Bugojno 1986 White tried to achieve an advantage by 15 ♖fd1 ♕e8 16 ♗g3 ♘fe4 17 ♘xe4 ♘xe4 18 ♗e5 ♗f6 19 ♗xf6 (19 ♗c7 ♕xa4 20 f3 ♗xd4 21 exd4 ♘f6 22 ♗xb6 ♗d5 = Vaganian-Beliavsky, Montpellier Ct 1985) 19...♘xf6 20 ♕c2 ♖d8 = (20...♖c8 21 ♕b3 ♗d5 22 ♗xd5 ♖xc1 23 ♖xc1 ♘xd5 24 e4 ± Karpov).

**15...♕e8!?**

The queen eyes the weakness on a4; 15...♘h5?! 16 ♗f2 ♗d6 17 ♖fd1 ♕e7

18 b4 ♘d7 19 ♕d2! ♗xb4 20 ♘f5 exf5 21 ♕xd7 ± Portisch-Hjartarson, Reykjavik 1987, while after 15...♘d5 16 ♗xe7 ♕xe7 17 ♗xd5 exd5 White's position deserves preference.

**16 ♕c2**

16 b3 ♘fe4! 17 ♘xe4 ♗xh4 18 ♘d6 ♕e7 19 ♘xb7 ♕xb7 with an equal position.

**16...♖c8 17 ♗a2 ♘d5 18 ♗xd5**

18 ♗b1 g6! =.

**18...♗xh4!**

The game is equal, Portisch-Vaganian, Saint John Ct (1) 1988. Instead 18...exd5 19 ♗xe7 ♕xe7 20 ♖fe1 g6 is slightly better for White.

**D2)**

**9 ♗xf6 ♗xf6 10 cxd5 exd5** *(D)*

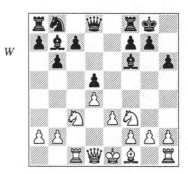

In this position White has three continuations:

Harmless is 11 ♕b3 c5! 12 ♗e2 (12 dxc5 d4 with the initiative) 12...cxd4 13 exd4 ♘c6 14 ♖d1 ♘a5 15 ♕c2 ♖c8 16 0-0 ♘c4 ∓ Garcia Gonzales-Geller, Moscow IZ 1982.

**D21)**
**11 ♗e2 ♛e7**
A typical manoeuvre. Black frees a place for the rook at d8, provides support for ...c5, and hinders White's b4 advance. Nevertheless, in practice Black has also sought equality in other ways: 11...♘d7 12 ♛b3 (12 0-0 ♗e7 13 ♛b3 ♘f6 14 ♖fd1 a6 15 ♘e5 ♛d6 16 ♗f3 ♖ab8 17 ♛c2 c5 = Dzindzi-chashvili-Hübner, Chicago 1982) 12...c6 13 0-0 ♖e8 14 ♗d3 (White wants to play e4, while Black will try to hinder this advance; 14 ♖fd1 ♘f8 15 ♛c2 ♛e7 16 ♛b1 ♖ac8 17 b4 ♘e6 = Tarjan-Liberzon, Lone Pine 1981) 14...♘f8 15 ♖fd1 ♘e6 = Hübner-Liberzon, Biel IZ 1976.

**12 0-0 ♖d8 13 ♛b3**
In the game Hort-Geller, Moscow 1975 White sought to prevent ...c5 directly by 13 ♘a4, upon which there followed 13...♘a6 (intending ...c5) 14 ♛c2 ♖ac8 15 ♖fd1 c5 16 ♗xa6 ♗xa6 17 dxc5 b5 18 ♘c3 ♖xc5 =; Black's bishop-pair and active counterplay compensate for the isolated pawn on d5.

**13...c5 14 dxc5 bxc5 15 ♖fd1 d4 16 ♘a4 ♘a6 17 ♛a3**
Beliavsky's recommendation; Garcia Gonzales-Beliavsky, Moscow IZ 1982 continued 17 ♗xa6 ♗xa6 18 ♘xc5 ♗e2 19 ♖xd4 ♖dc8! (19...♖ab8 20 ♛c2 ♗xf3 21 ♖xd8+ ♛xd8 22 gxf3 ♖xb2 23 ♛c4 ±) 20 ♛d5? (better is 20 ♖d5 ♖ab8 21 ♛c2 ♖xb2 22 ♛f5 ♖c7 23 h3 ♗xf3 24 ♛xf3 ♖xa2 ∓) 20...♗xf3 21 ♛xf3 ♗xd4 22 exd4 ♖ab8 23 b3 ♖d8 ∓.

**17...♖ac8**
According to Beliavsky, 17...dxe3 is insufficient for equality: 18 ♛xe3

♛xe3 19 fxe3 ♖xd1+ 20 ♖xd1 ♗c6 21 ♗xa6 ♗xa4 22 b3 ♗c6 23 ♖c1 ±.

**18 ♗xa6 ♗xa6 19 ♘xc5**
19 exd4 cxd4 20 ♛xe7 ♗xe7 21 ♖xc8 ♖xc8 22 ♘xd4 ♗f6 23 ♘c3 ♖b8 24 b3 (24 ♘b3 ♗c4 ∓) 24...♗xd4 25 ♖xd4 ♖c8 −+.

**19...♗e2 20 ♖xd4 ♗xf3 21 ♖xd8+ ♛xd8 22 gxf3 ♛d5**
In Beliavsky's opinion, Black has full compensation for the material.

**D22)**
**11 b4 (D)**

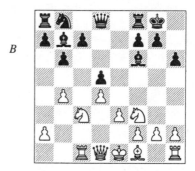

**11...c6**
A more active plan is also possible: 11...c5!? 12 bxc5 bxc5 and now:
a) 13 ♗b5!? ♘a6 14 0-0 ♘c7 15 ♛a4 cxd4 16 ♘xd4 ♗xd4 17 ♛xd4 (17 exd4 ♘e6 = 18 ♗a6? {better is 18 ♘e2 =} 18...♗xa6 19 ♛xa6 ♛g5! ∓ Høi-Geller, Malta OL 1980) 17...♘e6 18 ♛e5 a6 (18...♖c8!?) 19 ♗a4 (19 ♗d3 d4 ∓; 19 ♗e2 ♛b8!? 20 ♛xb8 {20 ♛f5 d4!?} 20...♖axb8 21 ♖fd1 ♖fd8 {intending ...d4} 22 ♗f3 d4 23 ♗xb7 ♖xb7 =) 19...d4! 20 ♖fd1 (20 exd4 ♛xd4 =) 20...♛h4 (Black seeks active counterplay) 21 exd4 ♘f4 22 d5 ♛g4 23 ♛e4 ♖ac8 (intending ...♖xc3) 24

🕏f1 a5 25 h3 (25 ♕f3!? ♗a6+ 26 ♗b5 ♕xf3 27 gxf3 ♗xb5+ 28 ♘xb5 ♖xc1 29 ♖xc1 ♘xd5 =) 25...♕g5 26 ♗b5 (26 ♗c6 ♗a6+) 26...♘xd5 27 ♘e2! = V.Raičević-Geller, Moscow 1986.

b) 13 dxc5 ♘d7 14 ♘b5 ♖c8! 15 ♗e2 (15 ♘d6 gives White nothing due to 15...♖xc5 16 ♘xb7 ♖xc1 17 ♕xc1 ♕b6 18 ♗d3 ♕b4+ 19 🕏e2 ♕xb7 20 ♕b1 ♖b8 =) and now 15...♘xc5 16 0-0 a6 17 ♘bd4 (Akopian-Short, Linares 1995) 17...♕a5 18 ♘b3 (18 ♖c2 ♘e4) 18...♘xb3 19 ♕xb3 ♗a8 is unclear according to Akopian, but I think that 15...♕a5+!? deserves serious attention: 16 ♕d2 (16 ♘d2 ♖xc5 =) 16...♕xd2+ 17 🕏xd2 (17 ♘xd2 ♖xc5 =) 17...♘xc5 18 ♖hd1 (18 ♘xa7 ♘e4+ and ...♖a8) 18...♘e4+ 19 🕏e1 ♘c3 =.

**12 ♗d3**

Also played, but without any particular success, is 12 ♗e2 ♕d6! 13 ♕b3 ♘d7 14 0-0 a5 15 a3 (15 bxa5 ♖xa5 16 a4 =; 15 b5 c5 ∞) 15...♖fe8 16 ♖fd1 ♗e7 17 ♖b1 (17 e4 axb4! 18 e5 ♕e6 19 axb4 b5! intending ...♘b6-c4 or ...f6) 17...♗f8 18 ♘e1 (Browne-Hort, Reykjavik 1978) and now Black should play 18...axb4! 19 axb4 b5 (intending ...♘b6-c4) 20 ♘d3 ♘b6 21 ♘c5 ♗c8 22 e4 dxe4 23 ♘3xe4 ♕g6 intending ...♗f5 and ...♘d5 =.

**12...♖e8**

Interesting is 12...♕d6!? 13 ♕b3 ♘d7 14 0-0 ♗e7 15 ♖b1 a5 = Ivkov-Gligorić, Bled/Portorož 1979.

**13 0-0 ♘d7**

But now 13...♕d6?! is dubious due to 14 b5! c5 15 dxc5 bxc5 16 ♘a4 ♘d7 17 ♗f5 ± Timman-Speelman, London Ct (1) 1989.

**14 ♕b3 ♘f8 15 ♖fd1 ♖c8 16 ♗b1 ♘e6**

= Korchnoi-Spassky, Belgrade Ct (11) 1977.

**D23)**
**11 ♗d3 (D)**

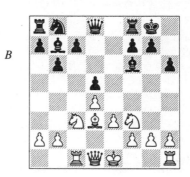

The most poisonous move: White plays to limit Black's counterplay.

**11...c5**

A logical reply: Black seeks play against the most exposed point in White's position – d4. Black can also play 11...c6:

a) 12 0-0 ♖e8 (12...a5 13 ♗b1 g6?! {13...♘d7 14 e4 ±} 14 ♘e5 ♘d7 15 f4 ±) 13 b4 a5 14 a3 ♘d7 15 ♕b3 axb4 16 axb4 b5 17 e4 ±.

b) 12 ♗b1 ♖e8 13 0-0 ♘d7. Now, in Lobron-Abramović, Belgrade 1988, White continued 14 ♘e2 ♘f8 15 ♘f4 g6 16 ♘d3 ∞, whereas I think that 14 b4!? a5 15 a3 (15 b5!? c5 16 dxc5 and now Black should play the unclear 16...♘xc5 rather than 16...♗xc3? 17 c6 ±) 15...axb4 16 axb4 b5 17 e4 ± deserves attention.

**12 0-0**

White can also try 12 ♗b1 cxd4 (12...♕e7!? 13 0-0 ♖d8 14 ♖e1 ♘d7 15 e4 dxe4 16 ♘xe4 cxd4 17 ♘c5 ♗xf3 18 ♕d3 ∞ Portisch-Beliavsky,

Linares 1990 – an interesting deployment by Black) 13 ♘xd4 ♘c6 14 ♘xc6 ♗xc6 15 0-0 ♕d7 16 ♘e2 ♗b5 17 ♖e1 ♖ac8 18 ♖xc8 ♖xc8 with equality.

**12...♘d7** *(D)*

The strongest continuation. Worse is 12...♖e8 13 ♗b5 ♖e7 (13...♖e6 14 dxc5 bxc5 15 ♘a4 c4 16 ♘d4 ♗xd4 17 ♕xd4 ♗c6 18 ♗xc4 {18 ♘c3 ♗xb5 19 ♘xb5 ♘c6 = Short} 18...♗xa4 19 ♗xd5 ♘c6 20 ♕c4 ±) 14 dxc5 bxc5 15 ♘a4 ♘a6 16 ♘xc5 ♘xc5 17 ♖xc5 ♗xb2 (17...♕a5 18 ♕a4 ♕b6 19 ♕c2 ♖e4 20 ♗d3 ♖b4 21 b3 ± I.Sokolov-Kotronias, Kavala 1990) 18 ♕c2 ♗f6 19 ♘d4 ± Topalov-Gomez Esteban, Las Palmas 1991.

White obtains a small but stable advantage after 12...cxd4 13 exd4 ♘c6 14 ♗b1 ♖e8 (14...g6 15 ♕d2 ♔g7 16 ♖fe1 ♕d6 17 ♘b5 ♕b8 18 ♖e2 ± I.Sokolov-Kotronias, Bled/Rogaška Slatina 1991) 15 ♕d3 g6 16 ♖fe1 (16 a3 ♘a5 17 ♗a2 ♔g7 18 b4 ♘c4 19 ♘xd5 ♗xd5 20 ♗xc4 ♗e4! 21 ♕b3 ♖e7 22 ♗a6 ½-½ Ljubojević-Short, Lucerne Wcht 1989) 16...♕d6 17 a3 ♖xe1+ 18 ♖xe1 ♖d8 19 ♗a2 ♘e7 20 ♘e5 ± Karpov-Portisch, Skellefteå 1989.

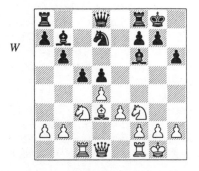

W

**13 ♗f5**

With this move, White seeks to simplify the position. However, 13 ♗b1 also deserves scrutiny:

a) 13...♖c8? 14 ♘b5 ± Portisch-Short, Rotterdam 1989.

b) 13...g6 14 ♕a4 ♖e8 15 ♖fd1 cxd4 16 exd4 ♘f8 17 ♗d3 a6 18 ♕b3 ♖c8 19 ♘a4 ♖e6 20 ♗f1 ♖d6 21 ♕e3 ♖xc1 22 ♖xc1 ♘e6 23 ♖d1 ♔g7 24 h4 ± Karpov-Short, Rotterdam 1989.

c) 13...a6!? 14 ♕c2 g6 15 ♖fd1 ♖c8 16 a4 ♗g7 17 ♗a2 cxd4 18 exd4 ♘f6 ∞ Züger-Bönsch, Graz 1993.

d) 13...♖e8 14 ♕a4 (14 ♕c2 g6 15 ♖fd1 ♖c8 16 ♕d2 ♘f8 17 ♗d3 ♘e6 gives Black good play, Lukacs-Kiss, Hungary 1992) 14...a6 15 ♖fe1 (after 15 ♖fd1 c4 16 ♕c2 g6 17 a4 ♗c6 18 ♘e2 b5 19 ♘f4 ♕e7 20 axb5 axb5 21 h4 ♗g7 22 h5 g5 23 ♘e2 g4 24 ♘h2 ♘f6 25 ♘g3 ♗d7 Black has created a queenside pawn majority, while also managing to defend his kingside, Gavrilov-Klovans, Pardubice 1993) 15...g6 16 dxc5 ♘xc5 17 ♕f4 ♔g7 18 ♘d4 ♘e6 19 ♘xe6+ ♖xe6 20 ♖ed1 ♖c8 = Lutz-Arlandi, Biel 1990.

**13...g6**

Bad is 13...♖c8?! 14 ♘e5! ♗xe5 15 dxe5 ♖a8 16 f4 ± I.Sokolov-Detreeuw, San Bernardino 1989; also inferior is 13...cxd4 14 exd4 g6 15 ♗d3 (15 ♗h3!? Hellers) 15...♗g7 16 ♕b3 a6 17 ♖fe1 ♖c8 18 a4 ♘f6 19 ♖cd1 ± I.Sokolov-Hellers, Biel 1989.

**14 ♗xd7 cxd4**

This is an important *zwischenzug*. 14...♕xd7? is no good due to 15 dxc5 bxc5 16 ♘e4 ♗xb2 17 ♘xc5 ♕e7 18 ♖b1! ♕xc5 19 ♖xb2 ♗a6 20 ♖e1 ♖ab8 21 ♖d2 ± L.Hansen-Campora, Biel 1991.

15 ♗c6 ♗xc6 16 ♘xd4 ♗b7
This position is important for the assessment of the variation: Black has an isolated pawn, but as practice shows, Black's bishop-pair compensates for this weakness, and the position is roughly equal.

17 ♕a4
White can also play 17 ♕f3 (17 ♕b3 ♕d7 intending ...♖fc8-c4) 17...♗e5 (17...♗g7!? 18 ♖fd1 ♕d7 ∞) 18 ♖fd1 ♖c8 19 ♖d2 (19 a3 ♕d7 20 h3 h5 21 ♖d2 ♖fd8 22 ♕d1 ♕e7 23 ♘ce2 ♖c5 =) 19...♕e7 20 ♖cd1 ♖fd8 21 ♘ce2 ♖c5 with a level position, Langeweg-Detreeuw, Forli 1991.

17...♕e7! 18 ♖fd1 ♖fc8 19 ♖d2 ♖c4 20 ♕b3 ♕c5! 21 ♖cd1 ♖d8
21...♖e8 deserves attention: 22 h3 ♖e5 23 ♕b5 ♕c8 24 ♘f3 ♖c5 25 ♕b3 ♖h5 ∞ L.Komljenović-Bode, Kassel 1993.

22 h3
22 a3 ∞ Dokhoian.
22...a6 23 ♘ce2 b5 24 ♕d3 ♕e7
= Dokhoian-Klovans, Berlin 1992.

E)
8 cxd5 (D)

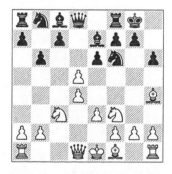

B

8...♘xd5

This is the modern interpretation of the Tartakower, though we should note that the idea of recapturing with the knight on d5 was known in the 1920s, for instance in Kostić-Tartakower, Bardejov 1926. Black avoids closing the a8-h1 diagonal and invites his opponent to do so. However, he can only do so at the cost of exchanging several more minor pieces, and this would reduce White's attacking possibilities. After 9 ♗xe7 ♕xe7 10 ♘xd5 exd5 the c8-bishop finds a favourable location on e6. Black can parry White's pressure on the c-file by playing the combative ...c5, taking on (after dxc5) a position with hanging pawns. In return, he obtains the semi-open b-file and piece-play.

Black can also play 8...exd5 but, in my opinion, Kasparov demonstrated a convincing route to an advantage for White in his match with Beliavsky in 1983. 9 ♗d3 ♗b7 10 0-0 and now:
a) 10...♘e4 11 ♗xe7 ♕xe7:
a1) 12 ♘e5 deserves attention: 12...♘d7 13 f4 ♘xe5 14 fxe5 c5 15 ♕e1 ♖ad8 16 ♖d1 ♕g5 (16...f6 17 ♗xe4! dxe4 18 exf6 ♖xf6 19 ♖xf6 ♕xf6 20 dxc5 bxc5 21 ♖xd8+ ♕xd8 22 ♘a4 ±/±) and now not 17 ♖f3, which led to a draw in Kasparov-Beliavsky, Moscow Ct (7) 1983 after 17...f6! 18 exf6 cxd4 19 exd4 ♖de8! 20 ♗b5 ♖d8 21 ♗d3 ♖de8 ½-½. Instead 17 h4!? ♕h5 18 ♘e2! presents Black with definite problems.
a2) 12 ♕b3 ♖d8 13 ♖ac1 c5 14 ♗b1 ♘c6 15 dxc5 ♘xc5 16 ♕c2 g6 17 ♖fd1 ♕f6 18 ♘b5 ♖ac8 19 ♕c3 ♕e7 20 ♕a3 a5 (Lautier-Ljubojević, Monaco Amber rpd 1997) and now 21 ♘bd4 gives White a stable advantage.

b) 10...c5 11 ♘e5 ♘bd7 (11...♘c6
12 ♗a6! ♕c8 13 ♗xb7 ♕xb7 14 ♗xf6
♗xf6 15 ♘g4! ♗d8 16 ♘xd5 ♘xd4 17
♘df6+! ± Kasparov-Beliavsky, Moscow Ct (1) 1983) 12 ♗f5! ♘xe5 13
dxe5 ♘e8 (13...♘e4? 14 ♘xd5! +—)
14 ♗g3 ♘c7 (14...g6 15 ♗c2 ±) 15
♕g4 ♕e8 (15...♗c8 16 ♖ad1 ♗e6?!
17 ♘xd5! ♗xd5 18 e4 ±) 16 ♗d7! ±
Kasparov-Beliavsky, Moscow Ct (5)
1983.

**9 ♗xe7**
Let's see how things turn out if
White does not want to exchange bishops. After 9 ♗g3 c5 White has three
continuations:

a) 10 ♘xd5 ♕xd5 11 a3 (11 dxc5
♕xc5 12 a3 ♖d8 13 ♕c1 ♕a5+ 14 b4
♕a4 gave Black the initiative in Zag-
oriansky-Stepanov, Moscow 1936)
11...♖d8 12 ♖c1 ♗a6 13 ♗xa6 ♘xa6
14 ♕e2 ♕b7 15 0-0 ♖ac8 16 ♖fd1 b5
= H.Steiner-Bondarevsky, USA-USSR
radio 1945.

b) 10 ♗d3 cxd4 11 exd4 ♗a6 12
0-0 ♗xd3 13 ♕xd3 ♘c6 14 ♖ac1 ♖c8
15 ♕a6 ♘db4! (15...♕d7?! 16 ♘xd5
♕xd5 17 ♘e5 ±) 16 ♕a4 (16 ♕b7
♘a5! 17 ♕xa7 f5! 18 ♗e5 ♖f7 19 ♘b5
♗c5! ∓) 16...a6 17 a3 b5 18 ♕d1 (18
♘xb5 axb5 19 ♕xb5 ♕d5! 20 ♕b7
♘xd4! 21 ♕xe2 ♘e2+ —+) 18...♘d5
with equality, Levenfish-Capablanca,
Moscow 1936.

c) 10 ♗c4 ♘xc3 11 bxc3 cxd4 12
cxd4 ♘c6 13 0-0 ♗b7 14 ♕e2 ♖c8 15
♖fd1 ♘a5 16 ♗d3 ♗d6! = Botvin-
nik-Bondarevsky, Leningrad 1939.

**9...♕xe7** (D)
At this point White has two continuations:

**E1: 10 ♖c1**    112
**E2: 10 ♘xd5**    113

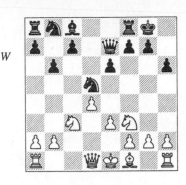

**E1)**
**10 ♖c1 ♗b7 11 ♘xd5**
Or:
a) 11 ♗d3 ♖c8 12 0-0 c5 13 ♕e2
(alternatively, 13 ♘xd5 ♗xd5 14 e4
♗b7 15 ♕e2 ♘d7 16 ♗a6 ♖ab8 17
♗xb7 ♖xb7 18 ♖c2 ♖bc7 19 ♖fc1
♘f6 = ½-½ Kluger-Ilivitsky, Budapest tt 1955) 13...♘d7 14 ♗a6 ♘xc3
15 ♖xc3 cxd4 16 ♖xc8+ ♗xc8 17
♘xd4 ♗xa6 18 ♕xa6 ♘c5 19 ♕c4 a5
½-½ Hort-Karpov, Tilburg 1980.

b) 11 ♗e2 ♖c8 12 0-0 c5 13 ♕a4
(13 ♘e5 ♘xc3 14 ♖xc3 ♘c6 15 ♘xc6
♖xc6 16 ♕a4 ♖cc8 17 ♖fc1 cxd4 18
♖xc8+ ♖xc8 19 ♖xc8+ ♗xc8 20 ♕xd4
½-½ Petrosian-Geller, USSR Ch (Tbilisi) 1959) 13...♘d7 14 ♗a6 (14 ♖fd1
♘xc3 15 ♖xc3 a6 16 ♕a3 ♔f8 17
dxc5 ♘xc5 18 ♖dc1 ♘d7 19 ♕xe7+
♔xe7 = Keres-Geller, USSR Ch (Moscow) 1955) 14...♘7f6 15 ♘xd5 ♘xd5
16 ♗xb7 (16 dxc5 ♗xa6 17 ♕xa6
♖xc5 18 ♖xc5 ♕xc5 19 ♕b7 ♕c8 =)
16...♕xb7 17 dxc5 ♖xc5 18 ♖xc5
bxc5 19 ♕c2 ♕a6 20 a3 c4 21 ♖c1
½-½ Vaganian-Ki.Georgiev, Wijk aan
Zee 1989.

**11...♗xd5 12 ♗e2**
In addition to this move, White can
employ the following continuations:

a) 12 ♕a4 ♖c8 13 ♗e2 c5 14 dxc5
♘d7! 15 c6 ♘c5 16 ♕a3 ♗xc6 17 0-0
a5 = Ghitescu-Kurajica, Wijk aan Zee
1967.

b) 12 ♗c4 ♗b7 13 0-0 ♖c8 14 ♕e2
♘d7 15 ♗a6 ♗xa6 16 ♕xa6 c5 17
♖fd1 (17 b4!? ♕e8 18 dxc5 bxc5 19
b5 ♘b6 ∞) 17...♕e8! ½-½ Furman-
Vasiukov, USSR Ch (Baku) 1972.

c) 12 ♗d3 ♖c8 13 0-0 c5 and now:

c1) 14 dxc5 ♖xc5 15 ♖xc5 ♕xc5
16 ♕a4 ♘c6 17 e4 ♘b4 18 exd5 ♘xd3
19 dxe6 fxe6 20 b3 (20 ♕e4 ♕d5 =)
20...♖d8! 21 ♕g4 (21 ♕xa7? ♘xf2
∓) 21...♕f5! 22 ♕xf5 exf5 23 ♖d1
♖d5! ½-½ Uhlmann-Spassky, Solin-
gen 1974.

c2) 14 b4 ♘d7 15 e4 ♗b7 16 bxc5
bxc5 17 ♕b3 ♘f6 18 dxc5 ♘xe4 19
c6 ♖xc6 20 ♗xe4 ♖xc1 21 ♕xb7
♖xf1+ 22 ♔xf1 ♕xb7 23 ♗xb7 ♖b8
is equal, Beliavsky-Geller, Erevan
1975.

**12...♖c8 13 0-0 c5 14 dxc5 ♖xc5
15 ♖xc5 ♕xc5 16 ♕a4 ♗c6 17 ♕f4**

17 ♕d4 ♘d7 18 ♕xc5 (18 ♕d2
♕d5 =) 18...bxc5! (18...♘xc5 19 b4
♘e4 20 ♖c1 ♗d5 21 ♗a6! is slightly
better for White, Chekhov-Klovans,
USSR 1985) 19 ♖c1 ♖b8 20 b3 ♔f8
21 ♘d2 ♔e7 22 ♔f1 g5 23 h3 f5 24
♗f3 ♗b5+ ½-½ Adorjan-Ki.Geor-
giev, Budapest 1993.

**17...♘d7 18 ♕c7**

18 b4 ♕f8! 19 ♕c7 ♖c8! = Kasparov-Timman, London (USSR vs RoW)
1984.

**18...♗xf3 19 ♕xc5 ♘xc5 20 ♗xf3
♖d8**

with a roughly level ending.

**E2)**
**10 ♘xd5 exd5** *(D)*

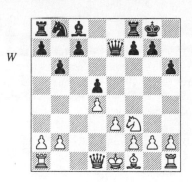

Now:
**E21: 11 ♗e2    113**
**E22: 11 ♖c1    114**

Or: 11 ♕d2 ♗e6 12 b4 c6 13 ♖b1
♘d7 14 ♗e2 c5 15 bxc5 bxc5 16 dxc5
♘xc5 17 0-0 ♘e4 18 ♕a5 ♖fc8 19
♖bc1 ♖xc1 20 ♖xc1 ♕f6! with equal
chances, Petrosian-Tal, Tallinn 1979.

**E21)**
**11 ♗e2 ♗e6 12 0-0**

White gains nothing by 12 ♘e5 c5
13 0-0 ♘d7 (13...c4 14 b3 ±) 14 f4
♘xe5 (14...♘f6 15 ♗f3 ♗f5 16 g4
♗e4 17 g5 hxg5 18 fxg5 ♘h7 19
♗xe4 dxe4 20 g6 ±) 15 dxe5 ♖ad8 =
Pachman-Darga, Varna OL 1962.

**12...c5 13 ♕d2**

Other continuations also fail to give
White an advantage:

a) 13 dxc5 bxc5 14 ♘e5 (14 ♕a4
♕b7! 15 ♕a3 ♘d7 16 ♘e1 a5 17 ♘d3
c4 18 ♘f4 ♖fb8 ∓ Bertok-Fischer,
Stockholm IZ 1962) 14...♘d7 15 ♘d3
♖fb8 16 b3 a5 17 ♘f4 ♘f6 18 ♕c2 a4
= Agdestein-Short, Reykjavik 1990.

b) 13 b3 ♖c8 14 ♖c1 a5 15 ♗b5
♘d7 16 ♕d3 ♖a7 17 dxc5 ♘xc5 18
♕d4 ♖ac7 19 ♕b2 ♘e4 = Najdorf-
Gheorghiu, Lugano OL 1968.

**13...♘d7 14 b3**

Or 14 ♖fc1 ♖ac8 (14...c4!? deserves serious attention: 15 b3 b5 16 ♕a5 ♖fb8 with sharp play, Larsen-Portisch, Poreč Ct (4) 1968) 15 b3 ♘f6 16 ♕b2 a5 17 ♘e5 ♘e4 = Krasenkow-Beliavsky, Pula Echt 1997.

**14...a5 15 ♗b5 ♘f6 16 ♖ac1**

Black equalized easily in Portisch-Ki.Georgiev, Linares 1988 after 16 ♖fc1 ♖fc8 17 ♕b2 ♗d7 18 ♗f1 ♘e4 19 ♘e5 a4! =.

**16...♖fc8 17 ♕b2**

17 ♘e5 is interesting, but promises nothing: 17...♘e4 18 ♕b2 (18 ♕e2 ♕b7! intending ...♘d6 =) 18...♘d6 19 ♗e2 a4 20 bxa4 ♖xa4 21 ♕xb6 c4! gives Black full compensation for the pawn, Najdorf-Spassky, Lugano OL 1968.

**17...♗d7 18 ♗d3 a4 19 ♖c2 ♗e6 20 ♖fc1 ♕a7**

= Larsen-Spassky, Malmö Ct (8) 1968

**E22)**
**11 ♖c1** (D)

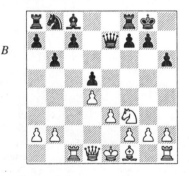

Now:
**E221: 11...♗b7** 114
**E222: 11...♗e6** 114

**E221)**
**11...♗b7**

The favourite continuation of the young Spassky.

**12 ♕a4**

Nothing is achieved by 12 ♗d3 c5 13 0-0 ♘d7 14 b3 ♖fc8 15 ♖c2 a5 16 ♗b5 ♘f6 with an equal position, Loginov-Gusev, 1983.

**12...c5 13 ♕a3 ♖c8 14 ♗e2**

14 ♗d3 ♔f8!? intending ...c4 – Karpov.

**14...♘d7 15 0-0 ♕f8**

15...♘f8!?, intending ...♘e6, deserves attention: 16 ♖fd1 ♖c7 17 dxc5 bxc5 18 ♗a6 (18 ♘d2!?) 18...♗xa6 19 ♕xa6 ♖d8 20 ♕d3 ♘e6 21 ♕f5 d4 22 exd4 ♘xd4 23 ♘xd4 cxd4 24 ♖xc7 ♕xc7 is equal, Flohr-Vidmar, Groningen 1946.

**16 dxc5 bxc5 17 ♖c2 ♕d6 18 ♖fc1 ♕b6 19 ♘d2!**

Intending ♗g4 and ♘b3.

**19...♖e8!?**

Now Petrosian gave 20 ♗f1 ±. Instead after 20 ♘b3 d4! 21 ♘xc5 ♘xc5 22 ♖xc5 dxe3 23 fxe3 (Petrosian-Spassky, Santa Monica 1966) Black can obtain counterplay by 23...♖ad8! 24 ♕c3 ♖e7! intending 25...♖de8 or 25...♖ed7 (Spassky).

**E222)**
**11...♗e6** (D)
Now:
**E2221: 12 ♕a4** 115
**E2222: 12 ♗d3** 115

White can also play 12 ♗e2 c5 13 ♘e5 ♖c8 14 dxc5 bxc5 15 0-0 ♘d7 16 ♘xd7 ♕xd7 17 ♕d2 c4 18 ♖fd1 ♕a4 with equality, Evans-Filip, Lugano OL 1968.

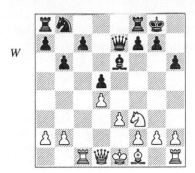

W

**E2221)**
**12 ♕a4**
The queen takes up an active position in the fight against the hanging pawns.
**12...c5 13 ♕a3 ♖c8**
Dubious is 13...♘d7?! 14 ♗a6 ± with a blockade of the queenside.
**14 ♗b5**
Other continuations are also encountered:
a) 14 ♘e5 ♘c6 15 ♗a6 ♖c7 =.
b) 14 ♗e2 a5 15 0-0 ♔f8 (intending ...c4) 16 dxc5 bxc5 17 ♖c3 (17 ♖c2 ♘d7 18 ♖fc1 ♖cb8 19 ♕c3 ♕d6 =) 17...♘d7 18 ♖fc1 (intending ♗b5) 18...♖cb8 19 ♖b3 a4! (19...c4?! 20 ♖xb8+ ♖xb8 21 ♕xa5 ♖xb2 22 ♘d4 ± Winants-Kasparov, Brussels 1987) 20 ♖b5 (20 ♖xb8+ ♖xb8 21 ♕xa4 ♖xb2 ∞ Kasparov) 20...c4!? 21 ♘d4 (21 ♕xe7+? ♔xe7 22 ♖xb8 ♖xb8 and b2 collapses; 21 ♖xb8+ ♖xb8 22 ♕c3 ♕b4 is good for Black) 21...♕xa3 22 bxa3 ♖xb5 23 ♘xb5 ♖b8 24 ♖b1 ♘e5 25 ♘c3 ♖xb1+ 26 ♘xb1 ♘d7 27 ♘c3 ♘b6 28 ♗d1 ♗d7 = intending ...♔e7-d6.
**14...♕b7!**
Geller's move, obliging White to go in for forcing play. In the famous game

Fischer-Spassky, Reykjavik Wch (6) 1972 Black quickly fell into a bad position after 14...a6?! 15 dxc5 bxc5 16 0-0 ♖a7 17 ♗e2 ♘d7 18 ♘d4! ♕f8 19 ♘xe6 fxe6 20 e4 d4 21 f4 ±.
**15 dxc5 bxc5 16 ♖xc5 ♖xc5 17 ♕xc5 ♘a6 18 ♗xa6**
18 ♕c6 ♕xc6 19 ♗xc6 ♖b8 (if 19...♖c8, then 20 ♗a4) 20 0-0 (20 b3? ♖c8 21 ♘d4 ♘b4 is winning for Black) 20...♖xb2 21 a4 ♘b4 22 ♘d4 ♖a2 and Black is slightly better, Zhidkov-Zarubin, Russia 1993.
**18...♕xa6 19 ♕a3**
This is necessary, since Black was threatening 19...♖c8.
**19...♕c4 20 ♕c3**
In Timman-Geller, Hilversum 1973 White continued with 20 ♔d2 but after 20...♕g4 21 ♖g1 d4! 22 ♘xd4 (22 exd4 ♖b8 intending ...♗d5) 22...♕h4 23 ♖e1 ♕xf2+ 24 ♖e2 ♕f1 25 ♘xe6 fxe6 he came under a strong attack.
Now Black can obtain an advantage by **20...♖b8!** ∓, but not 20...♕xa2 21 0-0 ♖b8 22 b4 ♕a4 23 ♖a1 with equality, Szabo-Kavalek, Amsterdam 1973.

**E2222)**
**12 ♗d3 c5 13 dxc5 bxc5 14 0-0** *(D)*

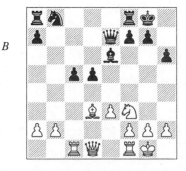

B

This is a critical position for the assessment of this whole variation. How should one view the hanging pawns – as a weakness or as a strength? Practice suggests that the position is roughly equal.

**14...♘d7**

14...a5!? deserves serious attention: 15 e4 (this is White's main idea in this position; he gains nothing by 15 ♗b5 ♖c8 16 ♕a4 ♘d7 =) 15...d4 16 a3 (16 ♘d2 ♗xa2 17 b3 a4 =; 16 b3 a4 17 ♘d2 axb3 18 axb3 ♘d7 19 f4 f6 =) 16...♘d7 17 h3 (17 ♘d2 ♘e5 is level) 17...♖fb8 18 ♕e2 ♖b3 with active play, Pantaleoni-Wagman, Forli 1988.

Karpov mentions 14...♖d8 15 ♘e5 (15 ♖e1 ♘d7 16 e4 dxe4 17 ♗xe4 ♘f6 18 ♗xa8 ♖xd1 19 ♖cxd1 ♕f8 is equal) 15...♕d6 16 f4 ♘d7 17 ♘xd7 ±.

**15 e4**

15 ♕a4 promises nothing: 15...♖fc8 (15...♕d6!? intending ...♕b6) 16 ♖fd1 ♘f6 17 ♕a3 a5 =. Or 15 ♗b1 ♖fc8 16 ♕c2 ♘f6 17 ♖fd1 a5 =.

**15...d4** *(D)*

15...dxe4 is also interesting. 16 ♗xe4 and then:

a) 16...♖ab8 17 b3 ♖fc8 (17...♖fd8 18 ♕e2 ±; 17...♘b6 18 ♖e1 ♖bd8 can be met by 19 ♕e2 ±, or 19 ♕c2 c4!? 20 bxc4 ♘xc4 21 ♗f5 ♗xf5 22 ♕xf5 ♕b4 23 ♕f4 ♖c8 24 ♘e5 ♕d2 25 ♕xd2 ♘xd2 26 ♘c6) 18 ♖e1 ♕f6 19 ♘d2 (19 ♕e2 c4! 20 bxc4 ♖b2 with compensation; 19 ♕d2 c4 20 bxc4 ♘c5 21 ♕e3 ♘xe4 22 ♕xe4 ♖b4 with compensation) 19...♘b6 20 ♕e2 =/±.

b) 16...♖ad8 and here:

b1) 17 ♖e1?! ♘f6 18 ♕c2 ♘xe4 19 ♖xe4 ♖d5 20 h3 ♖fd8 = Makogonov-Stolberg, USSR Ch (Moscow) 1940.

b2) 17 ♕a4?! can be answered by 17...♘b6 18 ♕a3 ♗xa2 19 ♖fe1 ♗e6 20 ♗f5 ♘d5 21 ♗xe6 fxe6 22 ♕xc5 ♕xc5 23 ♖xc5 ♘f4 24 ♖a5 ♖b8 ½-½ Sajtar-Katetov, Prague 1946 or 17...♖b8 18 ♕a3 ♗xa2 19 ♖fe1 ♗e6 20 ♕xa7 ♕f6 ½-½ Buturin-Kruppa, Kiev 1986.

b3) 17 ♗b1! ♘e5 (17...♘f6 18 ♕e2 ±; 17...c4 18 ♕e2 ♕f6 19 b3 ± Karpov) 18 ♕e2 ♘xf3+ 19 ♕xf3 c4 20 ♕e4 g6 21 ♕e3 ♕g5 22 f4 ♕f6 23 ♖c3 ♖fe8 24 f5 gxf5 25 ♕xa7 is slightly better for White, Danner-Van der Sterren, Albena 1983.

**16 ♗b1**

Or:

a) 16 ♖e1 a5 17 a4 ♗g4 18 e5 ♖ab8 19 h3 ♗xf3 20 ♕xf3 ♖xb2 21 ♕e4 g6 22 f4 ♖e8 23 ♗b5 ♖d8 24 f5 ♘f8 25 ♖f1 ♕g5 with compensation, Mochalov-Klovans, corr. 1992.

b) 16 ♕c2 ♖fc8 17 b3 a5 18 a4 ♖ab8 19 ♗b5 ♕f6 =.

c) 16 b3 a5 17 ♕c2 a4 18 bxa4 ♖fc8 with compensation.

d) 16 ♘d2 ♘e5 and now:

d1) 17 ♗a6 ♖fb8 18 b3 (18 f4 ♘g4) 18...♕d6 19 ♗c4 ♘xc4 20 ♘xc4 ♗xc4 21 ♖xc4 a5 = Druet-G.David, corr. Echt 1988-96.

d2) 17 ♗b1 c4 (17...f6 deserves attention: 18 h3 {intending f4} 18...♖ac8 19 f4 ♘d7 20 b3 ♘b6 21 ♗d3 a5 =) 18 h3 ♗xh3! 19 gxh3 ♕g5+ 20 ♔h1 ♕h4 21 ♘f3 ♕xh3+ 22 ♘h2 ♖ab8 23 b3 cxb3 24 axb3 ♖xb3 25 f3 ♖b2 26 ♖c2 ♖fb8 with compensation, Gatto-G.David, Italian corr. Ch 1980.

**16...a5 17 ♘d2 ♘b6 18 f4 f6 19 b3 a4 20 ♕c2 axb3 21 axb3 ♖fc8**

The game is equal. Note that White should avoid 22 e5 f5 23 g4?! c4!?, when Black intends to meet 24 gxf5 with 24...d3 ∓.

**F)**

**8 ♗d3** (D)

This is a fairly popular system, by which White prioritizes quick piece development. Now:
**F1: 8...dxc4**      117
**F2: 8...♗b7**      118

**F1)**

**8...dxc4 9 ♗xc4 ♗b7 10 0-0 ♘bd7 11 ♕e2**

Instead 11 ♖c1 transposes to Line D1, though an alternative is 11 ♗g3, upon which Black's best continuation is 11...a6! (11...c5!? 12 ♕e2 a6 13 a4

cxd4 14 exd4 ♘h5 15 ♖fd1 ♘xg3 16 hxg3 ♘f6 17 ♘e5 ±) 12 a4 ♗d6! (also possible is 12...♘h5 13 e4 ♘xg3 14 hxg3 ♗b4 15 ♕e2 ♕e7 16 ♖ad1 ♖fd8 17 e5 ± Sadler-Ljubojević, Monaco Amber rpd 1998) 13 ♕e2 ♗xg3 14 hxg3 c5 15 ♖fd1 ♕e7 =.

**11...♘e4**

A typical manoeuvre: Black tries to free his game by exchanges.

11...a6 is an alternative:

a) 12 ♖fd1 b5 13 ♗b3 (13 ♗d3 ♖c8 14 e4 c5 15 dxc5 ♖xc5 ∞ Savon-Zhidkov, 1974) 13...c5 14 dxc5 ♕c7 15 c6 ♕xc6 16 e4 ♗b4! = Larsen-Tisdall, Espoo Z 1989.

b) 12 a4! c5 13 ♖fd1 ♘e4 (13...cxd4 14 exd4 ♖e8 {14...♘d5 15 ♗xd5 ±; 14...♘h5 15 ♗xe7 ♕xe7 16 d5 ±} 15 ♘e5 ±; 13...♖c8 14 ♖ac1 g5 15 ♗g3 ♘h5 16 d5 ± Tatai-Purgimon, Andorra 1987) and then:

b1) 14 ♗xe7 ♘xc3 15 bxc3 ♕xe7 16 e4 ♘f6 =.

b2) 14 ♘xe4!? is an interesting idea: 14...♗xh4 (14...♗xe4?! 15 ♗xe7 ♕xe7 16 ♗xa6 ♗xf3 17 gxf3 ±) 15 ♘d6 ♗xf3 (15...♗c6 16 d5 ±) 16 ♕xf3 cxd4 17 exd4 (17 ♖xd4!? ∞) 17...♘f6 18 ♘b7 ♕e7 (18...♕c7 19 ♖ac1 ∞) 19 g3 ♗g5 20 h4 ♗xh4 21 gxh4 ♖fb8 ∞.

b3) 14 ♗g3 ♘xg3 15 hxg3 ♕c7 16 d5 exd5 17 ♘xd5 ±.

**12 ♗g3**

White tries to maintain the tension. Black has no particular problems after 12 ♗xe7 ♕xe7 13 ♗a6 (or 13 ♖ac1 ♘xc3 14 ♖xc3 c5 15 ♗b5 e5 =) 13...♘xc3 14 bxc3 ♗xa6 15 ♕xa6 c5 16 a4 ♖fe8 17 a5 ♕d8 18 h3 ½-½ Spassky-Andersson, Bugojno 1984.

Instead, 12 ♘xe4 ♗xe4 13 ♗g3 ♗d6 transposes to the main line.

**12...♗d6** *(D)*

Black continues his strategy of exchanges. Worse is 12...♘xg3 13 hxg3 c5 14 ♖fd1 ♗xf3 15 gxf3 cxd4 16 exd4 ♗d6 17 f4 ± Gavrikov-Dolmatov, Tallinn 1985.

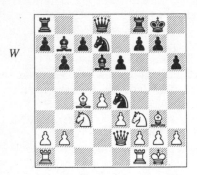

**13 ♘xe4 ♗xe4 14 ♗xd6**

White gains no advantage by 14 ♖fd1 ♕e7 15 ♖ac1 ♗xg3 16 hxg3 c5:

a) 17 dxc5 ♘xc5 18 b4 ♘d7 19 a3 ♖fd8 20 ♗a6 ♘f6 21 ♘e5 ♖xd1+ 22 ♖xd1 ♖d8 (22...♕c7!? 23 ♕b2 ♖d8 =) 23 f3 ♖xd1+ 24 ♕xd1 ♕c7 25 ♕d4 ♗c6 26 ♔f2 ♘d7 = Bernal-Campora, Spanish Cht 1993.

b) 17 ♘d2 ♗b7 18 ♗b5 ♖ac8 19 ♗a6 ♗xa6 20 ♕xa6 ♖fd8 21 ♘e4 (21 ♕xa7 ♖a8) 21...♘b8 22 ♕a3 ♕b7 =.

c) 17 ♗b5 ♖ad8 18 ♗xd7 ♖xd7 19 dxc5 ♖xd1+ 20 ♕xd1 bxc5 21 ♕a4 (21 ♘d2 ♖d8 22 ♕e1 ♗d3 23 b3 ♖d5 =) 21...♕b7 22 ♖xc5 ♗xf3 23 gxf3 ♕xf3 =.

**14...cxd6 15 ♖ac1**

A cunning move, by which White does not rush to play his bishop to a6. If immediately 15 ♗a6 then 15...♘b8 16 ♘d2 ♘xa6 17 ♘xe4 ♘c7 18 ♖ac1 d5 19 ♘d2 ♕d7 20 ♘f3 f6 21 ♖c2 ♖fc8 22 ♖fc1 ♘e8 =.

**15...♖c8!?**

Black fared worse in Kalinichev-Müller, Berlin 1995 after 15...♘f6?! 16 ♗a6! ♕e7 17 a3 e5 (17...♗b7!?) 18 ♘d2 ♗d5 19 ♕d3 e4 20 ♕b5 ♖ad8 21 ♖c2! ♖fe8 22 ♖fc1, when White had strong pressure on the c-file.

**16 ♗a6 ♖xc1 17 ♖xc1 ♕b8**

17...♕a8?! 18 ♖c7 ±.

**18 ♕c4**

If 18 ♘d2 then 18...♗b7 =.

**18...♘f6!**

18...♗b7?! 19 ♗xb7 ♕xb7 20 ♕c6! ±; 18...♗d5 19 ♕c7 ♘f6 20 a3! ♕a8 21 ♘e1 intending f3 and e4 ±.

**19 ♘d2**

19 ♕c7 ♗xf3 20 gxf3 ♘d5 =.

**19...♗b7**

Not 19...♗d5 20 ♕c7 ♗xa2? 21 b3 ♘d5 22 ♕c2 ♘b4 23 ♕c4 +−.

**20 ♗xb7 ♕xb7 ±**

It is hard for White to make immediate use of the c-file, since 21 ♕c7 ♕a6 gives Black counterplay.

**F2)**
    **8...♗b7 9 0-0 ♘bd7** *(D)*

This is the main position of the variation. White has the following continuations:

F21: **10 cxd5**    119
F22: **10 ♗g3**    119
F23: **10 ♖c1**    120
F24: **10 ♕e2**    121

**F21)**
    **10 cxd5 ♘xd5 11 ♗xe7**
11 ♗g3 c5 transposes to Line F22.
    **11...♕xe7 12 ♖c1**
Or:
    a) 12 ♖e1?! c5 13 e4 ♘f4 14 d5
exd5 15 exd5 ♕d6 16 ♗c4 ♘f6! (but
not 16...a6?! 17 ♘e4 ♕b8 18 a4 ♘e5
19 ♘xe5 ♕xe5 20 ♘c3 ♕g5 21 ♕f3
♖ad8 22 h4 ♕f6 23 ♘e4 ♕f5 24 g3
and White is clearly better, Nogueiras-
Wang Zili, Malta OL 1980) 17 ♘b5
♕d8 18 d6 ♘e4! ∓ Shirov-Beliavsky,
Linares 1993.
    b) 12 ♕e2 yields nothing due to
12...c5 (also possible is 12...♘xc3 13
bxc3 c5 14 ♗a6 ♗xa6 15 ♕xa6 cxd4
16 cxd4 e5 =) 13 ♗a6 ♘7f6 14 ♘xd5
exd5 15 b3 ½-½ Korchnoi-Spassky,
Moscow 1975.
    c) 12 ♘xd5 leads to simplifica-
tions: 12...♗xd5 (12...exd5!?) 13 ♕e2
(or 13 ♖c1 c5 =; 13 e4 ♗b7 14 ♕e2 c5
=) 13...c5 14 ♖fd1 ♖fd8 15 ♗b5 ♖ac8
16 b3 ♘f6 = De Waal-Dutreeuw, Bel-
gian League 1998/9.
    **12...c5 13 ♘xd5**
    13 ♗b1 cxd4 14 ♘xd5 (14 ♕xd4
♘7f6 =) 14...♗xd5 15 e4 ♗b7 and
now 16 ♕xd4 =; note the interesting
trap 16 ♖c7? ♕d8! 17 ♖xb7 ♘c5 with
a clear advantage for Black.
    **13...♗xd5 14 e4**
    Other moves are harmless: 14 b3
cxd4 15 ♘xd4 ♘f6 16 ♕e2 ♖ac8 =;
14 ♗b5 ♖fd8 15 ♕e2 ♖ac8 16 ♗a6
♖c7 =; or 14 ♗b1 ♖fd8 15 ♕c2 g6 =.
    **14...♗b7 15 b4!?**

An interesting tactical idea: White
wants to create a pawn majority on the
queenside.
    **15...♖fc8**
    The pawn is poisoned: 15...cxb4 16
♖c7.
    **16 dxc5 bxc5 17 b5 a6 18 a4 axb5
19 axb5**
    19 ♗xb5 is well met by either
19...♘f6 or 19...♘b6 with good play.
    **19...♘b6**
    The game is level. Note that 19...c4!?
also deserves attention.

**F22)**
    **10 ♗g3** *(D)*

    Romanishin's favourite move. White
drops back the bishop to parry the
freeing manoeuvre ...♘e4, which would
now fail, viz. 10...♘e4 11 ♗xe4 dxe4
12 ♘d2 f5 (12...♘f6 13 ♕c2 ±) 13
♘b5 ±.
    **10...c5**
    10...♗d6!? deserves serious atten-
tion: 11 cxd5 (11 ♗xd6 cxd6 12 cxd5
♘xd5 13 ♘xd5 ♗xd5 14 e4 ♗b7 15
♖c1 ♘f6 =; 11 ♖c1 ♗xg3 12 hxg3 c5
=) 11...♘xd5 12 e4 (12 ♘xd5 ♗xg3
13 hxg3 ♗xd5 14 ♕a4 a6 15 b4 c5 16
bxc5 bxc5 17 e4 ♗b7 18 ♖ab1 ♖b8 19

♖fd1 cxd4 20 ♕xd4 ½-½ Yermolinsky-Anastasian, New York 1996) 12...♘xc3 13 bxc3 ♗xg3 14 fxg3 e5! 15 ♕e2 ♕e7 16 ♘h4 g6 17 ♗c4 ♔h7 =.

**11 cxd5**

11 ♕e2 transposes to Line F241.

**11...♘xd5**

Worse for Black is 11...exd5 12 ♖c1 a6 13 ♗b1 ♖e8 14 ♘e5 ± Novikov-M.Gurevich, Lvov 1987.

**12 ♖c1**

12 e4 yields nothing owing to 12...♘xc3 13 bxc3 ♖c8 14 ♕e2 ♘f6 15 ♖ad1 cxd4 16 cxd4 ♖c3!, when Black has active play on the queenside; or 12 ♕e2 cxd4 13 exd4 ♘7f6 14 ♖ac1 ♖c8 15 ♘e5 ♘xc3 16 bxc3 ♕d5 17 ♘f3 ♘e4 18 c4 ♘xg3 19 hxg3 ♕d6 =/∓.

**12...♘7f6**

12...cxd4?! is unpleasantly met by 13 ♘xd5! (White gains nothing by 13 exd4 ♖c8 {13...♘7f6 14 ♖e1 ♖c8 15 ♗b1 ♖e8 16 ♘e5 ∞} 14 ♗b1 ♘7f6 15 ♗e5 {15 ♖e1!? ♖e8 16 ♘e5 ∞} 15...♘xc3 16 ♖xc3 ♕d5 ∞ Yermolinsky-Beliavsky, Groningen PCA qual 1993) 13...♗xd5 14 e4 ♗b7 15 ♗c7 ♕e8 16 ♘xd4 ♘c5 17 ♗b5 ♕c8 18 ♗e5 a6 (18...♗xe4? 19 b4 ♕b7 20 bxc5 bxc5 21 ♕g4 ±) 19 ♕g4! ♗g5!? (19...f6 20 ♗c4! ±) 20 f4 f5 21 exf5 exf5 22 ♗c4+ ♔h8 23 ♕h3! ±/± Khalifman-Asrian, Las Vegas FIDE 1999.

**13 ♕e2 cxd4**

An interesting alternative continuation is 13...♘xc3 14 bxc3 ♘e4 15 ♘e5 ♗g5 16 f3 ♘xg3 17 hxg3 ♖c8 18 g4 ♕e7 19 ♗b1 cxd4 20 f4 ♗f6 21 ♕d3 g6 22 exd4 ♖c7 23 ♖fe1 ♖fc8 24 ♖e3 ♗xe5 25 dxe5 ♕h4 with counterplay

for Black, Korobov-Faibisovich, Pardubice 1997.

**14 exd4**

Instead 14 ♘xd5 leads to equality: 14...♕xd5 15 ♖c7 ♗d8 16 ♗c4 ♕e4 17 ♗d3 ♕d5 =.

**14...♘xc3 15 bxc3 ♘h5 16 ♘e5 ♘xg3 17 hxg3 ♖c8**

A position of dynamic equality has arisen. In Epishin-Pushkov, Rostov 1993 there followed 18 ♗b1 ♕d5 19 f3 ♕a5 20 ♕d3 f5 21 ♘g6 ♗a3 22 ♘xf8 ♗xc1 23 ♖xc1 ♔xf8 24 c4 and here 24...♗a6! would have fully equalized.

**F23)**
**10 ♖c1 c5 (D)**

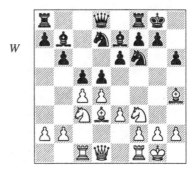

**11 ♕e2**

No advantage is given by 11 ♗g3 due to 11...cxd4 12 exd4 dxc4 13 ♗xc4 a6 14 a4 ♘h5 15 d5 ♘xg3 16 hxg3 exd5 17 ♘xd5 (17 ♗xd5 ♗xd5 18 ♘xd5 ♘f6 19 ♘xe7+ ♕xe7 20 ♖e1 ♕b4 {20...♕b7!?} 21 ♕d4 ♕xd4 22 ♘xd4 ♖fd8 23 ♘c6 ♖d6 =) 17...♗xd5 18 ♕xd5 ♘c5 19 ♕f5 ♕d7 with equality, Romanishin-Van der Wiel, Sarajevo 1984.

**11...♘e4**

Also interesting is 11...♖c8 12 ♗g3 (12 ♖fd1 cxd4 13 ♘xd4 ♘e5 14 ♗xf6 ♗xf6 15 cxd5 ♘xd3 16 ♕xd3 ♗xd5 17 ♕b1 ♕d7 = Ftačnik-Sr.Cvetković, Stary Smokovec 1983) 12...cxd4 13 exd4 dxc4 14 ♗xc4 ♘h5 15 ♗a6 ♘xg3 16 hxg3 ♗xa6 17 ♕xa6 ♖c7 18 ♘b5 ♘b8 19 ♕a4 ♖xc1 20 ♖xc1 a6 = Najdorf-Hort, Lugano OL 1968.

**12 ♗g3**

After 12 ♗xe7 ♕xe7 Black's defensive resources are greater:

a) 13 ♖fd1 ♖fd8 14 cxd5 ♘xc3 (14...exd5 15 dxc5 bxc5 16 ♗a6 ♘df6 17 ♘xe4 ♘xe4 18 ♗xb7 ♕xb7 19 ♘e5 c4 20 ♖c2 a5 = Trifunović-Ivkov, Belgrade 1964) 15 ♖xc3 ♗xd5 16 e4 ♗b7 17 h3 ♖ac8 18 a3 cxd4 19 ♖xc8 ♖xc8 20 ♘xd4 ♘e5 = Gheorghiu-Spassky, Buenos Aires OL 1978.

b) 13 cxd5 ♘xc3 14 ♖xc3 ♗xd5 15 e4 (15 ♗c4 ♗xf3 16 ♕xf3 cxd4 17 exd4 ♘f6 ∓ M.Gurevich-Lputian, USSR 1981) 15...♗b7 16 ♖fc1 ♖fd8 17 h3 ♕d6 18 dxc5 ♘xc5 = Vilela-Lengyel, Trnava 1979.

**12...♘xg3 13 hxg3 dxc4**

Black has also tried 13...cxd4 14 exd4 (14 ♘xd4 ♘f6 =) 14...dxc4 15 ♗xc4 ♘f6 16 ♖fd1, and then:

a) 16...♗b4!? 17 ♘e5 ♕e7 18 a3 ♗xc3 19 ♖xc3 ♖ac8 20 ♖e3 ♖c7 ∞ Lobron-Greenfeld, Biel 1986.

b) 16...a6 17 a4 ♗b4 18 ♘e5 ♕e7 19 f4 (Beliavsky-Ki.Georgiev, Linares 1988) and now, according to Ki.Georgiev, the chances are level after 19...♘d7 20 g4 ♘xe5 21 fxe5 ♖fd8 =.

**14 ♗xc4 ♗xf3 15 gxf3**

In the opinion of M.Gurevich, chances are equal after 15 ♕xf3 cxd4 16 exd4 ♗g5 17 ♖cd1 ♕c7 intending ...♖ad8.

**15...cxd4 16 exd4 ♘f6 17 ♖fd1 ♖c8 18 ♗a6 ♖c6! 19 ♘b5 ♕d7 20 a3 ♘d5 21 ♖c4 ♗g5! 22 ♘c3**

½-½ Torre-M.Gurevich, Leningrad 1987.

**F24)**
**10 ♕e2 c5** *(D)*

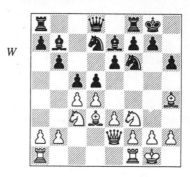

This is the key position of the 8 ♗d3 line. White has two main continuations:

**F241: 11 ♗g3**   121
**F242: 11 ♖fd1**   122

11 cxd5 was tried in Andersson-Beliavsky, Reykjavik 1991, but after 11...♘xd5 12 ♘xd5 ♗xh4 13 ♘c3 cxd4 14 exd4 ♗e7 15 ♗a6 ♗xa6 16 ♕xa6 ♖c8 17 ♕e2 ♖e8 18 ♖ac1 ♕b7 the chances were level.

**F241)**
**11 ♗g3 ♘e4**

White's chances, as practice shows, are better after 11...cxd4 12 exd4 dxc4 13 ♗xc4 a6 (13...♗b4?! 14 ♘b5 ♘e4 15 ♗c7! ♕e8 16 a3 ♗e7 17 ♗f4 ♕d8 18 ♖ac1 ♘df6 19 ♘c7 ♖c8 20 ♘xe6! ±; 13...♘h5 14 ♗a6 ±) 14 a4 ♗b4 15 ♖ac1 ♘h5 (15...♗xc3 16 bxc3 ♘e4

17 ♗h4 ♕c7 18 ♗d3 ♕c6 19 c4 ±
Mikhalchishin-Ivanchuk, Lvov 1987)
16 d5! ♘xg3 17 hxg3 exd5 18 ♘xd5 ±
Vyzhmanavin-Beliavsky, Novosibirsk
1995.

**12 cxd5 exd5 13 ♖ad1**
Or 13 ♖ac1 ♖e8! (13...♖c8?! 14
♗a6! ♘xg3 15 hxg3 ♕c7 16 ♗xb7
♕xb7 17 ♖fd1 ♗f6 18 ♕d3 ♖fd8 19
♕f5 ♘f8 20 dxc5 ♗xc3 21 ♖xc3 bxc5
22 b3 ± Timoshchenko-A.Marić, London Lloyds Bank 1990; 13...♘df6 14
♖fd1 ♘xc3 15 ♖xc3 c4 16 ♗b1 b5 17
♖cc1 ± Nenashev-Vaganian, USSR
1991) 14 ♖fd1 ♘xc3 15 bxc3 c4 16
♗c2 (16 ♗f5 g6 17 ♗c2 ♗f6 18 ♖b1
♖c8 19 ♘d2 ♕e7 20 ♗a4 ♖ed8 21
♗f4 ♗g7 22 ♕f3 ♘f8 23 ♗c2 ♘e6 ∓/∓
Wells-Lputian, Ubeda 1996) 16...b5
17 ♘e5 ♘xe5 18 dxe5 ♕b6 19 f4 ♗c5
20 ♖e1 f6 21 ♔h1 ♖f8 22 ♖cd1 f5 ∞
Naumkin-Epishin, Vilnius 1988.

**13...♘df6**
Weaker is 13...♗f6 because of 14
♗xe4 dxe4 15 ♘e5 cxd4 16 exd4
♕e7 17 ♘xe4 ♗xe5 18 dxe5 ♘xe5 19
♘c3 ♖fe8 20 ♖fe1 Vyzhmanavin; or
13...♘xg3 14 hxg3 ♘f6 15 dxc5 (15
♘e5!? intending f4) 15...bxc5 16 ♗a6
♕b6 17 ♗xb7 ♕xb7 18 ♖d2 ♖fd8 19
♖fd1 ♖d6 20 ♘e1 ♖ad8 21 ♘d3 ♘e4
(Vyzhmanavin-Kolev, Burgas 1993)
22 ♘xe4 dxe4 23 ♘e5 ±.

**14 dxc5 ♘xc3 15 bxc3 ♗xc5 16
♘d4**
White's chances appear slightly
better due to the strong knight on d4
and his better development. However,
Black has a precise route to equality:

**16...♕c8!**
16...♕e7 17 ♗h4 ♕e5 18 ♗xf6 ♕xf6
19 ♗a6! ± Timoshchenko-A.Petro-
sian, USSR 1990.

**17 f3 ♖e8!**
Weaker is 17...♕e8?! 18 ♖fe1 ♕e7
19 ♗h4 ♖fe8 20 ♗c2 a6 21 ♕d3 g6 22
♘b3 ±/± Novikov-A.Petrosian, Erevan open 1996.

**18 ♗h4 ♘d7 19 f4 ♗f8 20 ♗f5
♕c7**
= Vyzhmanavin-Gavrilov, Novgorod 1995.

## F242)
**11 ♖fd1 (D)**

**11...♘e4**
This is the most popular move, but
11...cxd4 also looks very solid:
a) 12 exd4 a6 13 a4 ♘h5 14 ♗g3
♘xg3 15 hxg3 ♘f6 16 ♘e5 dxc4 17
♗xc4 (17 ♘xc4?! b5!? 18 axb5 axb5
19 ♘xb5 ♖xa1 20 ♖xa1 ♗c6 is at least
OK for Black, Gheorghiu-Beliavsky,
Baden 1980) 17...♕e8 = 18 ♕c2 ♗d6
19 ♕e2 ♕e7 is comfortable for Black,
Vyzhmanavin-Li Wenliang, Lucerne
Wcht 1993.
b) 12 ♘xd4 ♘e5 13 ♗xf6 ♗xf6 14
cxd5 ♘xd3 15 ♕xd3 exd5 (15...♗xd5
is also OK) 16 ♖d2 ♕d7 17 ♖ad1
♖fd8 18 ♕e2 ♖ac8 = Ghitescu-Liang
Jinrong, Timisoara 1987.

**12 ♗g3**

12 ♗xe7 ♕xe7 13 cxd5 ♘xc3 (or
13...exd5 14 ♖ac1 ± Nenashev-Schlos-
berg, Regensburg 1998) 14 bxc3 exd5
with equality, Rejfir-Sefc, Czechoslo-
vak Ch (Prague) 1955.

**12...cxd4**

12...♘xg3 13 hxg3 cxd4 (13...♗f6
14 ♖ac1 ♕e7 15 cxd5 ♗xd5 16 ♘xd5
exd5 17 ♗b5 ± Lesiège-Duong Thanh
Nha, Quebec Ch (Montreal) 1999) 14
♘xd4 (14 exd4 transposes to the main
line) 14...♘f6 15 ♖ac1 ♖c8 16 cxd5
♘xd5 is pleasant for Black, Halkias-
Nenashev, Korinthos 1999.

**13 exd4**

13 ♗xe4?! dxc3! 14 cxd5 cxb2 15
♕xb2 ♗f6 16 ♘e5 ♕e8! ∓ Mirallès-
Renet, Lyons Z 1990.

**13...♘xg3 14 hxg3 ♘f6**

14...dxc4 15 ♗xc4 ♘f6 16 ♘e5
♗b4 17 ♕d3 (17 ♖ac1 transposes to
note 'a' to Black's 13th move in Line
F23) 17...♗xc3 18 bxc3 ♖c8 19 ♗b3
♗e4 20 ♕e3 b5 ∞ Portisch-Karpov,
Brussels 1988.

14...♗f6 15 cxd5 ♗xd5 16 ♘xd5
exd5 17 ♗a6 gives White pressure,
Stefansson-Asrian, Erevan OL 1996.

**15 ♘e5 ♖c8**

15...♗b4 16 ♖ac1 ♗xc3 (16...♖c8
is a better idea) 17 bxc3 ♖c8 18 cxd5
(18 f4 is a good alternative) 18...♕xd5
19 f3 ± ♖xc3? 20 ♗h7+ ♘xh7 21
♖xc3 ♕d8 22 ♕c2 ♘f6 23 ♖c7 ♕b8
24 ♖c1 ± Rogers-Lutz, Bundesliga
1998/9.

**16 ♖ac1 dxc4 17 ♗xc4 ♘d5 18
♗xd5**

18 ♗b3 ♘xc3 19 bxc3 ♖c7 = Gav-
rikov-Yusupov, Tunis IZ 1985.

18...exd5 19 ♕d3 ♗f6 20 ♖c2 g6
21 ♖e2 ♗g7 22 ♖de1 a6 23 ♕d1 b5
= Ftačnik-Lutz, Bundesliga 1998/9.

**G)**

**8 ♗e2 ♗b7 9 ♗xf6 ♗xf6 10 cxd5**

This is one of the most popular systems of recent years.

**10...exd5** *(D)*

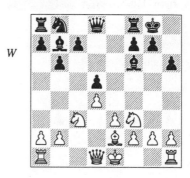

At this point White has two continuations:

**G1: 11 0-0**    123
**G2: 11 b4**    127

**G1)**
**11 0-0**

For the time being White does not
reveal his plan. Now Black has tried
several continuations:

**G11: 11...♘c6**    124
**G12: 11...♘d7**    124
**G13: 11...♕e7**    125

There are also some secondary continuations:

a) 11...♕d6 12 ♖c1 a6 13 a3 ♘d7
14 b4 b5 (Karpov-Spassky, Leningrad
Ct (11) 1974) 15 ♘d2! ±/±.

b) 11...c5 12 dxc5 ♗xc3 13 bxc3
bxc5 14 ♕b3 (14 ♘e5!? ♕e7 15 ♖b1
±/±) 14...♕c7 15 ♖ab1 ♗c6 16 c4 dxc4
17 ♕xc4 ♘d7 18 ♖bc1 ♖ab8 19 ♕c3
♗d5 (M.Gurevich-Dolmatov, Reykjavik 1988) 20 ♖c2 ±.

c) 11...♖e8?! 12 b4! and now, rather than 12...a6?! 13 a4 (13 ♕b3!?) 13...a5 14 b5 ♕d6 15 ♕b3 ♘d7 16 ♘e1 ♘f8 17 ♗f3 ♖ad8 18 ♘d3 ♘e6 19 g3 g6 20 ♗g2 ± Groszpeter-Thorsteins, Copenhagen 1988, better is 12...c6 13 ♕b3 ±.

## G11)
   **11...♘c6 12 ♖c1** *(D)*

### 12...♖e8
Also played, but without particular success, is 12...a6 (12...♘e7 13 b4 c6 14 a4 ±; 12...a5 13 ♘b5! ±) 13 ♘e1 ♘e7 (13...♕d6!? intending ...♘d8-e6) 14 ♘d3 (14 ♗f3!? ♕d6 15 ♘d3 g6 16 b4 with a slight advantage for White, Gligorić-Kurajica, Ljubljana/Portorož 1977) 14...♖b8 (14...♘f5 15 ♕b3 ♖b8! 16 ♘f4 ±) 15 b4 ♘f5 (15...c6!? 16 a4 b5 17 ♘c5 ±) 16 a4 ♖e8 (16...c6?! 17 b5 axb5 18 axb5 ±) 17 b5! ± Vaganian-Lobron, Haifa Echt 1989.

### 13 ♘e1 a5!
Intending to answer 14 ♘d3 with 14...♘b4.

### 14 ♘b5!
Timman-Short, Lucerne Wcht 1989 continued 14 a3 (White obtains nothing by 14 ♗b5 ♖e6 =) 14...♘e7 15

♘d3 ♘f5 16 ♗f3 (16 ♗g4 ♘d6 17 ♗f3 c6 18 b4 axb4 19 axb4 ♗a6 =) 16...♘h4! (only move) 17 ♗g4 c5 18 g3 ♘g6 19 dxc5 d4 with compensation.

### 14...♖e7 15 a3
In Timman's opinion, White has the better chances: he plans to exert pressure on the d5-pawn by ♘d3-f4 and ♗f3; meanwhile it is difficult for Black seek counterchances.

## G12)
   **11...♘d7** *(D)*

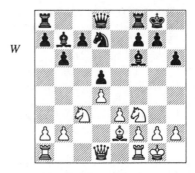

### 12 ♕b3
One drawback of Black's 11th move is that White can, by 12 b4!?, force Black to transpose to a well-known position: 12...c5 13 bxc5 bxc5 and now:

a) 14 ♖b1 and now:

a1) 14...♘b6?! is bad: 15 a4 ♕e7 16 a5 ♘c4 17 a6 ♗c6 18 ♗xc4 dxc4 19 d5 ♖ad8 20 ♕e2 ± Podgaets-Klovans, USSR 1977.

a2) 14...♗c6 transposes to Line G222.

b) However, White should consider 14 ♕b3!? cxd4 15 ♘xd4 ♗xd4! (15...♘c5 16 ♕b4 ♕b6 17 ♖ab1 ±) 16

exd4 ♘b6 17 a4 ♖b8 18 a5 ♘c4 19
♗xc4 dxc4 20 ♕xc4 ♕d6 21 ♕c5 (the
only try for advantage; 21 ♖fd1? ♖fc8!
22 ♕d3 ♕c6; 21 a6 ♗xg2! 22 ♔xg2
♕g6+ 23 ♔h1 ♖fc8; 21 ♖fc1 ♖fd8 22
♖ab1 ♖bc8 23 ♕b4 ♕xd4! 24 ♕xd4
♖xd4 25 ♖xb7 ♖xc3 =) 21...♕xc5 22
dxc5 ± Karpov-Kasparov, Seville Wch
(19) 1987.

**12...c6 13 ♖ad1**
White gradually prepares the e4 advance. The direct 13 e4 gives White
nothing due to 13...dxe4 14 ♘xe4 c5
15 ♘d6 ♕b8 16 ♘xb7 ♕xb7 17 ♗c4
(17 ♘e5 ♕c7 =) 17...♖ad8 18 ♗d5
♕a6 19 ♖ad1?! cxd4 20 ♘xd4 ♘c5 ∓
G.Kuzmin-Forintos, Bath Echt 1973.
   Or 13 ♖fe1 ♖e8 14 e4 c5! 15 ♘xd5
cxd4 16 ♘xf6+ ♕xf6 17 ♕a4 ♘c5 18
♕xd4 ♕xd4 19 ♘xd4 ♖xe4 20 ♘b5
♗c6 ½-½ Timman-Spassky, Bugojno
1982.

**13...♖e8 14 ♖fe1**
   Or 14 ♗d3 ♘f8 15 e4 (15 ♕c2 ♖c8
16 b4 c5 17 bxc5 bxc5 18 dxc5 ♖xc5
19 ♕b3 ♕b6 = Barlov-Yusupov, Dubai
OL 1986) 15...♘e6 16 e5 ♗e7 17 ♗f5
♗f8 is equal, Barlov-Schüssler, Han-
inge 1988.

**14...♘f8 15 e4 g6**
   Also possible is 15...♘e6 16 e5 ♗e7
17 a3 ♗f8 18 g3 ♖c8 19 ♖d2 g6 with
an equal position, Timman-Spassky,
Hilversum 1983.

**16 e5**
   Or 16 a4 ♘e6 17 exd5 cxd5 18 a5
♖e7 19 a6 ♗c6 with equality, Ftačnik-
Haba, Prague 1989.

**16...♗g7**
   Also possible is 16...♗e7 17 a3 ♘e6
18 g3 ♗f8 19 h4 h5 20 ♗f1 ♕e7 is
equal, Gaprindashvili-A.Marić, Cetinje
wom 1991.

17 ♕c2 ♕e7 18 ♖b1 ♘e6 19 ♗f1
♖ad8 20 b4 ♗a8
   = Ki.Georgiev-Portisch, Sarajevo
1986.

**G13)**
**11...♕e7 (D)**

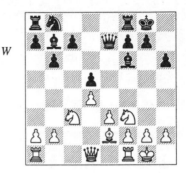

Black wants to carry out the ...c5
advance in comfort.

**12 ♕b3**
A cunning response to 12 ♖b1 was
revealed in the game Cvitan-Beliav-
sky, Bern 1995: 12...c5 13 dxc5 ♗xc3
14 bxc3 ♕xc5! (14...bxc5, Kasparov-
Torre, Moscow 1981, 15 ♕a4! ♘c6 16
♕a3 ± Kasparov) 15 ♕b3 ♘d7 16 ♘d4
♘f6 17 ♖fd1 ♖fc8 18 ♖bc1 ♕e7 =.

**12...♖d8**
12...c6 is inconsistent with Black's
general plan: 13 ♖fe1 ♗c8 14 ♖ac1
♗e6 15 ♕a4 a5 16 ♗d3 ♖c8 17 e4 ±/±
Korchnoi-Cuellar, Leningrad IZ 1973.

**13 ♖ad1**
13 ♖fe1 only leads to equality:
13...c5 14 dxc5 ♗xc3 15 ♕xc3 bxc5
16 ♖ac1 ♘d7 17 ♕a3 ♖dc8 18 ♘d4
♕g5 19 ♘f3 ♕e7 20 ♖c2 a5 = Ribli-
Vaganian, Nikšić 1978.
   Or 13 ♖fd1 c6 14 a4 ♘a6! 15 a5
♕b4 16 ♕c2 ♕e7 17 ♘a4 b5 18 ♘c3

♗c8 = Nikolić-Beliavsky, Reykjavik 1991.

**13...c5!?**

Worse is 13...c6 14 ♖fe1!? ♘d7 (or 14...♗c8?! 15 ♕c2! c5 16 e4! dxe4 17 ♘xe4 ♘c6 18 dxc5 ♗f5 19 ♘xf6+ ♕xf6 20 ♕c1! ± Karpov-Beliavsky, Reggio Emilia 1991/2) 15 ♗f1 (but not 15 ♗d3 ♘f8 16 e4 dxe4 17 ♘xe4 ♗c8! 18 ♘c3 ♗e6 19 ♗c4 b5 = Portisch-Beliavsky, Reggio Emilia 1991/2) 15...♘f8 16 e4 dxe4 17 ♘xe4 ♘e6 18 ♗c4 ± Beliavsky-T.Georgadze, USSR 1979.

**14 dxc5 ♗xc3 15 ♕xc3 bxc5** (D)

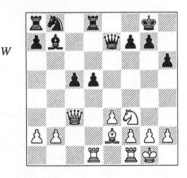

**16 ♖d2**

White prepares to besiege the hanging pawns. He obtains nothing from either 16 ♖c1 ♘d7 17 ♖c2 ♖dc8 18 ♕a3 a5 19 ♖fc1 ♕f6 20 ♗b5 ♗c6 21 ♗xc6 ♖xc6 22 ♕d3 ♖d6 ½-½ Veingold-Tal, Tallinn 1983, or 16 ♘e5 ♘d7 17 ♘xd7 ♖xd7 18 ♗g4 ♖c7! (but not 18...♖dd8? 19 ♖c1 ± Ribli-Vaganian, Skellefteå 1989) 19 ♖d2 ♖d8 20 ♖c1 ♖d6 with equality, P.Nikolić-Liang Jinrong, Lucerne Wcht 1989.

**16...♘d7**

We have reached the critical position of the variation. The assessment

hinges on to what extent White can show the hanging c- and d-pawns to be weak. Currently the verdict is that the chances are equal.

**17 ♖c1 a5!**

But not 17...♖dc8?! 18 ♖dc2 ♕d6 19 ♗d3 g6 20 ♗b5 ♘f8 21 ♕e5 ♕b6 22 ♗a4 a5 23 a3! ♖c7 24 h4 ± Nikolić-Short, Barcelona 1989.

**18 ♕a3 ♕e4**

Also possible is 18...♕f6 19 ♖cd1 ♕b6 20 ♘e1 ♘e5 21 ♕c3 ♖e8 22 ♘f3 ♘d7 23 ♖c2 ♖ac8 = Timman-Yusupov, Rotterdam 1989.

**19 ♗b5**

On 19 ♘e1 there would follow 19...♕b4, while on 19 ♗d3 fully possible is 19...♕e6!? and White has achieved nothing.

**19...d4! 20 exd4**

Or:

a) 20 ♗d3 ♕e6 21 exd4 ♗xf3 22 gxf3 ♕f6! 23 ♖cd1 cxd4 24 ♗e4 ♘e5 with an attack.

b) If 20 ♗e2 ♘e5! 21 ♖xc5? then 21...d3 22 ♖xe5 (22 ♗d1 ♘c4 −+) 22...dxe2 23 ♖xe4 ♖xd2 24 ♘e1 ♖d1 25 f3 (25 ♕c3 ♖c8 26 ♕xa5 ♗xe4 27 f3 ♗b1 −+) 25...♖xe1+ 26 ♔f2 ♖g1! 27 ♔xe2 ♖xg2+ 28 ♔f1 ♖xh2 ∓.

c) 20 ♗f1!? dxe3 21 ♕xe3 ♕xe3 22 fxe3 ♔f8! = with the point 23 ♗b5 ♗xf3! 24 gxf3 ♘e5.

**20...♘e5! 21 ♘e1**

Or 21 ♗f1 ♘xf3+ 22 ♕xf3 ♕xf3 23 gxf3 ♖xd4 24 ♖xd4 cxd4 25 ♔g2 intending ♗d3 =.

**21...cxd4 22 ♕g3! ♕f5**

Also possible is 22...♖ac8 23 ♖cd1 =.

**23 ♗f1 ♗a6!?**

= Timman-Ivanchuk, Hilversum (3) 1991.

**G2)**

**11 b4** *(D)*

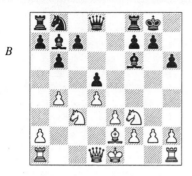

B

White seizes space on the queenside and threatens, by playing b5, to dislocate Black's c7- and d5-pawns. Black has two ways to counter White's plan: either 11...c6, preventing the further advance of White's b-pawn and preparing to attack it by ...a5; or 11...c5, immediately trying to free his game.

**G21: 11...c6** 127
**G22: 11...c5** 130

11...♘c6 cannot be recommended: 12 ♕b3 ♘e7 13 0-0 c6 14 ♖ac1 ♖c8 15 ♖fd1 ♖c7 16 a4 ♕b8 17 e4 dxe4 18 ♘xe4 ♘d5 19 ♗c4 ♗e7 20 b5 gives White a clear advantage, Furman-Yuferov, Leningrad 1971.

**G21)**

**11...c6 12 0-0**

12 ♕b3 seems premature due to 12...a5:

a) 13 b5 c5 14 ♖d1 (14 0-0 ♕d6 15 ♖ac1 ♘d7 16 ♖fd1 ♖ac8 = T.Georgadze-Lputian, Volgograd 1985) 14...c4 15 ♕c2 ♕d6 16 0-0 ♖e8 17 ♖d2 ♘d7 =/∓.

b) 13 bxa5 b5! 14 0-0 ♕xa5 15 e4! b4 16 exd5 bxc3 (16...cxd5 17 ♘b5 intending a4) 17 ♕xb7 cxd5 18 ♖ac1 ♖a7 19 ♕b5 (only move) 19...♖c8 20 ♖c2 ♘d7! ∓ Dokhoian-Portisch, Wijk aan Zee 1990.

Now Black has a choice: either to hold back ...a5 for now and make a useful move, or else to play it immediately:

**G211: 12...♖e8** 127
**G212: 12...a5** 129

Black can also use an alternative plan: 12...♕d6 (intending ...♘d7) 13 ♕b3 (13 ♖b1!? ♘d7 14 ♘e1 ♗d8 15 ♘d3 ♗c7 16 g3 ♕e7 17 ♗f3 ♘f6 18 ♕c2 ♖ad8 19 ♖fc1 h5 with counterplay on the kingside, Meduna-Bönsch, Trnava 1988) 13...♘d7 14 ♖fe1 (14 ♖fd1 a5 15 a3?! {15 bxa5!? ♖xa5 16 a4 ∞} 15...axb4 16 axb4 ♗e7 17 ♖ab1 ♘f6 18 ♘e5 ♕e6 19 ♘d3 ♗d6 = Ekström-Sr.Cvetković, Liechtenstein 1988) 14...♖ad8 15 ♖ab1 (15 a4!? intending a5 ±) 15...♖fe8 16 ♗d3 and White is slightly better, Speelman-Short, London Ct (1) 1988.

**G211)**

**12...♖e8** *(D)*

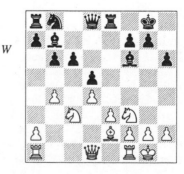

W

**13 ♕b3**

13 ♖c1!? is an interesting interpretation of the line for White: 13...♘d7 (13...a5 14 b5 c5 15 dxc5 bxc5 16 ♘a4 ±) 14 ♕b3 a5 15 b5 c5 16 ♘xd5 ♗xd4 17 ♗c4 a4 18 ♕c2 ± Beliavsky-Gomez Esteban, Lyons 1994.

**13...a5**

13...♘d7?! is dubious in view of 14 ♖ad1, intending b5: 14...a6 15 a4 ♘f8 16 a5 bxa5 17 bxa5 ♖b8 18 ♘a4 ♘e6 19 ♕c3 ± Kasparov-Ehlvest, Belgrade 1989.

However, Black quite often plays 13...♕d6:

a) 14 ♖fe1 (with this move White aims to prepare an advance in the centre, viz. e4) 14...♘d7 15 ♗f1 (in Karpov's opinion, the position is pleasant for White after 15 ♗d3 ♘f8 16 e4 dxe4 17 ♘xe4 ♕f4) 15...♗e7 16 ♖ab1 a5 17 bxa5 ♖xa5 18 a4 ♗f8 (18...♗a6 19 ♗xa6 ♖xa6 20 e4! dxe4 21 ♘xe4 ♕g6 22 ♖e3 with a slight advantage for White, Karpov-Bönsch, Baden-Baden 1992) 19 ♕c2 g6 20 e4 dxe4 21 ♘xe4 ♕f4 22 ♗c4 ♗g7 23 ♖e2 ± Karpov-Ki.Georgiev, Tilburg 1994.

b) There is also another plan: 14 a4!? ♘d7 15 a5 (15 ♖fc1 a5 16 bxa5 ♖xa5 17 ♖ab1 g6 18 ♕c2 ♗g7 19 g3 ♖c8 20 h4 {20 ♗f1 c5 21 ♗h3 f5 22 ♗g2 ∞ Ki.Georgiev} 20...c5 ∞ Beliavsky-Ki.Georgiev, Yugoslavia 1994) 15...♖ad8 16 axb6 axb6 17 ♖a7 ♕b8 18 ♖a2 (18 ♖fa1 gives White nothing: 18...b5 19 ♘e1 ♘b6 20 ♘d3 ♘a4 21 ♖a5 ♗xd4 22 exd4 ♘xc3 23 ♕xc3 ♖xe2 24 ♘e5 f6 25 ♕d3 ♖b2 26 ♕c3 = P.Nikolić-Short, Belgrade 1989) 18...b5 19 ♘e1 ♗e7 20 ♘d3 ♗d6 21 g3 ♘b6 22 ♗f3 ♗c8 23 ♖fa1 ♗f5 24 ♘c5 and White's position deserves

preference, P.Nikolić-Short, Manila IZ 1990.

**14 bxa5**

Or:

a) 14 a3 gives White nothing after 14...♘d7 and now:

a1) 15 ♖ad1 axb4 16 axb4 b5 17 ♗d3 (17 ♘e1?! ♕b6 18 ♘d3 ♗c8 19 ♘c5 ♗f5 20 ♖a1 ♗e7! 21 ♖a2 ♖xa2 22 ♕xa2 ♗d6 ∓ Speelman-Lputian, Kropotkin 1995) 17...♕b6 18 e4 (18 ♖a1 ♘c4 19 e4 dxe4 20 ♗xe4 ♕b6 =) 18...♘c4! (18...dxe4 19 ♘xe4 ♘d5 20 ♘c5 ±) 19 exd5 (19 e5? ♖a3 20 ♕c2 ♗e7 ∓) 19...cxd5 20 ♘xb5 ♕b6 21 ♘c3 (21 ♗xc4? dxc4 22 ♕xc4 ♗a6 −+) 21...♖a3 22 ♕c2 ♕xb4 23 ♖b1 = (23 ♘e2 ♖c8 24 ♖b1 ♕e7 ∓).

a2) 15 b5 c5 16 ♘xd5 ♗xd4 17 ♖ad1 ♘e5 18 ♘xe5 ♗xd5 19 ♘c4 ♕g5 20 g3 ♕f5! 21 ♖fe1 ♕e4 22 f3 ♕xe3+! = Karpov-Short, Amsterdam 1991.

b) Timman's move 14 b5 leads to very sharp play: 14...c5 15 dxc5 bxc5 16 ♖ac1 ♗xc3 17 ♕xc3 ♘d7 18 ♖fd1 (18 ♖c2 ♕b6 19 ♖d1 ♖e7 ∞ Timman-Short, San Lorenzo del Escorial Ct (1) 1993) 18...♕b6 19 ♗f1 ♖ac8 ∞ Timman-Short, San Lorenzo del Escorial Ct (3) 1993.

**14...♖xa5 (D)**

**15 Ⅱfe1 ♘d7**

If 15...Ⅱe7, then 16 a4 ♘d7 17 ♗f1 is slightly better for White, Lputian-Portisch, Kropotkin 1995.

**16 a4**

Instead, 16 e4?! is premature in view of 16...c5 17 ♘xd5 cxd4 (17...♗xd5 18 exd5 cxd4 19 ♗b5 ♘c5 20 ♕c4 Ⅱe4 21 Ⅱad1 Ⅱa3, Hulak-Short, Debrecen Echt 1992, 22 Ⅱxe4 {only move} 22...♘xe4 23 ♘xd4 ♘d6 24 ♕e2 ♗xd4 25 Ⅱxd4 ♕f6 = Short) 18 ♗c4! ♘c5 19 ♕xb6 ♕xb6 20 ♘xb6 Ⅱxe4 21 ♘d5! ♗xd5 22 ♗xd5 Ⅱxe1+ 23 Ⅱxe1 ♔f8 24 ♗b3! = Epishin-Vaganian, Rostov 1993.

**16...♗a6**

If 16...g6, then 17 Ⅱab1 ♗g7 18 ♗f1 ♗a6 19 ♗xa6 Ⅱxa6 20 Ⅱec1 ♗f8 21 ♘e1 ♗d6 22 ♘d3 ♘f6?! (Epishin-Lutz, Dortmund 1994) 23 ♘a2! ♕a8 (23...♗xh2+ 24 ♔xh2 ♘g4+ 25 ♔g1 ♕h4 26 ♘ab4 Ⅱaa8 27 ♘xc6! ♕h2+ 28 ♔f1 ♕h1+ 29 ♔e2 ♕xg2 30 Ⅱg1 ♕e4 31 ♘ce5 +−) 24 ♘ab4 Ⅱxa4 25 ♘xc6 ± Epishin.

**17 ♗xa6**

White gets nothing from 17 Ⅱac1 ♗xe2 18 Ⅱxe2 c5 19 ♘xd5 cxd4 20 ♘xf6+ ♕xf6 21 ♘xd4 ♘c5 22 ♕d1 Ⅱea8 23 h3 Ⅱxa4 = Lutz-Lobron, Munich 1993.

**17...Ⅱxa6 18 Ⅱe2**

The direct 18 e4 is less effective due to 18...dxe4 19 ♘xe4 Ⅱe6 20 Ⅱa2 (Lputian-A.Petrosian, Erevan 1995), when, according to Lputian, 20...Ⅱa8! equalizes.

However, 18 Ⅱad1 deserves attention: 18...Ⅱa5 19 Ⅱe2 (the time is still not right for 19 e4 dxe4 20 ♘xe4 Ⅱe6 21 Ⅱe3 Ⅱd5 22 ♘xf6+ ♕xf6 23 Ⅱxe6 ♕xe6 24 Ⅱe1 Ⅱe5 25 ♕xe6 Ⅱxe6 26

Ⅱa1 ½-½ M.Gurevich-Van der Sterren, Wijk aan Zee 1993) 19...Ⅱe6 20 Ⅱc2 (20 Ⅱde1!? intending e4 deserves attention) 20...♕a8 21 Ⅱdc1 ♔h7 (21...g6!? 22 ♘e1 ♔g7 23 ♘d3 ♗g5 24 ♘b4 h5 ∞ Van Wely-Tisdall, Gausdal 1993) 22 g3 ♗d8 (Epishin suggests 22...g6!? intending ...♔g7) 23 ♘e1!? c5 24 ♕b1 (24 ♘xd5? c4 −+) 24...g6 25 ♘d3 (Epishin-Goldin, Novosibirsk 1993) 25...cxd4! =.

**18...Ⅱe6 19 Ⅱc2 ♗e7 20 Ⅱac1 ♗f8 21 ♘e1**

White has the preferable position, H.Leyva-Arencibia, Holguin 1995. According to H.Leyva, Black should continue 21...♕a8 22 ♘d3 (22 ♘xd5 cxd5 23 Ⅱc8 ♘c5!) 22...Ⅱa5 23 g3 ♔h7 24 ♘f4 Ⅱe8 25 e4 ±.

**G212)**

**12...a5** *(D)*

This seems to be the strongest continuation.

**13 bxa5**

Or:

a) 13 a3 ♕d6 (if 13...axb4 14 axb4 Ⅱxa1 15 ♕xa1 ♘d7, then 16 ♕b1 ♕c7 17 Ⅱd1 ±; 13...♘d7 14 ♕b3 Ⅱe8 transposes to note 'a' to White's 14th

move in Line G211) 14 b5 (White gets
nothing from 14 e4 dxe4 15 ♘xe4
♕f4 16 ♘xf6+ ♕xf6 17 ♕b3 ♘d7 18
♖ac1 axb4 19 axb4 ♖fe8 = Kraai-
Bönsch, Bundesliga 1998/9) 14...c5 15
dxc5 ♕xc5 (15...bxc5?! 16 ♘e4 ♕e7
17 ♘xf6+ ♕xf6 18 ♖c1 ♘d7 19 ♘d2
d4 20 exd4 ♕xd4 21 ♘b3 ±) 16 ♘a4
±.
　　b) 13 b5 c5 14 ♖c1 (14 ♖e1!? ♖e8
15 ♖c1 ♘d7 16 g3 ♘f8 17 ♘a4 c4 18
♗f1 ♕d6 19 ♗g2 ♖ad8 20 h4 ♘e6 21
♘c3 g6 = Topalov-Kramnik, Linares
1998) 14...♘d7 (14...♕d6? 15 dxc5
bxc5 16 ♘e4 ±) 15 dxc5 (15 ♕d2
yields nothing in view of 15...c4! 16
♖fd1 ♖c8 17 g3 ♕e7 18 ♘e1 ♕e6 19
♘g2 ♗e7 20 ♘f4 ♕d6 21 ♗f3 ♘f6 =)
15...♘xc5 16 ♘d4 ♖c8! (worse for
Black is 16...♕d6 17 ♗g4 ♖ad8 18
♘ce2 g6 19 ♕c2 h5 20 ♗h3 ♔g7 21
♖fd1 ± Nikolić-Beliavsky, Groningen
1993; however, 16...♗xd4 17 ♕xd4
♘e6 18 ♕e5 ♖e8 ∞ deserves attention) 17 ♗g4 ♖c7 18 ♘ce2 (or 18 ♘a4
♘e4 19 ♕d3 ♖c4 20 ♘b2 ♖c5 21 ♘a4
♗xd4 22 exd4 ♖c4 23 ♘c3 ♕c7 24
♘e2 f5 25 ♗h3 g5 26 f3 ♘d6 = Gre-
tarsson-Yusupov, Groningen FIDE
1997) 18...♗e5 19 g3 g6 20 ♗h3 ♕d6
21 ♖c2 h5 22 ♗g2 h4 = Lutz-Van der
Sterren, Munich 1994.
　　**13...♖xa5 14 a4**
　　14 ♕b3 ♗c8! 15 ♘a4 (15 a4!?)
15...♗a6 16 ♗xa6 ♘xa6 17 ♖ac1 (17
♖ab1?! b5 18 ♘b2 c5 19 dxc5 ♘xc5
20 ♕b4 ♘e4 21 ♘d4 ♗xd4, Hulak-
Lutz, Wijk aan Zee 1995, 22 ♕xd4
♖xa2 23 f3 ♘f6 24 ♘d3 is slightly
better for Black – Lutz) 17...c5 ∞
Siegel-Lutz, Bundesliga 1994/5.
　　14 ♖b1 is only justified after 14...c5?
15 ♕b3! cxd4 16 exd4 ♘d7 17 ♗b5 ±

Lobron-Van der Sterren. Wijk aan
Zee 1993. However, Black can calmly
reply 14...♘d7.
　　**14...c5**
　　Beliavsky's continuation 14...♗c8!?
deserves serious attention: 15 ♕c2
♗e6 16 ♖fc1 (or 16 ♖ab1 ♘d7 and
now: 17 ♖fe1 ♕c7 18 ♗d3 ♖aa8 19 e4
dxe4 20 ♘xe4 ♗d5 21 ♗c4 ♖fc8 22
♗xd5 cxd5 23 ♘xf6+ ♘xf6 24 ♕xc7
♖xc7 25 ♖xb6 ♖xa4 =; or 17 ♖fc1
♕a8 18 ♗d3 c5 19 ♗h7+ ♔h8 20 ♗f5
♕c6 =) 16...♕e7 17 ♘d2 c5 18 ♘b3
cxd4! 19 exd4 (19 ♘xa5 dxc3 20 ♘b3
♘c6 with compensation) 19...♖a8 =
Nikolić-Beliavsky, Tilburg 1993.
　　**15 ♕b3 ♘a6**
　　15...c4?! is dubious: 16 ♕b2 ♘d7
17 ♖fb1 ♗c6 18 ♘e1 ♗e7 19 ♘c2
♕a8 20 ♗f3 ±.
　　**16 ♖fb1**
　　16 ♖fd1 ♘b4 17 ♗b5 ♕a8 18 ♘e1
♖c8 19 ♖ac1 ♗e7 ½-½ Bischoff-Lutz,
Bremen 1998.
　　**16...♘b4 17 ♘a2 ♘xa2 18 ♖xa2
♗a6 19 ♗xa6 ♖xa6 20 ♕b5 ♕a8 21
dxc5 bxc5 22 ♕xc5 ♖xa4 23 ♖xa4
♕xa4 24 h3**
　　½-½ Lautier-Kramnik, Belgrade
1997.

**G22)**
　　**11...c5** *(D)*
　　Black provokes an immediate crisis
in the centre.
　　**12 bxc5 bxc5 13 ♖b1**
　　According to analysis by Seirawan,
13 ♕b3 yields nothing owing to
13...♗c6 (dubious is 13...♕b6?! 14
♘xd5 ♗xd5 15 ♕xd5 cxd4 16 ♖c1!?)
14 dxc5 ♕a5 (14...♘d7 15 ♘d4 ♘xc5
16 ♕b4 ♗e7 17 ♘xc6 ♘d3+ 18 ♗xd3
♗xb4 19 ♘xb4 ∞) 15 ♖c1 ♘d7 16

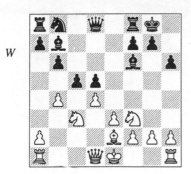

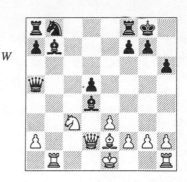

②d4 ②xc5 17 ②xc6 ②xb3 18 ②xa5 ②xc1 =.

At this point Black has two continuations:

**G221:** 13...♕a5 131
**G222:** 13...♗c6 132

As practice shows, the latter gives Black better chances of equality.

### G221)
**13...♕a5 14 ♕d2**

Seirawan's move 14 0-0 does not yield an advantage: 14...cxd4 15 ②xd4 ②c6! 16 ②db5 (16 ♖xb7 ②xd4 17 exd4 ♕xc3 18 ♗f3 =; 16 ②xd5 ♕xd5 17 ♗f3 ♕xa2! 18 ②xc6 ♗xc6 19 ♗xc6 ♖ad8 20 ♕f3 ♖d6 21 g3 a5 = Seirawan-Beliavsky, Barcelona 1989) 16...②e7 17 ♕a4 ♕xa4 18 ②xa4 ♗c6 19 ②c5 ♖fc8 20 ♖fc1 ♗xb5 21 ♗xb5 d4 (also possible is 21...♖c7 22 ②d7 ♗c3 23 ♖b3 ♗a5 24 ♖xc7 ♗xc7 = Seirawan-Karpov, Brussels 1988) 22 ②d7 dxe3 23 ②xf6+ gxf6 24 fxe3 ♖ab8 25 ♗a4 ♔g7 26 ♖xb8 ♖xc1+ 27 ♔f2 ♖c7 ½-½ Timman-Karpov, Amsterdam 1988.

**14...cxd4 15 ②xd4 ♗xd4 (D)**
**16 exd4**

16 ♕xd4!? is probably best met by 16...②c6 17 ♕d2 d4! 18 exd4 ♗a6,

with sufficient compensation, rather than 16...♖c8 17 ♖xb7 ♖xc3 18 0-0 ②c6 19 ♕d2 ♖a3 20 ♕xa5 ♖xa5 21 ♖c1 ②e5 22 ♖c2 ±.

**16...♗a6**

16...♗c6 leaves Black worse:

a) 17 ②b5!? ♕d8 18 0-0 ②d7 (or 18...a6 19 ②a3! ♖e8 20 ②c2 ♖xe2?! {better is 20...②d7!? 21 ②b4 ♕a5 22 ♖b2 ♗b5 23 ♗xb5 ♕xb5! ± Geller} 21 ♕xe2 ♗b5 22 ♖xb5 axb5 23 ♕xb5 ♖xa2 24 ②e3 ± Kasparov-Karpov, Moscow Wch (40) 1984/5) 19 ♖fc1 ♗xb5 20 ♖xb5 ②f6 (20...②b6 21 ♕b4 intending a4 ±) 21 f3 ♕e7 22 ♔f2!? ♖ab8 23 ♖cc5 ♖xb5 24 ♗xb5 ♖b8 25 a4 ♕d6 26 g3 ♕e6 27 ♕f4 ± Vaganian-Gomez Esteban, Haifa 1989.

b) 17 ②d1! ♕d8 (17...♕xd2+ 18 ♔xd2 ②d7 19 ♖c1! ± Chernin-Beliavsky, Debrecen Echt 1992) 18 0-0 intending ②e3, ♗f3 and ♖fc1 ± (Chernin).

**17 ②b5 ♕d8**

Bad is 17...♕xd2+ 18 ♔xd2 ②c6 19 ♖hc1! ②a5 20 ②c7 ♗xe2 21 ♔xe2! ♖ad8 22 ♖c5 ±.

**18 0-0 ②c6**

White obtains a stable advantage after 18...②d7 19 ♖fc1 ②f6 20 f3 ♖e8 21 a4 ♖e7 22 ♗d3 ±/± Vaganian-Geller, New York 1990.

**19 ♖fd1**
19 ♖fc1?! is suspect in view of
19...♕f6! 20 ♘c7 ♗xe2 21 ♘xa8 ♘xd4
(intending ...♘f3+) 22 ♖b4 ♗c4 ∓.
However, White can play 19 a4 ♕f6
20 ♖fd1 ♖fd8 21 ♖b3 ♖ac8 22 h3! ±
Azmaiparashvili-Short, Manila OL
1992.
**19...♕f6**
Bad is 19...♕d7? 20 a4 ♖ab8 21
♖bc1 ♗b7 22 ♕f4! ± Ki.Georgiev-
Beliavsky, Biel 1992.
**20 ♗f1!**
White achieved nothing in Yusu-
pov-Beliavsky, Linares 1988: 20 ♗f3
♖ab8 21 a4 ♖fd8 22 ♕c3 ♗c8 23 ♖bc1
a6 24 ♕xc6 ♕xc6 25 ♖xc6 axb5 26
axb5 ½-½.
**20...♖ab8 21 a4 ♖fc8 22 ♖b3 ♗xb5
23 axb5 ♘d8 24 ♕a2!**
Intending 25 ♖a3, 25 ♖e3 or 25 ♖f3.
**24...♖c7**
24...♖b7 25 ♖e3 intending 26 ♕xd5
or 26 ♖e8+.
**25 ♖a3!**
± Karpov-Short, Linares Ct (7)
1992.

**G222)**
**13...♗c6 14 0-0 ♘d7 15 ♗b5**
White tries to exchange the light-
squared bishops, as this would enhance the weakness of the d5-pawn.
15 ♕d2 c4 16 ♘e1 ♕a5 17 ♘c2 ♖ab8
18 ♗f3 ♘c5 19 ♘e4 ♕xd2 20 ♘xd2
c3 21 ♖xb8 ♖xb8 22 ♖b1 ♖c8 23 ♘b3
♘e4 ∞ Dokhoian-Pigusov, Kharkov
1985.
**15...♕c7 (D)**
We have reached the critical position for the whole variation. In practice White has tried various moves in
the quest for an advantage.

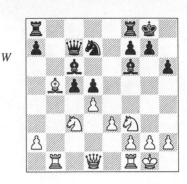

W

**16 ♕d3**
This is the most common continuation. Others:
a) 16 ♕a4 (Salov's move, by which
White immediately tries to provoke a
crisis) 16...♘b6 17 ♕a5 cxd4 18 exd4
♖fc8 19 ♗xc6 (according to analysis
by Salov, equal chances also result after 19 ♗a6 ♘c4 20 ♕c5 ♗e7 21 ♘xd5
♗xc5 22 ♘xc7 ♖xc7 23 dxc5 ♗xf3 24
♗xc4 ♖xc5 25 ♗xf7+ =) 19...♕xc6 20
♖b3 ♕c4 21 ♖d1 ♖c6 22 g3 g6 23
♔g2 ♔g7 = Salov-Hjartarson, Belgrade 1987.
b) 16 ♕c2 (this move was tried
several times in the 1984/5 Karpov-
Kasparov match) 16...♖ab8 (Black
fared worse in Karpov-Kasparov, Moscow Wch (39) 1984/5 with 16...♖fd8
17 ♖fc1 ♖ab8 18 a4 ♕d6 19 dxc5
♘xc5 20 ♗xc6 ♕xc6 21 ♘b5 ♗e7 22
♘xa7 ♕a6 23 ♘b5 ♕xa4 24 ♕xa4
♘xa4 25 ♘fd4 ±; however, fully possible is 16...♖fc8 17 ♖fc1 ♗xb5 18
♘xb5 ♕c6 19 dxc5 ♘xc5 20 ♕f5
♕e6 21 ♘fd4 ♕xf5 22 ♘xf5 ♘e6 23
♖xc8+ ♖xc8 24 ♘xa7 ♖c2 with equality, Kasparov-Karpov, Moscow Wch
(42) 1984/5) 17 a4 ♕d6 18 ♖fd1 ♖fc8
19 ♕a2 cxd4 20 ♘xd4 (Dorfman-Stu-
rua, Forli 1994) and now, according to

Sturua, Black should play 20...♗xd4 21 ♖xd4 ♘f6 22 ♖bd1 ♗xb5 23 ♘xb5 ♕c5 24 ♖4d3 a6 25 ♘c3 ♕c4 =.

c) 16 ♕d2 ♖ab8 (worse is 16...♖fd8 17 ♖fc1 ♖ab8 18 a4 ♕d6 19 h3 cxd4 20 exd4 ± Epishin-Lugovoi, St Petersburg 1996) 17 ♗xc6 ♕xc6 18 dxc5 ♗xc3 19 ♕xc3 ♕xc5 20 ♕xc5 ♘xc5 21 ♘d4 ♖fc8 22 f3 g6 = Hübner-Ivanchuk, Dortmund 1992. White cannot derive any particular advantage from Black's isolated pawn in the endgame.

**16...♖fd8**

Or 16...♖fc8 17 ♖fc1 ♖ab8 18 h3, and now:

a) 18...g6?! 19 ♗xc6 ♖xb1 (not 19...♕xc6? 20 ♖xb8 ♖xb8 21 dxc5 ♗xc3 22 ♖xc3! ♘xc5 23 ♕c2 ♖c8 24 ♘d4 +−) 20 ♕xb1! ♕xc6 21 dxc5 ♕xc5 (21...♘xc5 22 ♘e2 ♕a8 23 ♘f4 ±) 22 ♘e2 ± Kasparov-Karpov, Seville Wch (18) 1987.

b) Nor does Black equalize by 18...cxd4 19 ♘xd5 ♗xb5 20 ♖xc7 ♗xd3 21 ♖xb8 ♖xb8 22 ♖xd7 dxe3 23 ♘xf6+ gxf6 24 fxe3 ♗e4 25 ♖xa7 ±.

c) 18...c4 19 ♕c2 (19 ♕f5 g6 20 ♕f4 ♕xf4 21 exf4 ♗xb5 22 ♘xb5 ♘f8 ∞) 19...♗xb5 (Kasparov suggested 19...♗a8, but, according to Khalifman, White keeps the initiative after 20 ♕f5 ♘b6 21 e4!) 20 ♘xb5 ♕a5 21 ♘c3 g6 (recommended by Khalifman; 21...♖xb1 22 ♖xb1 ♖b8 23 ♖xb8+ ♘xb8 24 e4! dxe4 25 ♘xe4 ♕d5 26 ♘xf6+ gxf6 27 ♘d2! ♕xd4 28 ♘xc4 ± Khalifman-Chandler, Bundesliga 1994/5) 22 ♖xb8 ♖xb8 23 e4 dxe4 24

♘xe4 ♖c8 25 ♘d6 ♖c6 26 ♘xc4 ♕d5. In Khalifman's opinion Black has compensation for the pawn.

**17 ♖fd1**

In Dydyshko-E.Vladimirov, Moscow 1983, 17 ♕f5 cxd4 18 exd4 g6! 19 ♕h3 (or 19 ♘xd5 ♗xd5 20 ♕xd5 ♘e5 =) 19...♗xb5 20 ♘xb5 ♕f4 gave Black good play.

**17...♖ab8 18 ♗xc6 ♕xc6**

The preliminary 18...♖xb1, which aims to lessen the pressure on the d5-pawn, allows White to generate some pressure on the queenside by 19 ♕xb1 ♕xc6 20 ♕b5! ♘b8 21 ♕a5 ♕b6 22 ♕xb6 axb6 23 ♖b1.

**19 ♖xb8**

Instead, 19 ♖bc1 can be answered by 19...♖b2, or 19...c4 with a fully equal game for Black.

**19...♖xb8 20 dxc5 ♗xc3 21 ♕xc3 ♕xc5 22 ♕xc5 ♘xc5 23 h3 ♘e4**

Not, of course, 23...♖d8? due to 24 ♘d4 ±.

**24 ♖xd5 ♖b1+ 25 ♔h2 ♘xf2 26 ♖d8+ ♔h7 27 ♖d7 a5 28 ♖xf7 ♖b2 29 a4! ♘d1**

Black's activity is sufficient for equality, Karpov-Kasparov, Moscow Wch (8) 1985.

**Conclusion:** The Tartakower Variation leads to lively piece-play. There frequently arise positions with hanging pawns. In recent times 8 ♗e2 and 8 ♗d3 have been especially popular, but Black's results have not been at all bad, which is a testament to the vitality of the Tartakower Variation.

# 9 The Exchange Variation

**1 d4 d5 2 c4 e6 3 ♘c3 ♘f6**

This move allows White to play the most challenging form of Exchange Variation, with ♗g5 and retaining possibilities of ♘ge2.

**4 cxd5 exd5 5 ♗g5** *(D)*

White has several possible middlegame plans in this line, of which the main ideas are: 1) A queenside minority attack with b4-b5; 2) Attack in the centre with (e3-)e4.

Black's possible plans are: a counterattack using his kingside pawns; a kingside attack based on piece-play; positional methods of defence, involving the creation of a defensive barrier by ...b5 or piece control of c4 and b5.

It is important to bear these plans in mind as they subtly affect the opening play for both sides.

Getting back to specifics, Black has two main continuations here:

**A: 5...♗e7**    134
**B: 5...c6**    137

Other continuations have also been tried in practice, but without success:

a) 5...♗e6?! 6 e3 c5 7 ♗b5+ ♘c6 8 ♗xf6 gxf6 9 ♘ge2 a6 10 ♗xc6+ bxc6 11 0-0 ♖g8 12 ♔h1 f5 13 dxc5 ♗xc5 14 ♘f4 ♗d6 15 ♘ce2 ± Furman-Spassky, USSR 1958.

b) 5...c5?! 6 ♗xf6 gxf6 7 e3 ♗e6 8 ♘ge2 ♘c6 9 g3 ± Pillsbury-Steinitz, Hastings 1895.

## A)

**5...♗e7 6 e3**

In this position Black can, if he wishes, transpose to Line B24 by playing 6...c6. Other continuations have also been tried in practice:

**A1: 6...h6**    134
**A2: 6...♘bd7**    135
**A3: 6...0-0**    136

## A1)

**6...h6 7 ♗h4 0-0 8 ♗d3** *(D)*

**8...b6**

Black can try 8...♖e8, hoping for 9 ♕c2?! c5! 10 ♘ge2 ♘c6 11 dxc5 d4 12 ♖d1 g5 13 ♗g3 dxc3 14 ♗c4! ♕a5 15 ♕g6+ ♔h8, when 16 ♕xh6 ♘h7 is unconvincing for White, and 16 ♗xf7? loses to the attractive sequence 16...cxb2+ 17 ♔f1 (Azmaiparashvili-Sr.Cvetković, Stary Smokovec 1983) 17...♖d8! 18 ♗d6 ♗f5! 19 ♕xf5 ♖xd6! 20 ♖xd6 ♕xc5! –+. However, simpler and stronger is 9 ♘ge2 ♘bd7 10 0-0 c6 (or 10...♘f8 11 ♕c2 c6 12 f3 ♗e6 13 ♖ad1 ♖c8 14 ♔h1 ± Malaniuk-Kasperek, Katowice 1991) 11 f3 c5 12 ♕c2 b6 13 ♗b5 ♗b7 14 ♗xf6 ♗xf6 15 dxc5 bxc5 16 ♖ad1 d4! 17 exd4 cxd4 18 ♘xd4 ♕b6 19 ♕f2 ♖ed8 20 ♘b3 ± Botvinnik-Porath, Amsterdam OL 1954.

White has a stable advantage after the straightforward 8...c5 9 dxc5 ♘bd7 10 ♘ge2 ♘xc5 11 ♗c2 ♗e6 12 0-0 ♖c8 (or 12...♘ce4 13 ♕d3 ♖c8 14 ♗xf6 ♘xf6 15 ♖fd1 ♕b6 16 ♗b3 ♖fd8 17 ♘f4 ♗d6 18 ♘fxd5 ♘xd5 19 ♘xd5 ♗xd5 20 ♗xd5 ♕xb2 21 ♖ab1 ♕c3 22 ♕xc3 ♖xc3 23 ♖xb7 ± Gulko-Lputian, Tashkent 1984) 13 ♕d4 ♕b6 14 ♖ab1 ♖fd8 15 ♖fc1 ± Portisch-Pfleger, Skopje OL 1972.

**9 ♘ge2 ♗b7 10 0-0**

10 ♗xf6 is overly hasty: 10...♗xf6 11 b4 c5 12 bxc5 bxc5 13 ♖b1 cxd4 14 exd4 ♗c6 = Antoshin-Zinn, Germany 1966.

**10...♘bd7 11 ♖c1**

11 ♗g3 c5 12 ♘f4 c4 13 ♗b1 ♖e8 14 f3 ♗b4 15 ♗f2 ♘f8 16 ♘fe2 a6 is unclear, Polugaevsky-Ab.Khasin, USSR 1956. However, 11 f3!? deserves attention: 11...c5 12 ♕d2 ♖e8 13 ♗f2 ♗f8 14 g4 with the initiative, Lama-Gomez Velasco, Argentina 1992.

**11...♖e8**

If 11...c5 then 12 ♗b1 a6 13 dxc5 bxc5 14 ♕c2 g5 15 ♗g3 ♕b6 16 ♖fd1 with a slight advantage for White, Draško-Dervishi, Panormo Z 1998.

**12 ♗b1 c6 13 f3 c5 14 ♗f2 ♗d6 15 ♖e1 a6 16 ♘g3 ♕b8 17 ♖c2 ♘f8 18 a3 ♘e6 19 ♗a2 cxd4 20 exd4 b5 21 ♔h1!**

Intending ♘f5.

**21...g6 22 ♘f1 ♗c6 23 ♗h4**

± Bagirov-Abramović, Erevan 1982.

**A2)**

**6...♘bd7 7 ♗d3 ♘f8 (D)**

Black's idea is to play ...♘e6, meeting ♗h4 with ...g6, ...♘g7 and ...♗f5, with a favourable exchange of light-squared bishops.

**8 ♘f3**

8 ♘ge2!? deserves serious attention: 8...♘e6 9 ♗h4 g6 10 0-0 ♘g7 11 f3 ±/±.

Beliavsky's idea 8 f4!? is also interesting: 8...c6 9 f5 ♘e4 10 ♗xe7 ♕xe7 11 ♕f3 ♕b4 12 ♘ge2 ♕xb2 13 ♗xe4 ♕xa1+ 14 ♗b1 ♘d7 (Beliavsky-Ljubojević, Linares 1989) 15 ♕g3 0-0 16 f6 g6 (16...♘xf6 17 0-0 intending 18 ♖f6 or 18 ♗h7 ±) 17 0-0 ♕b2 18 h4!

♖e8 19 h5 ♕d2 20 ♖f3 ♘xf6 21 hxg6 hxg6 22 ♗xg6 ± Beliavsky.

**8...♘e6 9 ♗h4 0-0 10 0-0 g6 11 b4!?**

White gains nothing from 11 ♘e5 due to 11...c5 12 ♗e2 cxd4 13 exd4 ♘g7 14 f4 ♘f5 15 ♗xf6 ♗xf6 16 ♕d2 ♗e6 17 ♖ad1 ♖c8 18 ♔h1 ♗g7 = Uhlmann-Westerinen, Siegen OL 1970.

However, Portisch's recommendation 11 ♕c2 ♘g7 12 ♗xf6 ♗xf6 13 b4 ± deserves attention.

**11...c6**

Black is worse after 11...a6 12 a4 c6 13 ♕b3 ♘g7 14 b5 axb5 15 axb5 ♗f5 16 ♘e5 ± Petrosian-Birbrager, USSR Cht (Moscow) 1966. Also not very good is 11...♘g7 12 b5 ♗f5 13 ♘e5 ♗xd3 14 ♘xd3 c6 15 bxc6 bxc6 16 ♖c1 ± Gligorić-Medina, Palma de Mallorca 1967.

**12 ♕b3 a5!**

The strongest move. If 12...a6 then 13 a4 ±, while 12...♘e4 is met by 13 ♗xe7 ♕xe7 14 ♗xe4 (also possible is 14 b5 ♘xc3 15 ♕xc3 cxb5 16 ♗xb5 ♘g5 17 ♘xg5 ♕xg5 18 ♖fc1 ± Zharkov-Ufimtsev, corr. 1991) 14...dxe4 15 ♘d2 ♘g5 16 h4 ♘e6 17 d5 ♘g7 18 ♘dxe4 ♕xh4 19 ♖ad1 ± Zelinsky-Ufimtsev, corr. 1991.

**13 b5 c5 14 ♗xf6 ♗xf6 15 ♘xd5 cxd4 16 ♘xf6+ ♕xf6 17 ♕b2 ♔g7 18 ♖ac1**

18 ♘xd4 ♘xd4 19 ♕xd4 ♕xd4 20 exd4 ♖d8 =.

**18...dxe3 19 ♕xf6+ ♔xf6 20 fxe3 ♔e7 21 ♘e5 ♗d7**

= Miladinović-Ljubojević, Belgrade 1995.

**A3)**

**6...0-0 7 ♗d3 ♘bd7** *(D)*

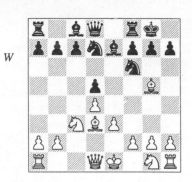

**8 ♘ge2**

The main continuation. We should also note Lerner's idea 8 ♕f3!? c6 9 ♘ge2 ♖e8 10 h4!? ♘f8 11 ♗xf6 ♗xf6 12 0-0-0 ♕d7 13 e4 dxe4 14 ♗xe4 ♕g4 15 ♕d3 ± Lerner-A.Petrosian, Jurmala 1983.

**8...♖e8**

Here 8...b6?! is dubious due to 9 ♘g3! (intending ♘f5) 9...g6 10 h4 c5 11 ♕c2 ♖e8 12 0-0-0 c4 13 ♗e2 a6 14 ♗f3 ♗b7 15 h5 ± Gulko-Chiburdanidze, Frunze 1985. White has an attack.

**9 0-0**

An important alternative is 9 ♕c2 ♘f8 10 0-0-0 ♗e6:

a) 11 ♘f4!? ♖c8 12 ♔b1 a6?! 13 ♘xe6 fxe6 14 f4 ± E.Vladimirov-Klovans, Frunze 1988.

b) 11 ♔b1!? ♘e4 (11...♘g4 12 ♗xe7 ♕xe7 13 ♘f4 ♘f6 14 f3 c5 15 g4 ± Kasparov-Campora, Thessaloniki OL 1988; 11...♖c8 12 ♘f4 h6 13 ♘xe6 fxe6 14 ♗f4 c5 15 dxc5 ±) 12 ♗xe7 ♘xc3+ 13 ♘xc3 ♕xe7 14 f4 gives White the initiative and a slight advantage – Kasparov.

c) 11 f3 ♖c8 12 ♔b1 a6 (12...c5 13 dxc5 ♖xc5 14 ♘d4 a6 15 h4 ♕b8 16 g4 ± Shirov-Ambartsumian, Frunze 1989) 13 g4! c5 14 dxc5 ♗xc5 15

♘d4 ♗b4 16 ♕b3 ♗xc3 17 bxc3 ±
Shirov.

**9...♘f8 10 b4!**

This pawn thrust gives Black the
most serious problems.

**10...♗xb4**

Or:

a) 10...a6 does not ease Black's
problems:

a1) 11 ♕b3!? c6 12 ♘a4 is slightly
better for White.

a2) 11 a3 c6 12 ♕c2 g6 13 f3 ♘e6
14 ♗h4 ♘h5 15 ♗xe7 (Kasparov-
Short, London PCA Wch (15) 1993)
15...♕xe7 16 ♖ae1 a5 17 ♕b2 axb4
18 axb4 ±.

a3) 11 a4 ♗xb4 12 ♗xf6 gxf6 13
♕b3 ♗xc3 (Bareev-Nenashev, Lucerne Wcht 1993) 14 ♕xc3! intending
to meet 14...b6 with 15 ♘g3 ♗e6 16
♖ac1 ± Kasparov.

b) Or 10...♘g6 11 b5 ♘g4 12 ♗xe7
♖xe7 13 ♗xg6! hxg6 14 ♘f4 c6 15
h3 ♘f6 (Istratescu-Notkin, Bucharest
1997) 16 bxc6 bxc6 17 ♘d3! ♗a6! 18
♖e1 ♗xd3 19 ♕xd3 ♘e4 20 ♖ec1!
♘xc3 21 ♕xc3 ♖e6 22 ♖ab1 ± Istra-
tescu.

c) Kasparov recommends 10...h6!?
11 ♗xf6 ♗xf6 12 b5 ± (or 12 ♕b3!?
±).

**11 ♗xf6 gxf6 12 ♘xd5**

White gains nothing from 12 ♕b3
due to 12...♗xc3 13 ♘xc3 (13 ♕xc3
with compensation) 13...c6 with equality, Gutman-Razuvaev, USSR 1976.

**12...♕xd5 13 ♕a4 ♗h3 14 ♘f4
♕a5 15 ♕xa5 ♗xa5 16 ♘xh3 ♘e6 17
♖fd1**

± Kasparov.

**B)**

**5...c6** *(D)*

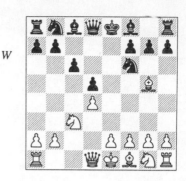

W

The main move, enabling Black to
maintain a choice of plans. White has
three continuations:

**B1: 6 ♘f3**          137
**B2: 6 e3**           138
**B3: 6 ♕c2**          145

**B1)**

**6 ♘f3 h6**

It is very important to insert this
move. The immediate 6...♗f5 is bad
due to 7 ♕b3:

a) 7...b5? 8 e3 ♗d6 9 ♗xb5! cxb5
10 ♗xf6 ♕xf6 11 ♕xd5 and White
wins.

b) 7...♘bd7 8 e4! ♗xe4 (8...dxe4?!
9 ♘e5 ♗e6 10 ♗c4 ♗xc4 11 ♕xc4
♕e7 12 ♘xd7±) 9 ♘xe4 dxe4 10 ♘e5
♕e7 11 ♕xb7 ♕b4+ 12 ♕xb4 ♗xb4+
13 ♔e2 ♘xe5 (13...♘d5 14 ♘xc6
♗d6 15 ♔d2 ±; 13...♖c8 14 ♖c1 ±;
13...c5 14 a3 ±) 14 dxe5 ♘g4 15 ♗f4
♗c5 16 ♖c1 ♗d4 17 ♖c4 c5 18 f3! ±
Savon-Magerramov, Moscow 1992.

c) 7...♕b6 8 ♗xf6 gxf6 (8...♕xb3
9 axb3 gxf6 10 e3 ♘d7 11 ♔d2 ♖g8
12 ♘h4 ♗e6 13 ♗d3 with an advantage for White in the endgame, Green-
feld-Pinter, Budapest 1989) 9 e3 ♘d7
10 ♔d2 ♕a5 11 ♘h4 ♗g6 12 ♗d3 b5
13 a4 ♗xd3 14 ♔xd3 b4 15 ♘e2 ♖d8

(Gretarsson-Stripunsky, Wijk aan Zee 1996) 16 ♖hc1! intending ♔d2-e1 ±.

**7 ♗h4**

White obtains nothing by 7 ♗xf6 ♕xf6 8 ♕b3 ♗d6 9 e3 ♘d7 10 ♗d3 ♕e7 11 0-0-0 ♘f6 12 ♖he1 ♗e6 13 ♕c2 0-0-0 = Lilienthal-Botvinnik, USSR Ch (Moscow) 1945.

**7...♗f5 8 e3**

The principled 8 ♕b3 is well met by 8...g5! 9 ♗g3 (9 ♕xb7? gxh4 10 ♕xa8 ♕b6 −+) 9...♕b6 10 e3 ♘a6 (10...♘e4?! is weaker due to 11 ♘xe4 ♗xe4 12 ♘d2! ♗f5 13 0-0-0 ♘d7 14 h4 ♖c8 {14...g4 15 ♗d3 ±} 15 ♗d3 ♗xd3 16 ♕xd3 c5 17 hxg5 ♗g7 18 gxh6 ± Seirawan-Zviagintsev, Groningen FIDE 1997) 11 ♗e5 (11 ♕xb6 axb6 12 a3 ♘b8 {12...♘b4?! 13 ♔d2! ±} 13 ♔d2 ♘bd7 14 ♗d3 ♗e6 15 ♘e5 ♖g8 is equal, Seirawan-Zviagintsev, Groningen FIDE 1997) 11...♗e7 12 ♕xb6 axb6 13 h4 g4 14 ♘g1!? ♘b4!? (14...♖g8!? ∞; 14...b5 15 ♘ge2 ♘b4 16 ♔d2 ♘d3 17 ♘g3 ♘xe5 18 ♘xf5 ♘c4+ 19 ♗xc4 bxc4 20 f3 gxf3 21 gxf3 ♔d7 22 a3 b5 23 e4 ± Beliavsky-Shirov, Biel 1992) 15 ♔d2 ♖g8 16 a3 b5 17 ♖c1 ♘a6 ∞.

**8...♘bd7**

8...♕b6!? 9 ♗d3!? (9 ♕c1 ♘bd7 10 ♗e2 ♗d6 11 0-0 0-0 12 ♗g3 ♗xg3 13 hxg3 ♖fe8 with equality, Arkell-Kruppa, Bratislava 1996) 9...♕xb2 10 0-0 (10 ♗xf5!?) 10...♗xd3 11 ♕xd3 with compensation – G.Georgadze.

**9 ♗d3 ♗xd3 10 ♕xd3 ♗d6 11 0-0-0**

White also obtains nothing by 11 0-0 0-0 12 ♖ab1 ♕e7 13 ♖fe1 ♕e6 14 b4 (14 ♘d2 ♖fe8 15 f3 ♘f8 16 e4 dxe4 17 fxe4 ♘g6 18 ♗xf6 gxf6 ∞ Burmakin-G.Georgadze, Krasnodar

1997) 14...a6 15 ♘a4 b5 16 ♘c5 ♗xc5 17 dxc5 ♘e5 18 ♘xe5 ♕xe5 19 ♗xf6 = or 11 a3 a5 12 ♘e2 0-0 13 0-0 ♖e8 14 ♖fc1 ♖a6 15 ♖c2 ♕b8 16 ♗g3 ♘e4 17 ♗xd6 ♘xd6 18 ♘d2 a4 = Landa-Bareev, Vienna 1996.

**11...♗b4**

Black prevents the intended continuation 12 e4. Worse is 11...♕a5 12 e4! ±, or 11...0-0 12 g4 ±.

**12 ♘d2 0-0 13 ♔b1**

If 13 f3 then 13...♗xc3! 14 ♕xc3 ♘e4! =.

**13...♖e8 14 ♖c1 ♘f8 15 f3 ♖c8 16 ♘b3 b6 17 a3 ♗e7 18 ♖hd1 ♕d7** = Illescas-Bareev, Ubeda 1997.

**B2)**
**6 e3** *(D)*

Now:
**B21: 6...♗f5    138**
**B22: 6...♕b6    140**
**B23: 6...♘bd7   141**
**B24: 6...♗e7    142**

**B21)**
**6...♗f5**

This prevents White from putting his bishop on d3, which is very important in the Exchange Variation. Since the exchange of light-squared bishops (7 ♗d3) would be to Black's advantage, White generally takes the opportunity to damage Black's kingside pawn formation by...

**7 ♕f3 ♗g6**

Vaganian's move 7...♗e6 also seems interesting: 8 ♗xf6 ♕xf6 9 ♕xf6 gxf6 and now:

a) White gains no advantage by 10 ♘f3 ♘d7 11 ♗d3 ♘b6 12 0-0-0 ♘c8!? 13 ♘e2 (or 13 e4 ♘b6 14 ♖he1 0-0-0 15 ♘h4 ♗b4 16 a3 dxe4 17 ♖xe4 ♗xc3 18 bxc3 ♖d5 = Ehlvest-Andersson, Reggio Emilia 1989/90) 13...♘d6 14 ♘g3 h5 15 ♘h4 0-0-0 16 ♖df1 ♗e7 17 ♘gf5 ♘xf5 18 ♘xf5 ♗b4 19 g3 ♔c7 20 ♔b1 ♖dg8 21 ♖c1 ♗xf5 ½-½ Ionov-Vaganian, Moscow 1990.

b) 10 ♗d3 ♘d7 11 ♘ge2 ♘b6 12 ♘g3 ♗d6 (or 12...a5 13 f4!? ♗e7 14 f5 ♗c8 15 ♘h5! ♖g8 16 ♖g1 ♗d7 17 g4 0-0-0 18 ♔f2 ± Ibragimov-Shabanov, Russian Club Cup (Maikop) 1998) 13 0-0-0 0-0-0 14 ♘f5 ♗f8 15 g4 ♔c7 (15...h5!?) 16 ♘e2 ♘c8 17 h3 ♘d6 18 ♘fg3 ± Aleksandrov-Dokuchaev, Smolensk 1997. White has managed to blockade the kingside and his chances are better.

**8 ♗xf6 ♕xf6**

Black's best chance is to go for the endgame! He is clearly worse after 8...gxf6?! 9 ♕d1! ♕b6 10 ♕d2 ♘a6 11 ♘f3 0-0-0 12 a3 ♘c7 13 b4 ♘e8 14 ♗e2 ♘d6 15 ♕a2 ± Petrosian-Barcza, Budapest 1955.

**9 ♕xf6 gxf6 (D)**

Black's kingside structure is chronically weak. It is true that it is not so easy to exploit this weakness without queens on the board. One should also note the harmony between Black's

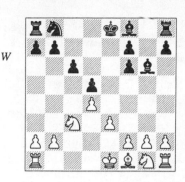

bishops and his pawns. The g6-bishop and the f6-pawn work together to stop the enemy knights penetrating. The f8-bishop and the pawns on c6 and d5 perform a similar function. Black's position in fact appears perfectly viable. One of the first players to take on this position as Black was Boris Spassky, while in recent times its most enthusiastic adherent has been Nigel Short.

**10 h4!?**

White tries to provoke further weaknesses in Black's position. Practice has also seen other continuations:

a) 10 ♘ge2 ♗d6 11 g3 ♘d7 12 ♘f4 a5 13 h4 a4 14 h5 ♗f5 15 ♗d3 ♗xd3 16 ♘xd3 f5! 17 ♔e2 ♖g8! = Miladinović-Azmaiparashvili, Burgas 1995.

b) 10 ♘f3 ♘d7 11 ♘h4 ♗e7 12 g3 ♘b6 13 ♖d1 (13 0-0-0 f5 14 ♘g2 h5 15 ♗d3 ♘c8 = Averbakh-Damjanović, Rijeka tt 1963) 13...♗b4! 14 a3 ♗xc3+ 15 bxc3 ♘a4 16 ♔d2 b5 = Piket-Van der Sterren, Wijk aan Zee 1998.

c) 10 ♖d1 ♘d7 11 ♗d3 ♘b6 12 ♘ge2 ♔d7 = Timman-Short, San Lorenzo del Escorial Ct (5) 1993.

d) 10 0-0-0 ♘d7 11 ♗d3 ♖g8 (also possible is 11...0-0-0 12 ♘ge2 ♖g8 13

♘f4 ♘b6 14 g3 ♔b8 15 ♔b1 ♘c8 =
Gligorić-Porath, Moscow 1956) 12 g3
♘b6 13 ♘f3 ♗h5 14 ♗e2 ♗b4! 15
♘h4 ♗g6 16 ♗d3 ♗xc3 17 bxc3 ♗xd3
18 ♖xd3 ♔d7 19 ♖d2 ♘c4 20 ♖e2
♘d6 21 ♘g2 a5 22 ♘f4 a4 23 ♔c2 f5
= Beliavsky-Short, Batumi Echt 1999.

e) 10 ♔d2 ♘d7 11 ♗d3 (or 11 h4
♘b6 12 h5 ♗f5 13 b3 ♖g8 14 g3 ♗a3!
15 ♗d3 ♗xd3 16 ♔xd3 ♗b2 17 ♖e1
♗xc3 18 ♔xc3 ♘c8 intending ...♘d6
=, Vaiser-Ruban, Novosibirsk 1993)
11...♘b6 (but not 11...a5 12 f4!? f5 13
♘ge2 ♘f6 14 ♘g3 ♘e4+ 15 ♗xe4
dxe4 16 ♖ac1 ±) 12 b3 ♗a3! 13 ♘ge2
♔d7 14 ♘g3 ♘c8 15 h4 ♘d6 16 h5
♗xd3 17 ♔xd3 ♗b2 18 ♖ab1 ♗xc3
19 ♔xc3 ♖hg8 20 ♔d3 a5 = Gulko-
Short, New York PCA Ct (12) 1994.

f) 10 g3!? ♘d7 11 ♗h3 ♘b6 12
♘ge2!? ± Tal (12 ♘f3?! ♘c4 = Tal-
Spassky, Sochi 1973).

**10...h5**
Denying White any more space on
the kingside. Or 10...♘d7 11 h5 ♗f5,
and now:

a) 12 ♘f3 ♖g8 (or 12...a5 13 ♘h4
♗e6 14 ♗d3 a4 15 0-0 a3 16 b3 ♗b4
17 ♘e2 ♘b6 18 f3 0-0 19 ♔f2 ♘c8
20 g4 ± Knaak-Filip, Polanica Zdroj
1976) 13 ♘h4 ♗e6 14 ♗d3 h6 15 f3
♘b6 16 ♔f2 ♗d6 17 ♘e2 ± Vaïsser-
Pigusov, Las Palmas 1996.

b) Mikhalchishin's recommendation 12 ♘ge2!? ♗d6 13 ♔d2, intending f3 and g4 ±, deserves attention.

**11 ♘ge2**
11 ♘h3!? deserves attention. Then
11...♗d6 should be answered by 12
g3!? intending ♘f4 (Dautov) rather
than 12 ♗e2?! ♘d7 13 ♖c1 ♘b6 14
g3 (I.Sokolov-Dautov, Nussloch 1996)
14...♔d7 =.

11...♗d6 12 g3
Mikhalchishin recommends 12 f4!?
intending ♘g3 ±.

12...♘d7 13 ♗h3 ♘b6 14 0-0-0
♘c4 15 ♖de1 ♔d8 16 ♘f4! ♔c7 17
♘xg6 fxg6 18 e4 dxe4 19 ♖xe4 f5 20
♖e6 ♖hg8 21 ♖he1 ♖ad8 22 d5
± Draško-H.Pedersen, Copenhagen
1989.

**B22)**
**6...♕b6** *(D)*

Black steps out of the pin and at-
tacks the b2-pawn, forcing White to
solve some concrete problems.

**7 ♕d2!?**
Or:

a) White gains nothing from either
7 ♕c2 ♘e4 8 ♗f4 (8 ♗h4 ♘a6 9
♘xe4 ♘b4 10 ♕b1 dxe4 11 ♕xe4+
♗e6, Skomorokhin-S.Ivanov, Katowice 1993, 12 ♘f3 ♘d5 13 ♕c2 ♕a5+
14 ♘d2 c5 ∞ S.Ivanov) 8...♗f5! (but
not 8...♘a6 9 f3! ♘d6 10 0-0-0!, Sem-
kov-Kelečević, Cannes 1989, 10...♗e7
11 g4 h5 12 gxh5 ♖xh5 13 ♘ge2 intending ♘g3 ±) 9 ♗d3 ♘a6 10 a3 ♕a5
= N.Zilberman-Faibisovich, Pula 1989.

b) 7 ♗xf6 also gives White nothing: 7...♕xb2 8 ♕c1 ♕xc1+ 9 ♖xc1

gxf6 10 ♘xd5 ♗a3 11 ♖c4 ♘a6 (not
11...♔d8?! 12 ♖a4 ± Kondratiev-Rad-
ashkevich, USSR 1969; 11...b5!?) 12
♘xf6+ ♔e7 13 ♘e4 b5 14 ♖xc6 ♗b7
15 ♖h6 ♗xe4 16 ♖xa6 ♗b4+ 17 ♔d1
♖hc8 with compensation – Faibiso-
vich.

c) However, Scherbakov's idea 7
♗d3!? ♕xb2 8 ♘ge2 deserves careful
attention: 8...♗e7 9 0-0 0-0 10 e4 dxe4
11 ♘xe4 ♘bd7 12 ♘2g3 with compensation, Scherbakov-S.Ivanov, Podolsk 1992.

**7...♘e4 8 ♘xe4 dxe4 9 ♘e2 ♗e6
10 ♘c3 ♗b4 11 ♗e2 ♕a5 12 ♗h4**

12 ♗f4 also deserves attention:
12...♘d7 13 0-0 ♘b6 14 ♕c2 ♗xc3
15 bxc3 ♘d5 16 c4 (16 ♕xe4?! ♘xc3
17 ♕c2 ♘xe2+ 18 ♕xe2 0-0, as in
Knaak-Faibisovich, Berlin 1989, does
not give White an advantage; Knaak
now gives 19 e4 f5!? =) 16...♘c3 17
♗d6 ±.

**12...♘d7 13 0-0 ♘b6 14 ♕c2**

White gets no advantage from 14
♖fc1 ♘c4! (14...0-0 15 a3 ♗xc3 16
♕xc3 ♕xc3 17 ♖xc3 ± Dydyshko-
A.Ivanov, USSR Cht (Azov) 1991) 15
♗xc4 (15 ♕c2 ♗xc3 16 bxc3 f5 =)
15...♗xc4 16 ♕d1 ♗xc3 17 ♖xc3 ♗e6
= (17...♗d5?! 18 ♕g4 ±) Bönsch-
Rabiega, Bundesliga 1993/4.

**14...f5 15 a3 ♗xc3 16 bxc3 ♘c4 17
♕b3 ♕b5 18 ♕xb5 cxb5 19 a4 bxa4
20 ♖xa4**

± Dragomaretsky-Faibisovich, Moscow 1988. White's chances are better.

**B23)**
**6...♘bd7 7 ♗d3** *(D)*
**7...♗d6**

Black intends 8...♘f8 followed by
...♘e6. Instead 7...♗e7 is Line B242,

and leads to positions of a more standard type.

**8 ♘ge2**

This is the best move.

**8...♘f8 9 f3**

Also possible is 9 ♕c2 ♘g6 (or
9...♘e6 10 ♗h4 g6 11 f3 {11 0-0??
♗xh2+! –+} 11...♘g7 12 0-0 intending e4 ±; 9...h6 10 ♗h4 ♕e7 11 a3
♗d7 12 e4 g5 13 ♗g3 ± Spielmann-
Capablanca, Karlsbad 1929) 10 ♘g3
0-0 (10...h6 11 ♗xf6 ♕xf6 12 ♘h5
♕g5 13 ♘xg7+ ♔f8 14 ♘f5 ±
Bagirov-Raičević, Vrnjačka Banja
1974) 11 ♘h5!? ♗e7 12 ♘xf6+ ♗xf6
13 ♗xf6 ♕xf6 14 h4 ♖e8 15 h5 ♘f8
16 0-0-0 ± Uhlmann.

**9...♘e6**

Dubious is 9...♘g6?! (intending
...h6) 10 e4! dxe4 11 fxe4 ♗e7 12 0-0
0-0 (12...♘xe4? 13 ♗xe7 ♘xc3 14
♗xd8 ♘xd1 15 ♖axd1 ♔xd8 16 ♖xf7
+–) 13 ♕b3 c5! 14 e5 ♘g4 15 ♗xg6!
hxg6 (15...♗xg5 16 ♗xf7+ ♔h8 17
e6 ♗e3+ 18 ♔h1 ♕h4 19 h3 ♘f2+ 20
♖xf2 ♕xf2 21 ♘g1!! intending 22 e7
or 22 ♘e4 ± Seirawan) 16 ♗xe7 ♕xe7
17 ♘f4 ♕h4 18 h3 ♘e3 19 ♖f2 ♗e6
20 d5 g5 21 ♘fe2 ± Seirawan-Ljubo-
jević, Barcelona 1989.

**10 ♗h4 ♕c7**

Black is also worse after 10...0-0 11 ♕c2 g6 12 0-0 ♗e7 13 ♖ad1 ♘g7 14 ♔h1 ♗e6 15 ♗f2 ± Berg-Blazar, Næstved 1988 or 10...♗e7 11 ♕c2 g6 12 0-0-0 0-0 13 g4 c5 14 dxc5 ♘xc5 15 ♗c4 ± Urday-Castellano, Las Palmas 1993.

**11 ♖c1 g5 12 ♗f2**

12 ♗g3 ±.

**12...h5 13 ♕d2**

Intending ♘b5.

**13...♕b8 14 ♗g3 h4 15 ♗xd6 ♕xd6 16 ♗f5 ♖g8 17 e4**

± Klima-Ševčak, Prerov 1994.

**B24)**

**6...♗e7 7 ♗d3 (D)**

Now, in addition to 7...0-0, which will transpose to main lines (8 ♕c2 ♘bd7 is Line B3 of Chapter 10), Black has the following continuations:

**B241: 7...♗g4     142**
**B242: 7...♘bd7     143**

**B241)**

**7...♗g4**

Black's idea is to exchange the light-squared bishops after ...♗h5-g6.

**8 ♕c2**

8 ♘ge2 does not lead to an advantage: 8...♗xe2 9 ♕xe2 ♘bd7 10 0-0 0-0 11 ♖ab1 a5 12 ♕c2 g6 13 a3 ♔g7 14 b4 axb4 15 axb4 ♖c8 16 ♖fd1 (16 b5 c5 =) 16...♗d6 17 h3 h6 18 ♗xf6+ ♘xf6 19 ♗f1 ♗b8 = Sokolov-Gavrilov, Moscow 1992.

8 f3!? is interesting: 8...♗h5 9 ♘ge2 ♗g6 10 0-0 0-0 11 ♗xf6 ♗xf6 12 ♗xg6 hxg6 13 e4 dxe4 14 fxe4 c5 (Gutman-Knežević, Bregenz 1984), when, according to Gutman, White should continue 15 e5! cxd4 16 exf6 dxc3 17 fxg7 ♔xg7 18 ♘xc3 ♘c6 19 ♕f3 ±.

**8...♗h5**

Black continues with his general plan. 8...♘bd7 is worse due to 9 h3 ♗e6 (9...♗h5 10 f4! ± intending g4) 10 ♗f4 ♘h5 11 ♗h2 g6 12 ♘ge2 ♘g7 (intending ...♗f5) 13 g4 ♘b6 14 0-0-0 ♗d6 15 ♘f4 ♕c7 16 ♔b1 0-0-0 17 ♖c1 intending ♘b5 ± Reshevsky-Gligorić, New York 1952.

**9 ♗xf6**

White does not obtain an advantage by 9 ♘ge2 ♗g6 10 ♘g3 ♘a6! 11 ♗f5 (11 a3 ♘c7 =) 11...♘h5! 12 ♗xe7 ♕xe7 13 ♘xh5 ♗xh5 14 ♕b3 ♗g6 = Furman-Kan, Moscow 1955.

**9...♗xf6 10 f4!**

White bases his play on the unfortunate position of the bishop on h5.

**10...♗g4**

If 10...♗e7, then 11 h3!? (11 ♔f1!?) 11...♗h4+ 12 ♔f1 ♗g3 13 h4! ♗g4 14 ♗xh7 ±.

**11 f5**

11 ♗xh7?! is met by 11...♗xd4! with the point 12 exd4 ♕h4+.

**11...g6 12 h3**

A dubious idea is 12 fxg6?! hxg6 13 ♗xg6? ♗h4+! 14 ♔d2 (the only

move) 14...♕g5! 15 ♗d3 ♗f2 and Black wins.
**12...♗xf5**
If 12...♗h4+ then 13 ♔d2 ± or 13 ♔f1 ♗xf5 14 ♗xf5 gxf5 15 ♘f3! ± Glek.
**13 ♗xf5 gxf5 14 ♘ge2**
Possible is 14 ♕xf5 ♘d7 intending ...♕e7-e6 ± (Glek).
**14...♗h4+!**
14...♗g5 15 0-0! ♗xe3+ 16 ♔h1 with the initiative.
**15 g3 ♗g5 16 0-0 ♗xe3+ 17 ♔h2**
White has compensation for the pawn, Glek-Yudasin, Tilburg 1994.

**B242)**
   **7...♘bd7** *(D)*

W

White must make an important decision: to develop the knight on e2 or f3:
**B2421: 8 ♘ge2**    143
**B2422: 8 ♘f3**    144

**B2421)**
   **8 ♘ge2 ♘h5**
Andersson's favourite continuation. After 8...0-0 play tends to lead to main lines (9 ♕c2 is Line B31 of Chapter 10), but 9 ♘g3!? is interesting: 9...h6

(9...♘e8? 10 h4! ± Alekhine-Capablanca, Buenos Aires Wch (32) 1927) 10 h4 ♘b6! 11 ♕c2 ♖e8 (11...♘g4!?) 12 0-0-0 hxg5 (12...♗d6!? ∞) 13 hxg5 ♘e4 14 ♗xe4 dxe4 15 f4! ♘d5 16 ♘gxe4! ♘xe3 17 ♕f2! ♘xd1 18 ♕h4 f5 19 ♕h5!. Now the game Gulko-Van der Sterren, Amsterdam 1988 continued 19...♔f8? 20 ♕g6 ♔g8 21 ♖h7 ♕xd4 22 ♕h5 ♕e3+ 23 ♔c2 1-0. In Gulko's opinion, chances are level after 19...fxe4! 20 g6 ♗h4 21 ♖xh4 ♔f8! 22 ♕c5+ ♔g8 23 ♕h5 =.
   **9 ♗xe7 ♕xe7 10 g4**
White must play energetically. He gains nothing by 10 0-0-0 0-0 11 ♕c2 g6 12 ♖ab1 a5 13 a3 ♘df6 14 b4 ♘g7 intending ...♗f5 =, or 10 ♖b1 g6 11 b4 a6 12 a4 0-0 13 b5 axb5 14 axb5 ♘df6 15 ♖a1 ♗d7 16 ♖a4 ♖fe8 17 0-0 ♘g7 = Ivanchuk-Andersson, Novi Sad OL 1990. However, White can play 10 ♕c2, transposing to Line B2 of Chapter 10.
   **10...♘hf6 11 ♘g3**
11 h3 ♘b6 12 b3 ♗d7 13 ♕d2 0-0-0!? ∞.
   **11...♘b6**
Worse for Black are:
   a) 11...h6 12 h3 ♘b6 13 ♕d2 ♗d7 14 b3 g6 15 a4 a5 16 f3 ± Kasparov-Spassky, Barcelona 1989.
   b) 11...g6 12 g5! (12 h3?! ♘b6 13 ♕b3 ♗e6 14 a4 0-0 15 a5 ♘c4 16 ♗xc4 dxc4 17 ♕a3 ♕xa3 18 bxa3 c5! 19 0-0-0! cxd4 20 ♖xd4 ♘d7 intending ...♘e5-c6 with equality, Brenninkmeijer-Zsu.Polgar, Amsterdam 1990) 12...♘g8 13 h4 h6 14 gxh6! ♘df6! 15 h5 ♗g4 16 ♗e2 ♗xe2 17 ♕xe2 ♘xh5 18 ♘xh5 gxh5 19 ♖xh5 ♖xh6 20 0-0-0 ± Yakovich-A.G.Panchenko, USSR Ch (Moscow) 1991.

**12 g5 ♘g8 13 h4 g6**

We have reached the critical position of this variation. Black wants to break up White's pawn phalanx on the kingside by playing ...h6.

**14 ♔d2!?**

White derives no real benefit from other moves:

a) 14 ♕c2 h6 15 gxh6 (15 0-0-0 hxg5 16 hxg5 ♖xh1 17 ♖xh1 ♕xg5 18 ♖h8 ♔f8) 15...♘xh6 16 h5 g5 ∞.

b) 14 ♖g1 ♗d7 15 ♕c2 0-0-0 16 ♘ge2 ♔b8 17 0-0-0 h6 18 ♘f4 hxg5 19 hxg5 ♕d6 20 ♔b1 ♘e7 21 ♘a4 ♘xa4 22 ♕xa4 ♖h2 with counterplay, Van der Sterren-Kelečević, Winterthur 1996.

c) 14 ♕e2 h6 15 0-0-0 (15 f4!?) 15...hxg5 16 h5! gxh5 17 ♘xh5 ♖h6! 18 ♖dg1 ♔d8! 19 ♕f3 ♗d7 20 ♕g3 f6 21 f4 ♗e8 22 fxg5 fxg5 23 ♕xg5 ♕xg5 24 ♖xg5 ♘f6 25 ♘g3 ♖xh1+ 26 ♘xh1 ♔e7 27 ♘g3 ½-½ Vyzhmanavin-Kharitonov, Helsinki 1992.

**14...h6 15 f4 hxg5 16 fxg5**

16 hxg5!? ♖xh1 17 ♕xh1 ♗d7 18 ♖e1 ±.

**16...♗e6 17 ♕f3 0-0-0 18 ♘ge2 ♕d7 19 a4**

± V.Milov-Andersson, Groningen FIDE 1997.

## B2422)

**8 ♘f3 (D)**

**8...♘h5**

8...0-0 transposes to Line B32 of Chapter 10.

Also possible is 8...♘b6 9 h3 ♘c4 10 ♗xc4! dxc4 11 ♘e5 ♗e6 12 0-0 ± Dydyshko-Smagin, Passau 1994.

8...♘e4 9 ♗xe7 ♕xe7 10 ♕c2 f5 11 0-0 0-0 12 ♖fe1 a5 13 ♘d2 ♘xd2 14 ♕xd2 ♘f6 15 f3 ♗e6 16 ♘a4 ♘d7 17

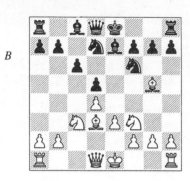

♖ac1 and White has a slight advantage, Taimanov-Janošević, Vrnjačka Banja 1974.

**9 ♗xe7**

Piket experimented with 9 ♘d2?! but it did not prove justified: 9...♗xg5 10 ♕xh5 ♗e7 11 h3 g6 12 ♕e2 ♘b6 13 a3 ♗e6 14 g4 ♗d6 15 f4 ♕e7 16 ♘f3 f6 17 0-0-0 0-0-0 18 ♔b1 ♔b8 = Piket-Timman, Amsterdam (5) 1995.

**9...♕xe7 10 0-0 ♘hf6**

10...0-0 gives White the possibility of supporting the b4 advance with gain of tempo: 11 ♕b1! ♘hf6 12 b4 ♖e8 13 ♖c1! (13 b5 c5 =) 13...a6 14 a4 g6 15 ♕b2! ± a5 16 bxa5 ♖xa5 17 ♘d2! ♘g4 18 ♘b3 ♕d6 19 g3 ♖a7?! (better is 19...♖a8) 20 e4! dxe4 21 ♘xe4 ± Kramnik-Timman, Belgrade 1995.

On 10...g6 White can immediately launch a minority attack: 11 ♖b1 (11 e4 dxe4 12 ♗xe4 0-0 13 ♖e1 ♕b4 14 d5 ♘c5 ∞ Peev-Makropoulos, Plovdiv 1981) 11...0-0 (11...a5!?) 12 b4 a6 13 a4 ♘hf6 14 ♕c2 ♖e8 15 ♖fe1 ♘e4 16 b5 axb5 17 axb5 ♘df6 18 bxc6 bxc6 19 ♘e5 ♘g4 20 ♘xe4 ♘xe5 21 dxe5 dxe4 22 ♗xe4 ♕xe5 23 ♗xc6 ♗f5 24 e4 ♖ac8 25 ♕a4 ± Stefansson-Vera, Winnipeg 1997.

11 ♕c2 0-0 12 ♖fe1 g6 13 a3
13 ♖ab1!?.
**13...♘b6**
13...a5!?.
**14 b4 ♖e8 15 b5 c5 16 dxc5 ♕xc5
17 e4**
± Piket-Timman, Wijk aan Zee
1996.

**B3)**
6 ♕c2 *(D)*

Now Black can try to take immediate advantage of the white queen's location on c2 or develop more classically:
**B31: 6...♘a6** 145
**B32: 6...♗e7** 146

6...g6!? deserves serious attention:
7 e3 (7 ♘xd5 ♕xd5 8 ♗xf6 ♗b4+ 9
♔d1 0-0 10 e4 ♖e8 11 ♗d3 ♕e6! 12
♗e5 c5 with compensation – Vladimirov) 7...♗f5 8 ♕b3 ± Vaganian.

**B31)**
**6...♘a6 7 e3**
7 ♘f3 yields nothing due to
7...♘b4 8 ♕d2 ♗f5 =.
White can deny the knight the b4-square by 7 a3 ♘c7 8 e3 ♘e6 (also

possible is 8...♗e7 9 ♗xf6 ♗xf6 10
♗d3 ♕e7 11 ♘ge2 ♗g4 12 0-0 ♗xe2
13 ♘xe2 g6 14 b4 0-0 15 ♖ab1 ♖fc8
16 ♘c3 ♕d6 17 a4 ♘e6 = Bronstein-
An.Bykhovsky, Moscow 1962) 9 ♗h4
and now:
a) On 9...♗e7 may follow 10 ♗d3
(or 10 ♘f3 g6 11 ♗d3 ♘g7 12 b4 a6!
{12...♗f5 13 b5 ♖c8 14 bxc6 ♕a5 15
cxb7 ♖b8, Vaganian-Westerinen, Moscow 1982, 16 ♘e5 +–} 13 0-0 ♗f5 ±)
10...g6 11 ♘ge2 ♘g7 12 f3! 0-0 13
0-0 ♖e8 14 ♗f2 ♗d6 15 h3! c5 16
dxc5 ♗xc5 17 ♘b5 ± A.Sokolov-
Stromer, Viernheim 1992.
b) 9...g6 10 ♗d3 ♘g7 11 f3 ♗e7
12 ♘ge2 0-0 13 0-0 ♘f5 14 ♗f2 c5 ∞
S.Ivanov.
**7...♘b4 8 ♕b1**
White has also tried 8 ♕d1 ♗f5 9
♖c1 ♕a5 10 ♗xf6 gxf6 (10...♘xa2!?
11 ♗h4 ♗b4 12 ♕d2 ♘xc1 13 ♕xc1
0-0 14 ♘f3 b5 15 ♗e2 ∞ Ehlvest) 11
♕d2 ♘xa2 12 ♖a1 ♘xc3 13 ♖xa5
♘e4 14 ♖xd5 ♘xd2 15 ♖xf5 ♗b4 16
♔e2 ♔e7 17 ♘f3 ♘c4 18 ♔d1 ♘d6
19 ♖f4 a5 = Ehlvest-Short, Manila OL
1992. The puzzling complications
have led to an equal ending.
However, fully possible is 8 ♕d2!?
♗f5 9 ♖c1 a5 10 a3 ♘a6 11 ♘ge2 h6
(11...♘c7 12 ♘g3 ♗g6 13 ♗e2 ♗e7
14 0-0 0-0 15 ♘a4 ♘d7 16 ♗xe7
♕xe7 17 ♘c5 ± Spassky-Szabo, Amsterdam Ct 1956; or 11...♗e7 12 ♘g3
{but not 12 ♘f4 0-0 13 ♗d3 ♗xd3 14
♘xd3 ♘d7 15 ♗xe7 ♕xe7 16 0-0
♘b6 = Petrosian-Spassky, Amsterdam
1973} 12...♗g6 13 ♗d3 0-0 14 ♘f5 ±
Shirov-Barkhagen, Gausdal 1991) 12
♗f4 ♗d6 (12...♗e7 13 ♘g3 ♗h7 14
♗d3 ♗xd3 15 ♕xd3 g6 16 e4 ±
Petursson-Hartman, Stockholm 1991)

13 ♘g3 ♗h7 14 ♗xd6 ♕xd6 ∞ Barsov-S.Ivanov, Germany 1994.

**8...h6**

8...g6?! is dubious due to 9 ♕d1! a5 10 a3 ♘a6 11 ♗d3 ♗g7 12 ♘f3 0-0 13 0-0 ± Dokhoian-Vaganian, Tilburg 1994.

**9 ♗h4 g6 10 ♕d1**

In S.Ivanov's opinion, 10 f3 g5 11 ♗g3 c5 leads to unclear play. Or 10 a3 ♗f5 11 e4 dxe4 12 axb4 ♕xd4 ∞.

**10...♗f5 11 ♖c1 g5 12 ♗g3 ♕a5 13 ♗e5! ♗e7 14 ♗xf6 ♗xf6 15 ♕f3**

White wins material.

**B32)**

**6...♗e7**

White has two moves at his disposal. The main line, 7 e3, is the subject of the next chapter. Here we discuss...

**7 ♘f3** *(D)*

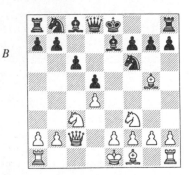

Black can again harass the white queen:

**B321: 7...♘a6**     146
**B322; 7...g6**     147

The latter move intends ...♗f5.

**B321)**

**7...♘a6 8 e3**

8 a3 is also fully possible:

a) 8...♘c7 9 e3 ♘h5 and then:

a1) White gets no advantage from 10 ♗xe7 ♕xe7 11 ♗e2 g6 12 0-0 0-0 13 ♘e5 (13 b4!?) 13...♘g7 14 b4 a6 15 ♘a4 ♘ge8! 16 ♘b6?! (16 ♖fc1!?) 16...♖b8 17 a4 ♘d6 = 18 ♕c5 f6 19 ♘f3 ♖f7! 20 ♖fc1 ♗d7 (intending ...♗e8) 21 ♗d3?! (better is 21 ♘xd7 =) 21...♗e8! ∓ Gofman-Janjgava, Kramatorsk jr 1989; Black has seized the initiative.

a2) 10 h4! h6! (but not 10...♗xg5?! 11 hxg5 g6 12 ♗d3 ♘g7? {better is 12...♗e6 ⩲} 13 ♗xg6! fxg6 14 ♖xh7 ± Wallace-Janjgava, Erevan OL 1996) 11 ♗xe7 ♕xe7 12 ♘e5 ♘f6 ⩲.

b) 8...g6 and here:

b1) 9 e4 is interesting: 9...♘xe4! 10 ♘xe4 ♘c7! (10...♗f5?! 11 ♗xa6 ♗xe4 12 ♕c3 bxa6 13 ♕xc6+ ♔f8 14 ♗xe7+ ♔xe7 15 ♘e5 ♖c8 16 ♖c1 ± Lautier-Geller, Sochi 1989) 11 h4 dxe4 12 ♕xe4 ♘d5 13 ♗c4 ♗f5 14 ♕e2 0-0 15 0-0 ♖e8 =.

b2) 9 e3 ♗f5 10 ♗d3 ♗xd3 11 ♕xd3 ♘c7 12 0-0 0-0 (also possible is 12...♘e6!? 13 ♗h4 0-0 14 b4 ♖c8 15 ♖ab1 a6 16 a4 b5 17 ♖fe1 ♖e8 18 ♘d2 ♘d7 19 ♗xe7 ♕xe7 20 a5 ♘g5 = Portisch-Yusupov, Rotterdam 1989) 13 b4 (13 ♗xf6 ♗xf6 14 b4 ♕e7 is equal) 13...♘e4 14 ♗f4 ♘xc3 15 ♗xc7 (15 ♕xc3? ♗d6 16 ♗xd6 ♘b5! 17 ♕b3 ♘xd6 ∓ Portisch-Kasparov, Skellefteå 1989) 15...♕xc7 16 ♕xc3 = Kasparov.

**8...♘b4** *(D)*

**9 ♕b1**

The game is level after 9 ♕d2 ♗f5 10 ♗xf6 ♗xf6 11 ♖c1 a5 12 a3 ♘a6 13 h3 ♘b8 14 ♗d3 ♗xd3 15 ♕xd3 0-0 16 0-0 ♘d7 17 ♖c2 ♗e7 18 ♖b1

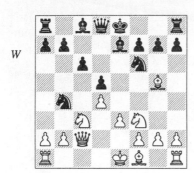

W

½-½ Andersson-Ehlvest, Reggio Emilia 1991.

White can also play 9 ♕d1 ♗f5 10 ♖c1 ♕a5! (Black is worse after 10...a5 11 ♗e2 0-0 12 0-0 ♘d7 13 ♗xe7 ♕xe7 14 ♕b3 ♖fb8 15 ♘a4 ♘a6 16 ♗xa6 ♖xa6 17 ♘c5 ± Karpov-Yusupov, Rotterdam 1989):

a) Very interesting complications result after 11 ♕d2 ♘xa2 12 ♗xf6 (12 ♖a1 ♘xc3! 13 ♖xa5 ♘ce4 14 ♕d1 ♗b4+ 15 ♔e2 ♗xa5 16 ♗xf6 ♘xf6 is slightly better for Black, Gretarsson-Kharitonov, Berlin 1995) 12...♘xc1 13 ♗xe7 ♕a1 14 ♗a3 ♘d3++ 15 ♔e2 ♘c1+ 16 ♔e1 ♘d3++ ½-½ Lerner-Kharitonov, Simferopol 1988.

b) 11 ♗xf6 ♗xf6 (11...gxf6!? 12 ♕d2 ♘xa2 13 ♖a1 ♘xc3 14 ♖xa5 ♘e4 ∞) 12 ♕d2 0-0 13 a3 ♘a6 14 ♗d3 ♗xd3 15 ♕xd3 ♖fe8 16 0-0 ♖ad8 = Ivkov-Shocron, Mar del Plata 1959.

**9...g6 10 ♕d1 ♗f5 11 ♖c1 ♕a5**
Bad is 11...a5? 12 a3 ♘a6 13 ♕b3! ♕b8 (the only move) 14 ♘a4 0-0 15 ♘e5 ♖d8 16 ♗e2 ♔g7 17 0-0 ♘c7 18 g4! (intending f4-f5) with a clear advantage for White, Vaganian-Rogozenko, Bundesliga 1996/7.

**12 ♗xf6**
12 ♕b3 ♕b6 =.

**12...♗xf6 13 ♕d2 0-0 14 ♗e2 ♔g7 15 0-0 ♖fe8 16 a3 ♘a6 17 ♖a1**
Intending b4.

**17...♘b8 18 b4 ♕d8 19 b5**
Now after 19...♕a5 20 ♖fc1 ♘d7 21 ♕b2 ♖ec8 22 ♘d2 ♕d8 23 ♘b3 White's advantage has increased, Portisch-Pinter, Hungary 1997. Instead Black should play 19...♘d7!, when, in Pinter's opinion, Black should prepare ...♖c8 followed by ...♗e6 and ...c5, when White's advantage is minimal.

**B322)**
**7...g6 (D)**

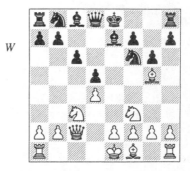

W

Now White has two continuations:
**B3221: 8 e3** 147
**B3222: 8 e4** 148
The latter is sharper.

White gets no advantage from 8 ♗xf6 ♗xf6 9 e3 ♗f5 10 ♗d3 ♗xd3 11 ♕xd3 ♘d7 12 0-0 ♗e7 13 ♖ab1 a5 14 a3 0-0 15 ♕c2 ♗d6 16 b4 axb4 17 axb4 ♘b6 intending ...♘c4, Inkiov-Yusupov, Dubai OL 1986.

**B3221)**
**8 e3 ♗f5 9 ♗d3 ♗xd3 10 ♕xd3 ♘bd7 11 0-0**

Other continuations yield no advantage:

a) 11 ♖b1 a5! 12 ♗h6 ♗f8! 13 ♗xf8 ♔xf8 14 0-0 ♔g7 15 ♕c2 ♕e7 16 a3 ♖hc8 17 ♖fc1 ♘e8! 18 b4 ♘d6 = Andersson-Farago, Dortmund 1978.

b) 11 h4 0-0 12 ♗h6 ♖e8 13 h5 ♘e4 14 hxg6 hxg6 15 ♔f1 ♗f8 = Spassky-Petrosian, USSR Ch (Tbilisi) 1959.

c) 11 ♗h6 ♗f8! 12 ♗xf8 (or 12 ♗f4 ♗e7 13 h3 0-0 14 0-0 ♖e8 15 ♖ab1 ♗f8 16 ♕c2 ♘b6 17 ♘e5 ♘fd7 18 ♖bd1 ♘xe5 19 ♗xe5 ♗d6 20 ♗xd6 ½-½ Bönsch-Zsu.Polgar, Brno 1991) 12...♔xf8 13 b4 (13 0-0 ♔g7 14 ♖fc1 ♕e7 15 ♘d2 h5! 16 b4 h4 17 h3 ♖h5 18 ♘e2 a6 19 a4 ♖f5 20 f3 ♖e8 with counterplay for Black, Bönsch-Yusupov, Munich 1990) 13...♔g7 14 0-0 ♕e7 15 b5 (15 ♕c2 ♖he8 16 b5 cxb5 17 ♕b3 ♕e6 18 ♕xb5 ♖ec8 19 ♘e2 ♖c7 = Rogers-M.Gurevich, Biel IZ 1993) 15...♖hc8! intending ...c5 with counterplay.

**11...0-0 12 ♖ab1**

If 12 ♘d2 then 12...♖e8 13 ♖ae1 (13 ♖ab1 ♘e4 14 ♗xe7 ♕xe7 15 b4 a6 = Padevsky-Antoshin, Moscow 1963; 13 ♖ac1 ♔g7 14 ♘b3 ♗d6 15 h3 h6 16 ♗h4 g5 17 ♗g3 ♗xg3 18 fxg3 ♖e6 = Taimanov-Korchnoi, USSR 1983) 13...♘e4 14 ♗xe7 ♕xe7 15 ♘cxe4 dxe4 16 ♕b3 ♖ab8 17 f3 exf3 18 gxf3 ♘b6 19 f4 ♖bd8 20 ♘f3 c5 = Ftačnik-Lukacs, Baile Herculane Z 1982.

**12...a5 13 ♕c2**

Black has no problems after 13 a3 ♖e8 14 ♖fc1 (or 14 ♕c2 ♘e4 15 ♗xe7 ♕xe7 16 ♘xe4 ♕xe4 17 ♖fc1 ♕xc2 18 ♖xc2 ♘b6 19 ♘e5 f6 20 ♘d3 ♘c4 21 a4 ♘d6 22 b3 ♔g7 23 h3 ½-½ Novikov-Chernin, Debrecen 1990)

14...♘e4! 15 ♗f4 ♗f8 16 ♘d2 ♘xd2 17 ♕xd2 ♘b6 ½-½ Miladinović-Janjgava, Panormo Z 1998.

**13...♖e8 14 ♗xf6 ♗xf6**

Possible is 14...♘xf6 15 a3 ♗d6 = Benko-Bilek, Stockholm IZ 1962.

**15 a3 ♘b6**

15...♖e6 16 e4 dxe4 17 ♘xe4 ♕e7 18 ♖fe1 ♖e8 = T.Georgadze-Bagirov, USSR 1978.

**16 ♘d2 ♕e7 17 b4 axb4 18 ♖xb4 ♘c8 19 ♖fb1 ♘d6 20 a4 ♖a7 21 g3 h5**

= Szilagyi-Suetin, Albena 1970.

**B3222)**
**8 e4** *(D)*

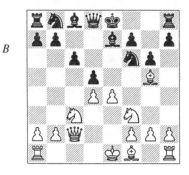

**8...dxe4**

8...♘xe4?! is dubious in view of 9 ♗xe7 ♔xe7 (9...♕xe7? 10 ♘xd5 +−) 10 ♘xe4 dxe4 11 ♕xe4+ ♗e6 12 ♗c4 ♕a5+ 13 ♔f1! ± Karpov-Yusupov, USSR Ch (Moscow) 1988.

However, 8...0-0!? is interesting: 9 e5 ♘e4 10 ♗h6 ♖e8 11 ♗d3 (11 h3?!) ♘xc3 12 bxc3 c5 13 ♗b5 ♘c6 14 0-0 ♗f5 15 ♕d2 ♕a5 16 ♗xc6 bxc6 17 dxc5 ♕xc5 18 ♘d4 ♗d7 = Hall-Renet, Cannes 1989) 11...♘d6! (11...♘xc3? 12 bxc3 c5 13 h4 ± Kamsky-Shirov,

Dortmund 1992) 12 0-0 ♘f5 13 ♗f4 ♘g7 ± Shirov.

**9 ♗xf6 ♗xf6 10 ♕xe4+ ♔f8**

Fully possible is 10...♕e7 11 ♗c4 0-0 12 0-0 (12 ♕xe7 ♗xe7 13 0-0 ♗f5 14 ♖fe1 ♗f6 15 h3 h5 16 ♘e5 ♘d7 17 ♘e4 ♗xe5 18 dxe5 ♘xe5! 19 ♘f6+ ♔g7 20 ♘xh5+ gxh5 21 ♖xe5 ♔f6 22 ♖ae1 ♖ad8 = Murshed-Serper, Dhaka 1995) 12...♗f5 13 ♕f4 ♕b4 14 ♗b3 (14 ♘e5 ♗xe5 15 dxe5 ♗e6 16 ♘e4 ♕xc4 17 ♖ac1 ♕b5 18 a4 ♕a5 19 ♘f6+ ♔g7 20 ♘h5+ gxh5 21 ♕g5+ ♔h8 22 ♕f6+ ½-½ Gulko-Yusupov, Munich 1990) 14...♘d7 15 ♖fe1 a5 16 g4 ♗e6 with equality, Ruban-Dreev, Tbilisi 1989.

**11 ♗c4 ♔g7 12 0-0 (D)**

According to Oll, 12 0-0-0 deserves attention; he provided the following analysis: 12...♖e8 13 ♕f4 ♗e6 14 ♗xe6 ♖xe6 15 h4 ♕d6 16 ♕d2 ♘d7 17 h5 ♘f8 ∞.

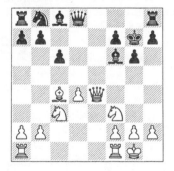

**12...♖e8 13 ♕f4 ♗e6 14 ♗xe6 ♖xe6 15 ♖fe1**

White gets nothing from 15 ♖ad1 ♕d6 16 ♕c1 ♘d7 17 d5 ♖ee8 18 dxc6 ♕xc6 19 ♘d4 ♗xd4 20 ♖xd4 ♘f6 = Sokolovs-Belikov, Jurmala 1991.

**15...♕d6!**

The strongest move. 15...♖xe1+ 16 ♖xe1 ♘d7 17 ♘e4 ♗e7 18 h4 ± Timman-Short, Belgrade 1987.

**16 ♕xd6 ♖xd6 17 ♘e4 (D)**

Or 17 ♖e8 ♖d8 18 ♖xd8 ♗xd8 19 ♖e1 ♘d7 20 g4 h6 21 ♔g2 ♔f8 22 ♖e2 ♘f6 23 h3 ♗b6 = Beim-Korneev, Frankfurt 1997.

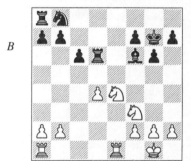

**17...♖d8 18 ♘xf6 ♔xf6 19 g4**

19 ♖e4 ♘a6 20 ♖ae1 ♖d7 = Lastin-Korneev, Russia 1996.

**19...h6 20 h4 ♘d7 21 g5+ hxg5 22 hxg5+ ♔g7 23 ♖e7 ♔f8 24 ♖ae1 ♖ab8 25 ♔g2 ♘b6 26 ♔g3 ♘d5 27 ♖7e4 ♔g7**

=/∓ Lautier-Oll, Moscow 1989.

# 10 Exchange Variation: Main Line

1 d4 d5 2 c4 e6 3 ♘c3 ♘f6 4 cxd5
exd5 5 ♗g5 c6 6 ♕c2 ♗e7 7 e3 ♘bd7
*(D)*

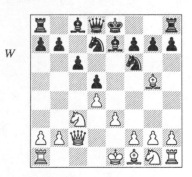

*W*

Now White can immediately put
the knight on f3 or continue to delay
its development:

A: 8 ♘f3      150
B: 8 ♗d3      151

**A)**
**8 ♘f3 ♘h5**
We are by now quite familiar with
this relieving manoeuvre, which works
well for Black here.
**9 ♗xe7 ♕xe7 10 h3**
White seeks to gain space on the
kingside by playing g4. He can also
play 10 0-0-0:
a) 10...g6 11 g4 ♘hf6?! (better is
11...♘g7) 12 ♖g1 0-0 13 ♗d3 ♖e8 14
h3 ♘e4 (14...b6 15 g5 ♘h5 16 ♔b1

♕d6 17 ♕d2 ♗b7 18 ♖g4 ♖e6 19 ♖h4
♖ae8 20 ♖xh5! gxh5 21 ♘e2 is clearly
better for White, Portisch-Andersson,
Reggio Emilia 1987/8) 15 ♗xe4 dxe4
16 ♘d2 ♘f6 17 ♖de1 h6 18 f3 exf3 19
♘xf3 ±.
b) 10...♘b6 11 ♗d3 ♗e6 (possible
is 11...g6 12 h3 ♗e6 13 ♔b1 0-0-0 14
♖c1 ♔b8 15 ♘a4 ♘xa4 16 ♕xa4 ♘f6
17 ♖c3 ♘e4 18 ♖a3 ♘xf2 19 ♕a7+
♔c7 ½-½ Geller-Cirić, Oberhausen
Echt 1961) 12 ♔b1 0-0-0 (or 12...g6
13 ♖c1 ♘g7 14 ♖he1 0-0 15 h3 a5 16
g4 a4 17 ♔a1 ♘e8 18 ♖g1 ♘d6,
which gives Black counterplay on the
queenside, P.Nikolić-Greenfeld, Ljubljana 1989) 13 ♘a4 ♘f6 14 ♘c5 ♔b8
15 ♖c1 (15 ♔a1!? intending ♖b1,
♖hc1 and b4) 15...♖c8 16 ♔a1 ♖c7 17
♖b1 ♘e8 18 h3 ♘d6 19 ♘e5 g6 20 g4
f6 21 ♘f3 g5 22 ♕e2 h5 with equality,
Bagirov-Nei, Leningrad 1960.
**10...g6 11 0-0-0 ♘b6 12 ♗d3 *(D)***
**12...♗e6**
Fully possible is 12...♘g7 13 g4
♗d7 14 ♔b1 0-0-0 15 ♕b3 (intending
a4-a5; 15 ♘a4 ♘xa4 16 ♕xa4 ♔b8 17
♖c1 ♖c8 18 ♖c3 ♖c7 19 ♘e5 ♗e8 20
♖a3 b6 21 ♖c1 c5 22 ♗b5 ♗xb5 23
♕xb5 ♖hc8 24 ♖ac3 ♘e6 = Speel-
man-Andersson, Lyons ECC 1991; 15
♘e5 ♔b8 16 ♖c1 ♗e8 17 ♘a4 f6! 18
♘f3 ♘xa4 19 ♕xa4 g5! 20 ♖c3 h5 21
♖a3 a6 22 ♖g1 hxg4 23 hxg4 ♖h3 ∞

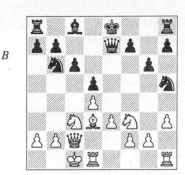

B

Makarychev) 15...♔b8 (15...♗e6!? 16 ♖c1! ♘c4!? {16...♔b8 17 ♘a4! ± Epishin-Ivanchuk, Tilburg 1992} 17 e4 ♔b8 18 ♘a4 intending ♘c5 ± Epishin) 16 a4 c5 (Mozetić-Cirić, Sveti Sava 1994) 17 a5!? is very interesting, since after 17...c4 18 ♕a2 cxd3 19 axb6 axb6?! 20 ♖xd3, 20...♕f6?! 21 ♘e5 ♕xf2? loses to 22 ♘xd7+ ♖xd7 23 ♘b5 +−.

**13 g4 ♘g7 14 ♔b1**
Nor does White gain an advantage by 14 ♘e2 0-0-0 15 ♘f4 ♔b8 16 ♗e2 ♘e8 (also possible are 16...♗c8 17 ♘e5 g5 18 ♘g2 f6 19 ♘d3 h5 = Malaniuk-Savon, Baku 1988 and 16...♘c8 17 ♘d2 ♘d6 18 h4 ♗c8 19 ♘b3 ♘e4 20 ♗f3 f5 ½-½ Komliakov-Bratchenko, Cherepovets 1997) 17 ♘d2 ♘d6 18 h4 ♗c8 19 ♘b3 ♘e4 20 ♗f3 f5 ½-½ Kasparov-Smyslov, USSR Ch (Moscow) 1988.

**14...0-0-0**
Epishin recommends 14...♖d8!? intending ...♘c8-d6, but this has not yet been tried in practice.

**15 ♘a4 ♘xa4 16 ♕xa4 ♔b8 17 ♖c1 ♗d7**
Or:
a) 17...♖c8?! 18 ♖c3 h5 19 ♖g1 hxg4 20 hxg4 ♗d7 21 ♖a3 a6 22 ♘e5

♗e8 23 ♗xa6! bxa6 24 ♕xa6 ♔c7 25 ♕a5+ ♔d6 26 e4! ♘e6 27 exd5 ♘xd4 28 ♘c4+ ♔d7 29 ♕a7+ 1-0 Oll-Bosch, Hoogeveen 1997.
b) 17...f6?! 18 ♖c3 ♖d6 19 ♖hc1 ♖c8 20 ♖a3 b6 21 g5! ± Ioseliani-Hort, Roquebrune (Ladies vs Veterans) 1998.
c) 17...♘e8!? 18 ♖c3 ♘d6 19 ♖hc1 (19 ♖b3 ♘c4 20 ♕b4 ½-½ Ivanchuk-Van der Sterren, Munich 1994) 19...♗d7! 20 ♖a3 ♘c8 21 ♘e5 ♗e8 22 ♕b3 ♘b6 23 ♕c3 f6 24 ♕a5 ♘c8 25 ♘f3 g5 = Van der Sterren-Ree, Dutch Ch 1993.
**18 ♖c5 ♗e8 19 ♖hc1 ♘e6 20 ♖5c3 f6!**
Black intends ...♘g5; the game is equal, P.Nikolić-Timman, Tilburg 1988.

**B)**
**8 ♗d3** (D)

B

Now:
**B1: 8...♘f8**    151
**B2: 8...♘h5**    152
**B3: 8...0-0**    153

**B1)**
**8...♘f8**
With this move Black intends to play ...♘e6-g7.

**9 ♘f3 ♘e6 10 ♗h4 g6 11 0-0 ♘g7**

Black is worse after 11...0-0 12 ♖ab1 ♘g4 (12...a5 13 a3 ♘g7 14 b4 axb4 15 axb4 ♗f5 16 b5 ± Szabo-Ståhlberg, Zurich Ct 1953) 13 ♗xe7 ♕xe7 14 h3 ♘h6 15 ♖be1 (but not 15 ♕c1 ♖d8 16 e4 dxe4 17 ♗xe4 ♔g7 18 d5 cxd5 19 ♗xd5 ♕c7 20 b3 ♕f4 21 ♖d1 ♕xc1 22 ♖bxc1 ♘f5 = Portisch-Ljubojević, Linares 1988) 15...f5 16 ♘e2 ♘f7 17 ♘f4 ± Timman-Ljubojević, Amsterdam 1986.

**12 b4**

Interesting is 12 ♗xf6 ♗xf6 13 b4 a6 14 a4 0-0 15 b5 ♗g4 (15...♗f5 16 bxc6 bxc6 17 ♖ab1 ± Botvinnik-Keres, Leningrad/Moscow 1941; 15...a5 16 bxc6 bxc6 17 ♘e2 ♗d7 18 ♘f4 ♕e7 19 ♖ab1 ± Kaidanov-Rogers, Calcutta 1988) 16 bxc6 bxc6 17 ♘d2 a5! 18 ♖ab1 ♗e7 19 ♘a2 ♗d7 20 ♘b3 ♘e6 21 ♘ac1 ♖b8 with counterplay for Black, Collas-Skembris, Cappelle la Grande 1995.

**12...a6**

12...♗xb4 fails to 13 ♗xf6 ♕xf6 14 ♘xd5 ±; 12...0-0 13 b5 ♗f5 14 bxc6 bxc6 15 ♘e5 ♖c8 16 ♘a4 ± Stein-Rossetto, Mar del Plata 1966.

**13 ♖ab1 ♗f5 14 a4 0-0 15 b5**

Or 15 ♗xf5 ♘xf5 16 ♗xf6 ♗xf6 17 b5 axb5 18 axb5 ♕a5 19 bxc6 bxc6 20 ♖fc1 with a stable advantage for White, Polugaevsky-Milev, Cuba 1962.

**15...axb5 16 axb5 ♗xd3**

16...♖c8 17 ♖fc1 ♗xd3 18 ♕xd3 ♘f5 19 ♗xf6 ♗xf6 20 ♘a4! ± Novikov-Kharitonov, Sevastopol 1986.

**17 ♕xd3 ♘f5**

Or 17...♖a3 18 bxc6 bxc6 19 ♕c2 ♘d7 20 ♗xe7 ♕xe7 21 ♘e2! ♕d6 22 ♖fc1 ♖c8 23 ♘f4 ± Vera-Yu.Hernandez, Mondariz Balneario 1996.

**18 ♗xf6**

Also possible is 18 ♗g3 ♘xg3 19 hxg3 ♗d6 20 ♕c2 ± Larsen-Smyslov, Copenhagen 1985. 18 ♗g5!? is another interesting idea.

**18...♗xf6 19 ♖fc1!**

19 bxc6 does not give White an advantage: 19...bxc6 20 ♘e2 ♖a2! 21 ♖fc1 ♕a8 22 ♖c2 ♘d6 23 ♖bc1 ♖c8 = Dlugy-Christiansen, USA 1987.

**19...♖a3 20 bxc6 bxc6 21 ♕c2**

White is aiming to play against Black's weakness on c6.

**21...♕a8**

After 21...♕a5 22 ♘e2 ♖a2!? 23 ♕xc6 ♖xe2 24 ♕xf6 ♕a2 25 ♖a1 ♕b2 26 ♖cb1 ♕c2 27 ♖f1 Black was a pawn down for no compensation in Stohl-Chernikov, Rimavska Sobota 1990.

**22 ♘e2 ♖a6 23 ♘f4 ♘d6 24 ♘d2 ♗e7 25 h3! ♖d8 26 ♘d3 ♘b5 27 ♖b3 ♗d6**

27...♖a2 ± Timman.

**28 ♘b4 ♗xb4 29 ♖xb4**

White has a stable advantage, Timman-Andersson, Tilburg 1987.

**B2)**

**8...♘h5 9 ♗xe7 ♕xe7 10 ♘ge2!** (D)

B

Developing the knight on e2 gives White additional possibilities.
**10...g6**
Practice has also seen:
a) 10...♘f8 11 0-0-0 ♗g4 12 ♔b1 ♗xe2 13 ♕xe2 ♘f6 14 ♖c1 0-0-0 15 ♖c2 ♔b8 16 ♔a1 ♘e6 17 ♖b1 ♕d6 18 g3 ♖he8 19 ♕f1 ± Antoshin-Chistiakov, USSR 1960.
b) 10...♘b6 11 0-0 g6 12 ♖ab1 (12 ♘a4!? ♘xa4 13 ♕xa4 0-0 14 b4 ± Byrne-Eliskases, Helsinki OL 1952) 12...0-0 13 b4 ♘g7 (13...♘c4 14 ♗xc4 dxc4 15 e4 ±; 13...a6 14 a4 intending a5 and ♘a4-c5 with the initiative and a slight advantage for White; 13...♗e6 14 b5 ♖ac8 15 bxc6 ♖xc6 16 ♕b3 ♖fc8 17 ♖fc1 ±) 14 b5 (14 ♘a4!? ♘xa4 15 ♕xa4 intending ♖fc1 and b5 ±) 14...♗f5 15 bxc6 bxc6 16 ♖b3 ± Mozetić.
**11 0-0-0**
The most aggressive plan.
**11...♘b6 12 h3**
12 ♔b1 is also possible:
a) 12...♘g7!? 13 ♘g3 ♗d7 14 ♖c1 0-0-0 15 ♘a4 ♘xa4 16 ♕xa4 ♔b8 17 ♖c3 b6 and then:
a1) 18 ♗a6!? ♘e6 19 ♖hc1 ♖he8 20 ♕b3 ♕d6 21 ♘f1 ♔a8! 22 ♘d2 ♘c7 23 ♗f1 (Kasparov-Andersson, Reykjavik 1988) 23...♕xh2 24 ♘f3 ♕d6 25 ♘e5 ♖xe5! 26 dxe5 ♕xe5 ∞ Kasparov.
a2) 18 ♖a3 ♗e8 19 ♕c2 ♖c8 20 ♖c1 ♗d7 21 ♕d2 h5 22 ♖b3?! (22 ♖b3 ±) 22...♘e6 23 ♖bc3 h4 24 ♘e2 ♕d6 ∞ Timman-Short, San Lorenzo del Escorial Ct (11) 1993.
b) 12...♗e6 13 h3 0-0-0 14 ♘a4 ♘f6 15 ♘c5 ♘fd7 16 ♘b3 ♔b8 17 a3 ♖c8 18 ♖c1 ♘c4 = Bareev-Vladimirov, Tilburg 1993.

**12...♘g7**
Also possible is 12...♗e6 13 g4 ♘f6 14 ♘f4 0-0-0 15 ♔b1 ♔b8 16 ♖he1 ± Videki-Shipkov, Györ 1990.
**13 g4 ♗d7 14 ♔b1**
14 ♘f4 is too hasty: 14...g5! 15 ♘fe2 h5 = Malaniuk-Vaganian, USSR Ch (Moscow) 1988.
**14...0-0-0 15 ♘f4 ♔b8 16 ♗e2 ♘e6 17 ♘d3 ♖c8 18 b4 ♘c4 19 ♔a1 b6 20 ♕b3 ♖hd8 21 ♖c1 ♗e8 22 ♖hd1**
White's chances are better, Granda-Nogueiras, Buenos Aires 1991.

**B3)**
**8...0-0** (D)

Now White must decide how to develop his knight:
**B31: 9 ♘ge2** 153
**B32: 9 ♘f3** 157

**B31)**
**9 ♘ge2 ♖e8**
Botvinnik-Larsen, Noordwijk 1965 featured an original treatment of Black's position, viz. 9...h6 10 ♗h4 ♖e8 11 f3 c5 12 0-0 a6 13 ♖ad1 b5 14 ♗f2 c4 15 ♗f5 ♘b6 16 ♘g3 ♗f8 17 a3 ♗b7 18 e4, but nothing good came

of it, as White has broken through in the centre and has an advantage.

**10 0-0 ♘f8**

Black aims for a classical formation. Other moves are worse: 10...g6 11 f3 ♘h5 12 ♗xe7 ♕xe7 13 e4 ♘b6 14 ♖f2 ± Timman; 10...h6 11 ♗h4 b6?! 12 f3 c5 13 ♖ad1 ♗b7 14 ♔h1! (intending dxc5 and e4) 14...a6 15 ♗f5 cxd4 16 ♘xd4 ± Kouatly-Benko, Augsburg 1988/9.

We have reached the basic starting position of the variation. White has two plans: preparing a minority attack or aiming for play in the centre and on the kingside:

**B311: 11 a3**      154
**B312: 11 ♖ab1**   155
**B313: 11 f3**      155

Other continuations have also been tried in practice:

a) 11 ♖ae1!? ♘g6 (if 11...♘h5 then 12 ♗xe7 ♕xe7 {12...♖xe7 13 b4 a6 14 ♘a4 ± Petrosian-Letelier, Buenos Aires 1964} 13 ♖b1! g6 14 b4 a6 15 a4 ♘g7 16 b5 axb5 17 axb5 ♗f5 18 ♗xf5 ♘xf5 19 ♘a4 ± Portisch-I.Almasi, Hungarian Cht 1993) 12 ♘g3 ♗d7 13 f3 ♖c8! (intending ...c5) 14 ♘f5 ♗xf5 15 ♗xf5 ♖c7 = I.Sokolov-Vaganian, Sarajevo 1987.

b) 11 ♖ad1 ♘h5 (11...♘g4 12 ♗xe7 ♖xe7 13 h3 ♘f6 14 ♘g3 ± Tukmakov-Timoshchenko, Sverdlovsk 1987) 12 ♗xe7 ♕xe7 and then:

b1) 13 ♖fe1 ♗g4 14 h3 (14 ♖b1 ♖ad8 15 ♘g3 ♘xg3 16 hxg3 h5 17 b4 a6 18 ♘a4 ♖d6 19 ♘c5 ♗c8 = Azmaiparashvili-Campora, San Roque 1996) 14...♗xe2 15 ♕xe2 ♘f6 16 f3 ♘e6 17 ♕f2 c5 = Tukmakov-Lputian, Sochi 1987.

b2) 13 ♖b1 a5 14 ♘a4 ♗g4 15 ♕c5 ♗xe2 16 ♕xe7 ♖xe7 17 ♗xe2 ♘f4 18 ♗g4 ♘4e6 19 ♖fc1 g6 = Guliev-Smagin, Moscow 1995.

**B311)**
**11 a3** *(D)*

**11...♘h5**

Black has also played:

a) 11...a5 and then:

a1) 12 ♗xf6 ♗xf6 13 b4 g6 =.

a2) 12 ♖ab1 ♗e6 13 b4 axb4 14 axb4 b5 15 ♘f4 ♘6d7 16 ♘xe6 fxe6 17 ♗xe7 ♕xe7 18 e4 ♘b6 = Speelman-Beliavsky, Barcelona 1989.

a3) 12 f3! ♘g6 (12...♘h5?! 13 ♗xe7 ♖xe7 14 ♕d2 ± Spassky-Timoshchenko, USSR 1972) 13 e4 dxe4 14 fxe4 ♗g4 15 ♗xf6 ♗xf6 16 e5 ♗g5 17 ♗c4 ± Salov-Beliavsky, Reykjavik 1991.

b) 11...♘g4 12 ♗xe7 ♕xe7 13 h3 ♘h6 14 ♘g3 ♘g6 15 ♖fe1 (15 ♕d1!? intending ♕h5) 15...♕h4 16 ♗f1 ± Salov.

**12 ♗xe7 ♕xe7 13 b4 ♕g5**

Entirely sufficient for equality is 13...a6 14 ♘a4 and now 14...g6 15 ♘c5 ♘g7 16 a4 ♗f5 17 b5 axb5 18 axb5 ♘fe6 19 ♘xe6 ♗xd3 20 ♕xd3

♘xe6 21 ♕b3 ♕d6 22 ♘c3 h5 23 h3 ♖ed8 24 ♖a4 ♖xa4 25 ♘xa4 c5 26 dxc5 ♘xc5 27 ♘xc5 ♕xc5 28 ♖d1 d4 ½-½ Gulko-Spassky, Cannes 1987 or 14...♗g4!? 15 ♘ec3 ♘g6 16 ♖ae1 ♖ad8 17 f3 ♗c8 = Wallace-Asrian, Erevan OL 1996.

**14 ♖ae1 ♗h3 15 ♘g3 ♘xg3 16 hxg3 ♗d7 17 e4 dxe4 18 ♘xe4 ♕e7 19 ♘c5!?**

19 ♕c3 ♗e6 20 ♘c5 ♕c7 21 ♗e4 ♖ad8 22 ♖e3 ♖d6 = H.Olafsson-Baburin, Las Vegas 1997.

**19...♕xe1 20 ♖xe1 ♖xe1+ 21 ♔h2 ♖ae8 22 ♘xb7 ♖a1! 23 ♘c5 ♖ee1 24 g4 ♗xg4**

The position is unclear – Baburin.

**B312)**
**11 ♖ab1 (D)**

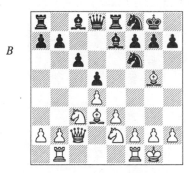

**11...♗e6**
Or:
a) Black can transpose via 11...a5!? 12 a3 to note 'a2' to Black's 11th move in Line B311.
b) 11...♘e4?! 12 ♗xe7 ♕xe7 13 ♗xe4 dxe4 14 b4 a6 15 ♘g3 f5 16 d5 ± Spraggett-King, London 1985.
c) 11...♘g6 12 ♗xf6 ♗xf6 13 b4 a6 14 a4 ♗e6 15 b5 ±.

d) 11...a6 12 b4 ♗g4 13 ♘a4 ♗xe2 14 ♗xe2 ♘e4 15 ♗xe7 ♖xe7 16 ♘c5 ♘d6 17 a4 ± Veingold-Nei, Tallinn 1983.
e) 11...♘h5 12 ♗xe7 ♕xe7 13 b4 a6 14 a4 ♕g5 15 b5 ♖e6 16 bxa6 bxa6 17 ♗f5 ♖h6 (Hodgson-Crouch, Dublin Z 1993) 18 ♘xd5! ±.
f) 11...♘g4!? 12 ♗xe7 (12 ♗f4 ♗d6 13 b4 ♗xf4 14 ♘xf4 ♕d6! 15 h3 g5 16 hxg4 gxf4 17 ♕e2 ♕h6 ∞) 12...♕xe7 13 h3 (13 b4 ♕d6 14 ♘g3 h5 ∞) 13...♘f6 14 b4 (14 ♘f4 ♘g6 15 ♘ce2 ♘h4 16 g3 ♘f3+ 17 ♔g2 ♘g5 18 h4 ♘ge4 19 ♖be1 ♘d6 20 ♘c3 h6! 21 ♖h1 {21 h5!?} 21...g5 22 hxg5 hxg5 23 ♘h3 ♗xh3+ 24 ♖xh3 ♔g7 with equality, Chernin-Inkiov, Saint John 1988) 14...♘e6 =.

**12 b4 ♖c8**
Black is worse after 12...a6 13 ♘a4 ♘6d7 14 ♗xe7 ♕xe7 15 ♘c5 ± Portisch-Yusupov, Bugojno 1986.

**13 b5 c5 14 dxc5 ♗xc5 15 ♕a4 h6 16 ♗h4 ♘8d7 17 ♖fd1 ♗d6 18 ♗g3 ♗xg3 19 hxg3 ♘c5 20 ♕d4 ♘xd3 21 ♕xd3 ♕a5**
= Yrjölä-Wedberg, Finland 1989.

**B313)**
**11 f3 (D)**

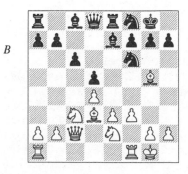

Botvinnik's favourite plan: White intends e4.

**11...♘g6**

Or:

a) 11...b5?! 12 ♗h4 a6 13 ♗f2 ♗b7 14 e4 dxe4 15 ♘xe4 ±.

b) 11...c5?! 12 ♗xf6! ♗xf6 13 dxc5 ♖xe3 14 ♖ad1 ♗e6 15 ♗e4! d4 16 ♘b5! ± Mozetić-Abramović, Yugoslavia 1995.

c) 11...♘h5!? 12 ♗xe7 ♕xe7 13 e4 dxe4 14 fxe4 ♗e6! (14...♗g4 15 e5! ±) 15 ♖f2! (15 e5 c5 16 d5 ♗d7 −+; 15 ♖ad1 ♖ad8 intending ...c5 =) 15...♘f6 (15...c5!? 16 ♘d5 ♗xd5 17 exd5 cxd4 18 ♘xd4 ∞) 16 h3 ♖ad8 17 ♖af1 ♘g6! 18 a3 ♖f8 19 b4 a5 = (19...b6 intending ...c5 =; 19...a6? 20 ♘a4 ± Bareev-Ahlander, Næstved 1988).

d) 11...♗e6!? and then:

d1) 12 ♖ae1 ♖c8 13 ♔h1 ♘6d7 (13...c5?! 14 dxc5 ♖xc5 15 ♘d4 ±) 14 ♗xe7 and now:

d11) 14...♖xe7?! 15 ♘f4 ♘f6 (not 15...♖c7?! 16 ♕f2 ♘f6 {16...♘b6!? intending to meet 17 e4 by 17...dxe4 18 fxe4 ♗c4!} 17 e4 dxe4 18 fxe4 ♖cd7 19 d5! cxd5 20 ♗b5 ♖c7 21 exd5 ♗d7 22 ♗e2! ± Kasparov-Andersson, Belfort 1988) 16 ♕d2 ♖d7 (16...♕d6?! 17 e4! ±) 17 b4 ± Kasparov.

d12) 14...♕xe7! 15 ♕d2 ♘b6 16 b3 ♖cd8 (intending ...♘c8-d6) 17 a4 ♕b4 18 ♘e4 ♕xd2 19 ♘xd2 ♗d7! = Lutz-Yusupov, Tilburg 1993.

d2) 12 ♖ad1 and here:

d21) 12...♖c8!? deserves serious attention: 13 e4 (13 a3 a6 14 ♘a4 ♘6d7 15 ♗xe7 ♕xe7 16 b4 a5 17 ♖b1 axb4 18 axb4 b6 = Gelfand-Piket, Wijk aan Zee 1998) 13...dxe4 14 fxe4 ♘g4 15 ♗f4 ♘g6 16 e5 ♗g5 17 ♗xg6 hxg6 18 ♕d2 ♗xf4 19 ♘xf4 ♗c4 20

♖fe1 c5! ∞ Timman-Yusupov, Riga 1995.

d22) 12...♘g6 and here:

d221) 13 ♔h1 ♖c8 14 ♘g3 (14 a3 ♘d7 15 ♗xe7 ♕xe7 16 ♗xg6 hxg6 17 e4 g5 18 ♘g3 ♕f6 = Moskalenko-Gelfand, Norilsk 1987) 14...♘h5 15 ♗xe7 ♘xg3+ 16 hxg3 ♕xe7 17 ♔g1 c5 18 ♗xg6 hxg6 19 dxc5 ♕xc5 = Tukmakov-Miladinović, Burgas 1995.

d222) 13 ♘g3 ♖c8 (13...a6?! 14 ♗f5 ±) 14 ♖de1 (14 ♘f5 ♗f8 ∞; 14 ♗f5 ♕a5 ∞) 14...c5 15 f4 ♘f8! 16 ♔h1 h6 17 ♗h4 a6 18 ♕d2 cxd4 19 exd4 ♘e4! 20 ♘cxe4 ♗xh4 21 ♘c5 ♖c7! 22 f5 ♗g5! 23 ♕d1 ♗d7 = Bareev-Yusupov, Munich 1994.

**12 e4**

12 ♖ad1 ♗e6 transposes to note 'd22' to Black's 11th move.

**12...dxe4 13 fxe4** *(D)*

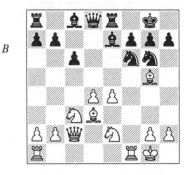

**13...♗e6**

An interesting idea is 13...c5!? 14 dxc5 ♗xc5+ 15 ♔h1 ♗e7 16 ♖ad1 ∞ (Smagin).

**14 h3**

White stops Black's knight intruding on g4. If 14 ♖ad1, then 14...♘g4!: 15 ♗c1 c5 16 d5 ♗d7 17 h3 ♕b6 18 hxg4 c4+ 19 ♔h1 cxd3 20 ♕xd3 ♗xg4

21 ♕g3 h5 with counterplay, Naumkin-Dreev, Vilnius 1988; 15 ♗xe7 ♕xe7 16 ♕d2 c5 17 d5 ♗d7 18 h3 ♘4e5 19 ♘g3 c4 20 ♗c2 ♕c5+ 21 ♔h1 ♖ad8 = Padevsky-Panchenko, Moscow 1989.

**14...c5**

Or:

a) 14...♘h5!? 15 ♗xe7 ♕xe7 16 e5 ♕h4 17 ♘e4 (17 ♕d2!? ∞; f4 is an important square) 17...♘hf4 18 ♘xf4 ♘xf4 19 ♘d6 ♘xh3+! 20 gxh3 ♕g3+ with compensation, A.Petrosian-Akopian, Erevan 1989.

b) 14...♖c8 15 ♖ad1 b5 16 ♔h1 ♕a5 17 e5 ♘d5 18 ♗xe7 ♖xe7 19 ♕d2 ♘xc3 20 ♘xc3 ♖d7 21 ♕f2 ♖cd8 is unclear, Dokhoian-Dreev, Pavlodar 1987.

**15 ♗xf6**

Or 15 d5 ♗d7 (15...♗c8 16 ♖ad1 ±) 16 d6!? ♗xd6 17 ♗xf6 gxf6 18 ♖ad1 (18 ♘d5!? ♗e5 19 ♕xc5 ∞) 18...♗c6! 19 ♗c4 ♕e7 20 ♘d5 ♗xd5 21 ♗xd5 and White has enough compensation for the pawn, but no more than that.

**15...♗xf6 16 e5 ♗g5!**

Bad is 16...cxd4?! 17 exf6 dxc3 18 bxc3 gxf6 19 ♘g3! ±.

**17 d5 ♗c8**

Also possible is 17...♗d7!? 18 e6 fxe6 19 ♗xg6 hxg6 20 ♕xg6 exd5 21 ♘g3 ♖e5 22 ♕f7+ ♔h8 23 ♕h5+ = Baburin-Gleizerov, Voronezh 1988.

**18 e6 fxe6 19 ♗xg6 hxg6 20 ♕xg6 exd5 21 ♖f7 ♗e3+! 22 ♔h1 ♗h6 23 ♘f4 ♖f8**

The only move.

**24 ♖xf8+ ♕xf8 25 ♘fxd5 ♔h8!**

Intending ...♗f5.

**26 ♖e1 ♗f5 27 ♕h5 ♗h7**

½-½ Vaiser-Pigusov, Pula 1988.

**B32)**
**9 ♘f3 ♖e8** (D)

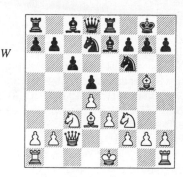

W

White has a choice: castle queenside, kingside, or else make a useful waiting move:

**B321)**
**10 0-0-0**

This aggressive move leads to sharp and unclear play in many variations.

**10...♘f8**

In addition to this standard move, other continuations have also been tried in practice:

a) 10...h6 and now 11 ♗h4?! b5 12 h3 (12 ♔b1!?) 12...a5 13 g4 ♘e4 14 ♗xe7 ♕xe7 15 ♔b1 ♗a6 gives Black the initiative, J.Rodriguez-Zinn, Havana OL 1966. However, 11 ♗f4! may be recommended for White: 11...♘f8 (11...b5? 12 ♘xb5 +– intending to meet 12...cxb5 with 13 ♗c7; 11...b6? is also met by 12 ♘b5 +–) 12 h3 ♗e6 13 g4 b5 14 ♔b1 ±.

b) 10...a5!? (a typical counterattacking plan for Black) 11 g4! (11 h3 a4 12 ♔b1 b5 13 g4 {13 ♘e5!?} 13...g6

14 ♖dg1?! {14 ♖c1!?; 14 ♘e2!?; 14 ♗f4!?} 14...a3 15 b3 b4 16 ♗xf6! ♗xf6 17 ♘a4 ♗a6 = Shulskis) 11...♘f8 12 h3 b5 13 ♘e5 ♗b7 14 ♔b1 a4 15 f4 ± Stohl-Salac, Czech Ch (Prague) 1992.

**11 h3 (D)**

White prepares to attack on the kingside. Other continuations are also encountered: 11 ♗xf6 ♗xf6 12 h3 ♗e6 13 ♔b1 ♖c8 14 g4 (Korchnoi-Yusupov, Dortmund 1994) 14...c5! 15 ♗b5 ♘d7 16 ♘e5 (16 dxc5 ♖xc5 17 ♘d4 a6 ∞) 16...cxd4 = Yusupov; 11 ♔b1 ♗e6 12 h4 ♕a5 (12...♖c8!?) 13 ♗xf6 ♗xf6 14 ♘g5 g6 15 ♕e2 c5 16 ♕f3 ♗g7 17 h5 cxd4 18 exd4 ♖ac8 19 ♘e2 ♕d8 20 ♕g3 ♕f6 21 hxg6 hxg6 with an unclear position, Dydyshko-Faibisovich, 1971.

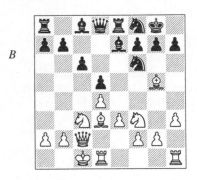

B

**11...♗e6**

White is better after 11...♘e4 12 ♗xe4 (12 ♗xe7!? ♕xe7 13 g4 ±) 12...♗xg5 13 ♗d3 ♗e7 14 ♔b1 ♗e6 15 ♘e2 ♖c8 16 ♘f4 ± Bagirov-Van Scheltinga, Beverwijk 1965.

11...a5!? deserves attention:

a) 12 ♔b1 a4 13 ♘xa4 (13 ♗xf6 ♗xf6 14 ♘xa4 ♕a5 15 b3 ♕b4 16 ♔a1 ♗e6 17 g4 g6 18 ♕d2 ♕a3 19 ♕b2 ♕d6 20 ♘e5 b5 21 ♘c5 ♗xe5 22

♘xe6 ♖xe6 23 dxe5 ♖xe5 with equality, Annageldiev-Nenashev, Pavlodar 1987) 13...♕a5 14 b3 b5 15 ♘c5 ♗xc5 16 dxc5 (16 ♗xf6?! ♗b4 17 ♗h4 ♖e6 with compensation, Anastasian-Lputian, Erevan 1996) 16...♘8d7 is unclear according to Lputian.

b) 12 g4 a4 13 ♘xa4 ♕a5 14 ♘c3 b5 15 ♗xf6 ♗xf6 16 g5 ♗d8 gives Black compensation.

**12 g4**

Or 12 ♔b1 ♘6d7 13 ♗xe7 ♕xe7 14 g4 ♖ac8 15 ♖c1 a6 16 g5 c5 17 dxc5 ♘xc5 18 h4 b5 19 ♕d2 ♘e4!? 20 ♗xe4 dxe4 21 ♘d4 ♗c4 22 ♔a1 (Lobron-M.Gurevich, Munich 1992) 22...b4!? 23 ♘a4 ♗b5 ∞ M.Gurevich.

**12...♕a5**

Also possible:

a) 12...♖c8 13 ♔b1 c5?! (13...♘e4 ∞) 14 dxc5 ♖xc5 15 ♘d4 ± Hort-Beliavsky, Haifa Echt 1989.

b) 12...a5 13 ♖dg1 a4 14 ♘xa4 ♕a5 15 ♘c3 b5 16 ♗xf6 ♗xf6 17 ♘d2 b4 18 ♘e2 ♕xa2 19 ♘b3 (Gretarsson-Gabriel, Matinhos jr Wch 1994) 19...c5!? 20 ♘xc5 (20 dxc5 ♗d7! with compensation) 20...♘d7 21 ♘xe6 ♖ec8! 22 ♘c5 ♘xc5 23 dxc5 b3 24 ♕b1 ♖xc5+ 25 ♔d2 ♗xb2 with compensation – Gretarsson.

c) 12...♘e4!? 13 ♗xe7 ♕xe7 14 ♖hg1 (14 ♗xe4 dxe4 15 ♕xe4 {15 ♘d2 ♗d5 16 h4 a5 17 g5 a4 ∞ Sapis-Pinkas, Poland 1993} 15...b5 16 ♘d2 b4 17 ♘a4 ♕f6 ∓ Cebalo-Kovačević, Vinkovci 1982) 14...♘xc3 15 ♕xc3 ∞ intending ♔b1, ♖c1 and h4 – V.Kovačević.

**13 ♔b1 ♖ac8**

The relieving manoeuvre 13...♘e4!? deserves serious attention: 14 ♗xe4 (14 ♗xe7 gives White nothing due to

14...♘xc3+ 15 ♕xc3 ♔xc3 16 bxc3 ♖xe7 =) 14...dxe4 15 ♗xe7 ♖xe7 16 ♘d2 ♖ae8 17 ♘dxe4 (or 17 ♕a4 ♕xa4 18 ♘xa4 ♗d5 19 ♘f1 h6 20 ♘g3 g6 21 ♘c3 ♔g7 22 ♖c1 ♖d8 = Baumbach-Csom, Kapfenberg Echt 1970) 17...♗xa2+ 18 ♘xa2 ♖xe4 19 ♘c3 ♖4e7 20 e4!? (20 h4 ♘d7 21 ♕a4 ♕xa4 22 ♘xa4 ♘f6 23 ♖hg1 ♘e4 24 ♖g2 f6 ∓ Moskalenko-A.N.Panchenko, Belgorod 1990) 20...♖d8 21 ♖d2 ♖ed7 22 ♖hd1 =.

**14 ♖c1 ♘e4 15 ♗xe4 dxe4 16 ♗xe7 ♖xe7 17 ♘d2 ♖ce8 18 a3 ♗d5** ½-½ Knaak-Bönsch, Stara Zagora Z 1990.

**19 g5 ♕d8 20 h4 ♕d6 21 ♖cg1 ♘d7 22 ♖g4 f5 23 gxf6 ♘xf6 24 ♖f4 ♔h8 25 h5 h6** ∞ Quinteros-Andersson, Mar del Plata 1981.

## B322)
**10 h3 (D)**

This move was introduced into practice by Portisch.

**10...♘f8 11 ♗f4**

White can, if he wishes, play 11 0-0, transposing to Line B3235. Instead 11 g4 is too hasty in view of

11...♘e4! 12 ♗xe7 ♕xe7 13 ♖g1 ♘xc3 14 ♕xc3 ♘e6 15 0-0-0 ♘g5 = Lombardy-Drimer, Leipzig OL 1960.

**11...♗d6**

Black has also tried:

a) 11...♗e6 12 ♗e5 (12 0-0 transposes to note 'b' to Black's 12th move in Line B3235) 12...♘6d7! 13 ♗g3 a6 14 ♖d1 ♖c8 15 0-0 ♕b6 (Hort-T.Georgadze, Porz 1981/2) 16 ♖d2! ±.

b) 11...♘g6 12 ♗h2 ♗d6 13 ♗xd6 ♕xd6 14 0-0-0 and here:

b1) 14...b5?! 15 ♔b1 ♗d7 16 ♘d2! ♕e7 17 ♘b3! ♘e4 18 ♗xe4 dxe4 19 ♘c5 ±; White has an ideal position.

b2) 14...♕e7?! 15 g4 ♗e6 16 g5 ♘e4 (16...♘d7 17 ♖dg1 ±) 17 ♗xe4 dxe4 18 ♕xe4 b5 19 h4! b4 20 ♘a4 ♕d6 (20...♗xa2 21 ♕xe7 ♖xe7 {or 21...♘xe7 22 ♘d2 ♗e6 23 ♘c5 ♘d5 24 ♖de1} 22 ♘d2 ♗d5 23 ♖h2 ±) 21 h5! ± Portisch-Larsen, Rotterdam Ct (4) 1977.

b3) 14...♗e6 15 g4 (15 ♔b1?! wastes time: 15...♖ac8 16 ♖c1 b6 {intending ...c5} 17 ♖hd1 ½-½ Matlak-Klovans, Cappelle la Grande 1996) 15...♖ac8 (or 15...b5 16 ♔b1 ♘f8 17 ♘e5 ♘6d7 18 ♘xd7 ♗xd7 19 ♘e2 ♖ec8 20 ♖c1 ♖ab8 21 ♘f4 ♖b7 22 ♗f5 ± Spraggett-A.Hernando, Saragossa 1994) 16 g5 ♘d7 17 ♔b1 (an important prophylactic move; the immediate 17 h4? is bad due to 17...♗g4 18 ♗e2 ♘f4! 19 ♘g1 ♘xe2+ 20 ♘gxe2 c5 21 ♔b1 b5! 22 dxc5 ♕xc5 23 ♖d4 ♗xe2 24 ♕xe2 b4! ∓ Krivoshei-Asrian, Minsk 1998) 17...c5 18 h4 ♗g4 19 ♗e2 a6 20 h5 ♘gf8 21 ♖h4 ± Dautov-Shaboian, Dresden 1989.

c) 11...♘e6 12 ♗h2 (also possible is 12 ♗e5!? g6 13 0-0-0 ♘g7 14 g4 a5 15 ♗g3 a4 16 ♘e5 ♘d7 17 ♔b1 ♕a5

18 f3 ± Beliavsky-Ivanović, Yugoslavia 1993) 12...g6 (or 12...♗d6 13 ♗xd6 ♕xd6 14 0-0 g6 15 ♖ab1 a5 16 a3 ♘g7 17 b4 axb4 18 axb4 ♗f5 19 ♖fc1 ♗xd3 20 ♕xd3 ♘e4 21 b5 ♖a3 22 ♘d2 ± Kasparov-Rabinovich, Tel-Aviv simul 1994) 13 0-0-0 c5 14 ♗b5 ♖f8 (Illescas-Nogueiras, Spanish Cht (Ponferrada) 1997) 15 dxc5 ♘xc5 16 ♘d4 ±.

**12 ♗xd6 ♕xd6 (D)**

**13 0-0-0**
13 0-0 ♕e7 (13...♗e6 14 a3 {14 ♖ab1 a5 15 ♖fc1 ♘8d7 16 a3 h6 17 ♘a4 ♘e4 18 ♗xe4 dxe4 19 ♘d2 ♗d5 20 ♘c5 ♘xc5 21 ♕xc5 ±} 14...♕e7 {14...♖ad8!? intending ...♗c8} 15 b4 ♖ac8 16 ♖fc1 ♘6d7 17 ♘e2! ± Karpov-Beliavsky, Tilburg 1986) 14 ♖ab1 ♘e4 15 b4 ♗f5 16 ♖b3 (if 16 ♘a4, then 16...♖ac8 = Beliavsky) and now:
a) 16...♖ad8?! 17 b5 c5 18 dxc5 ♕xc5 19 ♘d4 ♗g6 20 ♘xe4 ♕xc2 21 ♗xc2 ♗xe4 22 ♗xe4 ♖xe4 23 ♖a3 ± Portisch-Beliavsky, Brussels 1988.
b) 16...♖ac8!? 17 b5 c5 18 dxc5 (18 ♘xd5? ♕d7 ∓) 18...♕xc5 19 ♘d4 ♗g6 20 ♘xe4 dxe4 ∞.
c) 16...a6 17 a4 ♖ad8 18 b5 axb5 19 axb5 c5 20 dxc5 ♕xc5 21 ♘d4 ♗g6

leaves Black very well placed in the centre, while the weakness of the isolated d5-pawn is very hard to exploit, Tunik-Shabanov, Krasnodar 1991.
**13...♗e6**
13...b6?! is dubious due to 14 g4 ♗b7 15 g5 ♘e4 (15...♘6d7 16 h4 ±) 16 ♗xe4 dxe4 17 ♘d2 c5 18 d5 ± Eingorn-Beliavsky, USSR Ch (Moscow) 1988. However, 13...a5!? appears interesting: 14 ♔b1 ♗e6 15 g4 ♖ac8 16 ♘g5 b5 17 f4 ♗d7 18 ♕e2 a4 19 ♖c1 a3 ∞ Topalov-Piket, Linares 1997.
**14 ♔b1 ♖ac8 15 g4 c5**
15...♘e4? is bad due to 16 ♗xe4 dxe4 17 ♘d2 f5 18 gxf5 ♗xf5 19 f3 ± Gofshtein-Ubilava, Erevan 1981. Also inferior for Black are 15...b6 16 ♖c1 a5 17 g5 ♘6d7 18 h4 c5 19 ♗f5 c4 20 h5 g6 21 hxg6 fxg6 22 ♗xe6+ ♖xe6 23 a4 ± Komarov-Levin, Leningrad 1989, and 15...b5 16 ♘d2 a6 17 ♘b3 ♘6d7 18 ♘e2 c5 19 dxc5 ♘xc5 20 ♘xc5 ♖xc5 21 ♕d2 and White has a slight advantage, Dautov-Proehl, Bad Wörishofen 1998.
**16 dxc5 ♕xc5**
16...♖xc5 17 ♘d4 a6 18 f3 ♘6d7 19 ♕h2 ♕e7 20 ♖he1 ♘b6 21 ♖c1 is slightly better for White, Gabriel-Lobron, Bundesliga 1995/6.
**17 ♘d4 a6**
In this position the game Gavrikov-Barbero, San Bernardino 1991 was agreed drawn, although I think White's chances are better.

**B323)**
**10 0-0 ♘f8 (D)**
This is the main position of the Exchange Variation. White has a wide choice of continuations:

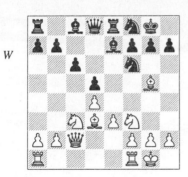

W

B3231: 11 &xf6    161
B3232: 11 &ab1    161
B3233: 11 a3      162
B3234: 11 &ae1    163
B3235: 11 h3      166

**B3231)**
**11 &xf6 &xf6 12 b4 &g4**
12...a6 is also possible:

a) 13 ♘a4 &e7 (but not 13...g6 14 ♘c5 ♕d6 15 &ab1 b6 16 ♘b3 ♘d7 17 &fc1 &b7 18 a4 &d8 19 a5 ± Vera-Lputian, Sochi 1985) 14 ♘c5 &d6 15 &f5 ♕e7 16 &ab1 &xf5 17 ♕xf5 b6 18 ♘a4 b5 19 ♘c5 a5 20 a3 axb4 21 axb4 &xc5 ½-½ Granda-Bönsch, Novi Sad OL 1990.

b) 13 a4 g6 (or 13...&g4 14 ♘d2 &e7 15 b5 a5 16 bxc6 bxc6 17 ♘e2 &b4 18 ♘b3 ♕f6 19 &fc1 &ac8 20 ♘c5 ♘g6 21 ♘g3 ♔h8 22 &f5 ± Yuneev-Akopian, Daugavpils 1989; 13...&e7 14 b5 a5 15 bxc6 bxc6 16 &fc1 &d6 17 &f5 ±) 14 b5 a5 15 bxc6 bxc6 16 ♘b1 ♕d6 17 ♘bd2 ♘e6 (Timman-Spassky, Tilburg 1979) 18 ♘b3 ±.

**13 ♘d2 &e7**
13...&c8 14 &f5 &xf5 15 ♕xf5 ♘e6 (15...♕d7 16 ♕xd7 ♘xd7 17 a4 &e7 18 &fb1 ♘f6 19 a5 a6 20 ♘a4

gives White the more pleasant ending, Korchnoi-Karpov, Baguio City Wch (31) 1978; 15...g6 16 ♕d3 ♕d6 17 &fb1 &g7 18 a4 ± Reshevsky-Miagmasuren, Sousse IZ 1967; 15...&e7!? 16 &ab1 a6 17 &fc1 &d6 18 a4 g6 19 ♕d3 f5 ∞) 16 &ab1 g6 17 ♕d3 &g7 18 ♘a4 (18 b5? c5 ∓) 18...b6 19 &fd1 ♕d7 20 ♘c3 &ed8 = Bagirov-Klovans, Leningrad 1963.

**14 &ab1 &d6 15 &f5**
Or 15 &fe1 &c8 16 &f5 &xf5 17 ♕xf5 a6 18 ♘a4 &c7 19 ♘c5 &ce7 20 ♘f3 ♕c7 21 &bc1 ♘d7 = Vera-Pigusov, Sochi 1985.

**15...&h5 16 &fc1 g6**
Also possible is 16...a6 17 ♘f1 ♕g5 18 ♘g3 &xg3 19 hxg3 &g6 20 &xg6 hxg6 = Matveeva-Timoshchenko, Frunze 1987.

**17 &d3 ♕g5**
Black becomes active on the kingside.

**18 ♘e2 ♘d7 19 h3 a6 20 a4 &ac8 21 ♘f1 &xe2 22 &xe2 ♕e7 23 ♕b3 ♘f6**
½-½ Timman-Kasparov, London (USSR vs RoW) 1984.

**B3232)**
**11 &ab1** (D)

B

**11...a5**

Or 11...♘g6:

a) 12 b4!? ♗d6 (12...a6 13 a4 ♗d6 14 ♖fe1! ♗g4! 15 ♘h4 ♗h5 16 ♘xg6 ♗xg6 17 ♗h4! ♗e7 18 ♗xf6 ♗xf6 19 ♗xg6 hxg6 20 b5 ± Knaak-Balashov, Berlin 1988) 13 b5 (13 ♖fe1 ♗g4 14 ♘h4 ♗h5 15 h3 h6 16 ♗xf6 ♕xf6 17 ♘f5 ♘h4 = Gligorić-Robatsch, Beverwijk 1967) 13...h6 14 ♗xf6 ♕xf6 15 e4 ♘f4! 16 e5 ♕e6 (intending ...♕g4) 17 ♘e1 ♗f8 18 ♘e2 ♘xd3 19 ♘xd3 cxb5! 20 ♘df4! (Dydyshko-Kveinys, Moscow OL 1994) 20...♕c6!? is unclear – Dydyshko.

b) 12 ♗xf6 ♗xf6 13 b4 ♗g4 14 ♘d2 ♗e7 15 b5 c5 16 ♗f5 (16 dxc5 ♗xc5 17 ♘b3 ♖c8 18 ♗f5 ♗xf5 19 ♕xf5 ♗d6 ½-½ A.Petrosian-Balashov, USSR Ch (Riga) 1985) 16...♗xf5 17 ♕xf5 cxd4 18 exd4 ♗f6 19 ♘f3 ♘e7 20 ♕d3 ♕a5 =.

**12 a3**

White gains nothing by 12 ♖fe1 ♘e4 13 ♗xe7 ♕xe7 14 ♘d2 ♘d6 15 ♘a4 ♕d8 with equality, Taimanov-Kholmov, USSR 1956, or 12 ♖fc1 ♘e4 13 ♗xe7 ♕xe7 14 a3 ♘d6 15 b4 axb4 16 axb4 b5 =. 12 h3!? is interesting though: 12...♘e4 (12...♗e6 13 ♘a4 ♘6d7 14 ♗f4 ♖c8 15 ♖fc1 ± Burmakin-Sitnik, Portorož 1995; 12...♗d6 13 ♖be1 ♗d7 14 e4 dxe4 15 ♘xe4 ♗e7 16 ♘c5 ♗c8 17 ♗c4 ♘d5 18 ♗xe7 ♖xe7 19 ♗xd5 cxd5 20 ♖xe7 ♕xe7 21 ♕b3 ♖b8 22 ♕b6 ± Eingorn-Pigusov, Sochi 1985) 13 ♗xe7 ♕xe7 14 ♗xe4 dxe4 15 ♘d2 f5 16 ♘c4 ♗e6 17 ♘b6 ♖ad8 18 a3 (18 ♕a4 ♕b4) intending ♕a4 ∞.

**12...♗d6**

White is better after 12...♘e4 (or 12...♘g6 13 ♗xf6 ♗xf6 14 b4 ±) 13 ♗xe7 ♕xe7 14 b4 ♗f5 (14...axb4 15 axb4 ♗f5 16 b5 ♘xc3 17 ♕xc3 ♗xd3 18 ♕xd3 ± Krogius-Ilivitsky, USSR 1958) 15 ♗xe4 dxe4 16 ♘e5 axb4 17 axb4 f6 (17...♕g5 18 ♘e2 ± Gligorić-Larsen, Copenhagen 1965) 18 ♘c4 ♗e6 19 ♘b6 ♖a6 20 ♘ba4 ± Eising-Unzicker, W.German Ch (Bad Pyrmont) 1961.

**13 ♖fe1 ♗g4 14 ♘d2 ♗h5 15 ♘f1 ♗g6 16 b4**

Or 16 ♘a4?! ♗xd3 17 ♕xd3 h6 18 ♗h4 ♘g6 = Tomaszewski-Bönsch, Polanica Zdroj 1987.

**16...axb4 17 axb4 h6**

Also possible is 17...♗xd3 18 ♕xd3 h6 =.

**18 ♗xf6 ♕xf6 19 b5 ♗xd3 20 ♕xd3 ♘g6 21 bxc6**

½-½ Alterman-Gabriel, Bad Homburg 1996. After 21...bxc6 the game is absolutely equal.

**B3233)**

**11 a3** *(D)*

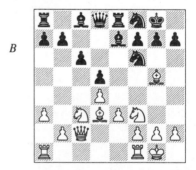

White prepares b4.

**11...a5**

Or:

a) 11...g6 is insufficient for equality: 12 b4 a6 (12...♘e6 13 ♗xf6 ±) 13

♘e5 ♘g4 14 ♗xe7 ♕xe7 15 ♘xg4
♗xg4 16 ♘a4 ♖ad8 17 ♖ae1 ♖c8 18
f4 ± Chernin-Darcyl, Mendoza U-26
Wcht 1985.
  b) 11...♗d6 12 ♖ae1 ♗g4 13 ♘d2
♗d7 (13...♗h5 14 f4! h6 15 ♗h4 ♘g6,
Chernin-Morović, Tunis IZ 1985, 16
♗g3! {intending h3} 16...♘g4 17 ♘d1
±) 14 h3 ♗e7 15 ♗f4 ± Bareev-Sma-
gin, USSR 1986.
  c) 11...♘e4 12 ♗f4 ♘xc3 (12...♘g5
13 ♘xg5 ♗xg5 14 ♗xg5 ♕xg5 15
♖ae1 ± Petrosian-Beliavsky, USSR
Ch (Moscow) 1983) 13 bxc3 c5 14 c4
♗f6 15 cxd5 cxd4 16 ♘xd4 ± (16 exd4
♕xd5 = Knaak-Inkiov, Varna 1985).
  d) 11...♘g6 12 ♘e5 ♘g4 13 ♗xe7
♕xe7 14 ♘xg4 ♗xg4 15 ♖ae1! ♗d7
16 f4 ♘f8 17 f5 ♕d6 18 ♕f2 ± Tal-
Saeed, Taxco IZ 1985.
  **12 ♘e5**
  12 ♖ae1 seems interesting; e.g.,
12...♘e4 13 ♗xe7 ♕xe7 14 ♗xe4
dxe4 15 ♘d2 f5 16 ♘c4 ∞.
  **12...♘g4**
  White intended 13 f4, so this relieving manoeuvre is entirely logical for
Black.
  **13 ♗xe7 ♕xe7 14 ♘xg4 ♗xg4 15
♖ae1**
  White seeks play in the centre and
on the kingside.
  **15...♗h5**
  Or: 15...♕h4?! 16 f4 ♘e6 17 ♕d2 g6
18 ♗b1 ♗f5 19 e4 dxe4 20 ♗xe4 ♖ed8
21 ♗xf5 gxf5 22 d5 ± Psakhis-Šibare-
vić, Banja Luka 1985; 15...♖ad8?! 16
f4 ♗c8 17 ♘a4 h6 18 ♕c3 ♕c7 19 b4
axb4 20 axb4 ♕e7 21 b5 ± Goldin-
Ruban, Andropov 1986; 15...♗e6!?
16 ♘a4 g6 17 ♘c5 b6 18 ♘xe6 ♕xe6
19 ♖c1 ♖ec8 20 ♕d2 c5 = C.Hansen-
Bönsch, Tilburg 1994.

  **16 f4 f6 17 ♕f2**
  White achieved nothing in Kiria-
kov-Asrian, Moscow 1996 after 17
♘a4 ♗g6 18 f5 ♗f7 19 ♘c5 ♕c7 20
b4 b6 21 ♘a4 axb4 22 axb4 ♘d7 23
♖f3 ♕d6 24 ♖b1 ♖ec8 25 ♗f1 ♕e7 26
h3 ♖c7 ½-½.
  **17...♗f7**
  17...♗g6!? intending to meet 18 f5
with 18...♗f7.
  **18 h3 b5 19 e4 dxe4 20 ♘xe4 ♕d7
21 ♖d1 ♖ab8!?**
  21...♔h8 22 ♘c5 ♕d6 23 ♗e4 ♗d5
24 ♖fe1 ♗xe4 25 ♘xe4 ♕d5 26 ♘c3
♖xe1+ 27 ♖xe1 ♕d7 28 f5 ♔g8 29 d5
b4 30 dxc6 ½-½ Bagirov-Avshalu-
mov, Sevastopol 1986.
  **22 ♘c5 ♕d6 23 ♗e4 b4 24 a4**
  The position is equal.

**B3234)**
  **11 ♖ae1** (D)

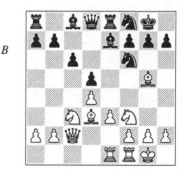

  White is aiming for play in the centre.
  **11...♘e4**
  Black seeks simplifications. However, other plans are also possible:
  a) 11...g6 12 ♘e5 ♘e6 13 ♗h4 (13
f4?! ♘g7 =) 13...♘g7 14 f3 ♗e6 15 g4
♘d7 16 ♗xe7 ♖xe7 17 ♗e2 f5 18

♘d3 ♖f7 19 ♗d1 ± Hjartarson-Ivkov, Lone Pine 1981.

b) 11...♘g4!? 12 ♗xe7 ♖xe7 (or 12...♕xe7 13 e4 ±) 13 b4 ♕d6 14 b5 c5 15 e4 c4 16 ♗e2 (16 e5 ♕d8 17 ♗f5 ♗xf5 18 ♕xf5 ♘h6 19 ♕c2 ♘e6 ∞ Khalifman-Lputian, Erevan 1996) 16...dxe4 17 ♘xe4 ♕f4 (17...♕g6 18 ♗xc4 ±) 18 ♗xc4 ♗f5 19 ♗d3 ♖ae8 20 ♕d2 ♖xe4 21 ♕xf4 ♖xf4 22 ♖xe8 ♗xd3 23 ♖c1 ♘f6 24 ♖d8 ± Lputian.

c) 11...♗e6 *(D)* and then:

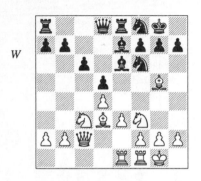

c1) Portisch's move 12 ♕b1 (preparing b4) seems interesting: 12...a5 (12...♖c8 13 b4 b5 14 ♖c1 {14 a4!?} 14...a5 15 a3 axb4 16 axb4 ♘6d7 17 ♗xe7 ♕xe7 18 e4 dxe4 19 ♘xe4 ♗d5 20 ♖fe1 ± Bondarenko-Izsak, Budapest 1994) 13 a3 ♘6d7 (13...♘g6 14 ♘e5 ±) 14 ♗xe7 ♖xe7 (14...♕xe7 15 b4 axb4 16 axb4 b5 {16...♖a3 17 ♕b2 ♖ea8 18 b5 ±} 17 e4 ±) 15 b4 axb4 16 ♕xb4 ♘b6 17 a4 ♘c8 18 ♖a1 ± Portisch-Larsen, Rotterdam Ct (6) 1977.

c2) 12 ♘e5 ♘6d7 13 ♗xe7 (13 ♗f4!?) 13...♖xe7 14 f4 (further simplification by 14 ♘xd7 only helps Black to equalize: 14...♕xd7 15 b4 ♖c8 16 ♖c1 ♕d6 17 ♕b1 ♖ec7 18 ♘e2 g6 19 ♖c3 ♘d7 20 ♘f4 ½-½

Portisch-Larsen, Rotterdam Ct (2) 1977) 14...f6 15 ♘f3 and then:

c21) 15...♕a5?! is dubious in view of 16 e4 dxe4 17 ♘xe4 ♔h8 18 ♘d6 ♕b4 19 ♘xb7! ± (19...♕xb7 is met by 20 f5) Todorović-S.Ilić, Niš 1993.

c22) 15...♖c8, preparing counterplay on the queenside, is interesting: 16 f5 ♗f7 17 g4 c5 18 ♕f2 a6 19 ♘h4 b5 20 a3 ±/= Rogers-Speelman, Spanish Cht (Cala Galdana) 1994.

c23) 15...♘b6 (Black wants to transfer the knight via c8 to d6, whence it will reinforce his control of the e4-square) 16 f5 ♗f7 17 g4 (17 h3 seems too sluggish due to 17...♕c7! 18 ♕f2 ♖ae8 19 ♖e2 ♘c8 = Novikov-Borges, Lucerne Wcht 1997; Black has managed to centralize his pieces) 17...♕d6 (17...h6?! is dubious due to 18 ♘h4 ♘c4 19 ♗xc4 dxc4 20 ♘f3 b5 21 e4 ± Leitão-Klovans, Groningen 1996, but 17...♘c8!? is fully possible: 18 ♕g2 ♘d6 19 g5 ♔h8 20 g6 ♗e8 21 gxh7 ♗h5 22 ♘h4 ♕e8 23 ♕h3 ♖d8 24 ♘g2 g5 25 fxg6 ♗xg6 26 ♗xg6 ♕xg6 27 ♕g3 ♕xg3 ½-½ Smejkal-Morović, Dubai OL 1986) 18 ♘h4 (somewhat hasty is 18 e4 dxe4 19 ♘xe4, because 18...♕c7 20 g5 ♘d5 21 ♗c4 ♔h8! is unclear, Yusupov-Spassky, Montpellier Ct 1985) 18...♖ae8 19 ♘g2 ♘c4 20 ♘d1 ♘d7 21 b3 ± Razuvaev-Beliavsky, Sochi 1986.

**12 ♗xe7** *(D)*

12 ♗f4 leads to equality: 12...♗f5 (12...♗b4!? 13 h3 ♘g6 14 ♗h2 f5!? 15 ♘d2 ♗d6 ∞ A.Sokolov) 13 ♗xe4 ♗xe4! 14 ♘xe4 dxe4 15 ♘d2 ♗b4 16 ♖d1 ♗xd2 17 ♖xd2 ♕d5! 18 b3 ♖ad8 19 ♖fd1 ♘e6 20 ♗g3 ♖d7 21 h3 ♖ed8 is equal, Sapis-Maciejewski, Polish Cht (Mikolajki) 1991.

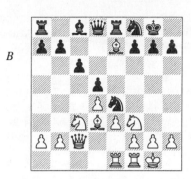

*B*

**12...♕xe7 13 ♗xe4 dxe4 14 ♘d2 f5**

14...b6 creates new weaknesses on the queenside. 15 ♕a4 b5 and now:

a) 16 ♕c2!? b4 17 ♘a4 (17 ♘e2 ♗a6 18 ♘b3 ♖ad8 19 ♘c5 ♗b5 20 ♖c1 ♘g6 21 ♖fe1 ♗xe2! ∞ Yusupov-Ribli, Lucerne Wcht 1985) 17...♗a6 18 ♘c4 ♘d7 19 ♖c1 ♕g5 20 ♕d2 ♖ab8 21 ♖fd1 ♖e6 22 ♘e5 ± Azmaiparashvili-Pigusov, Vilnius 1984.

b) 16 ♕a5 ♗f5 (16...f5 can be met by 17 ♖c1 ± or 17 d5!?) 17 ♖c1! ♖ad8 18 ♘e2 ♖d6 19 ♖c5 ♕d7 20 ♖fc1 ♘g6 21 ♘g3 ± Smejkal-Flear, Szirak 1986.

**15 f3**

White, trying to make use of his somewhat better development, opens the centre and undermines Black's pawn-chain. Another thrust does not yield any advantage: 15 d5 ♗d7 and now:

a) 16 f3 exf3 17 ♘xf3 cxd5 18 ♘xd5 (18 ♘d4 ♕c5 19 ♘xf5 ♘g6 20 ♔h1 ♗e6 =; however, in Murshed-Milos, Groningen FIDE 1997, White committed a curious oversight: 21 ♕b3?? d4 0-1) 18...♕e4 19 ♕xe4 ♖xe4 20 ♘d4 ♖ae8 = Spasov-Van der Sterren, Albena 1983.

b) 16 ♕b3 cxd5 17 ♕xb7 ♖eb8! (but not 17...♗e6 18 ♕xe7 ♖xe7 19 ♘b3 ♖b7 20 ♖b1 ♖ab8 21 ♖fd1 ± Khalifman-Zagorskis, Vilnius 1997) 18 ♕xd5+ ♗e6 19 ♕c6 ♗d7 20 ♕a6 ♖xb2 21 ♘b3 ♗e6 22 ♘d4 ♖b6! 23 ♕a5 ♕b4 = Azmaiparashvili-Zaid, USSR 1985.

**15...exf3 16 ♘xf3 ♗e6 17 e4 fxe4 18 ♖xe4**

18 ♕xe4?! gives White no advantage: 18...♖ad8 19 ♖e2 ♘g6 20 ♖fe1 ♕d7 intending ...♗f7 =, Semkov-Panchenko, Sochi 1982.

**18...h6** *(D)*

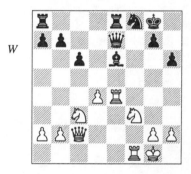

*W*

This is a critical position for the variation. Its assessment hinges on to what extent Black can limit the activity of the white pieces, and in particular how effectively he can challenge White's use of the e5-square.

**19 ♖fe1**

A logical move: White lines up his heavy artillery on the open e-file. Otherwise: 19 ♘e2 ♕b4! 20 a3 ♕b3 21 ♕d2 ♗d5 22 ♖xe8 ♖xe8 23 ♘e5 ♘e6 24 ♘c3 ♕b6 25 ♘xd5 ♕xd4+! (not 25...cxd5?! 26 ♘f3 ♘f8, Timman-Yusupov, Tilburg Ct (8) 1988, 27 ♖c1 ±) 26 ♕xd4 ♘xd4 27 ♘xc6 bxc6 28

♘c3 ♘e2+ 29 ♘xe2 ♖xe2 30 ♖f2
♖e1+ = Temirbaev-Kaidanov, Kuibyshev 1986.
**19...♖ad8 20 ♖1e3**
White has also tried:
a) 20 ♘e5 ♕g5 21 ♕f2 ♘g6 22
♘f3 ♕f5! ∞.
b) 20 ♖e5!? ♕f7 21 ♕e4 (weaker
is 21 b4?! ♘d7 22 ♖a5 ♗g4 23 ♘e5
♘xe5 24 dxe5 b6 25 ♖a4 ♖d4 ∓ Hjar-
tarson-Short, Dubai OL 1986) 21...♗d5
(21...♖d6 22 ♕e3 ♘d7 23 ♖a5 ♘f6 24
♕f4 ± Tal-Vaganian, Riga 1975) 22
♘xd5 ♖xe5 23 ♘f6+ ♕xf6 24 dxe5 ±
Tal.
c) 20 h3!? is interesting: 20...♕d6
21 ♖1e3 ♗f7 (21...♖e7 ±) 22 ♖xe8
♖xe8 23 ♖xe8 ♗xe8 24 ♕b3+ ♔h7 25
♕xb7 ♗h5 with compensation, Yusu-
pov-Kramnik, Vienna 1996.
**20...♕f7** *(D)*
20...♖d6 21 ♕e2 ±.

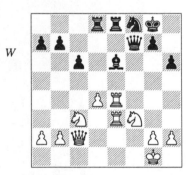

**21 ♘e5 ♕f5**
21...♕h5 is worse due to 22 ♕f2
♘g6 23 ♘xc6 bxc6 24 ♖xe6 ♖f8 25
♖f3 ♖xf3 26 ♕xf3 ♕xf3 27 gxf3 ♘h4
28 ♔f2 ♖xd4 29 ♖xc6 ♖d2+ 30 ♔g3
♘f5+ 31 ♔f4 ♖e7 32 ♖e6 ♔f7 33 ♖e2
± A.G.Panchenko-Masternak, Katowice 1992.

**22 ♖f3**
Bad is 22 ♖g3? ♖xd4 23 ♘g4 ♔h8
24 ♘xh6 gxh6 25 ♕c1 ♕f6 −+ Timman-Short, Amsterdam 1988.
**22...♕h5**
Also possible is 22...♕h7 23 ♕e2
♗d5 24 ♘xd5 cxd5 25 ♖g4 ♘e6 26
♕d1 ♘g5 27 ♖f1 ♖f8 28 h4 ♘e4 29
♖g6 ±; the black queen finds itself
misplaced.
**23 ♕f2 ♘d7 24 ♕e1 ♘xe5 25
♖xe5 ♕g6 26 ♖g3 ♕f7 27 ♖f3 ♕d7
28 ♖fe3 ♗f7**
with equality, Djurić-Savić, Nikšić
1997.

**B3235)**
**11 h3** *(D)*

**11...♗e6**
The main line. However, other continuations are also possible:
a) 11...♘e4 12 ♗f4 f5 (12...♘g5
13 ♗xg5 ♗xg5 14 b4 ♗e7 15 b5 ♗d6
16 bxc6 bxc6 17 ♗f5 ♕a5 18 ♗xc8
♖axc8 19 ♖ab1 ♘e6 20 ♖b7 ± Djurić-
Pfleger, Srbija-Bayern 1984) 13 ♘e5
♘g6 14 ♘xg6 hxg6 15 f3 ♘f6 16 ♕f2
♘h5 17 ♗e5 ♗h4 18 ♕d2 ♗g3 (I.Sok-
olov-Oll, Pula Echt 1997) 19 f4! and
White has a slight advantage.

b) 11...a6 12 ♖ab1 ♘g6 13 ♘e5
♘d7 14 ♗xe7 ♖xe7! 15 f4 ♘gf8 16
♖be1 f6 17 ♘f3 ♘b6 18 f5 ♗d7 19 b4
♗e8 20 a4 ♗f7 21 a5 ♘c8 22 e4 dxe4
23 ♘xe4 ♘d6 24 ♘c5 ♗d5 25 ♕f2 ±
I.Sokolov-Ziatdinov, Nikšić 1991.

c) 11...♘h5 12 ♗xe7 ♖xe7 (alternatively, 12...♕xe7 13 ♖ab1 a5 14 a3
g6 15 ♘a4 ♘d7 16 b4 axb4 17 axb4
b5 18 ♘c5 ♘xc5 19 dxc5 ♘g7 20 ♖a1
♗f5 21 ♘d4 ♗xd3 22 ♕xd3, Psakhis-
Ruban, Novosibirsk 1993, 22...♕d7
23 ♕c3 ♘e6 24 ♘f3 ±) 13 b4 ♗e6 14
b5 cxb5 15 ♘xb5 a6 16 ♘c3 ♖c8 17
♕b2 ♘f6 18 a4 ♕a5 19 ♘e2 ♖ec7 20
♕d2 ± Yermolinsky-I.Ivanov, USA
Ch (Parsippany) 1996.

d) 11...♘g6 and then:
d1) 12 ♘e5 deserves attention:
12...♘d7 (12...♘xe5?! 13 dxe5 ♘d7
14 ♗xe7 ♕xe7 15 f4 ♘f8 16 ♕f2 b6 17
e4 ± I.Sokolov-Akopian, Nikšić 1991)
13 ♗xe7 and then:
d11) 13...♕xe7 14 f4 f6 15 ♘xg6
♕xe3+ 16 ♔h2 hxg6 17 ♗xg6 ♖e7 18
♖ae1 (18 ♗h7+!? ♔h8 19 ♖ae1 ±
Rajković-Raičević, Yugoslavia 1989)
18...♕xe1 19 ♖xe1 ♖xe1 20 ♘e2 ♘f8
21 ♗d3 ♗d7 22 ♕d2 ♖a1 23 b4 ♘e6
24 f5 ♘g5 25 ♘c1 ♘e4 26 ♕b2 ±
Khenkin-Arkhipov, Protvino 1988.
d12) 13...♖xe7 14 f4 ♘gf8 15
♖ae1! (15 e4!? ♘f6 16 exd5 ♘xd5!
{16...cxd5? 17 ♖ae1 ♕b6 18 ♕f2 a6
19 g4 ± Annageldiev-Nadera, Manila
OL 1992} 17 ♘xd5 ♕xd5! ∞) 15...f6
16 ♘f3 ±.
d2) 12 ♗xf6 ♗xf6 13 b4 a6 (or
13...♗e7 14 b5 ♗d6 15 bxc6 bxc6 16
♘b1 {intending ♘bd2-b3; c5 is weak}
16...♕f6 17 ♘bd2 h6 18 ♖fc1 ♘e7 19
♕d1 ♖b8 20 ♘b3 ± Yermolinsky-
Gild.Garcia, St Martin 1993) 14 a4

♗e7 15 b5 a5 (15...axb5 16 axb5 ♗d7
17 bxc6 bxc6 18 ♘a4 ♖a5 19 ♘d2
♕c7 20 ♘b3 ♖a7 21 ♘ac5 ± Nikolić-
Ljubojević, Amsterdam 1988) 16 ♘e2
(16 bxc6 bxc6 17 ♘e2 ♕d6 18 ♖fc1
♗d7 19 ♗xg6 hxg6 20 ♘e5 ♖ec8 21
♘xd7 ♕xd7 = Mandekić-Lazović,
Croatian Cht (Medulin) 1997) 16...♕d6
17 ♘g3 c5 18 ♘f5 (18 dxc5 ♕xc5 19
♖ac1 b6 20 ♕b1 ♕b4 =) 18...♗xf5 19
♗xf5 c4 ∞ P.Nikolić-Seirawan, Nikšić 1983.

e) 11...g6 (D) and then:

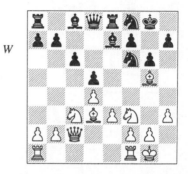

e1) 12 ♗h6!? ♘h5 (for 12...♘e6
13 ♘e5 see line 'e21') 13 ♖ab1 ♘g7
14 b4 a6 15 a4 (15 ♗xg7 ♔xg7 16
♘a4 ♗d6 17 ♘c5 ♕f6! = Karpov-
Short, Lucerne Wcht 1989) 15...♘f5
16 ♗f4 with a slight advantage for
White – Karpov.
e2) 12 ♘e5!? and now:
e21) 12...♘e6?! 13 ♗h6 ♘g7 14
g4! ♘d7 (14...♗d6 15 f4 ♘d7 16 ♖f3!
± Mirković-Todorović, Knjazevac
1989; White intends ♖af1 and f5) 15
f4 ♘xe5 16 dxe5 (16 fxe5?! ♗g5 =)
16...♗c5 17 ♕f2 f6 (17...d4? 18 ♘e4
dxe3 19 ♕e2 ±) 18 ♖ad1 ± intending
to meet 18...fxe5 by 19 ♘e4 with an
attack – Christiansen.

e22) 12...♘6d7! 13 ♗xe7 ♕xe7 14 ♘xd7 ♘xd7! (worse is 14...♗xd7 15 b4 a6 16 ♘a4 ♘e6 17 ♘b6 ♖ab8 18 ♖ab1 ± D.Byrne-Mednis, USA Ch (New York) 1963/4) 15 ♖ae1 (15 ♖ab1 ♕h4! 16 b4 ♘f6 17 b5 ♗xh3 18 gxh3 ♕xh3 19 ♗e2 ♘e4 with an initiative for Black, Nordahl-A.N.Panchenko, Gausdal 1991) 15...♘f6 16 f4 ♘e4 ∞.

e3) 12 ♗xf6 ♗xf6 13 b4 *(D)* and then:

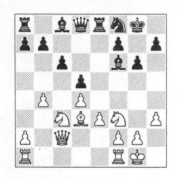

e31) 13...a6 14 a4 ♗e6 15 b5 axb5 16 axb5 ♘d7 17 bxc6 bxc6 18 ♘e2! ± Karpov-Ehlvest, Vienna 1996.

e32) 13...♗e6 14 b5 c5 15 dxc5 ♖c8 16 ♘d4 ♖xc5 17 ♕b2 ± Karpov.

e33) 13...♘e6!? 14 ♖fd1 a6 15 a4 (15 ♖ab1 ♘g5 =; 15 ♗f1 ♕d6 16 a3 ♘g5 =) 15...♕d6 16 ♕b3 ♖d8 17 ♗f1 ♗g7 18 ♖a2! ♘c7 19 ♘e1 ♗f5 20 ♘e2 ♗f8! 21 ♖b2 ♕f6 22 ♘f4 ± Karpov-Beliavsky, Belfort 1988.

e34) 13...♗e7 14 b5 ♗d6 15 bxc6 bxc6 16 ♖fc1 ♘e6 17 ♕d1 ♕f6 18 ♖ab1 ♖e7 (18...♔g7!? intending ...h6 and ...♘g5 ∞) 19 ♖b3 ♔g7 20 ♘a4 ♗d7 21 ♗a6 ♖ae8 22 ♘c5 (22 ♖b7 ♘g5 ∞ P.Nikolić-L.B.Hansen, Wijk aan Zee 1995; 22 ♗b7!? ♘d8 23 ♗a8

is unclear) 22...♗xc5 23 dxc5 =.

e4) 12 ♖ab1 *(D)* and now:

e41) 12...♘e6 13 ♗h6 (13 ♗h4!? ♘g7 14 b4 a6 15 a4 ♘f5 16 ♗xf6 ♗xf6 17 b5 ± Gelfand-Lobron, Munich 1994) 13...♘g7 (13...c5?! 14 dxc5 ♘xc5 15 ♖bd1 ♕a5 16 ♘d4 ♗d7 17 ♗g5 ± Yermolinsky-Kaidanov, USA 1994) 14 b4 a6 15 a4 (White gains nothing by 15 ♘a4 ♘f5 16 ♗f4 ♗d6! 17 ♘e5 ♘h5 18 ♗h2 ♘h4 19 f4 f6 20 ♘g4 ♔g7 21 ♕f2 ½-½ Bischoff-Bönsch, Hanover 1991) 15...♗f5 16 ♗xg7 (16 ♘e5 ♖c8 17 ♗xg7 ♗xd3 18 ♘xd3 ♔xg7 = Gelfand-Ivanchuk, Linares 1993; 16 b5!? cxb5?! {better is 16...axb5} 17 axb5 a5 18 ♗xf5 ♘xf5 19 ♗g5 ± Ivanchuk) 16...♗xd3 17 ♕xd3 ♔xg7 18 b5 (18 ♖fc1 ♗d6 19 b5 axb5 20 axb5 ♖a3 21 ♕c2 ♕a5 = Lobron-Smagin, Bundesliga 1991/2) 18...axb5 (18...cxb5 19 axb5 a5 20 ♘a4 ±) 19 axb5 ♖a3 20 bxc6 (20 ♕c2?! ♕a5 21 ♖b3 {21 ♖fc1 ♗b4 ∓} 21...♖c8! ∓ Van Wely-Hjartarson, Akureyri 1994) 20...bxc6 21 ♕c2 ♕a5 22 ♖fc1 ♗b4 23 ♖b3 (23 ♘e2!? ♖c8 {23...♖a2 24 ♖b2 ±} 24 ♘e5 c5 25 ♘d3 ♖a2 {25...♗d2!?} 26 ♖b2 ♖xb2 27 ♕xb2 ♗a3 28 ♕c3 ±) 23...♖c8 24

♖xa3 ♕xa3 25 ♘b1 ♕a6 = Ruban-A.N.Panchenko, Russian Ch (Elista) 1994.

e42) 12...a5 13 a3 ♘e6 14 ♗h6 ♘g7 (14...♗d6!? deserves attention: 15 ♖fe1 ♔h8 {intending ...♘g8} 16 e4 ♗f4 17 ♘e5 ♔g8 18 ♗xf4 ♘xf4 19 ♖bd1 ♘xd3 20 ♕xd3 ♗e6 21 exd5 {21 f3 ± Akopian} 21...♗xd5 22 ♘g4 ♘xg4 23 hxg4 ♕d6 = Akopian-Ivanchuk, Biel IZ 1993) 15 b4 axb4 16 axb4 ♗f5 17 b5 (17 ♗xg7 ♗xd3 18 ♕xd3 ♔xg7 19 b5 ♗d6 = Yermolinsky-Parma, New York 1994) 17...♖a3 (17...♗d6!?) 18 ♖a1 ♗xd3 19 ♕xd3 ♕a5 20 ♖xa3 ♕xa3 21 ♘e5 ♘e4 22 ♘xe4 ♕xd3 23 ♘f6+! ♗xf6 24 ♘xd3 ± Ivanchuk.

We now return to 11...♗e6 (D):

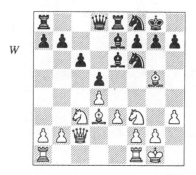

W

**12 ♘e5**
White can also try to develop an initiative in other ways:
a) 12 a3 ♘6d7 13 ♗f4 (13 ♗xe7 ♕xe7 14 b4 ♘g6 15 ♖fc1 ♕f6 16 ♕d1 ♖ac8 17 b5 c5 = Beliavsky) 13...a5! 14 ♘a4 ♘g6 15 ♗h2 ♗f8 16 ♖fb1 ♕f6 17 ♕d1 ♗f5 ½-½ Nikolić-Timman, Reykjavik 1991.
b) 12 ♗f4 ♖c8 13 ♘a4 ♗d6 14 ♘e5 ♖c7 15 ♖ab1 (15 ♗h2 ♗c8 16 f4

♘e4! =) 15...♘g6 (15...♗c8!? intending ...c5 and ...♘g6) 16 ♗h2 ♗c8 (16...c5!? 17 ♘xc5 ♘xe5! 18 dxe5 ♖xc5 = Krasenkow) 17 ♕c3 ♘e4 18 ♗xe4 dxe4 19 ♘c5 ♘xe5 20 dxe5 ♗xc5 21 ♕xc5 (Krasenkow-Yusupov, Pula Echt 1997) 21...b6 (intending ...♗a6) 22 ♕d6 = Krasenkow.
c) 12 ♖ab1 and now:
c1) 12...♘6d7 13 ♗f4 ♘b6 and then:
c11) 14 b4 ♘g6 (but not 14...♗d6 15 ♗xd6 ♕xd6 16 a4 a6 17 ♘d2 ♖e7 18 ♘b3! ♖c7 19 ♘c5 ♘bd7 20 f4 ± Beliavsky-Ivanchuk, Linares 1993) 15 ♗h2 (15 b5 c5 16 dxc5 ♗xc5 ∞) 15...♘c4!? 16 ♗xc4 dxc4 ∞.
c12) 14 ♘a4 ♘xa4 15 ♕xa4 ♘g6 16 ♗h2 ♗d6 17 ♘e5 ♕f6 18 ♕c2 ♘xe5 19 dxe5 ♗xe5 20 ♗xh7+ ♔h8 21 ♗xe5 ♕xe5 22 ♗d3 ∞ I.Sokolov-Yusupov, Amsterdam 1994.
c2) 12...a5!? 13 a3 (13 ♘e5 ♘6d7 14 ♗xe7 ♕xe7 15 f4 f6 16 ♘xd7 ♗xd7 =) 13...♘6d7 14 ♗xe7 ♕xe7 15 b4 (15 ♖fc1 ♕f6 16 ♕d1 ♘g6 17 ♘a4 h5 18 ♘c5 ♘xc5 19 ♖xc5 ♗f5 20 ♗xf5 ♕xf5 21 ♕c2 = Babula-Jirovsky, Czech jr Ch (Pardubice) 1991) 15...axb4 16 axb4 ♖ec8! 17 ♖fc1 (17 ♘a4 g6 {17...b6!? =} 18 ♖fc1 b5 19 ♘c5 ♘xc5 20 dxc5 ♖a4 21 ♘d4 ♗d7 22 ♕b2 ♖ca8 = Ellers-Klovans, Berlin 1993) 17...g6 18 ♘d2 ♘f6 19 ♘a4 ♘8d7 20 ♘c5 b6 21 ♘xe6 ♕xe6 22 ♖a1 ♖xa1 23 ♖xa1 ♕d6 24 ♕c3 c5 25 bxc5 bxc5 26 dxc5 ♕xc5 27 ♕xc5 ♖xc5 = Franco-Nogueiras, Las Palmas 1992.
d) 12 ♗xf6!? ♗xf6 13 b4 ♖c8 and here:
d1) Interesting is 14 ♖ac1!? g6 15 ♘a4 ♗e7 16 ♘c5 ♗xc5 17 dxc5 (17

♕xc5 is also slightly better for White) 17...♖c7 18 ♕b2 ♕e7 (18...♗c8 19 b5 cxb5 20 ♗xb5 ±) 19 ♖fe1! ± intending e4, Djurić-Nogueiras, Saint John 1988.

d2) 14 ♘a4 ♖c7 (14...g6 15 ♖ac1 ♗e7 16 ♘c5 ♖c7 17 ♕a4 a6 18 ♕b3 ♗d6 19 a4 ♗c8 20 b5 axb5 21 axb5 ♕f6 22 ♗e2 g5 23 ♘h2 ± Huss-Kelečević, Winterthur 1996) 15 ♖ac1 (15 ♘c5 ♗c8 ∞) 15...♗e7! 16 ♕b1 ♗d6 17 b5 ♕f6 18 bxc6 bxc6 19 ♘h2 ♕h4 20 ♗f5! ♕h5 21 ♗xe6 ♘xe6 22 ♘f3 ± Karpov-Campora, San Nicolas (2) 1994.

e) 12 ♖fc1!? ♘6d7 (or: 12...♘h5 13 ♗xe7 ♕xe7 14 ♖ab1 g6 15 b4 a6 16 ♘a4 ♘g7 17 ♘c5 ♗f5 18 a4 ± Khenkin-Grosar, Sochi 1989; 12...♖c8 13 a3 ♘6d7 14 ♗f4 ♘b6 15 ♘a4 ♘xa4 16 ♕xa4 ♕b6 17 b4 ± Spraggett-Lobron, Marseilles 1989) 13 ♗f4 ♘b6 14 ♖ab1 ♗d6 (14...♘g6!? 15 ♗h2 a5! ∞ deserves serious attention) 15 ♘e2 ♘g6 (15...a5 16 ♕b3 ♗xf4 17 ♘xf4 ♗c8 18 a4 ±) 16 ♗xd6 ♕xd6 17 a4! ± (17 b4 ♘c4 18 ♗xc4 dxc4 19 ♘c3 b5 20 a4 a6 21 ♖d1 ♕e7 ∞) Karpov-Kharitonov, USSR Ch (Moscow) 1988.

We now return to 12 ♘e5 (D):

**12...♘6d7 13 ♗xe7 ♖xe7**
Black has also played 13...♕xe7 14 f4 f6 15 ♘f3 (piece exchanges such as 15 ♘xd7 ♕xd7 = only help Black) 15...♗f7 (15...b6 16 ♖ae1 ♕d6 17 ♕f2 ♖ad8 18 ♘e2 c5 19 f5 ♗f7 20 g3 c4 21 ♗b1 b5 22 ♘f4 a5 23 g4 ± Polak-Pelletier, Bern 1993; White has brought all his forces to the kingside to enhance his attack) 16 ♖ae1 c5 17 ♕f2 ♘b6 18 ♘h4 (White probes Black's weaknesses) 18...cxd4 19 exd4 ♕c7 (intending 20...♖xe1 21 ♖xe1 ♖e8 =) 20 ♖c1 ♕d8 21 f5 (21 ♘b5 ♘c4 22 b3 a6 23 bxc4 dxc4 24 ♗xc4 ♗xc4 25 ♖xc4 axb5 26 ♖c5 ♘e6 27 ♖xb5 ♕xd4 is equal, M.Gurevich-Akopian, Barcelona 1992) 21...♖c8 22 g3 intending ♘g2-f4, and White is slightly better.

**14 f4 f6 15 ♘f3 ♘b6**
15...♗f7!? deserves attention: 16 ♖ae1 ♕c7 17 g4 ♖ae8 18 ♕f2 ♘b6 19 b3 ♘c8 ∞ intending ...♘d6 – analysis.

**16 ♖ae1 ♘c8 17 g4 ♘d6 18 ♕g2**
Kramnik recommends 18 f5!? ♗f7 19 ♕h2 ±.

**18...♔h8 19 f5 ♗f7 20 ♔h1 ♕e8!**
20...♕c7 21 ♖g1 g5 22 h4 h6 23 ♕h2 ♘e8 24 ♖g3 ♘h7 25 ♔g2 is slightly better for White, Kramnik-Renet, Paris 1995.

**21 ♕g3**
21 g5!? ∞.

**21...♖d8 22 ♕f4 b5 23 g5**
White is slightly better.

**Conclusion:** Practice shows that the Exchange Variation gives White a very pleasant game, since Black's possibilities for counterplay are limited.

# 11 The Catalan Opening

If Black chooses to defend the Queen's Gambit, then he must also be prepared to face the Catalan Opening, which can arise after the moves...

**1 d4 d5 2 c4 e6 3 ♘f3 ♘f6 4 g3** *(D)*

It is possible to recommend two moves for Black:
**A: 4...dxc4**  171
**B: 4...♗e7**  177

Note that in Line B we shall also focus on the active Open Catalan treatment with a later ...dxc4 (if permitted), rather than the Closed Catalan where Black maintains a pawn on d5 at the cost of a passive position.

## A)

**4...dxc4 5 ♗g2**

There are those who prefer 5 ♕a4+, to which Black can reply 5...♘bd7:
a) 6 ♕xc4 b6 7 ♗g2 ♗b7 8 0-0 c5 and now:
a1) 9 ♖d1 a6 10 dxc5 ♗xc5 11 b4 ♗e7 12 ♗b2 b5 13 ♕d4 ♖c8 14 ♘bd2

0-0 15 a3 ♖c2?! (15...♕b6 =; 15...♖c7 =) 16 ♘e1 ♖c7 17 ♗xb7 ♖xb7 18 ♘b3 ± Karpov-Korchnoi, Moscow Ct (22) 1974.
a2) 9 ♘c3 a6! (intending ...b5) 10 dxc5 ♗xc5 11 ♗g5 (11 a3?! b5 12 ♕f4 0-0 13 e4 ♖c8 = Arbakov-Kharitonov, Irkutsk 1983) 11...h6 12 ♗xf6 ♘xf6 (12...♕xf6!? 13 ♖ad1 ♖c8 14 ♕d3 ♘b8 15 ♘d2 ♗xg2 16 ♔xg2 0-0 = Andersson-A.Sokolov, Belfort 1988) 13 ♕a4+ ♘d7 14 ♖fd1 b5 15 ♕f4 g5 16 ♕d2 ♕e7 with equality, Andersson-Tal, Bugojno 1980.
b) 6 ♗g2 a6 *(D)* and now:

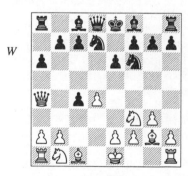

b1) 7 ♘e5?! c5 8 dxc5 ♗xc5 9 ♘xd7 ♗xd7 10 ♕xc4 ♖c8 ∓ Mate-Baburin, Budapest 1990.
b2) 7 ♘c3 ♖b8 8 ♕xc4 b5 and here:
b21) 9 ♕b3 ♗b7 10 0-0 (10 ♗f4 ♖c8 11 ♖d1 c5 12 dxc5 ♗xc5 13 0-0 ♕b6 = Panov-Makogonov, USSR Ch (Leningrad) 1939) 10...c5 11 ♗e3 ♗e7

12 dxc5 ♘xc5 13 ♕d1 0-0 14 ♕xd8 ♖fxd8 15 ♖fd1 ♔f8 is equal, Petrosian-Panno, Los Angeles 1963.

b22) 9 ♕d3 ♗b7 10 0-0 c5 11 ♗f4 (11 a3?! cxd4 12 ♕xd4 ♗c5 13 ♕h4 ♘d5 14 ♗g5 f6 15 ♗d2 ♘xc3 16 ♗xc3 0-0 17 ♖ad1 ♕e7 = Keres-Bondarevsky, Leningrad/Moscow 1941) 11...♖c8 12 dxc5 ♗xc5 13 ♖ad1 (13 ♘g5 ♗xg2 14 ♔xg2 ♕b6 15 ♖ad1 0-0 =) 13...0-0 14 ♘e5 ♗xg2 15 ♔xg2 ♘xe5 16 ♗xe5 ♗e7 17 ♕f3 ♕a5 18 ♕b7 ♖fe8 19 a3 b4 20 ♗xf6 gxf6 21 axb4 ♕xb4 22 ♕xb4 ♗xb4 23 ♘e4 ♔g7 24 ♘d6 ½-½ Andersson-Kasparov, Belgrade (6) 1985.

b3) 7 ♕xc4 b5 and then:

b31) 8 ♕d3 ♗b7 9 0-0 c5 10 a4 ♕b6 11 axb5 axb5 12 ♖xa8+ ♗xa8 13 ♘c3 b4 14 ♘a4 ♕a5 =.

b32) 8 ♕b3 ♗b7 9 a4 b4 10 0-0 c5 11 ♗g5 ♗d5 12 ♕e3 ♕b6 = Petursson-Hjartarson, Akureyri 1994.

b33) 8 ♕c2 ♗b7 9 0-0 c5 10 a4 cxd4!? 11 ♘xd4 ♗xg2 12 ♔xg2 ♗c5 13 ♘b3 ♗e7 14 ♗g5 0-0 15 axb5 axb5 16 ♘1d2 ♘b6 = Smyslov-Keres, Moscow 1967.

b34) 8 ♕c6 ♖b8 9 ♗f4 (9 ♗g5 ♗b7 10 ♕c2 c5 11 dxc5 ♗xc5 12 0-0 ♖c8 13 ♕d3 0-0 = Smyslov-Tal, Montpellier Ct 1985) 9...♘d5 10 ♗g5 ♗e7 11 ♗xe7 ♕xe7 12 ♘c3 (12 0-0 ♗b7 13 ♕c2 c5 14 dxc5 ♘xc5 15 ♘c3 0-0 16 ♘xd5 ♗xd5 17 ♖fc1 ♘a4 18 ♘e5 ♗xg2 19 ♔xg2 ♕b7+ 20 ♔g1 ♖bc8 = Portisch-Hübner, Turin 1982) 12...♗b7 13 ♘xd5 ♗xc6 14 ♘xe7 ♔xe7 15 0-0 (15 ♖c1 ♖b6 16 0-0 ♖c8 17 ♘g5 ♗xg2 18 ♔xg2 ♖d6! = Gleizerov-Serper, Moscow 1992) 15...♗xf3 16 ♗xf3 c5 17 dxc5 ♘xc5 18 ♖fc1 ♖hc8 19 ♖c2 ♘d7 20 ♖ac1 ♘b6 21 ♖xc8

♖xc8 22 ♖xc8 ♘xc8 23 ♗b7 ♘d6 24 ♗xa6 ♔d7 25 b3 ♔c6 26 a4 ♔b6 27 ♗xb5 ♘xb5 28 axb5 ♔xb5 29 ♔g2 ♔b4 30 ♔f3 ♔xb3 ½-½ Wojtkiewicz-Kaidanov, New York 1993.

**5...a6** (D)

This continuation has been the most popular in recent years.

**6 0-0**

Other continuations have also been tried:

a) 6 a4 ♘c6 7 0-0 ♖b8 (7...♘a5!? deserves attention: 8 ♘bd2 c5 9 dxc5 ♗xc5 10 ♘e5 c3! 11 bxc3 0-0 12 ♘ec4 {12 ♕c2 ♕c7 =; 12 ♘dc4 ♘xc4 13 ♕xd8 ♖xd8 14 ♘xc4 ♘d5 15 ♖d1 ♗d7 16 ♗xd5 ♗c6 17 ♗e3 ♗xd5 =} 12...♗e7 13 ♘xa5 ♕xa5 is equal, Gulko-Bronstein, Vilnius 1975) and now:

a1) 8 ♗g5!? ♗e7 9 ♘c3 0-0 10 e4 b5 11 axb5 axb5 12 ♖e1 ♘b4 13 b3! ♘d3 14 ♖e2 ∞ Simić-Krasenkov, Ptuj 1989.

a2) 8 ♘c3 ♗b4 9 ♕c2 (9 e4 ♗xc3 10 bxc3 ♘xe4 11 ♕c2 ♘d6 12 ♖e1 ♘e7 ∓; 9 ♗g5 h6 10 ♗xf6 ♕xf6 11 e4 0-0 12 e5 ♕e7 ∓) 9...♘xd4 10 ♘xd4 ♕xd4 11 ♖d1 ♕e5 12 ♗f4 ♕a5 13 ♘a2 ♗d6 14 ♖xd6 cxd6 15 ♗xd6 ♖a8

16 ♕xc4 ♕b6 17 ♗a3 ♗d7 ∞ Kožul-Rødgaard, Elista OL 1998.

a3) 8 a5 and then:

a31) 8...♗b4!? 9 ♕c2! ♘xa5 (alternatively, 9...♗xa5 10 ♘e5 ♘xd4 11 ♕a4+ ♗d7 12 ♕xa5 ♘b3 13 ♕a3 ♘xa1 14 ♕xa1 ±) 10 ♕a4+ ♘c6 11 ♘e5 ♘d5 12 ♘xc6 bxc6 13 ♕xc6+ ♗d7 14 ♕xc4 0-0 15 ♖d1 (15 ♕c2 ♗e7 is level, Alburt-Portisch, Malta OL 1980) 15...c5! 16 e4 (16 dxc5?! ♗b5 17 ♕c2 ♕e7 with compensation) 16...♘b6 17 ♕b3 a5! (17...♕e7? 18 ♗f4 ♖a8 19 d5! ± Gleizerov-S.Ivanov, Slupsk 1992) 18 ♗f4 ♖a8 19 dxc5 (19 d5? exd5 20 exd5 ♗g4 21 ♖c1 c4 ∓) 19...♗xc5 =.

a32) 8...b5 9 axb6 cxb6 10 ♗f4 (10 e4!?) 10...♗d6 11 ♘e5 ♘e7 12 e4 (12 ♘xc4 ♗xf4 13 gxf4 0-0 14 e3 ♘fd5 15 ♘e5 ♗b7 16 ♘d2 ♘g6 = Timoshchenko-Novikov, Nova Gorica 1997; 12 ♘c6 ♘xc6 13 ♗xc6+ ♔e7 14 ♗g5 h6 15 ♗xf6+ gxf6 16 ♘d2 b5 ∓ Hough-Kaidanov, Philadelphia 1993) 12...♗b7 13 ♘c3 0-0 (13...b5? 14 ♘xf7! ♔xf7 15 ♗xd6 ♕xd6 16 e5 ♕b6 17 ♗xb7 ♕xb7 18 exf6 gxf6 19 ♖e1 ± Petursson-Zlatilov, Andorra 1991) 14 ♗g5 b5 15 ♗xf6 gxf6 16 ♘g4 ♘g6 17 h4 b4 and now White should opt for 18 ♘a4! with compensation, rather than 18 ♘e2?! f5! 19 exf5 ♗xg2 20 ♔xg2 exf5 21 ♘h6+ ♔h8 22 ♘xf5 ♖b5! ∞ Petursson-Oll, Groningen FIDE 1997.

b) 6 ♘e5 c5 (D) and here:

b1) 7 ♘a3!? cxd4 8 ♘axc4 ♖a7! and now:

b11) 9 a4 b6 10 0-0 ♗b7 11 ♕b3 ♗xg2 12 ♔xg2 ♕d5+ 13 f3 ♗c5 (13...♘fd7!?) 14 e4 ♕b7 15 ♘d3 0-0 16 a5 ♘bd7 17 axb6 ♗xb6 18 ♗g5

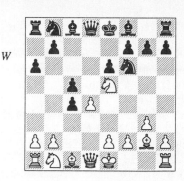

♖fa8 19 ♖a4 ♘c5 20 ♘xc5 ♗xc5 21 ♕xb7 ♖xb7 22 ♗d2 ♘d7 ∓ Berezin-Novikov, Donetsk Z 1998.

b12) 9 0-0 b5 10 ♘d2 ♗c5 11 ♘b3 ♗b6 12 ♗c6+?! ♘xc6! 13 ♘xc6 ♕d5 14 ♘xa7 ♗b7 15 f3 ♗xa7 intending ...h5, with the initiative, Hartung Nielsen-Kaluzhin, corr. 1979-81.

b13) 9 ♗d2 b6 10 ♕b3 ♗b7 11 ♗xb7 ♖xb7 12 ♘a5 ♖e7!? (12...♖a7!? 13 0-0 ♘e4 14 ♕a4+ b5 15 ♕c2 ♘xd2 16 ♕xd2 ♕d5 17 ♘f3 ♗c5 = Dizdar-Novikov, Lucerne Wcht 1997) 13 ♘ac6 ♘xc6 14 ♘xc6 ♕a8 15 ♖c1 (15 ♕xb6? ♘d7) 15...♖c7 16 ♕xb6 ♘d5 17 ♕b8+ ♕xb8 18 ♘xb8 ♖xc1+ 19 ♗xc1 ♗d6 20 ♘c6 (20 ♘xa6 ♔d7 21 b4 ♖c8 22 ♔d2 ♖a8 23 b5 ♘c3 24 a4 ♘xa4 25 ♔d3 ♘c3 26 ♔xd4 ♘xb5+ 27 ♔c4 ♖xa6 28 ♔xb5 ♖a2 ∓ Rashkovsky-A.Petrosian, Erevan 1984) 20...e5 21 ♘a5 ♔d7 22 ♘c4 =.

b2) 7 ♗e3 ♘d5! 8 dxc5 (8 0-0?! ♘d7 9 ♘xc4 b5 10 ♘cd2 ♘xe3 11 fxe3 ♖b8 12 ♘e4 f5! 13 ♘f2 ♗e7 14 e4 0-0 15 e3 ♗g5 16 ♕d3 ♘b6 ∓ Hort-Portisch, Nice OL 1974; 8 ♘c3!? ♘xe3 9 fxe3 ♘d7 10 ♘xc4 ♗e7 11 0-0 0-0 is equal, Verat-Rotshtein, Cannes 1992) 8...♘d7 (8...f6!? deserves serious attention: 9 ♘xc4 ♘xe3

10 ♕xd8+ ♔xd8 11 fxe3 {11 ♘xe3 ♗xc5 =} 11...♗xc5 12 ♘c3 ♖a7 13 ♘e4 ♗b4+ 14 ♔f2 b5 = Beliavsky-Csom, Vilnius 1978) and now:

b21) If 9 ♘xc4, then 9...♘xe3 10 ♘xe3 ♗xc5 11 ♘c4 ♕c7 (11...0-0!? 12 0-0 ♕c7 13 ♕b3 ♖b8 14 ♘c3 b5 15 ♘d2 ♗b7 16 ♗xb7 ♕xb7 17 a4 ½-½ Langeweg-Ree, Netherlands 1981) 12 ♘bd2 ♖b8 13 a4 ♘f6 14 0-0 0-0 15 ♖c1 b5 16 axb5 axb5 17 ♘e3 ♕b6 ∓ Basin-Razuvaev, Minsk 1985.

b22) 9 ♗d4 ♘xe5 10 ♗xe5 ♗xc5!? 11 ♗xg7 ♖g8 12 ♗c3 (12 ♗d4? ♘f4! −+; 12 ♗e5 ♕g5! 13 ♗d4 {13 f4 ♕d8 14 ♗xd5 ♕xd5 15 ♕xd5 exd5 ½-½ Tratar-A.Petrosian, Ljubljana 1995} 13...♗xd4 14 ♕xd4 ♕c1+ 15 ♕d1 ♕xb2 16 ♘d2 ∞ Vasiljević-Novikov, Tuzla 1989) 12...b5 (12...♘xc3 13 ♘xc3 ±) 13 ♗d4 ♕b6 14 ♗xc5 ♕xc5 15 ♘c3 ♗b7 16 ♘xd5 ♗xd5 17 ♗xd5 ♖d8 18 0-0 ♖xd5 = Salov-Portisch, Brussels 1988.

**6...♘c6** (D)

W

The most popular and, it seems, the strongest move.

**7 e3**

The main continuation. However, White may also choose:

a) 7 ♘a3!? (with this typical Catalan move, White, in return for a broken pawn formation, obtains the bishop-pair, the b-file and the possibility of active play in the centre) 7...♗xa3 8 bxa3 0-0 9 ♗b2 ♖b8 10 ♕c2 b5 11 ♖ad1 and now:

a1) 11...♘e7 12 e4 ♖b6 (12...♗b7 13 ♘g5 {13 ♘e5!?} 13...h6 14 ♘h3 ♘d7 15 ♘f4 ♕e8 ∞ Rashkovsky-A.Petrosian, Baku 1977) 13 ♖fe1 (13 ♘h4?! ♗b7 14 ♖fe1 ♕a8 15 ♕e2 ♘g6 16 ♘xg6 hxg6 17 g4 a5 ∞ Kožul-Davidović, Liechtenstein 1989) 13...♖e8 14 ♗c3 ♘g6 15 h4 h6 16 ♗a5 ♖b8 17 ♘e5 ♘e7 18 g4 with the initiative for White, Grebionkin-Kozirev, Ekaterinburg 1996.

a2) 11...♖b6!? 12 e4 (12 d5? exd5 13 ♘g5 g6 ∓; 12 ♘g5 h6 13 d5 hxg5 14 dxc6 ♕e7 15 ♗d4 {15 ♗c3 ♕xa3} 15...♖b8 ∓) 12...♗b7! (12...h6 13 ♘h4 ♕e7 14 ♗c3 ♘e8 15 ♗b4 with compensation, Zafirovski-Ostojić, Yugoslav Cht (Nikšić) 1997) and then:

a21) 13 d5? exd5 14 e5 (14 exd5 ♘e7 ∓) 14...♘d7 15 ♖xd5? ♘b4 −+.

a22) 13 ♘e5 ♘xe5 14 dxe5 ♘d7 15 ♗d4 (15 ♕d2 ♗c6) 15...♖c6 16 f4 ♕e7 ∓.

a23) 13 ♖fe1!? ♘e7 14 ♗c3 ♕a8 15 ♘e5 a5 ∞.

a24) 13 ♘g5 ♘d7 14 h4 (14 f4 h6 15 ♘f3 ♘e7 intending ...♕a8) 14...h6 15 ♘h3 (15 d5 hxg5 16 dxc6 ♗xc6 ∓) 15...♖e8! and here:

a241) 16 f4 f5!? intends to meet 17 exf5 with 17...exf5 18 ♕xf5 ♘e7 ∓.

a242) 16 ♘f4?! e5! 17 dxe5 (17 ♘d5 ♘xd4 18 ♗xd4 exd4 19 ♘xb6 ♘xb6 ∓) 17...♘cxe5 18 ♕c3 ♖d6 19 ♘d5 ♗xd5 20 ♖xd5 (20 exd5 ♘f6 ∓) 20...♖xd5 21 exd5 ♘f6 and Black has a clear advantage, Shipov-Se.Ivanov, St Petersburg 1998.

a243) 16 ♕c3!? f6 17 f4 ∞.

a244) 16 d5 exd5 17 exd5 ♘ce5 18 ♘f4 ♘c5!? 19 ♗d4 ♘cd3 20 ♗xb6 cxb6 21 ♘xd3 ♘xd3 22 ♖xd3 cxd3 23 ♕xd3 =.

b) 7 ♘c3 ♖b8 *(D)* and now:

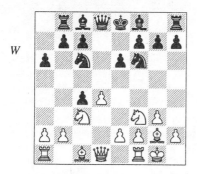

b1) 8 ♘e5?! ♘xe5 9 dxe5 ♕xd1 (9...♘d7!?) 10 ♖xd1 ♘d7 11 f4 b5 12 a4 b4 13 ♘e4 and then:

b11) 13...♗b7 14 ♘d2! (14 ♖d4? ♗d5 ∓) 14...♗xg2 (14...♗d5!? 15 e4 ♗c6 16 ♘xc4 ♘c5 17 ♗e3 ♘xa4 {17...♘b3 18 ♖a2 ∞} 18 ♖dc1 with compensation) 15 ♔xg2 c3 16 bxc3 bxc3 17 ♘c4 ∞ Rogers-Barsov, Netherlands 1997.

b12) 13...♘c5!? 14 ♗e3 ♘b3 15 ♖ac1! ♘xc1 16 ♘f6+! gxf6 17 ♗c6+ ♗d7 18 ♗xd7+ (18 ♖xd7 can be answered by 18...♘b3! = intending to meet 19 exf6? by 19...♗c5, while 18...♗e7!? also deserves serious attention) 18...♔d8 19 ♗xe6+ ♔e7 20 ♗xc4 with compensation.

b2) 8 e4 ♗e7! (8...b5?! 9 d5! ♘b4 10 b3! with compensation) and now:

b21) 9 ♕e2!? b5 10 ♖d1 0-0 11 d5 (11 ♗g5 ♘b4 12 ♘e5 ♘d7! 13 ♘xd7 ♗xd7 14 ♗e3 ♕c8 15 a4 ♖d8 ∓ Raetsky-Sveshnikov, Rostov-on-Don 1993) 11...exd5 12 e5 ♘d7 13 ♘xd5 ♘b4! 14 e6! (14 ♘xb4 ♗xb4 15 ♘d4 ♖b6 16 ♘c6 ♖xc6 17 ♗xc6 ♕e7 18 ♗f4 ♘c5 19 a3 ♗a5 with compensation, Summermatter-Sveshnikov, Bern 1992) 14...♘xd5 15 exd7 ♗b7 16 ♘e5 with compensation.

b22) 9 d5 exd5 10 exd5 ♘b4 11 ♘e5 ♗f5 12 a3 (12 ♗g5?! 0-0 13 a3 ♘bxd5! 14 ♘xd5 ♘xd5 15 ♗xd5 ♗xg5 16 ♕f3 ♕f6 17 ♖fe1 ♗e6! and Black has a clear advantage, Wojtkiewicz-Kveinys, Polish Cht (Mikolajki) 1991; 12 ♘xc4 ♗d3 ∓) 12...♘d3 13 ♘xc4 ♘xc1 14 ♖xc1 0-0 15 b4 (15 h3 ♘e8! 16 ♖e1 ♘d6 17 ♘e5 ♗f6 18 f4 ♖e8 19 ♕f3 h6 20 ♖e2 ♖e7 21 ♖ce1 ♕f8 = Sosonko-Am.Rodriguez, Amsterdam 1989) 15...♘e8! (another plan is 15...♖e8 16 ♕d4 ♗d6 17 ♖fe1 ♕d7 18 ♖xe8+ {18 ♘xd6 cxd6 19 ♕f4 h6 = Martin-Gligorić, Buenos Aires 1955} 18...♖xe8 19 ♘e3 ♗h3 (19...♗g6 20 ♕a7! ♕c8 21 ♘a4 ♕b8 22 ♕xb8 ♖xb8 23 ♘c4 ♗f5 24 ♘xd6 cxd6 25 ♘b6 ± Haba-Arbakov, Chemnitz 1997) 20 ♕a7 ♗xg2 21 ♔xg2 c6! =) 16 ♕f3 g6 17 ♖fe1 ♘d6 18 ♘xd6 ♗xd6 19 ♘e4 ♗xe4 20 ♖xe4 ♕g5 = Ruck-Tukmakov, Croatian Cht (Poreč) 1998.

**7...♗d7** *(D)*

**8 ♕e2**

Practice has also seen 8 ♘c3 ♖b8 9 ♘e5 (9 ♕e2 b5 10 ♖d1 ♗d6! 11 e4 e5 12 dxe5 ♗xe5! 13 ♘d5 ♗g4 14 ♗e3 0-0 and now, rather than 15 h3 ♗xf3 16 ♗xf3 ♘xd5 17 exd5 ♘b4 18 ♗a7 ♕f6! 19 ♗xb8 ♖xb8 20 ♖d2 c3 ∓ Veingold-Sveshnikov, Tallinn 1988, White should try 15 ♗c5, although

W

W

15...♗d6 16 ♘xc7 ♗xc5 17 ♖xd8 ♖bxd8 gives Black good compensation for the queen) 9...♘a5 (9...♘xe5?! 10 dxe5 ♘g8 11 ♕e2 b5 12 ♖d1 with compensation) and now:

a) 10 e4 ♗e7 (10...b5!? 11 g4 b4 12 g5 bxc3 13 bxc3! ♖b5 14 gxf6 gxf6 15 ♘xd7 ♕xd7 16 ♕f3 ♖g8 17 ♔h1 ½-½ Sosonko-Piket, Dutch Ch (Rotterdam) 1997; White has compensation) 11 ♗e3 0-0 12 ♕f3 b5 13 ♖ad1 b4 14 ♘e2 ♗b5 15 ♖fe1 ♘c6! ∓ Bernard-Korneev, Paris 1996.

b) 10 ♕e2 b5 11 ♖d1 ♗d6 12 e4 b4 13 ♘xd7 ♘xd7 14 ♘b1 0-0 15 e5 ♗e7 16 d5 ♗c5 17 ♘d2 ♕e7 18 ♘e4 ♖b5 19 ♗g5 ♕e8 with compensation, Tratar-Sveshnikov, Ljubljana 1994.

**8...b5 9 ♘c3**
Or:

a) 9 ♘e5 ♘xe5! 10 ♗xa8 (10 dxe5 ♘d5 11 ♖d1 c6 12 b3 cxb3 13 axb3 ♕c7) 10...♕xa8 11 dxe5 ♘e4 12 a4 (12 f3 ♘c5 13 e4 ♗e7 14 ♗e3 0-0 15 ♖d1 ♕c6 with compensation) 12...♕b7 13 axb5 axb5 14 f3 ♘c5 with compensation, Janssen-Piket, Dutch Ch (Rotterdam) 1999.

b) 9 ♖d1 ♗e7 *(D)* and now:
b1) 10 ♘c3 ♘d5! 11 e4 (11 a4?! 0-0 12 axb5 ♘xc3 13 bxc3 axb5 14

♖xa8 ♕xa8 15 d5 exd5 16 ♖xd5 ♕e8! 17 ♕d1 ♘b8! ∓ Beliavsky-Akopian, Pula Echt 1997) 11...♘xc3 12 bxc3 0-0 13 d5 exd5 14 exd5 ♘a5 15 ♘e5 with compensation.

b2) 10 b3 cxb3 11 axb3 0-0 12 e4 (12 ♘c3 b4 13 ♘e5 ♘xe5 14 dxe5 ♖a7 15 exf6 ♗xf6 16 ♕d3 ♗xc3 17 ♖a2 c5 18 ♗c6 ♕b6 19 ♗xd7 ♖d8 ∓ Ginting-Korneev, Jakarta 1997) 12...♕c8!? (12...♗c8 13 ♘c3 ♗b7 14 d5 with compensation, Polugaevsky-A.N.Panchenko, Sochi 1981) 13 ♘c3 ♖d8 ∞.

b3) 10 e4 0-0 11 ♘c3 ♖e8 12 ♘e5 ♖b8 (12...h6!? 13 a4 ♖b8 14 axb5 axb5 ½-½ Krasenkov-A.N.Panchenko, Belgorod 1990) 13 ♗e3 and then:

b31) 13...h6 14 ♘xf7 ♔xf7 15 e5 ♘b4 16 exf6 ♗xf6 17 ♘e4 ♔g8! (17...♕e7?! 18 ♘c5 ♗c6? {better is 18...♖b6 ∞} 19 ♗xc6 ♘xc6 20 ♘xa6 ± Cvitan-Dautov, Dresden Z 1998) 18 ♕g4 (18 ♘c5 ♗c6 19 ♗xc6 ♘xc6 20 ♘xa6 ♖a8 21 ♘c5 ♕d5 22 ♕g4 h5 23 ♕f4 ♖ad8 ∓) 18...♘c2 19 ♖ac1 ♘xe3 20 fxe3 ♖f8 21 ♘c5 ♖b6 22 ♖f1 with compensation.

b32) 13...♗f8 14 ♖ac1 h6 15 ♖d2 ♘a5 16 ♕f3 ♗c8 17 h4 ♗b7 18 ♕f4 ♕e7 19 g4 (White has compensation) 19...♘d7! 20 ♘xd7 ♕xd7 21 g5 hxg5

22 hxg5 ♗b4 23 ♕h4 ♘c6 24 a3 ♗xc3 25 bxc3 ♘e7 ½-½ Urban-Dautov, Pula Echt 1997.

We now return to 9 ♘c3 *(D)*:

**9...♗d6 10 e4 ♗e7 11 d5**

Or: 11 ♖d1 0-0 12 ♗g5 h6 13 ♗xf6 ♗xf6 14 e5 ♗e7 15 d5 ♘b4 16 ♘e1 exd5 17 ♘xd5 ♖b8! 18 ♘xb4 ♗xb4 19 ♗h3 ♗xh3 20 ♖xd8 ♖fxd8 with compensation, Kakhiani-Galliamova, Azov wom IZ 1990; 11 ♗g5 0-0 12 ♖ad1 (12 ♗xf6!?) 12...♖b8 13 ♖fe1 ♖e8 14 ♘e5 h6 15 ♗e3 again with compensation, Orlov-A.Shneider, Podolsk 1989.

**11...♘b4**

11...exd5?! 12 e5 ±.

**12 ♘e5**

12 dxe6 ♗xe6 13 ♖d1 ♕c8 ∞.

**12...exd5 13 exd5 0-0 14 a3 ♘d3 15 ♘xd3 ♗g4 16 ♕e3**

16 f3?! cxd3 17 ♕xd3 ♗h5 ∓.

**16...cxd3 17 ♕xd3**

17 h3 ♗f5 18 g4 ♗g6 19 f4 ♘d7! with counterplay for Black.

**17...♕d7 18 ♗f4**

18 ♖e1 ♖fe8 19 ♕f1 ♗d6 20 ♖xe8+ ♖xe8 21 ♗d2 ♗e5 = Aseev-Sveshnikov, Tashkent 1984.

**18...♗d6 19 ♗xd6 cxd6**

19...♕xd6 20 h3 ♗d7 21 ♘e4! ± Karpov-Gelfand, Dos Hermanas 1999.

**20 ♖fe1 ♖fe8 21 ♘e4 ♘xe4 22 ♗xe4 h6 23 ♖ac1**

White has a slight advantage.

**B)**

**4...♗e7 5 ♗g2 0-0** *(D)*

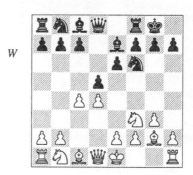

Now:

**B1: 6 ♕c2**    177
**B2: 6 ♘c3**    179
**B3: 6 0-0**    180

**B1)**

**6 ♕c2 c5**

The cunning point of White's queen move is seen in the line 6...dxc4 7 ♕xc4 a6 8 ♗f4! (8 0-0 transposes to Line B331):

a) 8...♘d5 9 ♘c3 b5 10 ♕d3 ♗b7 11 ♘xd5 ♗xd5 12 0-0 ♘d7 (12...c5 13 dxc5 ♗xc5 14 ♘g5 g6 15 ♖ad1 ±) 13 ♖fd1 c5 (13...f5 14 ♖ac1! ♗d6 15 ♘e5 ±) 14 e4 ♗b7 15 d5 exd5 16 exd5 ♗f6 17 ♕c2 ♖e8 18 h4! h6 19 ♘d2 ♕b6 20 ♘e4 ± Dorfman-Bönsch, Lvov 1984.

b) 8...♗d6 9 ♘e5 ♘d5 10 ♘c3 ♘xf4 11 gxf4 ♘d7 12 e3 ♕e7 13 0-0 ♖b8 14 ♘e4 and White has a slight advantage, Kasparov-Andersson, Belgrade (5) 1985.

**7 0-0**

The main continuation. However, in addition to the text-move, White can play:

a) 7 cxd5 and now:

a1) 7...♘xd5 8 dxc5 (8 0-0 cxd4 9 ♘xd4 ♘c6 10 ♘xc6 bxc6 11 ♘c3 ♖b8 12 ♗d2 ♗a6 13 ♖fd1 ♕c8 14 ♗f3 ♖d8 = Kengis-I.Zaitsev, Moscow 1986) 8...♕a5+ 9 ♗d2 ♕xc5 10 ♘c3 ♘c6 (10...b6!?) 11 ♖c1 ♘db4 (11...♘f6 12 ♗e3 ♕a5 13 0-0 ♗d7 14 ♖fd1 ±) 12 ♕b3 a5 13 a3 ±.

a2) 7...cxd4 8 ♘xd4 (8 dxe6 ♗xe6 =) 8...♘xd5 9 ♕b3 ♘c6 10 ♘xc6 bxc6 11 e4 ♘b4 12 0-0 c5! 13 ♘a3 ♘c6 14 ♗e3 ♖b8 15 ♕c3 ♘d4 16 ♔h1 ♗a6 17 ♖fd1 e5 18 b3 ♕c8 19 ♕a5 ♖b4 ∓ K.Grigorian-Vyzhmanavin, Pinsk 1996.

b) 7 dxc5 ♕a5+ *(D)* and now:

b1) 8 ♗d2 is met by 8...♕xc5.

b2) 8 ♕c3 ♕xc5 9 cxd5 ♘xd5 10 ♕xc5 ♗xc5 11 0-0 ♘c6 12 a3 ♗d7 13 ♘bd2 ♘d4 14 ♘xd4 ♗xd4 15 ♘f3 ♗b6 16 ♗d2 ♖ac8 17 ♖fc1 ♖xc1+ 18 ♖xc1 ♖c8 = Korchnoi-Tal, Moscow Ct (2) 1968.

b3) 8 ♘bd2 ♕xc5 and here:

b31) 9 0-0 b6 (9...b5!?; 9...♘c6!? 10 a3 dxc4 11 ♕xc4 ±) 10 a3 ♗b7 11 b4 ♕c7 12 ♗b2 ♘bd7 13 ♖ac1 ♖ac8 14 ♕b1 ♕b8 = Donchenko-Levin, Belgorod 1989.

b32) 9 a3 a5 10 0-0 (10 b4 ♕c7) 10...♘c6 11 ♕d3 a4 12 cxd5 ♕xd5 13 ♕xd5 ♘xd5 = Zara-Anikaev, Graz 1972.

b4) 8 ♘c3 dxc4 9 ♘d2 (9 0-0 ♕xc5 10 ♗e3 ♕h5 11 h3 ♘c6 12 ♖fd1 ♗d7 13 ♘e4 ♖fd8 14 ♕xc4 ♘xe4 15 ♕xe4 ♗e8 16 ♕c2 h6 = Ehlvest-Vyzhmanavin, Lvov 1985) 9...♕xc5 10 ♘a4 ♕a5 11 ♕xc4 (Korchnoi-Short, Lucerne Wcht 1989) 11...♘c6!? 12 0-0 (12 ♗xc6? bxc6 13 0-0 ♗a6) 12...♘e5!? 13 ♕c2 ♗d7 and Black has no problems.

**7...cxd4 8 ♘xd4 ♘c6 9 ♘xc6 bxc6 10 b3** *(D)*

White fianchettoes the bishop, and wants to exert pressure on Black's centre.

**10...♗a6**

Fully possible is also 10...a5!? 11 ♘c3 (11 ♗b2 a4! 12 ♘d2 axb3 13 axb3 ♗b7 14 ♖xa8 ♗xa8 15 e3 ♕b6 ½-½ Sher-Janjgava, Geneva 1995)

11...♗a6 12 ♖d1 ♘d7! 13 ♘a4 ♘h6 14 ♘xb6 ♕xb6 15 ♗e3 ♗c5 ½-½ Mochalov-Shariazdanov, Minsk 1998.

**11 ♗b2 ♖c8 12 e3**

12 ♘d2 is best met not by 12...d4 13 ♘f3 c5 14 e3! dxe3 15 fxe3, when 15...♗b7? loses to 16 ♘g5!, but by 12...c5 13 e3 ♕b6.

**12...♕b6 13 ♘d2 ♖fd8 14 ♖fd1 ♘d7 15 ♖ac1 ♗b7**

15...♗f6 =.

**16 ♘f3**

16 e4 e5 ∞; 16 ♕b1!? c5 17 ♕a1 ∞.

**16...c5 17 cxd5**

17 ♗c3?! ♘f6 18 ♕b2 ♗a6 with the initiative; 17 ♘e5? ♘xe5 18 ♗xe5 d4! ∓ Gulko-Karpov, Thessaloniki OL 1988.

**17...exd5 18 ♕f5 ♘f6 19 ♘g5**

The position is unclear.

**B2)**

**6 ♘c3 dxc4 (D)**

**7 ♘e5**

7 0-0 c5 8 dxc5 ♘c6 9 ♕a4 ♕a5 10 ♕xc4 ♕xc5 (10...e5!?) 11 ♕xc5 ♗xc5 12 ♗f4! (12 ♖d1 ♗d7 13 g4 h6 14 h4 ♖fd8 15 g5 hxg5 16 hxg5 ♘g4 17 ♘e4 ♗b6 18 ♗f4 e5 19 ♗g3 ♗e6 = Nogueiras-Armas, Havana 1991) 12...♗d7!

(12...♘d5 13 ♘xd5 exd5 14 ♖fd1 ♗e6 15 ♘e5 ±) 13 ♘e5 (13 ♖ac1 ♖fd8 =) 13...♘xe5 14 ♗xe5 ♘g4! (14...♗c6 15 ♗xc6 bxc6 16 ♗xf6 gxf6 17 ♖ac1 ±) 15 ♗f4 e5 16 ♖ad1 (16 ♗d2 ♖ab8 17 ♘e4 ♗e7 18 ♖ac1 ♖fc8 19 h3 ♘f6 20 ♘xf6+ ♗xf6 21 ♗e3 b6 is equal) 16...♖ad8 17 ♗g5 f6 18 ♗c1 b6 19 ♗d5+ (19 ♘e4 ♗e7 20 ♗h3?! ♗f5! 21 f3 ♘h6) 19...♔h8 20 h3 ♘h6 21 g4 ♘g8 22 ♘e4 ♗e7 23 ♘g3 ♗b5 24 ♗e3 ♗d6 = Tukmakov-Dokhoian, Lvov Z 1990.

**7...♘c6 8 ♗xc6 bxc6 9 ♘xc6 ♕e8 10 ♘xe7+ ♕xe7 11 ♕a4 c5 12 ♕xc4 cxd4 13 ♕xd4 e5 14 ♕h4 ♖b8**

14...♖d8 15 0-0 ♖d4 16 e4 ♗a6 17 ♖e1 h6 18 ♗e3 ♖c4 19 ♖ad1 ♖e8 20 f3 ♖c6 21 g4 ♗c4 22 ♕f2 ♕e6 23 b4 ± Karpov-Hjartarson, Belfort 1988.

**15 0-0**

If 15 ♗g5, then 15...♖xb2 16 0-0 ♕e6 17 ♗xf6 ♕xf6 18 ♕xf6 gxf6 19 ♖ab1 ♖xb1 20 ♖xb1 ♗e6 21 f3 ♖c8 22 ♖c1 ♖b8 23 ♖c2 ♖c8 24 ♔f2 ♗xa2 25 ♖xa2 ½-½ Korchnoi-Karpov, Baguio City Wch (15) 1978.

**15...♖b4 16 e4 ♕b7 17 ♖e1**

17 f3 ♕b6+ 18 ♖f2 h6 19 g4 ♖d8 20 g5 hxg5 21 ♗xg5 ♖xb2 22 ♗xf6 ♖dd2 23 ♘d1 ♖xf2 24 ♘xf2 ♕xf6 = Tukmakov-Levin, Riga 1988.

**17...♗g4!?**

A new continuation, instead of the previously seen 17...♗f5 18 f3 ♗e6 19 g4 ♖c8 20 ♖d1 a5 21 ♕e1 a4 22 ♗e3 ± Sorokin-Kruppa, Minsk 1990.

**18 ♗g5**

18 ♘d5?! ♘xd5 19 ♕xg4 f5! ∓; 18 ♗h6 ♗f5 19 ♕g5 ♗g6 20 ♕xe5 ♖e8.

**18...♘xe4 19 ♘xe4**

19 ♗e7? ♘xf2 −+; 19 ♕xg4? ♘xc3 is good for Black.

19...♖xe4 20 ♖xe4 ♕xe4 21 h3 ♗f3 22 ♕xe4 ♗xe4

The game is equal (analysis).

### B3)

6 0-0 dxc4 *(D)*

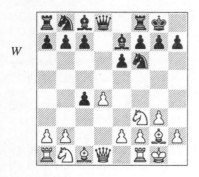

W

Now:

**B31: 7 ♘a3**    180
**B32: 7 ♘e5**    180
**B33: 7 ♕c2**    181

### B31)

7 ♘a3 ♗xa3 8 bxa3 ♗d7 9 ♘e5

Or: 9 ♕c2 ♗c6 10 ♕xc4 ♘bd7 11 ♗g5 h6 12 ♗xf6 ♘xf6 13 ♖fc1 ♕d6 14 ♘e5 ♗xg2 15 ♔xg2 ♘d5! 16 ♕b3 ♖ab8 17 ♖c2 c6 = Aseev-Rozentalis, Leningrad 1990; 9 ♗g5 ♗c6 10 ♗xf6 ♕xf6 11 ♕c2 ♘d7 12 ♕xc4 ♖fd8 13 ♖fd1 ♕e7 14 ♕d3 ♘f6 15 ♖ac1 ♗e4 = Murei-Geller, Moscow IZ 1982.

9...♗c6 10 ♘xc6

10 f3?! ♘d5! 11 ♕c2 ♘b6 12 ♗e3 ♗a4 13 ♕c1 ♘c6 14 ♘xc6 ♗xc6 15 ♗f2 f5 ∓ D.Gurevich-Janjgava, New York 1990.

10...♘xc6 11 ♗b2 ♘d5! 12 ♖b1

12 ♖c1 ♘b6 13 e3 (13 e4 ♘e7 14 ♕c2 ♕d7 15 ♗a1 f5!? is unclear) 13...♕d6 14 ♕g4 f6 15 ♖c2 ♘a4 16

♕h5 f5 ∓ Romanishin-Razuvaev, USSR Ch (Moscow) 1983.

12...♘b6 13 e3 ♕e7! 14 ♕c2 ♖fd8 15 ♖fd1 ♖d7! 16 ♕c3 ♕f8! 17 a4! a5 18 ♗a3 ♕d8 19 ♗c5 e5! 20 ♗xb6 cxb6 21 d5 ♘b4 22 ♕xc4 ♖c8 23 ♕b3 ♖d6 24 e4 ♘a6! 25 ♖dc1

½-½ San Segundo-Janjgava, Antwerp 1992.

### B32)

7 ♘e5 ♘c6 *(D)*

W

An idea of the Austrian grandmaster Robatsch: by giving back the pawn, Black obtains counterplay on the open b-file.

8 ♘xc6

White has another way to take the pawn: 8 ♗xc6 bxc6 9 ♘xc6 ♕e8 and then:

a) 10 ♕a4?! ♗d6! 11 ♕xc4 a5! 12 ♘e5 (12 ♘c3 ♗a6 13 ♘b5 {13 ♕a4 ♘d5 ∓} 13...a4! ∓; 12 ♗g5 ♘d5 intending ...f5-f4 and ...♕h5 ∓) 12...c5 13 ♘f3 ♗a6 14 ♕c2 ♖c8 ∓ Pigusov-Naumkin, Belgrade 1988.

b) 10 ♘xe7+ ♕xe7 11 ♕a4 a5!? 12 ♕xc4 ♗a6 13 ♕c2 e5 14 dxe5 ♕xe5 15 ♘c3 ♖fe8 16 ♖e1 (16 ♗f4 ♕h5 with compensation) 16...♗b7 17 ♗f4

♕c5! with compensation, C.Hansen-Vaganian, Esbjerg 1988.

**8...bxc6 9 ♘a3**

Or:

a) 9 ♕a4 ♕xd4 10 ♖d1 (10 ♘d2 ♖b8 11 ♕xc6 c3 12 bxc3 ½-½ Rashkovsky-Krogius, Sochi 1976) 10...♕b6!? 11 ♗e3 ♕xb2 12 ♗d4 ♕xe2 13 ♘c3 ♕h5 14 ♕xc6 ♖b8 15 ♕xc7 ♗d7! ∞.

b) 9 ♕c2 ♕xd4 (9...♖b8!? 10 ♖d1 ♘d5 11 ♕xc4 c5! ∞) 10 ♗e3 ♕d6 11 ♘d2 ♘d5 12 ♘xc4 ♘xe3 13 ♘xe3 ♗a6 14 ♖ac1 ♖ad8 15 ♗xc6 ♗g5 16 ♗f3 ♕b6 17 ♕c3 ♗f6 with equality, Larsen-Speelman, London 1980.

c) 9 e3!? ♗a6 10 ♗xc6 ♖b8 11 ♘c3 ♘d5 (11...♗d6!? intending to meet 12 e4 with 12...e5) 12 ♘xd5 exd5 13 ♕f3 ♗b7 14 ♗xb7 ♖xb7 15 b3 cxb3 16 axb3 c5 17 dxc5 ♗xc5 18 ♗a3 ♗xa3 19 ♖xa3 ♕d6 20 ♖fa1 g6 = Seirawan-Ivanchuk, Tilburg 1992.

d) 9 ♗xc6 ♖b8 10 ♘c3 (10 ♘a3 ♖b6 11 ♗f3 ♗xa3 12 bxa3 ♗b7 13 ♗xb7 ♖xb7 14 ♗g5 h6 15 ♗xf6 ♕xf6 16 ♖c1 ♖d8 17 ♖xc4 c5 18 ♖xc5 ♕xd4 with equality, Schmidt-Espig, Polanica Zdroj 1973) 10...♗b7! 11 ♗xb7 (11 ♗b5 ♗d5 12 b3 {12 ♕a4 a6} 12...cxb3 13 axb3 ♗a8 14 ♗c4 c5 =) 11...♖xb7 12 ♖b1 (12 e3 c5 13 ♕f3 ♘d5 14 dxc5 ♗xc5 15 ♖d1 ♖d7 =) 12...♕d7 (12...c5 13 dxc5 ♗xc5 14 ♕c2 ±) 13 e4 ♖fb8 intending ...♗b4 =.

**9...♗xa3 10 bxa3 ♗a6! 11 ♗xc6**

Or:

a) 11 ♕a4 ♗b5 12 ♕a5 c3 ∞.

b) 11 ♗g5 h6 12 ♗xf6 ♕xf6 13 ♕a4 (13 ♗xc6 ♖ab8 14 ♕a4 ♖b6 15 ♖fd1 ♖d8 16 ♗f3 c6! 17 ♔g2 ♕e7 18 e3 ♖c8! 19 h4 ♗b5 20 ♕b4 c5 ∓ Antunes-Karpov, Tilburg 1984) 13...♗b5 14 ♕a5 c3 =.

**11...♖b8 12 ♕a4 ♖b6 13 ♗g2**

13 ♗d2 ♕d6!? 14 ♗f3 ♘d5 15 ♖fb1 ♖fb8 16 ♖xb6 ♕xb6 17 ♖c1 ♕xd4 (17...♗b5!? 18 ♕a5 ♕xd4 19 ♖b1 h6 20 ♖xb5 ½-½ Ribli-Balashov, Dortmund 1987) 18 ♕xa6 ♕xd2 19 ♕xc4 g6 20 ♗xd5 exd5 21 ♕xc7 ± ♖e8 22 ♖c2 ♕d1+ 23 ♔g2 ♖xe2?? 24 ♖xe2?? (24 ♕b8+ ♔g7 25 ♕b2+ wins a rook − an astonishing oversight by both players!) 24...♕xe2 = Antunes-Janjgava, Moscow OL 1994.

13 ♗f3 ♘d5 14 ♕a5 (14 ♕c2 f5!; 14 e4 ♕f6! 15 ♔g2 ♕xd4 16 ♗g5 ♕e5) 14...c3 15 ♖e1 ♕f6 16 ♗xd5 exd5 17 ♕xc3 ♖c6 18 ♕b3 ♕xd4 19 ♗e3 ♕e4 20 ♖ad1 ♖c4 21 ♗xa7 c6 22 ♕e3 ½-½ Beliavsky-Geller, Moscow 1981.

**13...♘d5 14 ♕c2**

14 ♕a5 f5 =.

**14...f5 15 e4 fxe4 16 ♗xe4 h6 17 ♗g2 ♕f6 18 ♗e3 c3**

∓ E.Vladimirov-Vaganian, Moscow 1990.

## B33)

**7 ♕c2 a6** *(D)*

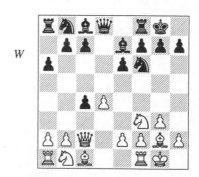

Now:

Or:

a) 8 e4 b5 9 ♘g5 (9 a4 ♗b7 10 ♘c3 ♘c6! 11 axb5 axb5 12 ♖xa8 ♕xa8 13 ♘xb5? ♘b4 14 ♕xc4 ♗a6!) 9...♘c6 10 e5 (10 ♗e3 h6 11 e5 ♘b4) 10...♘b4 11 ♕d1 ♘fd5 ∓.

b) 8 ♖d1 b5 9 ♘g5 c6 10 e4 h6 11 ♘h3 c5 12 d5 (12 dxc5 ♕c7 13 e5 ♘d5 14 ♘f4 ♘xf4 15 ♗xf4 ♗b7 16 ♗xb7 ♕xb7 17 b3 cxb3 18 axb3 ♘c6 ∓ Chiburdanidze-Hjartarson, Linares 1988) 12...e5 13 a4 ♗b7 14 axb5 axb5 15 ♖xa8 ♗xa8 16 f4 ♗d6 ∓.

c) 8 ♗g5 b5!? 9 ♗xf6 ♗xf6 10 ♘g5 ♗xg5 11 ♗xa8 ♕xd4 12 ♗g2 ♘d7 13 ♘c3 f5! 14 b3! cxb3 15 axb3 ♕c5 16 ♖a2 ♗e7 17 e3 ♗d6 = Korchnoi-Vaganian, Montpellier Ct 1985.

d) 8 ♘bd2!? b5 9 ♘g5 c6 10 b3 (D) and now:

d1) 10...c3! 11 ♘de4 (11 ♘df3 h6 12 ♘h3 ♗b7 13 ♕xc3 ♘bd7 14 ♗b2 c5 =) 11...♘d5!? (11...♘xe4 12 ♘xe4 f5 13 ♘xc3 ♕xd4 14 ♗e3 ♕f6 15 ♖ad1 ♗d7 16 a4 with compensation) 12 ♘f3! (12 ♘xh7? ♘b4 −+) 12...b4 13 a3 a5 (13...f5 14 ♘c5 ♗xc5 15 dxc5 a5 16 e4 with compensation, Ehlvest-Short, Riga 1995) 14 axb4 ♘xb4 15 ♕xc3 ♗a6 16 ♖e1 ♘d7 = Short.

d2) 10...cxb3 11 ♘xb3 a5! 12 ♖d1 ♗d7! 13 ♘c5 h6 14 ♘f3 ♗e8 15 ♗b2 ♘a6 16 ♖ac1 ♕c8 17 ♕b1 ♘xc5 18 dxc5 ♘d7 ∓ Shabalov-Aseev, Barnaul 1988.

## B331)
### 8 ♕xc4 b5 9 ♕c2

9 ♕b3 promises nothing: 9...♗b7 10 ♖d1 ♘bd7 11 ♗g5 (11 ♘c3 c5 =) 11...c5 12 dxc5 ♕c7 13 ♘bd2 ♗xc5 ∓ Larsen-Portisch, Havana OL 1966.

9 ♕d3 ♗b7 10 ♗g5 ♘bd7 11 ♘bd2 c5 =.

**9...♗b7 (D)**

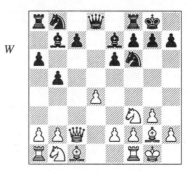

Now:
**B3311: 10 ♗g5** 182
**B3312: 10 ♗f4** 183
**B3313: 10 ♗d2** 184

## B3311)
### 10 ♗g5 ♘bd7 11 ♗xf6

11 ♘bd2 gives Black additional possibilities. 11...c5!? (11...♖c8 12 ♗xf6 ♘xf6 transposes to the main line) and now:

a) 12 ♗xf6 gxf6 13 ♖ad1 (13 a4 ♕b6 14 ♘b3 ♖ac8 15 dxc5 ♘xc5 16 ♘xc5 ♖xc5 17 ♕b3 ♖d8 ∓ Buturin-Klovans, Novosibirsk 1986) 13...♕b6

14 dxc5 ♘xc5 15 ♘d4 ♖ac8 16 ♕b1 ♖fd8 17 ♘2b3 ♗xg2 18 ♔xg2 f5 = Seirawan-Ivanchuk, Monte Carlo Amber rpd 1994.

b) 12 dxc5 ♘xc5 and then:

b1) 13 ♗xf6 gxf6 14 ♖fd1 (14 ♘b3 ♖c8 15 ♖ad1 ♕b6 16 ♘xc5 ♗xc5 17 ♕b1 ♖fd8 ∓ Khalifman-Aseev, Leningrad 1989) 14...♕b6 15 ♘d4 and now Black should play 15...♖ac8! = rather than 15...♗xg2 16 ♔xg2 f5 17 ♖ac1, which is slightly better for White, Van der Sterren-Renet, Lyons Z 1990.

b2) 13 ♖ad1 ♖c8 14 ♕b1 ♘d5 is equal, Kumaran-Wells, British League (4NCL) 1996/7.

**11...♘xf6 12 ♘bd2 ♖c8 13 ♘b3 (D)**

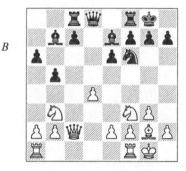

**13...c5**

13...♗e4!? is also fully possible: 14 ♕c3 (14 ♕c1 c5 15 dxc5 ♕c7 16 ♕f4 ♕xf4 17 gxf4 ♗xc5 18 ♘e5 ♗xg2 19 ♔xg2 ♗d6 20 ♘d3 ♘d5 21 e3 ♘b6 ½-½ Razuvaev-Hübner, London USSR-RoW 1984) 14...♘d5 15 ♕d2 (15 ♕c1 c5 16 ♘xc5 ♕b6 17 ♕d2 ♗xc5 18 dxc5 ♖xc5 19 ♖fc1 ♖fc8 20 ♖xc5 ♕xc5 21 ♘e1 ♗xg2 22 ♔xg2 ♕e7 ½-½ Andersson-Karpov, Moscow 1981) and now:

a) 15...c5!? 16 dxc5 ♗xc5 17 ♘xc5 ♖xc5 18 ♖ac1 ♖xc1 19 ♖xc1 ♕a8 20 ♕d4 (20 ♘e1 ♗xg2 21 ♘xg2 ♖c8 22 ♘e1 h6 23 ♘d3 ♘f6 = Fridmans-Berzinš, Tallinn 1998) 20...♘f6 21 ♕c5 h6 22 a3 ♖d8 23 h3 ♗b7 24 ♕b6 ♖b8 25 b4 ± Illescas-Epishin, Madrid 1995.

b) 15...♗b4 16 ♕d1 c5 17 a3 (17 dxc5 ♗xc5 18 ♘xc5 ♖xc5 19 ♖c1 ♕c7 20 ♖xc5 ♕xc5 = Dlugy-de Firmian, New York 1985) 17...c4 18 axb4 cxb3 19 ♕xb3 ♕d6 intending ...♘b4 =.

**14 dxc5 ♗d5 15 ♖fd1**

15 ♘e1 ♗xg2 16 ♘xg2 ♘d7 17 ♖fd1 ♕c7 18 c6 ♘b8 19 ♖ac1 ♕xc6 20 ♕xc6 ♖xc6 21 ♘f4 ½-½ Khalifman-Yusupov, USSR Ch (Moscow) 1988.

**15...♗xb3 16 ♕xb3 ♕c7 17 a4 ♕xc5 18 axb5 axb5 19 ♘d4**

19 ♘e1 ♘g4! 20 ♘d3 ♕c4 =.

**19...b4 20 e3 ♖fd8 21 ♖d2 ♕b6**

and at this point a draw was agreed in Kasparov-Karpov, London/Leningrad Wch (20) 1986.

**B3312)**

**10 ♗f4 ♘c6 (D)**

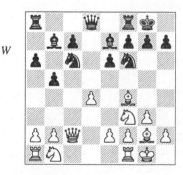

**11 ♖d1**

11 ♘c3 ♗b4 12 ♕b1 (12 ♕b3 c5 13 dxc5 ♗xc5 =; 12 ♕d2 c5 13 a3 ♘bd5 14 ♘xd5 ♗xd5 15 dxc5 ♗xc5 = Rossetto-Benko, Mar del Plata 1954) 12...♘bd5 13 ♘xd5 ♗xd5 14 ♖d1 ♕c8! 15 ♗e5 ♗e4 16 ♕c1 ♘d5 17 ♘e1 ♗xg2 18 ♘xg2 c5 19 dxc5 ♕xc5 ½-½ Schlosser-Lutz, German Ch (Binz) 1995.

11 ♘bd2 ♘xd4!? 12 ♘xd4 ♗xg2 13 ♘xe6 fxe6 14 ♔xg2 ♘d5 (14...c5 15 ♘f3 ♕b6 16 ♗e5 ±) 15 ♗e5 c5 16 ♘f3 ♕e8 17 a4 ♕h5 18 axb5 axb5 19 ♖xa8 ♖xa8 20 ♖d1 ♖f8 = Poluliakhov-Pigusov, Russian Ch (St Petersburg) 1998.

**11...♘b4 12 ♕c1 ♖c8**

12...♕c8!? 13 ♗g5 (13 ♘bd2 c5 14 dxc5 ♗xc5 15 ♘b3 ♗e7 16 ♘a5 ♗d5 = Andersson-Karpov, Tilburg 1982) 13...c5 14 ♗xf6 ♗xf6 15 dxc5 a5 16 ♘a3 ♗c6! 17 ♘c2 (17 ♘d4 ♗xg2 18 ♔xg2 ♗xd4 19 ♖xd4 ♕c6+ intending ...♖ac8 =) 17...♖a7! and here:

a) 18 ♘xb4 axb4 19 ♕c2 (19 ♘d4 ♗xg2 20 ♔xg2 ♖d8!; 19 a3 ♖a4! 20 ♘d2 ♗xg2 21 ♔xg2 ♕a8+ 22 ♘f3 bxa3 23 ♖xa3 ♗xb2! 24 ♖xa4 ♕xa4) 19...♕a8 20 ♕b3 ♖a4 21 ♘e1 ♗xg2 22 ♘xg2 ♖c8 =.

b) 18 ♘cd4 ♖c7 = Splosnov-Berzinš, Trinec 1988.

**13 ♘c3 ♘bd5 14 ♘xd5**

14 ♗e3 c6 15 ♘e5 ♕b6 16 ♘xd5 cxd5 17 ♕d2 b4 18 ♗g5 ♖c7 19 ♖ac1 ♖fc8 = Andersson-Beliavsky, Reggio Emilia 1989/90.

14 ♗g5 c5 15 ♘xd5 ♗xd5 16 ♕f4 ♕c7! 17 ♕xc7 ♖xc7 18 ♗f4 ♖cc8 19 dxc5 ♖xc5 20 ♘e1 ♗xg2 21 ♔xg2 ♘d5 22 ♖ac1 ♖fc8 = Renet-Mirallès, Epinal (4) 1986.

**14...♗xd5 15 ♗e3**

15 ♗g5 c5 16 ♕f4 ♕c7 =.

**15...c6**

15...♕d6!? 16 ♘e1 ♗xg2 17 ♔xg2 ♘d5 18 f3 ♘xe3+ 19 ♕xe3 ♕d5 20 ♕b3 ♖fd8 = Andersson-Geller, Las Palmas 1980.

**16 ♘e1**

16 ♕c3 ♕b6 17 ♖ac1 ♕b7 18 ♘e1 ♗xg2 19 ♘xg2 ♘e4 20 ♕b3 c5 = Azmaiparashvili-Geller, Moscow 1983.

**16...♕b6 17 ♘d3 ♗xg2 18 ♔xg2 ♘d5 19 f3**

19 ♘f4 ♘xf4+ 20 ♗xf4 c5 21 ♕e3 c4 22 d5 ♕xe3 23 ♗xe3 ♖fd8 ∓ Dizdarević-Khuzman, Pula Echt 1997.

**19...c5 20 dxc5 ♘xe3+ 21 ♕xe3 ♗xc5 22 ♘xc5 ♕xc5 23 ♕xc5 ♖xc5 24 ♖ac1 ♖cc8! 25 b4 g6**

= Khalifman-Lutz, Wijk aan Zee 1995.

**B3313)**
**10 ♗d2 ♗e4 11 ♕c1 ♗b7** *(D)*

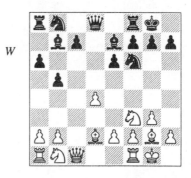

**12 ♗f4**

Or:

a) 12 ♗e3 ♘d5 13 ♘c3 ♘d7 14 ♖d1 ♖c8 15 ♘xd5 ♗xd5 16 ♘e1 c6! 17 ♘d3 ♕b6 18 ♕c3 b4 19 ♕d2 a5 20 ♖dc1 ½-½ Kasparov-Karpov, Moscow Wch (8) 1984/5.

b) 12 ♖d1 ♕c8 13 ♗a5 (13 ♗e3 ♘bd7 14 ♘bd2 c5 15 dxc5 ♘xc5 16 ♗xc5 ♗xc5 17 ♘b3 ♗b6 ∓ Kupreichik-Oll, Sverdlovsk 1987; 13 b4 ♘bd7 14 a4 ♗d6 15 axb5 axb5 16 ♘a3 ♕b8 17 ♘c2 ♗e4 18 ♘fe1 ♗xg2 19 ♘xg2 ♕b7 20 ♘ge1 ♕e4 21 ♗e3 ♘d5 22 f3 ♕g6 23 ♗d2 ♖xa1 24 ♘xa1 f5 ∓ Shipov-Kruppa, Minsk 1993; 13 a4 c5 14 dxc5 ♗xc5 15 axb5 axb5 16 ♖xa8 ♗xa8 17 ♗e3 ♗e7 18 ♕xc8 ♖xc8 19 ♘d4 ♗xg2 20 ♔xg2 b4 = Bareev-Aseev, Irkutsk 1986) 13...c5 (13...♘c6 14 ♗e1 ♖d8 15 e3 ♘a7 = intending ...c5, Pigusov-Panchenko, Tashkent 1986) 14 dxc5 ♕xc5 15 ♘bd2 ♘bd7 16 ♘b3 ♕xc1 17 ♖axc1 ♖fc8! 18 ♗c7 ♔f8 19 ♘e5 ♗xg2 20 ♘xd7+ ♘xd7 21 ♔xg2 ♔e8 22 ♘a5 ♘c5 is equal, Chernin-Gurevich, Vilnius 1985.

**12...♘d5 13 ♘c3 ♘xf4 14 ♕xf4 ♕d6 15 ♘e5**

Or:

a) 15 ♖ac1 ♘d7 16 ♕e3 (16 ♖fd1 ♖ac8 17 ♕e3 ♕b6 18 ♘e4 ♗xe4! 19 ♕xe4 c5 20 dxc5 ♖xc5 =) 16...♕b6! 17 ♘e4 ♗xe4 18 ♕xe4 c5! 19 dxc5 ♘xc5 20 ♕e3 ♖ac8 21 ♘e5 a5 22 b3 ♖c7 23 ♖c2 ♖fc8 = Yusupov-Vaganian, USSR Ch (Moscow) 1988.

b) 15 ♖fd1 ♘d7 16 d5!? and here:

b1) 16...exd5 17 ♘xd5 ±.

b2) 16...e5 17 ♘xe5! ♘xe5 (alternatively, 17...♕xe5 18 ♕xe5 ♘xe5 19 d6 ±) 18 ♘e4 ♘g6 (18...g5 19 ♕f5 ±) 19 ♘xd6 ♘xf4 20 ♘xb7 ♘xg2 21 ♔xg2 ±.

b3) 16...♕xf4! 17 gxf4 exd5 18 ♘xd5 ♗xd5 19 ♖xd5 ♘b6! 20 ♖dd1 ♗f6 21 ♖ac1! (21 ♘d4 ♖ad8; 21 ♘e5 ♖ae8) 21...♗xb2 22 ♖xc7 ♖ac8! with equality, Romanishin-Janjgava, Simferopol 1988.

**15...♗xg2 16 ♔xg2 c5 17 dxc5**
17 ♖fd1 ♘c6 18 ♘e4 ♕c7 ∞.

**17...♕xc5 18 ♘e4 ♕b6 19 ♖fd1 ♖a7! 20 ♖ac1 f6! 21 ♘f3 e5 22 ♕d2**
22 ♕f5 g6 23 ♕h3 f5 24 ♘eg5 ♗xg5 25 ♘xg5 ♖d8 ∞.

**22...♖d8 23 ♕c2 ♖xd1 24 ♕xd1**
24 ♖xd1 ♕c6! =.

**24...♕e6!**
The game is equal. 25 ♘c5 ♗xc5 26 ♖xc5 ½-½ Khalifman-Karpov, USSR Ch (Moscow) 1988.

**B332)**
**8 a4** *(D)*

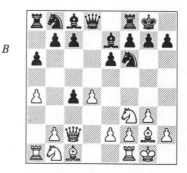

White prevents ...b5 and so makes it difficult for Black to develop his queenside.

**8...♗d7 9 ♕xc4**
White has also tried other continuations:

a) 9 ♘bd2 ♗c6 10 ♘xc4 (10 a5 b5 11 axb6 cxb6 12 ♘xc4 ♗e4 13 ♕d1 {13 ♕b3 ♗d5! =} 13...♘c6 14 ♗g5 ♘b4 15 ♕d2 a5 16 ♖fc1 ♖c8 = Kaidanov-Wells, London 1990) 10...♗e4 11 ♕c3 (11 ♕d1 ♘c6 12 ♘cd2 ♗g6 13 ♘b3 ♘b4 14 ♘e1 c6 = Smyslov-Kluger, Polanica Zdroj 1966) 11...♘c6 12 ♘ce5 ♘d5 13 ♕b3 ♘a5 14 ♕d1 c5

15 ♗d2 ♘b4 16 ♖c1 cxd4 17 ♗xb4 ♗xb4 18 ♕xd4 ♕xd4 19 ♘xd4 ♗xg2 20 ♔xg2 ♖fd8 with equality, G.Kuzmin-Vaganian, USSR Ch (Vilnius) 1980/1.

b) 9 ♘e5 ♗c6 10 ♘xc6 ♘xc6 (D) and now:

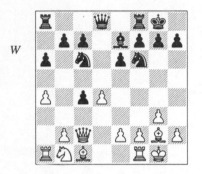

b1) 11 ♗xc6 bxc6 12 ♖d1 (12 ♕xc4 ♕d5! 13 ♘d2 ♖fd8 14 e3 c5 =; 12 ♘a3 ♕d5 13 ♘xc4 ♕h5! 14 ♘e5 c5 15 ♘f3 ♖ab8 = Liebert-Barczay, Szolnok 1975) 12...♕d5 13 ♘a3 c5 14 dxc5 ♕h5 = Khuzman-Kruppa, Lvov 1988.

b2) 11 e3 ♘a5 12 ♘d2 c5 13 dxc5 ♖c8 14 b4 cxb3 15 ♘xb3 ♘d5! 16 ♗a3 (16 ♗d2 ♘xb3 17 ♕xb3 ♖xc5 18 ♕xb7 ♕c8 19 ♕xc8 ♖fxc8 20 a5 ♗f6 21 ♖a3 ♘c3 22 ♗f3 ♖d8 23 ♗xc3 ♖xc3 24 ♖a2 ♗e5 25 ♗b7 ♖c5 ½-½ Cifuentes-Winants, Wijk aan Zee 1994) 16...♘xb3 17 ♕xb3 ♗xc5 18 ♕xb7 (18 ♗xc5 ♖xc5 19 ♕xb7 ♕a5 20 ♗xd5 ♖xd5 21 ♖fc1 h5 22 h4 ♖fd8 = Urban-Rozentalis, Polish Cht (Augustow) 1996) 18...♗xa3 19 ♖xa3 ♕a5 20 ♗xd5 ♖c7 21 ♕b1 (21 ♕b3 exd5 22 ♖b1 ♖c4 23 ♖a2 ♕c5 24 ♕b6 ♕c8 25 a5 ♖d8 26 ♖d2 h5 = Stajčić-Korneev, Werfen 1992) 21...♕xd5 22

♖c1 ½-½ Urban-A.Shneider, Cappelle la Grande 1993.

c) 9 ♖d1 ♗c6 10 ♘c3 (10 ♗g5 ♘bd7 11 ♕xc4 ♗d5 12 ♕c2 ♗e4 13 ♕c1 h6 14 ♗xf6 ♘xf6 15 ♘c3 ♗c6 16 ♕c2 ♗b4 17 ♘e5 ♗xg2 18 ♔xg2 c5 19 dxc5 ♕c7 20 ♘d3 ♕c6+ 21 f3 ♗xc5 22 ♘xc5 ♕xc5 23 ♕b3 ♖ab8 is equal, Piket-Z.Almasi, Tilburg 1996) 10...♗xf3 11 ♗xf3 ♘c6 (D) and then:

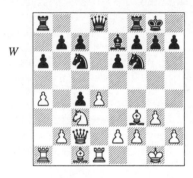

c1) 12 e3 ♘d5!? (12...♘a5 13 d5 e5 14 ♘e4 ½-½ Rashkovsky-Razuvaev, Dubna 1979) 13 ♕e2 ♘a5 14 ♖b1 c6 15 e4 ♘b4 16 d5 ♘d3 17 ♗e3 ♘b3 18 ♕c2 ♘b4 19 ♕e2 ♘d3 ½-½ Romanishin-Geller, USSR Ch (Vilnius) 1980/1.

c2) 12 ♗xc6 bxc6 and now:
c21) 13 a5 ♕b8 14 ♕a4 (14 ♖a4 ♕b3! 15 ♕xb3 cxb3 16 ♖c4 c5! 17 dxc5 ♖fd8 18 ♖xd8+ ♖xd8 19 ♗e3 ♘d5 20 ♘xd5 ♖xd5 21 ♖b4 h6 22 ♖xb3 ♗xc5 = Krasenkov-Khalifman, Vilnius 1988) 14...c5 15 ♕xc4 (15 dxc5 ♗xc5 16 ♕xc4 ♕a7 17 e3 ♖fd8 18 ♗d2 ♖ab8 19 ♗e1 ♖xd1 20 ♖xd1 ♗d6 21 ♘e2 e5 22 ♗b4 ♘e8 23 ♗xd6 ♘xd6 24 ♕d5 ♖xb2 25 ♘c3 h6 26 ♕xe5 ♕b7 = Van der Sterren-Kalinin, Wijk aan Zee 1997) 15...cxd4 16 ♖xd4

c5 17 ♖d1 ♕b4 18 ♖a4 ♕xc4 19 ♖xc4 ♖fd8 20 ♖xd8+ ♖xd8 21 ♗e3 ½-½ Gorelov-Khalifman, Minsk 1985.

c22) 13 ♗g5 ♖b8 14 ♗xf6 (14 a5 ♖b4 15 ♖a4 ♕b8 16 ♖xb4 ♕xb4 17 ♗xf6 gxf6 18 ♘a2 ♕b5 19 ♖c1 ♖d8 20 e3 c5 = Kochiev-Aseev, Leningrad 1989; 14 e3 ♘d7 15 ♗xe7 ♕xe7 16 ♘e4 ♖b4 17 ♘d2 c5 = Dizdar-Sadler, Pula Echt 1997) 14...♗xf6 15 ♘e4 ♖b4 16 e3 ♕d5! 17 ♖ac1 (17 a5!?) 17...♖fb8 18 ♘c5 a5 19 ♘a6! (19 ♕e2? ♗e7 20 e4 ♕d8 ∓ Illescas-Beliavsky, Madrid 1998) 19...♖xb2 20 ♕xc4 ♕f3 21 ♖f1 ♖8b6 22 ♘c5 ♗g5! 23 ♘d3!? (23 ♘d7 ♗xe3 24 ♖c2 ♖xc2 25 ♕xc2 ♗xd4 26 ♘xb6 cxb6 −+; 23 ♖c2 ♖b1 ∓) 23...♗xe3 24 ♖ce1! ♗d2 25 ♖d1 ∓.

**9...♗c6** (D)

**10 ♗g5**
Other possibilities:

a) 10 ♘c3?! is dubious due to 10...b5! 11 ♕d3 (11 ♕a2 b4 12 ♘d1 ♗d5 13 b3 c5 14 dxc5 ♘e4 ∓ Polugaevsky-Braga, Mar del Plata 1982) 11...b4 12 ♘b1 (12 ♘d1? ♗e4 13 ♕d2 ♘c6 14 e3? ♘a5 −+ Poldauf-Tischbierek, Dresden 1978) 12...♗e4 13 ♕d1 (13 ♕c4 ♗d5 14 ♕c2 c5 15

dxc5 ♘bd7 ∓ Schinzel-I.Zaitsev, Graz 1979) 13...c5 14 ♗f4 (14 ♘bd2 ♗d5 15 dxc5 ♘bd7 ∓) 14...♘bd7 15 ♘bd2 ♗d5 16 ♖e1 ♖c8 17 e4 ♗b7 ∓ Sveshnikov-Ivanchuk, Minsk 1986.

b) 10 ♗f4 a5!? 11 ♘c3 ♘a6 12 ♖ac1 (12 ♖fe1 ♗d5 13 ♘xd5 exd5 14 ♕b5 ♕c8 15 ♕b3 c6 16 ♘e5 ♗b4 17 ♖ed1 ♕e6 = Donchenko-Geller, USSR 1979; 12 ♖ae1 ♗d5! 13 ♘xd5 exd5 14 ♕b5 ♕c8 intending ...c6 =; 12 ♕d3 ♘b4 13 ♕b1 ♗xf3 14 ♗xf3 c6 15 ♖d1 ♗d6 16 ♗d2 ♕e7 =) 12...♘b4 (12...h6!? 13 ♖fe1 ♗b4 14 ♗e5 ♗xf3 15 ♗xf3 c6 16 ♖ed1 ♕e7 17 ♗f4 ♘d5 18 ♗d2 ♖fd8 = Kramnik-Lautier, Dortmund 1995) 13 ♖fe1 ♗d6 14 e3 (14 ♘e5!?; 14 ♗g5 ♗d5 15 ♘xd5 exd5 16 ♕b3 h6 17 ♗xf6 ♕xf6 18 e3 ♖ae8 19 ♕d1 ♖e7 = Kasparov-Gelfand, Moscow 1996) 14...♘fd5 15 ♕e2 ♘xf4 16 gxf4 f6! 17 ♔h1 ♕e8 18 b3 e5 19 fxe5 fxe5 20 d5 e4! 21 ♘xe4 ♗xd5 22 ♘xd6 cxd6 ∓ Lautier-Beliavsky, Belgrade 1995.

**10...♗d5 11 ♕d3**
Or 11 ♕c2 ♗e4, and now:

a) 12 ♕c1 ♘c6 (12...a5!?) 13 e3 ♘b4 14 ♘c3 ♗c6 15 a5 ♖c8 16 ♖d1 ♗xf3 17 ♗xf3 ♘fd5 18 ♗xe7 ♕xe7 19 ♘a4 ± Pigusov-Liang Jinrong, Beijing 1997.

b) 12 ♕d1 and then:

b1) 12...♘bd7 13 ♘c3 ♗c6 14 ♕c2 ♗b4 15 ♖fe1 ♗xf3 16 ♗xf3 c6 17 ♖ed1 ♕a5 18 ♗f4 (18 ♘a2 ♗d6 19 ♗d2 ♕c7 20 ♗g2 a5 = Tkachev-Z.Almasi, Senec ECC 1998) 18...e5 19 dxe5 ♘xe5 20 ♗g2 ♖ad8 21 ♘a2 is slightly better for White, Filipov-Gutov, Perm 1998.

b2) 12...c5 13 ♘bd2 (13 dxc5 ♗xc5 14 ♘c3 ♗c6 15 ♘e5 ♗xg2 16 ♔xg2 h6 17 ♕xd8 ½-½ Polugaevsky-Geller, USSR Ch (Leningrad) 1977) 13...♗c6 (13...♗d5 14 dxc5 ♘bd7 15 b4 a5 =) 14 dxc5 ♗xc5 and here:

b21) 15 ♘b3 ♗e7 16 ♕xd8 ♖xd8 17 ♘a5 ♗d5 18 ♘e5! ♗xg2 19 ♔xg2 ♘bd7 20 ♘d3 h6! 21 ♗f4 g5 22 ♗e3!? (22 ♘xb7 gxf4 23 ♘xd8 ♖xd8 24 gxf4 a5 = Ribli-Donev, Austria 1997) 22...♖db8 23 ♖fc1 ♘d5 ∞.

b22) 15 ♕c2 ♘bd7 16 ♗xf6 gxf6 17 ♘b3 ♖c8 18 ♘xc5 ♘xc5 19 ♕xc5 ♗xf3 20 ♕b4 ♗xg2 21 ♔xg2 ♕d5+ 22 ♔g1 ♖c4 23 ♕e7 ♔g7 = Timoshchenko-Pigusov, Irkutsk 1983.

**11...c5** *(D)*

**12 dxc5**
Or:

a) 12 ♗xf6?! ♗xf6 13 e4 ♗c6 14 ♖d1 (14 e5?! ♗e7 intending ...♘d7 ∓) 14...cxd4 15 e5 ♗e7 16 ♘xd4 ♗xg2 17 ♔xg2 ♕d5+ 18 ♘f3 (18 ♕f3 ♖d8 19 ♘c3 ♗xf3+ 20 ♘xf3 ♘c6 is a little better for Black) 18...♕xd3 19 ♖xd3 ♘c6 20 ♖d7 (20 ♘c3 ♖fd8 21 ♖ad1

♖xd3 22 ♖xd3 ♖d8 ∓) 20...♖ab8 = Kožul-Ki.Georgiev, Sarajevo 1998.

b) 12 ♘c3 ♗c6 13 e4 (13 ♖fd1 cxd4 14 ♘xd4 ♗xg2 15 ♔xg2 ♕a5 16 ♗xf6! ♗xf6 17 ♘e4 ♗xd4 18 ♕xd4 ♘c6 19 ♕c5 and now, rather than 19...♖ac8 20 ♕xa5 ♘xa5 21 ♘d6 ♖c2 22 b4 ± Tukmakov-Beliavsky, Portorož 1996, Black should play 19...♖fd8 =) 13...cxd4 14 ♕xd4 h6 15 ♗f4 ♘bd7 16 ♕c4!? (16 b4 b6 17 ♖fd1 a5 =) 16...♖c8 17 ♕e2 ♗c5 18 ♘d2 e5 19 ♗e3 ♗xe3 20 ♕xe3 ♕a5! 21 ♖fc1 (21 ♖fd1 ♕b4! ∓) 21...♖fd8 22 ♗h3 ♖b8 = Beliavsky-Ki.Georgiev, Ulcinj 1998.

**12...♘bd7 13 ♘c3 ♘xc5 14 ♕e3 ♕a5 15 ♘xd5**

15 ♖ad1 ♗c6 16 ♖d4 ♘b3 17 ♖c4 ♖ad8 18 ♗xf6 ♗xf6 19 ♘e4 ♗xe4 20 ♖xe4 ♘d2 = Gulko-Beliavsky, Amsterdam 1989.

**15...♘xd5 16 ♕a3! ♗xg5 17 ♘xg5 h6 18 ♖fc1 ♘d7 19 ♘e4** *(D)*

19 ♗xd5 ♕xd5 20 ♖d1 ♕xg5 21 ♖xd7 b5 22 a5 ♕e5 23 ♖d2 ♖ad8 24 ♖ad1 ♖xd2 25 ♖xd2 ♕c7 26 ♕c3 ♕xc3 27 bxc3 ♖c8 28 ♖d6 ½-½ Stohl-Ribli, Bundesliga 1997/8.

**19...b5! 20 axb5**

20 b4 ♕xa4 21 ♕xa4 bxa4 22 ♘c5 ♘7b6 23 ♗xd5 exd5 24 ♘xa4 ♘xa4 25 ♖xa4 ♖ab8 26 ♖c5 ♖fd8 27 ♔f1 ♖d6 with equality, Gulko-Pigusov, Moscow 1990.

**20...♕xb5 21 ♘c3 ♘xc3 22 ♖xc3 ♖a7**

The game is equal.

# Index of Variations

## Chapter Guide

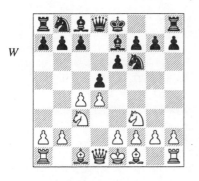
### 1: The Alatortsev Variation
1 d4 d5 2 c4 e6 3 ♘c3 ♗e7 *6* 4 cxd5 exd5 5 ♗f4 *6*
A: 5...c6 *6*
A1: 6 ♕c2 *6*
A2: 6 e3 *10*
B: 5...♘f6 *14*

### 2: The Eingorn Variation
1 d4 d5 2 c4 e6 3 ♘c3 ♗e7 4 ♘f3 ♘f6 5 ♕c2 *20* 5...0-0 6 ♗g5 *21* 6...dxc4 7 e4 *22* 7...♘c6 8 ♖d1 *23* 8...b5! 9 ♘xb5 ♘b4 10 ♕xc4 ♘xc4 11 ♗xe7 ♕xe7 12 a3 c6!? *23*

### 3: 5 ♗f4
1 d4 d5 2 c4 e6 3 ♘c3 ♗e7 4 ♘f3 ♘f6 5 ♗f4 *24* 5...0-0 6 e3 c5 7 dxc5 ♗xc5 *24*

A: **8 ♗e2** 24
B: **8 cxd5** 26 **8...♘xd5 9 ♘xd5 exd5**
26
B1: **10 ♗d3** 26
B2: **10 a3** 27
C: **8 a3** 28 **8...♘c6** 28
C1: **9 ♗e2** 28
C2: **9 ♖c1** 29
C3: **9 b4** 30
D: **8 ♕c2** 31 **8...♘c6** 31
D1: **9 ♖d1** 31
D2: **9 a3** 34 **9...♕a5** 34
D21: **10 ♘d2** 34
D22: **10 0-0-0** 35

## 4: The Classical QGD (with ...♘bd7)
**1 d4 d5 2 c4 e6 3 ♘c3 ♗e7 4 ♘f3 ♘f6**
**5 ♗g5 ♘bd7 6 e3 0-0** 39

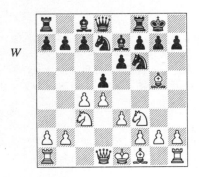

A: **7 cxd5** 39
B: **7 ♕b3** 40
C: **7 ♗d3** 41
D: **7 ♕c2** 43 **7...c5!** 43
D1: **8 0-0-0** 44
D2: **8 ♖d1** 45
D3: **8 cxd5** 46
E: **7 ♖c1** 48
E1: **7...h6** 49
E2: **7...dxc4** 49
E3: **7...b6** 51

E4: **7...a6** 52
E5: **7...c6** 55
E51: **8 ♕c2** 55
E52: **8 ♗d3** 58 **8...dxc4 9 ♗xc4 ♘d5**
**10 ♗xe7 ♕xe7** 60
E521: **11 ♘e4** 60
E522: **11 0-0** 61

## 5: 5 ♗g5 h6 6 ♗xf6
**1 d4 d5 2 c4 e6 3 ♘c3 ♗e7 4 ♘f3 ♘f6**
**5 ♗g5 h6 6 ♗xf6 ♗xf6** 66

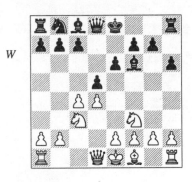

A: **7 e4** 66
B: **7 ♕d2** 67
C: **7 ♕b3** 68
D: **7 e3** 69 **7...0-0** 69
D1: **8 cxd5** 70
D2: **8 ♕b3** 70
D3: **8 ♕d2** 72
D4: **8 ♕c2** 76
D5: **8 ♖c1** 78
D51: **8...a6** 78
D52: **8...c6** 80 **9 ♗d3 ♘d7 10 0-0**
**dxc4 11 ♗xc4** 80
D521: **11...c5** 80
D522: **11...e5** 81

## 6: 5 ♗g5 h6 6 ♗h4 0-0 without 7 e3
**1 d4 d5 2 c4 e6 3 ♘c3 ♗e7 4 ♘f3 ♘f6**
**5 ♗g5 h6 6 ♗h4 0-0** 86

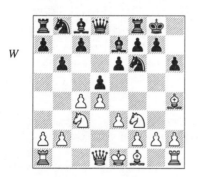

W

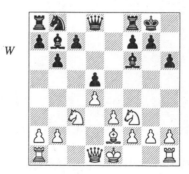

W

G222: 13...♗c6 *132*

## 9: The Exchange Variation
**1 d4 d5 2 c4 e6 3 ♘c3 ♘f6 4 cxd5 exd5 5 ♗g5** *134*

A: **5...♗e7** *134* **6 e3** *134*
A1: **6...h6** *134*
A2: **6...♘bd7** *135*
A3: **6...0-0** *136*
B: **5...c6** *137*
B1: **6 ♘f3** *137*
B2: **6 e3** *138*
B21: **6...♗f5** *138*
B22: **6...♕b6** *140*
B23: **6...♘bd7** *141*
B24: **6...♗e7** *142* **7 ♗d3** *142*
B241: **7...♗g4** *142*
B242: **7...♘bd7** *143*
B2421: **8 ♘ge2** *143*
B2422: **8 ♘f3** *144*
B3: **6 ♕c2** *145*
B31: **6...♘a6** *145*
B32: **6...♗e7** *146* **7 ♘f3** *146*
B321: **7...♘a6** *146*
B322: **7...g6** *147*
B3221: **8 e3** *147*
B3222: **8 e4** *148*

## 10: Exchange Variation: Main Line
**1 d4 d5 2 c4 e6 3 ♘c3 ♘f6 4 cxd5 exd5 5 ♗g5 c6 6 ♕c2 ♗e7 7 e3 ♘bd7** *150*
A: **8 ♘f3** *150*
B: **8 ♗d3** *151*
B1: **8...♘f8** *151*
B2: **8...♘h5** *152*
B3: **8...0-0** *153*
B31: **9 ♘ge2** *153* **9...♖e8 10 0-0 ♘f8** *154*
B311: **11 a3** *154*
B312: **11 ♖ab1** *155*
B313: **11 f3** *155*
B32: **9 ♘f3** *157* **9...♖e8** *157*
B321: **10 0-0-0** *157*
B322: **10 h3** *159*
B323: **10 0-0** *160* **10...♘f8** *160*
B3231: **11 ♗xf6** *161*
B3232: **11 ♖ab1** *161*
B3233: **11 a3** *162*
B3234: **11 ♖ae1** *163*
B3235: **11 h3** *166*

## 11: The Catalan Opening
**1 d4 d5 2 c4 e6 3 ♘f3 ♘f6 4 g3** *171*
A: **4...dxc4** *171*
B: **4...♗e7** *177* **5 ♗g2 0-0** *177*
B1: **6 ♕c2** *177*
B2: **6 ♘c3** *179*
B3: **6 0-0** *180* **6...dxc4** *180*
B31: **7 ♘a3** *180*
B32: **7 ♘e5** *180*
B33: **7 ♕c2** *181* **7...a6** *181*
B331: **8 ♕xc4** *182* **8...b5 9 ♕c2 ♗b7** *182*
B3311: **10 ♗g5** *182*
B3312: **10 ♗f4** *183*
B3313: **10 ♗d2** *184*
B332: **8 a4** *185*